The Book of the
JUBILEE 4-6-0s

A British Railways Illustrated Special

Edited by
CHRIS HAWKINS

ISBN1-903266-27-0
First published in the United Kingdom in 2002
by Irwell Press Limited, 59A, High Street, Clophill,
Bedfordshire MK45 4BE
Printed by Newton Printing

Below. One of Holbeck's finest, 45659
DRAKE at Kentish Town, 5 June 1960.
Photograph Peter Groom.

Acknowledgements

Little that is *wholly* new remains to be said concerning any major class of British steam locomotive, though of course there is still a lot to celebrate and illustrate. The same point was made in the preceding books of this series – *The Book of the BR Standards*, *The Book of the Coronation Pacifics*, *The Book of the Royal Scots*, *The Book of the Princess Royal Pacifics*, *The Book of the Merchant Navy Pacifics* and *The Book of the West Country and Battle of Britain Pacifics*. There are always a few nuggets to be had, and one or two particularly glistening ones, I like to think, have been introduced to the story of the Jubilees. For the great part, the photographs have not been seen before and my special thanks go to Barry Hoper, proprietor of the Transport Treasury, for help in this regard.

Many thanks go once again to Allan Baker, Stephen Summerson, Hamish Stevenson, Philip Atkins, E.W. Johnson, Alec Swain, Ian Sixsmith, Martin Smith, Geoff Goslin, Eric Youldon, and Peter Rowledge. Much of the hard task of typing the mountain of tabulated material was shouldered by Sue Hentschel; the hugely laborious and daunting task of checking the tables fell to Graham Onley. To him I feel an almost tearful sense of gratitude.

A good part of the finer detail or, rather, its marshalling into tabulated form, has come courtesy of John Jennison and David Clarke of Brassmasters. This outfit produces high quality kits in etched brass and other mysterious materials, largely for the love of it. For years before the production of a kit, an endless gathering of information goes on. I am profoundly grateful for the way they have made the fruits of these labours available. They have also put me right on many small points, enduring crass inquiries and many bad jokes. Not only that, but they also made available their very own copies of the original *one hundred and ninety one* complex multi-page Record Cards. By this kindness I was spared endless labour, and retained the will to live. These purveyors to the gentry of fine etched brass LMS locomotive kits (these are the blokes, after all, who put a *tipping driver's seat* into a 4mm Jubilee) will be happy to supply lists of their products, details and so on (SEND AN SAE): *BRASSMASTERS SCALE MODELS, PO BOX 1137, SUTTON COLDFIELD, WEST MIDLANDS B76 1FU*.

Contents

Bibliography

The Locomotive, The Railway Engineer, LMS Magazine, BR London Midland Magazine, The Railway Gazette, The Railway Observer, Journal of the Stephenson Locomotive Society, various record series at the Public Record Office Kew – principally RAIL 418, *The Stanier 4-6-0s of the LMS* (Rowledge and Reed, D&C 1977), *An Illustrated History of LMS Locomotives* (Essery and Jenkinson, SLP 1989), *London Midland Fireman* (Higson, Ian Allan 1972), *Engines of the LMS built 1923-1951* (Rowledge, OPC, 1974), *Crewe Locomotive Works and its Men* (Reed, D&C, 1982), *Derby Works and Midland Locomotives* (Radford, Ian Allan, 1971), *LMS Locomotive Names* (RCTS 1994) from which many of the naming dates have been derived, and various issues of all sorts of magazines.

Inside the Jubilee cab.

1. THE SECOND DIVISION

As is widely appreciated, the motive power situation on the LMS by the early 1930s was dire, and William Stanier was the man brought in to save the day. Any number of accounts attest to this, not least previous volumes in this series, such as *The Book of the Coronation Pacifics*, *The Book of the Royal Scots* and *The Book of the Princess Royal Pacifics*.

Stanier's 'poaching' from the GWR at an elegant London club culminated in the 'mighty re-stocking' of the LMS of the 1930s; from his arrival on 1 January 1932 he set about transforming the landscape of LMS motive power. From the muddle and demoralisation in the wake of the Depression years LMS locomotive thinking and practice came to wholly dominate unfolding events on the British Railways of the late 1940s and early 1950s.

The class of 191 Jubilees thoroughly bolstered the LMS passenger fleet, forming a secondary stiffening 'spine' behind the Pacifics and the Royal Scots. They became ubiquitous on the system and had the most effect, perhaps, on routes which did not have the benefit of the more powerful locos – on the Midland main line out of St Pancras, on the G&SW lines, on the Central Division and down to Bristol.

The first Jubilee to emerge was 5552 in 1934. One of the several black clouds jostling for position in the doom-laden LMS skies had been the parlous state of the Claughton 4-6-0s. Almost the last chance for Crewe to re-establish its position against the all-conquering Derby had been to bring the failing Claughtons up to scratch and from 1928 twenty had been equipped with new (Derby-designed) boilers ('G9½S'). Half these got Caprotti valve gear but the engines remained disappointing, prone to failure and expensive to run. It was this modest upgrading that saw these twenty Claughtons designated 5X instead of 5, indicating a power capability some way between the 5 of the Claughtons generally and the 6 of the Royal Scots.

As a 'Second Division' behind the Royal Scots the Claughtons, even 'beefed up' were still barely in the game so recourse was made instead to a thoroughgoing replacement ('rebuilding' officially) of these wayward charges. The LMS did have one solid success to build on, the Royal Scots, and in 1930 two of the Claughtons were transmogrified something after the fashion of the big 4-6-0s. These were 5902 SIR FRANK REE and 5971 CROXTETH which in 1934 became 5501 and 5500 respectively. These two embodied

Claughton frames (minus front end) and therefore the same driving wheel spacing, bogies and so on together with other odds and sods of the originals. Not so the rest, which were examples of that familiar British railway company concoction; a 'rebuild' that was in reality a new locomotive.

'Rebuilt' to replicate the best features of the Royal Scots the new engines (they used, effectively, a Royal Scot type chassis) looked very much like a smaller version of their bigger brethren and they were soon dubbed 'Baby Scots'. Forty more were 'rebuilt' in 1932-1933, marking the death-knell of the earlier LNW 4-6-0s. The new engines replaced a similar number of Claughtons, which were withdrawn, even though they were relatively youthful, less than twenty years old. In pre-war steam locomotive terms this can certainly be regarded as failure, though in their day some magnificent work was done; 1159 for instance, in its 1913 trials developed a drawbar horsepower better than ever recorded on a Star. The engines, classified '5XP' took the old Claughton numbers of the locos they replaced at first, though they were renumbered 5502-5541 from 1934.

With the '5XP' power grading established as what the LMS needed for this 'Second Division' of engine

5603 at Crewe (9 Shop behind, 10 shop to left). It was built at NBL Queen's Park in May 1935, named in 1936 and did not receive its first General until 1937. It would thus seem to be at Crewe after delivery from Glasgow in 1935. The North British batch, LMS 5557-5606, were built at the company's Hyde Park Works (Nos.24115-24139) and at Queen's Park (Nos.24140-24164). At £5,720 each they were quite a lot cheaper than most of the LMS-built engines. It is said NBL did not make much, if anything, on the deal. Hyde Park products got circular worksplates; 5603 carries the diamond plate of Queen's Park. Photograph courtesy E.M. Johnson.

NBL Hyde Park-built short firebox Jubilee 5573, suitably white-painted and polished to highlight detail. Crosshead driven vacuum pump prominent.

5560, an NBL engine, at Crewe Works, newly arrived and in original condition, 22 July 1934. It was named PRINCE EDWARD ISLAND in September 1936.

Long firebox 5681 ABOUKIR, more or less new at Crewe North.

5643 (later to become RODNEY) at Derby with indicator shelter and additional lagged pipework from the cylinders, 28 July 1935. What the test working might have entailed is not known; three Jubilees had been run in comparison with Patriots on the Western Division the previous year but 5643's activities seem not to have been recorded.

Facsimile

LONDON MIDLAND AND SCOTTISH RAILWAY COMPANY.   Euston Station.

MECHANICAL & ELECTRICAL   28th June, 1933.
ENGINEERING COMMITTEE.

Present :-

Charles Booth, Esq., in the Chair,

W. L. Hichens, Esq.,

J.W. Murray, Esq.

A.E. Pullar, Esq.

G.R.T. Taylor, Esq.

Sir Thomas Williams.

In Attendance :-

Sir Harold Hartley, Mr. W.A. Stanier,

Mr. F.A.C. Leigh and Mr. J. Shearman.

S.T.Jones - Secretary.

LOCOMOTIVE RENEWAL PROGRAMME, 1934. D.W.O. 3137.

       Submitted, with the approval of the
Executive Committee, reports (June 1933) from the Chief
Mechanical Engineer, the Chief Operating Manager and the
Chief Accountant, giving particulars of the original and the
revised renewals in 1933 and recommending that between the 1st
January and 31st December, 1934, the following new locomotives
be constructed to meet traffic requirements and in replacement
of locomotives which during 1934 would either reach the end
of their "useful" lives or arrive at a stage in such lives
when breaking up and substitution would be more economic
than the completion of their "useful" lives :-

LOCOMOTIVES.	No.	Cost. Engines and Tenders.	No.	Replace- ment Cost.	No.	Cost.
		£.		£.		£.
Tender - Passenger.						
(a) Improved 4-6-0 "Claughton".	58	382,800				
(b) Improved 4-6-0 "Prince of Wales".	10	65,000				
(c) Northern Division 4-6-0 Passenger.	10	56,500				
TOTAL ..	78	504,300	92		14	
Tender - Freight.						
(d) Experimental 2-8-0.	2	12,600	60		58	
TOTAL - TENDER	80	516,900	152		72	
Tank - Passenger.						
(e) Three-cylinder 2-6-4.	32	178,720				
(f) Standard 2-6-2.	20	92,000				
	52	270,720	49		-3	
Tank - Freight.	-	-	17		17	
TOTAL - TANK	52	270,720	66		14	
TOTAL - ENGINES	132)		218)		86)	
	)	787,620	)	829,863	)	42,243
TOTAL - TENDERS	80)		152)		72)	
RAIL MOTORS.	-		4	6,517		6,517

       The rail motor vehicles to be displaced were of
obsolete type and their work would be performed by existing locomotives
and carriage stock.

       In addition to the outlay on renewals it was
proposed to expend £1,210 on converting 13 locomotives from Westinghouse
to Vacuum brakes.

power, fifteen more were ordered in the 1932 Building Programme. Ten duly emerged as 'Baby Scots' 5542-5551 and five as the first Crewe 3A taper boiler 4-6-0 '5XP' engines – that is, pure Stanier products. It was a year or two before the general name 'Jubilees' came into use.

The Jubilees appeared like no other LMS class before them, now the 'mighty re-stocking' was under way. They began to come in bulk during the middle part of the 1930s and the first three batches were as follows:

1934:   5552-5556 (first 5, built Crewe)
1934-35: 5607-54 (total 48, built Crewe)
1934-35: 5655-5664 (total 10, built Derby)

The first batch of five, 5552-5556 (a quantity which looks almost tentative compared to events soon after) had been authorised in May 1933 but the much bigger second and the third batches of 1934-35, also to be built by the LMS, were part of the 1934 Locomotive Renewal Programme promulgated on 28 June 1933, a month after the initial batch of five. It's interesting to see that, though the engines would *start* to be called Jubilees within a few years (the name was far from general at first, particularly on the railway itself) they were at first referred to as 'Improved 4-6-0 Claughtons'. There has been confusion over the very names (a good start!) of these engines from the beginning, and in many subsequent published accounts. At first, *so far as the LMS Mechanical & Electrical Engineering Committee was concerned* [author's emphasis] the 'rebuilt' Claughtons (what we all came to know as the Patriots) were termed 'Superheated Converted Claughtons' (hardly a term likely to catch on) while what we all came to know as the Jubilees were called 'Improved Claughtons'.

Moreover, while the latter were also demonstrably in the '5XP' power rating and indeed carried this prominently, in the Minutes they are firmly just '5X' and this term took over from the cumbersome 'Improved Claughtons'. As the 1930s moved on and more of the new engines appeared they became 'three cylinder 5X taper boiler' 4-6-0s in the record. So, when the terms 'Patriot' and 'Jubilee' came into use it was a bit of a relief all round – see below, after the facsimile. The Building Programme shows the 1934-35 batch of 58 Jubilees (the 'Improved 3-cylinder Claughtons') to be built by Crewe and Derby, the fate of the ten 'Improved Prince of Wales' 4-6-0s and much besides.

The expected advantages of the new taper boiler 4-6-0s over the Patriots, it is clearly stated, were a reduction in axlebox troubles, an increase in power and lower maintenance costs. As is clear (not least from the facsimile minutes on these pages) the names of both the new types, whether 'Superheated Converted Claughtons' or 'Improved Claughtons' were hopeless, and both the familiar terms came about more or less by accident. 'Baby Scots' of course, was entirely unacceptable at official levels. In 1937 it was decided to transfer the LNWR war memorial plates from the Claughton PATRIOT and thereafter the class could logically be termed 'Patriots'. The name 'Baby Scot' of course refused to die, and was around in enthusiast circles (and others) to the end. 'Jubilee' came about in 1935 when the name SILVER JUBILEE was bestowed on 5642, then a few months old and one of the newest of the new engines. 5642, in red, ran with the name for a while before it was done up in the familiar special livery with raised chrome numerals and so on. A class name would only stick if the first one was given the name, so 5642 swopped identities with 5552. The name 'Jubilees' and various diminutives sufficed thereafter though, as with the Patriots, early history lived on in a propensity to call the engines '5XPs'. 'Red Staniers' was a favourite term which could still be found in use even when red was but a memory and at Crewe they called them 'Red 'Uns' to the end, to distinguish them (naturally) from the 'Black 'Uns' and the 'Big 'Uns'... When they weren't calling them 'Red 'Uns' they were described simply as 'the three cylinders'. What they were never called in professional railway circles, it seems, is 'Jubilees'.

Another fifty were ordered from North British in October 1933, followed by two more batches from Crewe, as follows:

1934-35: 5557-5606 (total 50, built NBL)
1935-36: 5665-5694 (total 30, built Crewe)
1934-35: 5695-5742 (total 48, built Crewe)
Total 191

Boilers, Fireboxes and Steaming
The first 3A boilers, fitted to 5552-5664, were domeless with vertical throatplate and short firebox (SFB). The boilers of LMS ones were built in mild steel and the North British in nickel steel.

Superheating modifications went on almost from the start, giving a transition that was also noticeable in other classes (see *The Book of the Princess Royal Pacifics* for instance). This is complicated stuff but fortunately the hard work has been done by Rowledge and Reed in *The Stanier 4-6-0s of the LMS* (D&C, 1977) which is reproduced on page 8, with grateful thanks.
 These superheating developments meant that by the time Crewe was ready to build 5665 onwards the back end of boilers had been re-arranged in

---

Facsimile

The total cost of the 1934 Locomotive Renewal Programme was therefore :-

New Locomotives		£787,620.
Expenditure on brakes		1,210.
Total expenditure in workshops		£788,930.
Consequent on reduction in separate types of locomotives certain stock parts will become obsolete at a loss of		£13,638.
		£802,468.
LESS residual value of locomotives and rail motors to be displaced	£27,150.	£775,318.

the Chief Accountant's allocation of which was :-

		New and Displaced Locomotives. £.	Conversion of Brakes on 13 Locomotives. £.	TOTAL. £.
Rolling Stock Renewal Fund		Dr. 775,583	-	775,583
Works & Equipment Maintenance Fund		Dr. -	2,149	2,149
Maintenance (Superintendence).		Dr. 31,032	49	31,081
Revenue Account (ultimate effect)		Dr. 806,615	2,198	808,813
Capital Account		Cr. 32,507	988	33,495
		£774,108	£1,210	£775,318.

Statements giving particulars of the costs per engine mile in respect of repairs, renewals and coal consumption for the new and old locomotives were submitted, shewing an estimated net saving of £17,423 per annum, the summarised effects of the programme being :-

Cost of Repairs, Renewals and Coal per mile.		Tender Locos. d.	Tank Locos. d.	Total.
New Locomotives	..	10.78	10.26	-
Old Locomotives	..	12.56	10.01	-
INCREASED or Decreased cost per mile	(dec) 1.78	(inc.) 0.25		-
Engine miles per annum	..	2,962,000	1,716,000	-
		£.	£.	£.
Total saving per annum	..	21,968	1,788	20,180
Deduct additional interest charges :-			£.	
Due to obsolescence.			4,432.	
Less decreased interest at 5% on capital credit of £33,495.			1,675.	2,757.
Estimated net saving per annum		..		£17,423.

Facsimile

Whilst the economies of maintenance and working had been the main determining factor in the range of the programme, it had the advantage of keeping the present staff employed for about five days per week and thus balancing shop work with maintenance.

The new locomotives to be constructed would be of increased unit power, compared with those to be displaced, to meet traffic requirements - the new tender locomotives shewing an average increased tractive power of 23% and the new tank locomotives 38% - which requirements could not, with economy, be covered by utilising the less powerful locomotives stored, or by further improving the workshop output which had probably reached its present practical limit, the number of locomotives under and awaiting repair having decreased from 19.02% of the total stock at 31st December 1923 to 3.86% at the end of 1932.

This reduction, combined with the provision of improved locomotives and decreased traffic demands, would enable the stock to be reduced since amalgamation by 1,964 at 31st December, 1933, whilst the present proposals would further reduce the stock in 1934 by 86, making the total reduction from 10,396, including Somerset and Dorset Railway transfers, to 8,346, or 2,050, apart from the storage of locomotives of which there were 954 stored at 27th May 1933.

Standardisation was proceeding and the result of the proposed 1934 programme would reduce the number of separate classes by 4, leaving the number of different classes in existence 210, compared with 393 in 1922.

The stock of superheater locomotives would be increased by 72 in 1934, making 3,877 or 46% of the total stock compared with 1,870 or 18% in 1922.

The justification of the new locomotives from the mechanical aspect was as follows :-

(a) 58 Improved 3-cylinder "Claughton" 4-6-0.

The present locomotives gave much trouble with the trailing axleboxes and were expensive on maintenance. The new locomotives would be of 12% increased tractive power, whilst the cost of maintenance and coal would be about 24% less.

(b) 10 Improved "Prince of Wales" 4-6-0.

The frames of the present locomotives gave a great deal of trouble, and the cost of maintenance and coal was heavy. The new locomotives would be of 17% increased tractive power, whilst the cost of maintenance and coal would be about 11% less.

Facsimile

(c)   10 Northern Division 4-6-0 Passenger.

       The present locomotives had reached the end of
their theoretical life, and it would not be economical to
reboiler them.   They were saturated engines, heavy on coal,
and not satisfactory in service, and the new locomotives
to replace them would reduce maintenance and coal costs by
about 6%.   The capacity would remain about the same, as the
weight was restricted by physical considerations.

(d)   2 Experimental 2-8-0 Freight

       To obtain mechanical and operating experience in
the use of larger freight locomotives.

(e)   32 2-6-4 Passenger Tanks.

       Improved design to meet the Southend traffic
requirements.

(f)   20 Standard 2-6-2 Passenger Tank.

       Present standards to replace various types of
locomotives which would be broken up.

       The displacements proposed included a number of
locomotives of inadequate power to meet modern requirements, and the
cost figures indicated that it was in the Company's interests to
replace them by modern units, so far as the power was now required.
The breaking up of these particular locomotives was due to obsolescence
and caused a departure from the lives assumed for renewal fund purposes.
The average expired life of the units was 32.93 years, compared with
the normal life of 41.01 years, giving an average unexpired life of
about 20%, which had been quantified by taking the portion of the
capital proposed to be displaced prematurely, £75,000, and treating
5% thereon = £3,750, as a reduction of the economies to be effected.

       As a consequence of the reduction of the number of
separate types of locomotives to be effected by the programme, certain
stock parts would become obsolete at a loss of £13,638, and 5% thereon
= £682, had been treated as a further reduction of the economies
to be effected.

       The total debit in respect of obsolescence
was thus £4,432 per annum.

Facsimile

Facsimile

So far as the 1933 Locomotive Renewal Programme was concerned; it was reported that consequent on the substitution of 15 improved 3-cylinder "Claughton" engines in place of 10 converted "Prince of Wales" locomotives (now included in the 1934 programme) and 5 2-8-0 freight tender locomotives authorised by Traffic Committee Minute No.3518 and Mechanical & Electrical Engineering Committee Minute No.287 of the 24th May, 1933, the original authorised gross expenditure had been increased by £2,500 from £741,435 to £743,935, the net expenditure for 1933 being estimated at :-

```
        New Locomotives      ..    ..   £743,935.
        Obsolete Materials   ..    ..     £2,403.
                                        ─────────
                                        £746,338.
    Less residual value of
    displaced locomotives    ..         £51,354.
                                        ─────────
                                        £694,984.

which the Chief Accountant had allocated :-
                                             £.
    Rolling Stock Renewal Fund   ..  Dr.  1,068,998.
    Maintenance (Superintendence) ..  Dr.    29,311.

    Revenue Account (ultimate effect)  Dr. 1,098,309.
    Capital Account       ..       ..  Cr.   403,325.
                                          ─────────
               TOTAL     ..    Dr.      £694,984.
```

The Chairman stated that the expenditure on the proposed programme had been recommended to the Board by the Traffic Committee to-day, subject to reference to the Mechanical and Electrical Engineering Committee.

Approved.

Diagram right. Inner/outer fireboxes on the Jubilees. Much has been said about the vertical throatplate and sloping throatplate boiler types, which are evidenced externally by the 'join' between boiler barrel and firebox. This drawing, adapted from Rowledge and Reed's *The Stanier 4-6-0s of the LMS* illustrates the increase in firebox volume so gained by employing the sloping front, as well as the 'steam collector' at the highest point, where there was the least chance of boiler water being carried over into the regulator and thence, possibly disastrously, to the cylinders. Priming would result for sure and, in extreme cases, the loss of cylinder covers when the pressure relief valves on the covers could not cope. (It must be stressed that this was far from being a common occurrence, for the relief valves had enormous capacity.) The later 'domed' boilers had the regulator therein, rather than incorporated in the smokebox superheater header. This not only put the steam collection point higher, it also made the job of attending to the regulator valve a much cleaner one.

It is worth making the point that the top feed cover, even when it incorporates what looks like a 'dome' on a 'domeless' boiler is not some form of dome, other than in the sense of its shape. In simple terms the top feed is the point at which feed water from the injectors enters the boiler; the steam collector/regulator valve is the point at which steam is taken for the cylinders. Only a dome on its own, with the top feed placed separately, contained a regulator valve.

Boilers/Fireboxes in the next section, *Devil in the Detail.*

order to improve steaming capacity (see later, also) These 3A boilers were domed with sloping throatplate and long firebox (LFB). Flues and tubes once more varied, as in the table below. The only faintly obvious external difference between these two variations of the 3A boiler was the length of the firebox. The join between firebox and boiler was all of eleven inches further forward on the long firebox boilers. In determining which was which, the giveaway was the number and arrangement of washout plugs – see

It was the steaming problems which shadowed the Jubilees in their first years. Their steaming reputation was probably the worst among the Stanier engines and though the Stanier 2-6-2Ts (remembered with a shudder in certain quarters) might have run the Jubilees close, the particular problems of the little Class 3 tanks were never so serious in their consequences – they could always be got rid of somewhere they could do relatively little harm.

Proportions were qualitative, as usual in British practice, and were altered on a similar basis. The blast nozzle was reduced

JUBILEES - HEATING SURFACE VARIATIONS									
Notes	Tubes No/Dia (inches)	Flues No/Dia (inches)	Heating Surface	Super-heater No/Dia (inches)	Elements SWG	Super-heating Surface Sq ft	Firebox Heating Surface Sq ft	Grate Area Sq ft	Free Gas Area Sq ft.
(a)	160/2	14/5$^{1}/_{8}$	1463	14/1$^{3}/_{8}$	11	228	162	29.5	3.90
(b)	158/2	14/5$^{1}/_{8}$	1447	14/1$^{3}/_{8}$	11	228	162	29.5	3.88
(c)	130/2	21/5$^{1}/_{8}$	1372	21/1$^{1}/_{8}$	11	256	162	29.5	4.27
(d)	128/2	21/5$^{1}/_{8}$	1357	21/1$^{1}/_{8}$	11	256	162	29.5	4.25
(e)	168/2	21/5$^{1}/_{8}$	1656	21/1$^{1}/_{4}$	11	290	162	29.5	4.78
(f)	159/1$^{7}/_{8}$	24/5$^{1}/_{8}$	1570	24/1$^{1}/_{4}$	11	331	162	29.5	4.55
(g)	138/2$^{1}/_{8}$	21/5$^{1}/_{8}$	1391	21/1$^{1}/_{8}$	11	235	181	31.0	4.75
(h)	105/2$^{1}/_{8}$	28/5$^{1}/_{8}$	1270	28/1$^{1}/_{8}$	11	312	181	31.0	4.80
(i)	168/1$^{7}/_{8}$	21/5$^{1}/_{8}$	1466	21/1$^{1}/_{8}$	11	235	181	31.0	4.54
(j)	159/1$^{7}/_{8}$	24/5$^{1}/_{8}$	1459	24/1$^{1}/_{4}$	11	307	181	31.0	4.55

Vertical throatplate boilers: (a) to (f)
Sloping throatplate boilers: (g) to (j)
(a) 5552-5641, 5647-5664 as built.
(b) as (a) but number of tubes reduced by two.
(c) 5642-5646 as built.
(d) as (c) but number of tubes reduced by two.
(e) boiler of 5554 re-tubed.
(f) boilers in (a) retubed and fitted with domes.
(g) 5665-5676, 5678-5701 as built (some of these boilers may have had the number of tubes reduced by two).
(h) 5677 – this boiler retained this arrangement throughout its existence.
(i) second boiler of 5665 – built as spare and later altered to (j).
(j) 5702-5742 as built – this became the standard arrangement for sloping throatplate boilers but the boiler first fitted to 5731 had one inch trifurcated elements with superheating surface of 357sq/ft for a trial period.

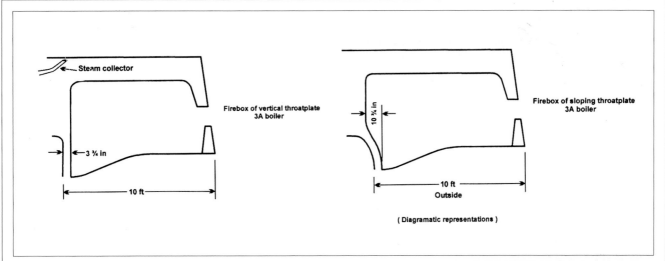

Steam collector

Firebox of vertical throatplate
3A boiler

3 ¾ in

10 ft

Firebox of sloping throatplate
3A boiler

10 ¾ in

10 ft
Outside

(Diagramatic representations)

on the Jubilees by various amounts, according to the number of boiler flues and tubes. The superheater element deflector plates in the smokebox were usually removed at the sheds (unofficially) as a sort of first step to see what happened. Further alterations to the draughting, principally the removal of the jumper top and improved superheating, solved the problems. The earlier vertical throatplate boilers were never rebuilt to the sloping form but their 14 element superheaters gave way to 24 elements. The low superheating that Stanier favoured at first was something he brought with him from Swindon but it apparently didn't suit the lower quality coal found on the LMS. As with the two Princess Royal Pacifics in 1933, *The Railway Gazette* wondered publicly at the low degree of superheating - see page 10.

In the 1930s the taper boiler engines poured forth. 5619 was built at Crewe in October 1934 and named NIGERIA in April 1936.

A new 5587; it later became BARODA. The new riveted steel plates in place of the old cast balance weights show well here – they're a less obvious feature than you'd think, in an era when it was the custom to photograph engines only when 'rods down', which meant the weights were usually obscured under the running plate.

The Jubilees kept a reputation for temperamental steaming more or less to the end; the early bad experiences lingered in the collective mind, possibly because they needed a more sensitive 'little and often' firing technique. As late as October 1958, with the end of the Jubilees on Midland expresses not far off, a fairly exasperated letter appeared in *Trains Illustrated*, to the effect that could the temperamental steaming troubles of the Class 6 Jubilees only be cured, then there would be none of the problems in timekeeping then being experienced. The Jubilees, it seemed, were sensitive to the least fault, such as a few blocked superheater flues. Injectors caused endless trouble (the writer described them as 'the bane of London Midland men's lives') and priming was a problem. Blow-down discharging into the ashpan was complained of because it was said to cause steam to rise and cool the fire. But latterly this became the norm due to complaints from the Civil Engineer regarding its deleterious effect when discharged onto the track so it was not really an issue when it came to steaming. Another point contemporary observers failed to appreciate was the steep slide in coal quality that could affect any area of BR by the late 1950s. The Jubilees might have had a fickle side – but they *were* beautiful!

April 27, 1934   *THE RAILWAY GAZETTE*

*   *   *

New L.M.S. Express Engines

THE new three-cylinder 4-6-0 express locomotive just completed at Crewe is the first of 113 being built to the designs of Mr. W. A. Stanier, Chief Mechanical Engineer of the L.M.S.R. The engines of this new series resemble in some respects those of the existing 5XP class, although differing therefrom in certain important respects, the most noteworthy being the substitution of a tapered boiler barrel equipped with Mr. Stanier's moderate form of superheater as applied by him already to other locomotives of his introduction on the L.M.S.R. We use the term " moderate " as distinct from " modified " in this connection as signifying the more clearly what is meant, namely, that, as things go with locomotives of this classification, the superheater appears to be on the small side and consequently may be expected to produce only moderate temperatures. Mr. Stanier's continued adherence to this plan can suggest only one thing, namely that his experience has proved to his satisfaction that the proportions adopted have, in spite of their apparent unorthodoxy, demonstrated their efficiency in service, which, of course, provides a sufficient justification.

We were enabled by the courtesy of Mr. Stanier to inspect the first Crewe-built engine, No. 5552, at Crewe works on the day it was turned out for its steam trials when opportunities were afforded for making a close inspection. We were much impressed by the well laid out features of design exhibited and particularly by the cab arrangements. On the footplate there is a sense of spaciousness and convenience and the lookout is facilitated by the ample window spacing in the front and at the sides, adjustable glass shields being fitted to the side windows so that when the enginemen are looking out through these windows in the forward direction protection is afforded. Great care and thought have obviously been expended in perfecting details with a view to producing a locomotive that shall not only be economical in running and maintenance costs, but shall also give a high overall efficiency. The comments we made upon Mr. Stanier's recent 2-6-4 tank engines, described in our issue of March 30, hold good in general for these new 4-6-0 express locomotives, which incorporate many of the standard components used on the former. Regarded as a whole the engine is a very good example of modern British locomotive design, and our inspection left us with a very clear impression of this fact. The new locomotives are illustrated and described on page 728 of this issue.

5613, later named KENYA, at Kentish Town in 1935.

5569 TASMANIA at Rugby shed along with another recent Fowler-tendered Jubilee, 1936. The mis-match between cab and tender is painfully clear here.

5584 in the old shed at Perth about 1935, before the LMS rebuilt the place into a modern depot. It was not named until 1938 – NORTH WEST FRONTIER. Photograph Gavin Whitelaw Collection.

This is 5635, completed at Crewe in November 1934, at Kentish Town shed. All the '5XPs' had the crosshead driven vacuum pump (showing well in the low light here, oily and glistening) driven off the left-hand crosshead when built; it was a feature which had an honourable ancestry, going back to Webb's time on the LNW and Dean's years on the GWR. The purpose was to maintain sufficient vacuum to keep the brakes off when the engine was running and so 'save' steam for actual running but their efficacy soon came into question. Late in the 1930s they were all removed, for it was found that the small ejector could do the work just as efficiently, without the expense of maintaining the pump. 5635 became TOBAGO in 1936. Photograph W. Hermiston, The Transport Treasury.

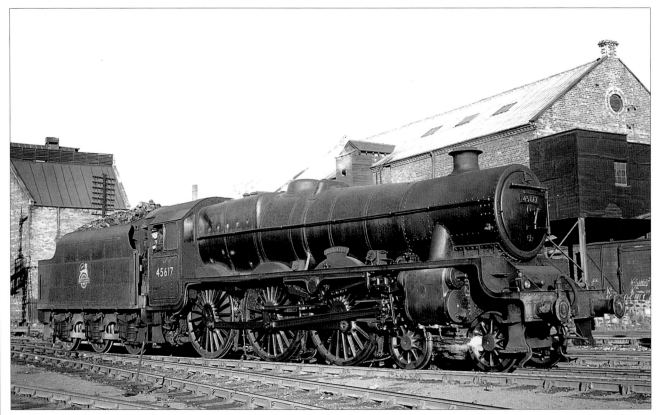

Devil in the Detail. 45617 MAURITIUS of Crewe North, at Edinburgh Dalry Road in August 1955. The standard Stanier bogie came into general use only once construction of the Jubilees was underway, which resulted in two sizes, or rather two different wheelbases – see 'Bogies'. There were of course visible differences; the 6ft 3in bogies had a FLAT cross-stay which could be discerned (as here) under the buffer beam in the unlikely event that the lighting was right. The 'lug' can be seen on the smokebox rim but the engaging bracket on the door itself is absent. The one-piece smokebox saddle shows well. These few photographs have been chosen to show such differences – don't forget the extra rivets on the smokebox front under the handrail... Photograph W. Hermiston, The Transport Treasury.

45612 JAMAICA (a Kentish Town engine) at Nottingham shed, 24 July 1955. It has the flat cross-stay denoting the earlier 6ft 3in wheelbase bogie, no lugs of any sort on the smokebox and one-piece smokebox saddle. The Fowler straight high sided tender is well-filled ready for the off and the rather bent handrail in front of the cab is something few would dare to model. It may have resulted from an exceptionally corpulent fitter attending the whistle/safety valves – a more likely culprit would be a heavy fire iron, carelessly put. Photograph Brian Morrison.

2. DEVIL IN THE DETAIL

Detail variation abounded among the Jubilees, though apart from different tenders which altered the overall appearance completely, very little of it was obvious at first glance. Built as they were in different batches, at different works, it was natural that changes should occur; these have been recounted elsewhere in almost fantastic detail, sometimes to the point of impenetrability, but I hope to be able to list some of the more important ones here. Differences in the bogie for instance, made it one of the few classes, surely, in which even the engine wheelbase varied… Watch out for BR Standard Class 4 chimneys – there is a brilliant comparison for instance, in the *British Railways Illustrated Summer Special* of 2002 – and some bizarre variants turned out by St Rollox, top feed only on some boilers and in one case two domes.

Bogies
The locomotives built with short fireboxes at Crewe (5552-5556, 5607-5654) had 6ft 3in wheelbase bogies; they followed the Patriot wheelbase dimensions precisely and were in fact ex-Claughton bogies. The LMS standard was being developed elsewhere as it were; this was the 6ft 6in wheelbase bogie devised for the 2-6-4T (trailing) which was to serve as the leading bogie for 4-6-0s. The ten Derby engines 5655-5664, the NBL engines 5557-5606 and the subsequent Crewe ones 5665-5742 all got the new, longer wheelbase bogie. The 6ft 3in wheelbase bogies were ex-Claughtons and were on the radial principle (hence 'LNWR' stamped on wheels on 45593 when it was preserved) while the 6ft 6in ones were on the Churchward/De Glehn principle.

Smokebox Saddle
The short firebox/vertical throatplate engines, 5552-5664, had a two-part casting for the smokebox saddle; this later gave way to a single-piece saddle, for the original double arrangement suffered from stress related flexing. The front section of the saddle was part of the inside cylinder casting and the rear one acted partly as a stay between the two outside cylinders. 5665-5742 got a much more conventional single saddle, completely separate from the inside cylinder casting and recognisable by a distinctive row of three vertical ribs. This was regarded as the standard arrangement and over time replaced the double saddle on the earlier engines, as the inside cylinders were renewed at overhaul.

Smokebox 'Lugs'
At the side of the smokebox was a 'lug' which engaged with a bracket on the smokebox door as it closed, to help locate the dart. Bracket and/or lug, or neither, might be present on individual engines at certain times.

Boilers/Fireboxes
With fundamental changes occurring as the engines were built, variations proliferated. In a sense the Jubilees were made up of two sub-classes; the original short firebox/vertical throatplate ones and the later long firebox/sloping throatplate examples.

Naturally we now use the terms short and long firebox willy-nilly but on the LMS/LMR the two boiler versions were differentiated as either vertical or sloping throatplate. The foundation ring of the firebox was of the same size in both and the extra heating surface and volume was achieved by adding a combustion

The 6ft 6in wheelbase bogie subsequently made standard was recognisable by the leading cross-stay which was not flat but was circular in cross section. It is even less obvious in most instances than the flat cross-stay but this picture of 45728 DEFIANCE leaving Perth on 3 September 1955 shows it well. One-piece smokebox saddle, lugs on smokebox door/rim and big Scottish Region cabside numbers. Photograph J. Robertson, The Transport Treasury.

Blackpool Jubilee 5588 KASHMIR in LMS red at Polmadie (to judge from the Caley engines). This view shows the two-piece smokebox saddle clearly, as well as the steam supply to the atomiser with its stop cock – just to the rear of the outside steam pipe. There is no smokebox door 'lug' and the bracket for the vacuum pump arm still forms part of the crosshead; 5588 still has gravity, or trickle, sanding – compare with other photographs. The engine is on an ashpit (note fire irons all over the place) having worked in off the Central Division; the pile of ash on the left presumably came from an earlier engine, unless the lads have carefully brushed the front running plate. The vacuum pipe leading down from the ejector just forward of the cab is fairly rigid copper with T-junction piece behind the valence. In later BR days this was modified with a central piece of rubber hose, following a number of fractures and subsequent total loss of vacuum and therefore unwanted application of the brakes. Photograph W. Hermiston, The Transport Treasury.

chamber. Of course the ordinary observer would not see that the lower part was the same, for it was hidden between the frames. The increase in grate area was obtained by making the water space less (each leg of the foundation ring was reduced in width). The prime reason that a sloping throatplate boiler could not be fitted to an earlier engine was the position of a frame stay just ahead of the firebox.

From 1936 the short firebox boilers were given domes and eleven of the short firebox engines had frames modified to take long fireboxes/boilers. Five short firebox boilers were never fitted with domes. These changes are summarised in Table 1. This was originally compiled by the proprietors of Brassmasters, a band of men dedicated to the creation of etched brass, lost wax and resin kits to breathtaking standards of accuracy and fine detail. The frets alone are works of art good enough to frame. (Which is about as far as I've got.) There is almost as much work in assembling the information on individual Jubilees as in producing the

kits themselves. I am inexpressibly grateful for their kindness in allowing me to reproduce the fruits of their labours here. See *Acknowledgements* for the Brassmasters trade address.

Recognition: A Note on Washout Plugs
The washout plugs on the firebox sides of the Jubilees are diagnostic. The short firebox vertical throatplate boiler engines had five on the left-hand side of the firebox and six on the right-hand side. They were so positioned that the boilerwashers could reach all parts of the inner firebox crown. The long firebox sloping throatplate engines, however, had six each side. A point for modellers is that the row of washout plugs, whether five or six, were not parallel to the handrail, their alignment rising upwards to the front, in order to lie parallel with the top of the inner firebox crown. The sloping throatplate boilers, moreover, also had 'handholes', two each side, sited right at the top of the firebox as it curved over. Boilerwashers called these 'mudholes' and they gave extra access

to the upper reaches of the inner firebox. All that was visible from the outside was the small domes of the protecting cover – sometimes, in the last dark days, left off, or, worse, left hanging by a single bolt. The table begins opposite.

Rivets
Even the rivets varied on the Jubilees, the engines representing the rivet counter's Nirvana. Patterns and types changed throughout the years as repairs, maintenance and modifications took place but there was a fundamental difference in the riveting of the bufferbeams and smokebox door rings from the beginning. On some engines flush rivets were used both on the buffer beam and the smokebox door rim while others had snaphead rivets. As the reader will have instantly guessed, other engines had both form of rivets. In later years further rivets appeared on the smokebox wrapper plates where inner liner plates were fitted. Table 1 has the fruits of the Brassmaster rivet counting labours for us to pore over –

TABLE 1. DETAIL CHANGES IN JUBILEE CLASS – ORIGINAL TABLE COMPILED BY *BRASSMASTERS* AND REPRODUCED WITH KIND PERMISSION

No.	Original Boiler/ firebox	Bogie	Sand	Original chimney	Double chimney	Buffer beam	Smoke-box rim	First Domed	SFB/ LFB conv.	Recon verted to SFB	Fitted with Domeless boiler
5552	SFB/VT	6'3"	Gravity	Tall		Flush	Riveted	9/40			4/43-5/45
5553	SFB/VT	6'3"	Gravity	Tall	1940	Flush	Riveted	2/37			
5554	SFB/VT	6'3"	Gravity	Tall		Flush	Riveted	6/36			
5555	SFB/VT	6'3"	Gravity	Tall		Flush	Riveted	10/38			6/52-2/56
5556	SFB/VT	6'3"	Gravity	Tall		Flush	Riveted	2/37			1/45-8/47
5557	SFB/VT	6'6"	Gravity	S/R		Riveted	Flush	2/37			
5558	SFB/VT	6'6"	Gravity	S/R		Riveted	Flush	11/37			
5559	SFB/VT	6'6"	Gravity	S/R		Riveted	Flush	10/37			
5560	SFB/VT	6'6"	Gravity	S/R		Riveted	Flush	6/37			
5561	SFB/VT	6'6"	Gravity	S/R		Riveted	Flush	2/38			
5562	SFB/VT	6'6"	Gravity	S/R		Riveted	Flush	6/37			10/47-2/52
5563	SFB/VT	6'6"	Gravity	S/R		Riveted	Flush	1/39			
5564	SFB/VT	6'6"	Gravity	S/R		Riveted	Flush	7/37			
5565	SFB/VT	6'6"	Gravity	Tall		Riveted	Flush	6/37			
5566	SFB/VT	6'6"	Gravity	Tall		Riveted	Flush	3/37			
5567	SFB/VT	6'6"	Gravity	Tall		Riveted	Flush	4/37	4/37		
5568	SFB/VT	6'6"	Gravity	Tall		Riveted	Flush	6/37			
5569	SFB/VT	6'6"	Gravity	Tall		Riveted	Flush	6/37			
5570	SFB/VT	6'6"	Gravity	Tall		Riveted	Flush	8/37			
5571	SFB/VT	6'6"	Gravity	Tall		Riveted	Flush	5/38			
5572	SFB/VT	6'6"	Gravity	Tall		Riveted	Flush	5/37			
5573	SFB/VT	6'6"	Gravity	Tall		Riveted	Flush	3/38			
5574	SFB/VT	6'6"	Gravity	Tall		Riveted	Flush	11/37			
5575	SFB/VT	6'6"	Gravity	Tall		Riveted	Flush	12/37			1/50-6/60
5576	SFB/VT	6'6"	Gravity	Tall		Riveted	Flush	6/41			12/37-5/41
5577	SFB/VT	6'6"	Gravity	Tall		Riveted	Flush	7/39			12/51-8/53
5578	SFB/VT	6'6"	Gravity	Tall		Riveted	Flush	4/38			12/52-8/57
5579	SFB/VT	6'6"	Gravity	Tall		Riveted	Flush	5/38			3/38-5/42&1/47-8/51
5580	SFB/VT	6'6"	Gravity	Tall		Riveted	Flush	6/37			8/41-6/42
5581	SFB/VT	6'6"	Gravity	Tall		Riveted	Flush	4/43			3/39-3/43
5582	SFB/VT	6'6"	Gravity	Tall		Riveted	Flush	11/37			
5583	SFB/VT	6'6"	Gravity	Tall		Riveted	Flush	1/38			
5584	SFB/VT	6'6"	Gravity	Tall		Riveted	Flush	8/38			
5585	SFB/VT	6'6"	Gravity	Tall		Riveted	Flush	6/37			
5586	SFB/VT	6'6"	Gravity	Tall		Riveted	Flush	2/37			2/61-1/65
5587	SFB/VT	6'6"	Gravity	Tall		Riveted	Flush	3/37			
5588	SFB/VT	6'6"	Gravity	Tall		Riveted	Flush	6/37			
5589	SFB/VT	6'6"	Gravity	Tall		Riveted	Flush	10/37			
5590	SFB/VT	6'6"	Gravity	Tall		Riveted	Flush	4/37	4/37		
5591	SFB/VT	6'6"	Gravity	Tall		Riveted	Flush	6/38			3/60-10/63
5592	SFB/VT	6'6"	Gravity	Tall		Riveted	Flush	5/37			6/44-3/49
5593	SFB/VT	6'6"	Gravity	Tall		Riveted	Flush	4/37			
5594	SFB/VT	6'6"	Gravity	Tall		Riveted	Flush	1/38			
5595	SFB/VT	6'6"	Gravity	Tall		Riveted	Flush	3/37			
5596	SFB/VT	6'6"	Gravity	Tall	1961-66	Riveted	Flush	11/37			
5597	SFB/VT	6'6"	Gravity	Tall		Riveted	Flush	2/38			
5598	SFB/VT	6'6"	Gravity	Tall		Riveted	Flush	6/37			
5599	SFB/VT	6'6"	Gravity	Tall		Riveted	Flush	8/37			
5600	SFB/VT	6'6"	Gravity	Tall		Riveted	Flush	2/38			12/40-11/42&7/54-6/58
5601	SFB/VT	6'6"	Gravity	Tall		Riveted	Flush	9/37			11/53-7/56
5602	SFB/VT	6'6"	Gravity	Tall		Riveted	Flush	4/37			
5603	SFB/VT	6'6"	Gravity	Tall		Riveted	Flush	10/37			
5604	SFB/VT	6'6"	Gravity	Tall		Riveted	Flush	7/37			
5605	SFB/VT	6'6"	Gravity	Tall		Riveted	Flush	4/38			
5606	SFB/VT	6'6"	Gravity	Tall		Riveted	Flush	2/38			
5607	SFB/VT	6'3"	Gravity	Tall		Flush	Riveted	6/36	6/36	4/38	12/42-10/46
5608	SFB/VT	6'3"	Gravity	Tall		Flush	Riveted	4/37	4/37		
5609	SFB/VT	6'3"	Gravity	Tall		Flush	Riveted	9/38			
5610	SFB/VT	6'3"	Gravity	Tall		Flush	Riveted	2/37	2/37		
5611	SFB/VT	6'3"	Gravity	Tall		Flush	Riveted	8/38			
5612	SFB/VT	6'3"	Gravity	Tall		Flush	Riveted	4/37			
5613	SFB/VT	6'3"	Gravity	Tall		Flush	Riveted	11/38			
5614	SFB/VT	6'3"	Gravity	Tall		Flush	Riveted	12/36			
5615	SFB/VT	6'3"	Gravity	Tall		Flush	Riveted	2/37			8/49-10/52
5616	SFB/VT	6'3"	Gravity	Tall		Flush	Riveted	7/36	7/36	2/38	
5617	SFB/VT	6'3"	Gravity	Tall		Flush	Riveted	12/37			
5618	SFB/VT	6'3"	Gravity	Tall		Flush	Riveted	4/37			1/43-4/44
5619	SFB/VT	6'3"	Gravity	Tall		Flush	Riveted	3/37			
5620	SFB/VT	6'3"	Gravity	Tall		Flush	Riveted	3/37			
5621	SFB/VT	6'3"	Gravity	Tall		Flush	Riveted	6/37	6/37		
5622	SFB/VT	6'3"	Gravity	Tall		Flush	Riveted	7/36	7/36	7/38	
5623	SFB/VT	6'3"	Gravity	Tall		Flush	Riveted	8/39			
5624	SFB/VT	6'3"	Gravity	Tall		Flush	Riveted	12/38			
5625	SFB/VT	6'3"	Gravity	Tall		Flush	Riveted	1/39			
5626	SFB/VT	6'3"	Gravity	Tall		Flush	Riveted	2/37			
5627	SFB/VT	6'3"	Gravity	Tall		Flush	Riveted	10/38			
5628	SFB/VT	6'3"	Gravity	Tall		Flush	Riveted	2/37			
5629	SFB/VT	6'3"	Gravity	Tall		Flush	Riveted	4/39			
5630	SFB/VT	6'3"	Gravity	Tall		Flush	Riveted	11/38			
5631	SFB/VT	6'3"	Gravity	Tall		Flush	Riveted	12/38			
5632	SFB/VT	6'3"	Gravity	Tall		Flush	Riveted	8/38			
5633	SFB/VT	6'3"	Gravity	Tall		Flush	Riveted	10/39			
5634	SFB/VT	6'3"	Gravity	Tall		Flush	Riveted	4/39			
5635	SFB/VT	6'3"	Gravity	Tall		Flush	Riveted	3/39			
5636	SFB/VT	6'3"	Gravity	Tall		Flush	Riveted	3/37			2/49-4/53
5637	SFB/VT	6'3"	Gravity	Tall		Flush	Riveted	10/38			
5638	SFB/VT	6'3"	Gravity	Tall		Flush	Riveted	11/36			
5639	SFB/VT	6'3"	Gravity	Tall		Flush	Riveted	3/37	3/37		
5640	SFB/VT	6'3"	Gravity	Tall		Flush	Riveted	8/36	8/36		
5641	SFB/VT	6'3"	Gravity	Tall		Flush	Riveted	4/37			
5642	SFB/VT	6'3"	Gravity	Tall		Flush	Riveted	12/39			
5643	SFB/VT	6'3"	Gravity	Tall		Flush	Riveted	6/44			9/42-6/44&3/56-8/60
5644	SFB/VT	6'3"	Gravity	Tall		Flush	Riveted	10/38			8/46-11/49
5645	SFB/VT	6'3"	Gravity	Tall		Flush	Riveted	9/37			10/57-10/63
5646	SFB/VT	6'3"	Gravity	Tall		Flush	Riveted	3/38			
5647	SFB/VT	6'3"	Gravity	Tall		Flush	Riveted	1/38			
5648	SFB/VT	6'3"	Gravity	Tall		Flush	Riveted	12/37			
5649	SFB/VT	6'3"	Gravity	Tall		Flush	Riveted	4/37			

(Continued overleaf)

No.	Original Boiler/firebox	Bogie	Sand	Original chimney	Double chimney	Buffer beam	Smokebox rim	First Domed	SFB/LFB conv.	Reconverted to SFB	Fitted with Domeless boiler
5650	SFB/VT	6'3"	Gravity	Tall		Flush	Riveted	1/37			
5651	SFB/VT	6'3"	Gravity	Tall		Flush	Riveted	10/37			3/57-11/62
5652	SFB/VT	6'3"	Gravity	Tall		Flush	Riveted	5/37			
5653	SFB/VT	6'3"	Gravity	Tall		Flush	Riveted	1/38			6/45-10/48
5654	SFB/VT	6'3"	Gravity	Tall		Flush	Riveted	5/37			
5655	SFB/VT	6'6"	Gravity	Short		Riveted	Flush	5/37			
5656	SFB/VT	6'6"	Gravity	Short		Riveted	Flush	3/37			
5657	SFB/VT	6'6"	Gravity	Short		Riveted	Flush	4/37	4/37		
5658	SFB/VT	6'6"	Gravity	Short		Riveted	Flush	6/37			
5659	SFB/VT	6'6"	Gravity	Short		Riveted	Flush	5/37			
5660	SFB/VT	6'6"	Gravity	Short		Riveted	Flush	7/37			
5661	SFB/VT	6'6"	Gravity	Short		Riveted	Flush	1/38			
5662	SFB/VT	6'6"	Gravity	Short		Riveted	Flush	7/38			2/61-11/62
5663	SFB/VT	6'6"	Gravity	Short		Riveted	Flush	7/38			
5664	SFB/VT	6'6"	Gravity	Short		Riveted	Flush	4/37			
5665	LFB/SL	6'6"	Gravity	Short		Riveted	Riveted				
5666	LFB/SL	6'6"	Gravity	Short		Riveted	Riveted				
5667	LFB/SL	6'6"	Gravity	Short		Riveted	Riveted				
5668	LFB/SL	6'6"	Gravity	Short		Riveted	Riveted				
5669	LFB/SL	6'6"	Gravity	Short		Riveted	Riveted				
5670	LFB/SL	6'6"	Gravity	Short		Riveted	Riveted				
5671	LFB/SL	6'6"	Gravity	Short		Riveted	Riveted				
5672	LFB/SL	6'6"	Gravity	Short		Riveted	Riveted				
5673	LFB/SL	6'6"	Gravity	Short		Riveted	Riveted				
5674	LFB/SL	6'6"	Gravity	Short		Riveted	Riveted				
5675	LFB/SL	6'6"	Gravity	Short		Riveted	Riveted				
5676	LFB/SL	6'6"	Gravity	Short		Riveted	Riveted				
5677	LFB/SL	6'6"	Gravity	Short		Riveted	Riveted				
5678	LFB/SL	6'6"	Gravity	Short		Riveted	Riveted				
5679	LFB/SL	6'6"	Gravity	Short		Riveted	Riveted				
5680	LFB/SL	6'6"	Gravity	Short		Riveted	Riveted				
5681	LFB/SL	6'6"	Gravity	Short		Riveted	Riveted				
5682	LFB/SL	6'6"	Gravity	Short		Riveted	Riveted				
5683	LFB/SL	6'6"	Gravity	Short		Riveted	Riveted				
5684	LFB/SL	6'6"	Gravity	Short	1937-38	Riveted	Riveted				
5685	LFB/SL	6'6"	Gravity	Short		Riveted	Riveted				
5686	LFB/SL	6'6"	Gravity	Short		Riveted	Riveted				
5687	LFB/SL	6'6"	Gravity	Short		Riveted	Riveted				
5688	LFB/SL	6'6"	Gravity	Short		Riveted	Riveted				
5689	LFB/SL	6'6"	Gravity	Short		Riveted	Riveted				
5690	LFB/SL	6'6"	Gravity	Short		Riveted	Riveted				
5691	LFB/SL	6'6"	Gravity	Short		Riveted	Riveted				
5692	LFB/SL	6'6"	Gravity	Short		Riveted	Riveted				
5693	LFB/SL	6'6"	Gravity	Short		Riveted	Riveted				
5694	LFB/SL	6'6"	Gravity	Short		Riveted	Riveted				
5695	LFB/SL	6'6"	Steam	Int.		Riveted	Riveted				
5696	LFB/SL	6'6"	Steam	Int.		Riveted	Riveted				
5697	LFB/SL	6'6"	Steam	Int.		Riveted	Riveted				
5698	LFB/SL	6'6"	Steam	Int.		Riveted	Riveted				
5699	LFB/SL	6'6"	Steam	Int.		Riveted	Riveted				
5700	LFB/SL	6'6"	Steam	Int.		Riveted	Riveted				
5701	LFB/SL	6'6"	Steam	Int.		Riveted	Riveted				
5702	LFB/SL	6'6"	Steam	Int.		Riveted	Riveted				
5703	LFB/SL	6'6"	Steam	Int.		Riveted	Riveted				
5704	LFB/SL	6'6"	Steam	Int.		Riveted	Riveted				
5705	LFB/SL	6'6"	Steam	Int.		Riveted	Riveted				
5706	LFB/SL	6'6"	Steam	Int.		Riveted	Riveted				
5707	LFB/SL	6'6"	Steam	Int.		Riveted	Riveted				
5708	LFB/SL	6'6"	Steam	Int.		Riveted	Riveted				
5709	LFB/SL	6'6"	Steam	Int.		Riveted	Riveted				
5710	LFB/SL	6'6"	Steam	Int.		Riveted	Riveted				
5711	LFB/SL	6'6"	Steam	Int.		Riveted	Riveted				
5712	LFB/SL	6'6"	Steam	Int.		Riveted	Riveted				
5713	LFB/SL	6'6"	Steam	Int.		Riveted	Riveted				
5714	LFB/SL	6'6"	Steam	Int.		Riveted	Riveted				
5715	LFB/SL	6'6"	Steam	Int.		Riveted	Riveted				
5716	LFB/SL	6'6"	Steam	Int.		Riveted	Riveted				
5717	LFB/SL	6'6"	Steam	Int.		Riveted	Riveted				
5718	LFB/SL	6'6"	Steam	Int.		Riveted	Riveted				
5719	LFB/SL	6'6"	Steam	Int.		Riveted	Riveted				
5720	LFB/SL	6'6"	Steam	Int.		Riveted	Riveted				
5721	LFB/SL	6'6"	Steam	Int.		Riveted	Riveted				
5722	LFB/SL	6'6"	Steam	Int.	1956-57	Riveted	Riveted				
5723	LFB/SL	6'6"	Steam	Int.		Riveted	Riveted				
5724	LFB/SL	6'6"	Steam	Int.		Riveted	Riveted				
5725	LFB/SL	6'6"	Steam	Int.		Riveted	Riveted				
5726	LFB/SL	6'6"	Steam	Int.		Riveted	Riveted				
5727	LFB/SL	6'6"	Steam	Int.		Riveted	Riveted				
5728	LFB/SL	6'6"	Steam	Int.		Riveted	Riveted				
5729	LFB/SL	6'6"	Steam	Int.		Riveted	Riveted				
5730	LFB/SL	6'6"	Steam	Int.		Riveted	Riveted				
5731	LFB/SL	6'6"	Steam	Int.		Riveted	Riveted				
5732	LFB/SL	6'6"	Steam	Int.		Riveted	Riveted				
5733	LFB/SL	6'6"	Steam	Int.		Riveted	Riveted				
5734	LFB/SL	6'6"	Steam	Int.		Riveted	Riveted				
5735	LFB/SL	6'6"	Steam	Int.		Riveted	Riveted				Rebuilt 5/42
5736	LFB/SL	6'6"	Steam	Int.		Riveted	Riveted				Rebuilt 4/42
5737	LFB/SL	6'6"	Steam	Int.		Riveted	Riveted				
5738	LFB/SL	6'6"	Steam	Int.		Riveted	Riveted				
5739	LFB/SL	6'6"	Steam	Int.		Riveted	Riveted				
5740	LFB/SL	6'6"	Steam	Int.		Riveted	Riveted				
5741	LFB/SL	6'6"	Steam	Int.		Riveted	Riveted				
5742	LFB/SL	6'6"	Steam	Int.	1940-55	Riveted	Riveted				

SFB/VT = Short firebox/Vertical throatplate, LFB/SL = Long firebox/sloping throatplate.
From 1938 existing dry Gravity sanding began to give way to steam sanding.
A useful distinguishing feature of the domeless short firebox engines was the absence of the prominent circular cover plate with four bolt fixings on the cylinder casings. This seems to have disappeared when domes were fitted, a result of modifications to the lubrication.
Note: The table is derived from photographs and various published sources; some are contradictory, and wherever possible the data has been verified to eliminate the error.

5579 PUNJAB in LMS red, with two-piece smokebox saddle. A prominent external feature was the steam supply to the atomiser which on the 'domeless' engines sat high on the smokebox (compare for instance with 5588). The stop valve was therefore not very accessible, though this became vital in the event of the pipe fracturing, as the escaping steam would thoroughly obscure the driver's vision. 5579 has a circular NBL Hyde Park worksplate (polished, as are the cylinder and piston valve cover casings); the circular ones denoted Hyde Park and the diamond type Queen's Park. Photograph J. Robertson, The Transport Treasury.

the golden rule remains, remember, that to perfectly model a particular locomotive at a particular period, get a photograph.

Vacuum Pump
The left-hand crossheads of the Jubilees had prominent vacuum pumps, after the fashion of the Royal Scots. They were there to maintain sufficient vacuum to keep the brakes off when the engine was running but late in the 1930s they were all removed. The small ejector, it was found, could do the work just as efficiently, without the trouble of maintaining the pump.

Cylinder Casing
There was a circular cover on the cylinder casings, fixed with four bolts and quite distinctive. They were

PUNJAB much later, with smaller atomiser cover, tablet catcher bracket now on the cab side, in what would look to be LMS black, rearranged cabside riveting, different (flush) tender, different top feed, steam instead of gravity sanding and recessed instead of 'knobbed' sandhole filler caps. It has also lost the six-hole bracket for the vacuum pump. Photograph J. Robertson, The Transport Treasury.

JUBILEE DOMELESS BOILERS

With the conversion of the bulk of the original domeless boilers to a domed type, five unconverted boilers remained (Nos.8748 to 8752) and were fitted to a number of locomotives as follows:

\multicolumn{2}{c}{8748}		\multicolumn{2}{c}{8749}		\multicolumn{2}{c}{8750}		\multicolumn{2}{c}{8751}		\multicolumn{2}{c}{8752}	
Loco	Date	Loco	Date	Loco	Date	Loco	Date	Loco	Date
5600	12/40 – 11/42	5642	New – 9/42	5644	New – 10/38	5645	New – 9/37	5646	New – 4/38
5618	1/43 – 4/44	5607	12/42 – 10/46	5579	3/39 – 5/42	5576	12/37 – 5/41	5579	4/38 – 3/39
5592	6/44 – 3/49	5579	1/47 – 8/51	5643	9/42 – 6/44	5580	8/41 – 6/42	5581	3/39 – 3/43
45615	8/49 – 10/52	45577	12/51 – 8/53	5644	8/46 – 11/49	5648	9/42 – 11/44	5552	4/43 – 5/45
45578	12/52 – 8/57	45600	7/54 – 6/58	45575	1/50 – 6/53	5556	1/45 – 8/47	5653	6/45 – 10/48
45645	10/57 – 10/63	45591	3/60 – 10/63	45601	11/53 – 7/56	5562	10/47 – 2/52	45636	2/49 – 4/53
				45575	9/56 – 6/60	45555	6/52 – 2/56	45575	6/53 – 9/56
				45562	2/61 – 11/62	45643	3/56 – 8/60	45651	3/57 – 11/60
						45651	11/60 – 11/62	45586*	2/61 – 1/65

It is notable that 45575 MADRAS was fitted with a domeless boiler no fewer than three times and 45651 SHOVELL was also fitted twice. The boilers were scrapped with the locos at last fitting.

*Listed as 45586, but photos fail to confirm it.

initially absent from the short firebox domeless engines but appeared when the lubrication was modified. The plates concealed a lubricating pipe to the cylinder.

Sanding
From 1938 the 'dry trickle' (better known as 'gravity') sanding on the earlier locomotives came to be replaced by steam sanding; Fowler pattern 'domed handle' sandbox lids were fitted at first but these were gradually replaced by the Stanier pattern with recessed handles, a process which appears to have been complete by the late 1940s.

Livery
Jubilee livery, otherwise known as the spawn of the devil was, it can be appreciated, somewhat complicated. What follows is a general outline; once again, if an engine is to be tied to a particular year, a photograph is the only 100% sure way.

1. The first Jubilees came out in red* with black and yellow lining, a marked contrast to the contemporaneous and very much black, Black 5s. They had the 1928 insignia, 12 inch numerals on the cab and 14 inch L M S on the tenders.

*Red: good enough for most of us though the prone to weathering 'crimson lake' is insisted upon by some. On reflection that may not be a correct statement. The LMS was more frugal than others with repaints so that an engine was obliged to perform longer between them than its contemporaries elsewhere. This is what probably produced the faded effect.

2. 1936-1938 new and repainted engines begin to get a plain lettering and numbering instead of the scroll type. These were made up of 10 inch gold with red shading numbers and 14 inch L M S on the tenders.

3. Come 1938 some numbers and letters revert to scroll type.

4. 1940 sees the wartime black livery, unlined with yellow shading letters and numbers. Few Jubilees, apparently, got anything like a full repaint in the war years, so many survived with pre-war red; no fewer than ten, Rowledge and Reed note, got their BR numbers while still in late 1930s red.

5. With many Jubilees well overdue for a decent paint job, the famously elegant LMS 1946 lined black with maroon and straw lining and block 12 inch numbers with 14 inch L M S begins to be widely applied.

6. Experiments included 5573 NEWFOUNDLAND about 1945-46 in blue grey with maroon lining and 5594 BHOPAL at about the same time in traditional LMS red.

7. M appears in front of the number on several in the first months of nationalisation, with BRITISH RAILWAYS on the tender and of course

45577 BENGAL with big Scottish numerals, at Carstairs on 1 June 1952 in BR green; top feed cover only, atomiser stop valve in low position and well lit in this view. There remains, however, a small pipe running down the smokebox from its former position – a lubricating pipe presumably, to the superheater/regulator valve. '6P' designation low on cabside, flush sided tender and NBL oval plate still in position. St Rollox provided nine sets of nameplates (5576-5578, 5580, 5581, 5583, 5584, 5644 and 5645) all distinguishable from the rest through the lettering, which was three inches high, thinner and more closely spaced. Photograph J. Robertson, The Transport Treasury.

5557 at Camden (it was named NEW BRUNSWICK in October 1936) showing the beautiful clean lines and satisfying proportions of the 'Red Staniers'. Purists abhor the description 'red', preferring 'crimson lake' but to posterity 'red' it has become. Fowler 'knobbed' sandbox filler lids and no smokebox door 'lugs'. The station in the background is Primrose Hill on the North London connection. Photograph W. Hermiston, The Transport Treasury.

the universal application of 40,000 to the numbers. Further experiments include 45565, 45604 and 45694 in light green. Others get BR mixed traffic lined black including 45630, 45676, 45672, 45678, 45679, 45700, 45735 and 45740.

8. From mid-1949 it's 'GWR' Brunswick green with the first emblem; second BR emblem appears from 1957. The unlined plain green and cab stripes of the last days are not worth mentioning.

5668 MADDEN at Polmadie in the sumptuous LMS post-war black; the time would be 1947-1948, MADDEN by now a Patricroft (10C) engine. Photograph J. Patterson, The Transport Treasury.

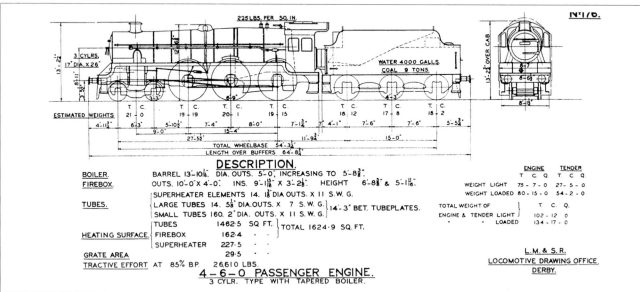

Above and right. Two officially-issued cards, together with the weight details and other measurements printed conveniently on the reverse. The side-on views show the principal left-hand differences (short firebox and five washout plugs on 5573 and long firebox/six washout plugs on 5721) as well as you can find anywhere. The 'join' between the short firebox of 5573 and its boiler falls somewhat short of the mid-point of the middle splasher while the 'join' of the long firebox 5721 falls exactly mid-way. 5721 moreover (see text) also has the two 'handholes' on the firebox curve; there were two each side but they were not sited opposite each other, they were off-set – again to provide maximum access across the firebox crown.

Double Chimney

The Jubilees would, you'd think, be good candidates for double chimneys but other than a few tinkerings, nothing happened. 5684 JUTLAND got a Kylchap exhaust in 1937, Rowledge and Reed (*The Stanier 4-6-0s of the LMS*) recording that it ran freely and developed impressive power returns on the Euston-Birmingham workings. Yet the Kylchap was removed in 1938. 5553 CANADA and 5742 CONNAUGHT were fitted with straightforward twin exhaust double chimneys in 1940, an unexpected development given the troubled times. CANADA's seems to have disappeared soon but CONNAUGHT retained the twin exhaust until late 1955.

In 1956 45722 DEFENCE spent time on the Rugby Testing Plant where among other arrangements, it was tried with a double blastpipe. This showed a marked improvement in steaming and economy but the Jubilees were never candidates for widescale equipping with double chimneys, despite the enormous aggregate increase in power and coal saving possible over a class of nearly two hundred. DEFENCE, after all (perhaps it should have been renamed OFFENCE) attained a 30% increase in indicated horsepower over 30mph with only modest coal, and a 40% increase in ihp above 60mph. It was not to be and the reasoning, no doubt, was cost. It did not, it seems, make sense to upgrade the Jubilees at considerable expense while dieselisation would allow the 'cascading' of more powerful classes to displace them. Witness events on the Midland main line, where Royal Scots and even Britannias became available for the top rank stuff.

The double exhaust was removed from DEFENCE and that seemed to be it until, oddly, another Jubilee got twin exhausts, 45596 BAHAMAS in 1961. In this distinctive condition it survived to the end.

6P or not 6P?

It was envisaged at one time that all the principal 4-6-0 classes, Royal Scots, Patriots and Jubilees would be converted to 6P form, something along the lines of the rebuilt FURY. This would give the LMS a truly prodigious stock of express engines and the proper precursors were two Jubilees, 5735 COMET and 5736 PHOENIX. What was odd, as it turned out, was that while all the Royal Scots and many of the Patriots would be converted, these would be the only Jubilees so dealt with. After the LMS authorised

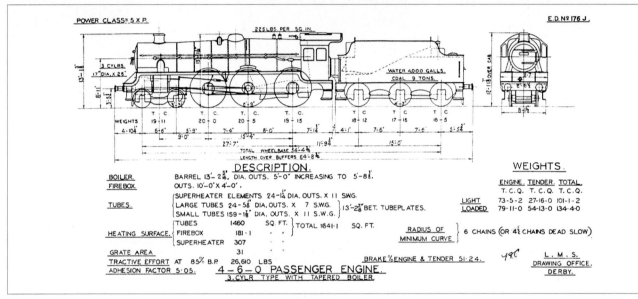

eighteen 'Baby Scots' for rebuilding as part of its post-war 'high speed' plans, BR completed the work but, with plans for the BR Standards coming along, no further conversions were authorised, and that was that.

The two engines appeared with new 2A boilers, with double exhaust, in April and May 1942, a month or so before the first ten Royal Scot conversions were authorised. Both new-style Jubilees went to Holbeck and it was their performances from there, over the Settle and Carlisle and so on, that ensured the authorisation of further Royal Scot conversions. Come 1946 the Patriots were drawn into the programme and, as indicated above, eighteen were transformed with 2A boilers, double exhaust and so on up to 1949. After that, conversion work stopped except for the Royal Scots (their conversion was not complete until 1955) and COMET and PHOENIX remained the only '6Ps' among the Jubilees. All the 2A boilered engines became 7P from 1951 under BR.

5XP to 6P
The Jubilees, including the 2A boilered pair COMET and PHOENIX, kept the 5XP classification until 1951, when BR re-ordered matters generally. In that year the 2A pair became 7P like the rebuilt Patriots and Scots and the rest of the Jubilees became 6P. From 1955 they were officially 6P5F but the engines continued to carry just 6P on the cab.

Speedos
BTH type speed indicators appeared on a few Jubilees in the late 1930s, the generators carried on brackets below the left-hand platform over the trailing wheels. They were soon removed but the brackets remained in place for some years. Early in the 1960s Stone-Deuta speedometers driven off the left-hand trailing crankpin began to appear on many BR classes and many Jubilees got this equipment.

AWS
BR standard AWS (Automatic Warning System) began to be generally fitted from 1959 and though not all the Jubilees got the equipment (with dieselisation their role was more 'Second Division' than ever, seeing them on non-AWS routes) all survivors had it by 1965. As on other classes, its presence was denoted by the running plate reservoir cylinders, the conduit (wiring within) clipped to the left-hand running plate and the protective shield for the receiver under the buffer beam.

Wheel Balances; 'Webbing'
The Jubilee wheels were weighted by steel plates riveted together either side of the spokes, with lead inserted between as required. They made a distinctive pattern, the balance weight plates covering six spokes on the middle (driving) axle and five spokes on the leading and trailing axles. While the leading and trailing wheel plates were the same size, they were riveted across different spokes, as revealed in good side views. This was a visible expression of the compromise between balancing the rotating and reciprocating parts. In a number of instances a distinctive 'webbing' appeared, to strengthen (it is

presumed) the spokes leading off the crankpin boss, giving it extra support. These wheels could be found distributed around all the 6P and 7P 6ft 9in engines, Jubilees, Royal Scots or Patriots in any number of combinations, and there was even a batch made for Black 5s.

PALESTINE with the distinctive webbed spokes bolstering the crankpin boss. Jubilees, as built, had distinctive driving wheels. The flat rimmed wheels of earlier Fowler vintage, notably on the Royal Scots, where prone to failure through tyre fractures, 17 to 18 per year. By the time Stanier took over, the LMS had established the 'V' or bevelled rim, which made for a stiffer wheel rim and virtually eliminated tyre failures, the tyre being fastened by a 'Gibson' ring (in effect a very large circlip). However, the four short spokes closest to the crankpin were still vulnerable to failure and were in turn 'stiffened-up' by half inch webs all around the three spaces. This was a Great Western practice for many years and it can be assumed that Stanier brought it with him. Since Royal Scots, Patriots and Jubilees all had 6ft 9in driving wheels with a 13 inch crank-throw, Crewe Works, to get an engine back into traffic as quickly as possible, would fit whatever suitable wheel-sets were on hand at the time. It was quite common to see any of the three types running with any combination of all three varieties – the flat rim, the bevelled rim and the bevelled rim with webs. On Jubilees the tyres were given their last turning when the thickness was down to 2 inches and were scrapped when they reached $1\frac{7}{8}$ inches, that is, when the 6ft 9in overall diameter was down to 6ft 6¾in.

5614 new (it was later named LEEWARD ISLANDS) at Kentish Town with its famous bottling plant. 5614 still has the vacuum pump under the slidebars and gravity ('trickle') sanding; domeless boiler and two-piece smokebox saddle, high straight sided tender. Photograph J.T. Rutherford, The Transport Treasury.

5607 FIJI with high (note the lining carried round the top edge) straight sided tender, in the red with the block style numbers and letters applied for a few years from 1936. Note also inexorable progress of grime/dust up the tender side, and loose coal dropped on the tender running plate, picked up from the coaling plant shortly before. Domed boiler, Fowler 'knobbed' sandhole filler lids and a good illustration of the 'join' between boiler and firebox – in this case a long firebox, coming mid-way in the centre splasher. The buckets are for sand and the wheelbarrow is of metal, for hot ashes. The side view and lighting shows the two-part smokebox saddle well. Photograph J.T. Rutherford, The Transport Treasury.

5580 BURMA on the turntable at Polmadie. Unlined black (this looks like it) officially displaced 'red' from 1941 though not many Jubilees seem to have received it; not many got a full repaint at all it seems, so by the end of the war most were in patched up pre-1941 red. Lining might disappear, as here, and a variety of lettering and numerals appeared, according to what might be available; 5580's cab numbers (a hand painted but fair attempt at the serif style) for instance have presumably been pushed up to take account of the new table catcher bracket. Photograph J. Robertson, The Transport Treasury.

LONDON MIDLAND & SCOTTISH RAILWAY COMPANY.   Euston Station.

25th January, 1939.

MECHANICAL & ELECTRICAL
ENGINEERING COMMITTEE.

Present :-

A.E. Pullar, Esq., in the Chair,
Sir Robert Burrows.
W. L. Hichens, Esq.
G.R.T. Taylor, Esq.

Attended by :-

Messrs. W.A.Stanier, C.E.Fairburn
and J. Shearman.

S.T.Jones - Secretary.

Fitting of Hinged Door Plates on Platforms.
of 4-6-0 Class 5X Engines. N.W.O. X.5610.

        The Chief Mechanical Engineer reported that the
joints of the mechanical lubricator oil pipe connections on the steam
chest of the 4-6-0 Class 5X engines required intermittent attention,
and in order to facilitate the carrying out of the work at the Motive
Power Depots and eliminate the necessity for removing the whole of the
main steam pipe casing which was fixed to the side of the smoke box,
it was proposed to fit hinged door plates on the platforms of these
engines.

        The Vice-President had already authorised the
fitting of hinged door plates to 191 taper boiler Class 5X engines
at an estimated cost of £466 (N.W.O. X.5610), and it was now considered
desirable to fit the plates on 52 Parallel Boiler Class 5X engines also,
making a total of 243 engines at an estimated cost of £554 (Capital).

Approved.

LMS 1946 black meets BR; the noble black remained but the block cab numbers looked crude, lowered as they were to accommodate the 'M'; in a number of instances a cast iron 'M' plate was made up (again crude compared to the existing style) and fixed slightly drunkenly to the smokebox door plate. VERNON is a visitor to Polmadie from the Central Division, a long-time Newton Heath resident. Photograph J. Robertson, The Transport Treasury.

5721 IMPREGNABLE was the first Jubilee to get the block, or 'sans' (that is, without serif) letters/numbers, in 1936. Here it is in grey and highlighting white, for the benefits of publicity.

More 'M' prefixing, this time on Kingmoor's 5714 REVENGE, at Polmadie. This is also a good indication of cleaning levels at the time. Photograph J. Robertson, The Transport Treasury.

BR numbering scarcely improved upon the look of the 'M' prefix block numbers. 45584 NORTH WEST FRONTIER at Polmadie looks hard done by, with smokebox door plate still awaiting delivery and the handpainted number and BRITISH RAILWAYS surely given over to an apprentice... Photograph J. Robertson, The Transport Treasury.

45693 AGAMEMNON makes for another sad renumbering, at its home shed of Corkerhill (the original 30A, not Stratford – were these plates ever sent south to end up on Sandringhams and all the rest – eventually indeed, on D200 diesels?). Photograph J. Robertson, The Transport Treasury.

'Hybrids' of course were not uncommon, as in the case of 45624 ST HELENA, at Polmadie in 1948, with BR numbers and LMS tender. The livery, by now without lining, would be red of sorts, though ST HELENA could well be fresh out of works (look at the buffer beam). A lovely early morning/late afternoon shot – and note the repair patch on the cabside. Photograph J. Robertson, The Transport Treasury.

Holbeck's 45694 BELLEROPHON, another Jubilee in a kind of post-war debased red without lining (or at least largely without lining) at Polmadie in 1948. Again, 'hybrid' BR numbers/LMS tender; the smokebox door numberplate is not cast but clumsily stencilled in white paint. Photograph J. Robertson, The Transport Treasury.

45604 CEYLON was one of three Jubilees (the other two were 45565 and 45694) which appeared in 1948 in light green, lined in red, grey and black. On 7 October 1948 CEYLON was on the 4pm Glasgow-Leeds at St Enoch. Proper Gill sans numerals were now of course in use. Photograph J.L. Stevenson, courtesy Hamish Stevenson.

Brunswick green (dirty in this case) comes to Kingmoor: 45564 NEW SOUTH WALES, still with 5XP below the number, outside the shed on 24 September 1950. Domed boiler, flush sided tender. The livery finally arrived at by BR (a few Jubilees got mixed traffic lined black before the final decision was made) might have unfortunate Swindon antecedents but it was certainly more stable and wore better than the 'red'. Lining was black-orange-black with 8in numerals except for those applied in Scotland, as here, which were 10in high. The nameplate looks as if it's been picked out in paint. Photograph A.G. Ellis, The Transport Treasury.

Green 45670 HOWARD OF EFFINGHAM at Dalry Road shed, 7 January 1953, now with 6P above the number; vacuum pump bracket still on crosshead. Photograph J. Robertson, The Transport Treasury.

Fowler tender Jubilee in BR green, Bristol Barrow Road's 45561 SASKATCHEWAN waiting in a siding with full tender at York, about to return south, 11 August 1952. Domed boiler. Here, surely, we have one of the BR Class 4 chimneys. Photograph J. Robertson, The Transport Treasury.

Above. 45700 AMETHYST outside the Erecting Shop at Crewe, 2 August 1962; its repair history had ended by now so far as the Record Card is concerned but it would appear that the 25kV warning flashes are being applied – hence the ladder. AWS (reservoir tank on footplate) was fitted the year before and there is a new dragbeam beneath cab, together with temporary three link coupling for shunting movements. Note period 'gricer' appearing just in time to annoy the photographer. Photograph The Transport Treasury.

Left. Protection shield for AWS shown to good effect, together with the supply conduit (note flexible connection) on grimy 45573 NEWFOUNDLAND (a Holbeck engine) stabled on one of the spurs off the outside turntable at Leicester shed, 20 April 1962. Photograph The Transport Treasury.

Above. 45565 with stripe and hand-painted nameplate backing piece VICTORIA, at Neville Hill of all places, in October 1965. Neville Hill's four A1 Pacifics 60118, 60131, 60134 and 60154 had been withdrawn; apparently this was a precipitate move, for Holbeck was then required to provide two Jubilees as standbys for diesel failures – though 45565 in fact came from Low Moor. Strange times! Photograph Mike Kinder.

Right. The be-striped cabside of 45562, showing that a good part of the 'rivets' we talk about were in fact boltheads – there is also a fair amount of speedo detail on view. Photograph The Transport Treasury.

LONDON MIDLAND AND SCOTTISH RAILWAY COMPANY.

Euston Station.

22nd February 1940.

MECHANICAL & ELECTRICAL
ENGINEERING COMMITTEE.

Present :-

        G.R.T. Taylor, Esq. in the Chair,

        W. L. Hichens, Esq.

        The Rt.Hon.The Earl Peel

        A.E. Pullar, Esq.

Attended by :-

        Sir Harold Hartley, Messrs. W.A.Stanier

        C.E.Fairburn and J.Shearman.

                S.T.Jones - Secretary.

Interchange of 3,500 gallon and 4,000 gallon
Tenders between Class 5X 4-6-0 and Class 4
0-6-0 Freight Engines. N.W.C.5621.

        The Chief Mechanical Engineer reported that, conse-
quent on the earlier Class 5X 4-6-0 engines undertaking more intensive
work necessitating their travelling.over routes where water troughs were
not available, it was necessary to replace the present 3,500 gallon
tenders with tenders of 4,000 gallons capacity. He, therefore, recommended
that the 4,000 gallon tenders of thirty Class 4 0-6-0 freight engines
built under the 1938 programme and the 3,500 gallon tenders on the Class
5X engines be interchanged and that certain alterations be carried out
to the Class 5X engines to effect the transfer.

        The estimated cost of the work was £1,621 allocated
by the Chief Accountant to :-

			£.
Works & Equipment Maintenance Fund			
(Revenue Account - ultimate effect)	Dr.		972.
Capital Account ..	..	Dr.	649.
TOTAL	..	Dr.	£1,621.

3. YET MORE VARIATION: TENDERS

We usually think, now, of Jubilees characteristically paired with the familiar high sided 4,000 gallon Stanier tender. In fact, these pairings only became ubiquitous (more or less) relatively late, in BR days. The Jubilees, it turns out, had had to make do with second-hand tenders at first, taken from other LMS express engines. There was constant swapping during the lifetime of the engines and few of the tenders originally paired with each locomotive remained attached for long.

There were four basic types, Fowler short and high sided and Stanier 3,500 and 4,000 gallons (in LMS documents these were identified as 'Old Standard' while the latter was simply '4,000 gallons'). The division into four types is the traditional one but on the basis of external appearance they can be subdivided to give seven or even eight 'varieties' in all. Many were second-hand.

1. 'Fowler' 3,500gall, 5½ tons. Straight sided, 13ft wheelbase, 7ft 1in wide, riveted, coal rails. Two variants Code FCR-R, FCR-U

2. 'Fowler' 3,500gall, 5½ tons. Plain sides, 13ft wheelbase, 7ft 1in wide, without rivet pattern, coal rails. Code FCR-P

3. 'Fowler' 3,500 gallon, 7 tons. High sides, 7ft 1 in wide, 13ft wheelbase. Code F-SS

4. Stanier 3,500gall, 7 tons. High, curved sides, riveted, 8ft 6in wide, 13ft wheelbase. Code S3.5

5. Stanier 4,000gall, 9 tons. High, curved sides, riveted, 8ft 6in wide, 15ft wheelbase. Code S4-R

6. Stanier 4,000gall, 9 tons. High, curved sides, welded, 8ft 6in wide, 15ft wheelbase. Code S4-W

7. Stanier 4,000gall, 9tons. High, curved sides, part riveted, part welded, 8ft 6in wide, 15ft wheelbase. Code S4-PW

A slight modification to the drawbar was necessary but tenders could be swapped at any time, really, throughout the life of individual engines. There were, however, identifiable main episodes, brought about by 'external' events. The original disposition of tenders *was* to be as follows.

5552-5556: Fowler type 3,500 gallon Nos.4469-4473.

5557-5606: Stanier 4,000 gallon Nos.9004-9053 built by North British.

5607-5616: The ten high sided 'Fowler' tenders, Nos.4564-4573

5617-5664: Fowler type 3,500 gallon

The principal change episodes were:
1. 1936, when many with 4,000 gallon riveted Stanier tenders intended for Jubilees were given up instead to the Royal Scots, and 3,500 gallon panelled ones fitted in return.

2. 1937-1941. During these years the opportunity was taken to replace a number of old-style 3,500 gallon tenders running with Jubilees; 4,000 gallon tenders ordered with 4F 0-6-0s being built during that time were attached instead to Jubilees. Thirty were so ordered in February 1940:

3. Later in the 1940s, between 1946 and 1949 the eighteen Patriots rebuilt to 6P were more suitably attached to 4,000 gallon tenders and these were donated by Jubilees, which got 3,500 gallon ones in return.

4. With the Fowler tenders deficient in coal trimming qualities as well as coal and water capacity, BR considered it

---

25th March, 1935.

Exchange of Tenders - 3-Cylinder 5X (Taper Boiler) and "Royal Scot" Class Engines. N.W.O. 4121.

In order to provide a safer margin of coal and water for the "Royal Scot" engines working through runs, the Chief Mechanical Engineer recommended that the present tenders which carry 5½ tons of coal and 3,500 gallons of water be removed from the "Royal Scot" class engines and coupled to the 3-cylinder 5X (Taper Boiler) engines; and that the 4,000 gallon tenders, carrying 9 tons of coal, provided for the latter engines, be coupled to the "Royal Scot" engines.

The proposal would necessitate the carrying out of certain alterations and additions to the tenders and locomotives concerned at an estimated cost of £5,880.

The scheme involved an improvement of the Company's existing Capital assets, the Chief Accountant's allocation being :-

		£.
Works & Equipment Maintenance Fund (Revenue Account - ultimate effect)	Dr.	4,857.
Capital Account	Dr.	1,023.
TOTAL ..	Dr.	£5,880.

Approved, and recommended to the Board.

TABLE 2 TENDER CHANGES. ORIGINAL COMPILED BY *BRASSMASTERS*

	Original		1936		1937-1939		1940-1943		1944-1947		1948-1951		1952-1955		1956-1959		Final	
	Type	No.	Type	No.	Type	No.	Type	No.	Type	No.	Type	No.	Type	No.	Type	No.	Type	No.
5552	S3.5	4619	S4-R	9006														
5553	FCR-R	4560			FCR-R	4562									S4-R	10301		
5554	FCR-R	4561									S4-W	10226						
5555	FCR-R	4562											FCR-P	3913	S4-W	10365		
5556	FCR-P	4563			S4-W	9757					FCR-R	4503	FCR-R	4483	S4-R	10216		
5557	S4-R	9004	FCR-P	3918	S4-W	9761			FCR-R	4486	S3.5	4648	FCR-P	4246			S4-W	10329
5558	S4-R	9005			S3.5	4622									S4-R	9149	S3.5	4615
5559	S4-R	9006	S3.5	4619													S3.5	4644
5560	S4-R	9007	FCR-P	2863	FCR-P	3903	S4-W	9777	S4-W	9062	S4-W	9362						
5561	S4-R	9008	FCR-P	3912	S4-W	9762					FCR-U	4492	FCR-U	4557	S4-W	10387		
5562	S4-R	9009	FCR-P	3903	FCR-P	2863	S4-W	9774										
5563	S4-R	9010	FCR-P	3897	S4-W	9756			FCR-U	4496			FCR-U	4495	S4-W	10418		
5564	S4-R	9011	FCR-P	3914	S4-W	9697												
5565	S4-R	9012	FCR-P	3900	S4-W	9768			S4-W	9696							S4-W	10152
5566	S4-R	9013	FCR-P	3932	S4-W	9766											S4-R	10780
5567	S4-R	9014	FCR-P	3924	S4-W	9688												
5568	S4-R	9015	FCR-P	3907											F-SS	4569	S4-W	10741
5569	S4-R	9016	FCR-P	3916	S4-W	9694												
5570	S4-R	9017	FCR-P	4249	S4-W	9700												
5571	S4-R	9018	FCR-P	3943											S4-W	10575	S4-W	9462
5572	S4-R	9019	FCR-P	4239	S4-W	9691							FCR-R	4483				
5573	S4-R	9020	FCR-P	3919	S4-W	9769												
5574	S4-R	9021	FCR-P	3939							FCR-P	3933	FCR-P	4242	S4-R	10758		
5575	S4-R	9022							S4-R	9023	S4-R	9366			S3.5	4637		
5576	S4-R	9023							S4-R	9022	S4-W	9258						
5577	S4-R	9024							S4-R	9027	S4-W	9278					S4-W	9696
5578	S4-R	9025					S4-R	9363										
5579	S4-R	9026			S4-R	9015	S4-W	9304	S4-W	9270	S4-W	9271					S4-W	9778
5580	S4-R	9027							S4-W	9190	S4-W	9254						
5581	S4-R	9028							S4-R	9077	S4-W	10524						
5582	S4-R	9029									S4-W	9265						
5583	S4-R	9030																
5584	S4-R	9031					S3.5	4621									S4-W	9828
5585	S4-R	9032	FCR-P	3915			S4-W	9781			FCR-U	4498	S4-R	10303			S4-R	10215
5586	S4-R	9033	FCR-P	3942									FCR-R	4504	FCR-P	3929	S4-W	10742
5587	S4-R	9034	FCR-P	4237	S4-W	9765					FCR-R	4507			FCR-U	4496	S4-W	9247
5588	S4-R	9035	FCR-P	3910	S4-W	9695											S4-W	9153
5589	S4-R	9036	FCR-P	3899									FCR-P	4238	FCR-P	3899	S4-W	10288
5590	S4-R	9037	FCR-P	3896	S4-W	9692									S4-R	9366	S4-W	9692
5591	S4-R	9038	FCR-P	3920	S4-W	9753					FCR-R	4504	FCR-R	4503			S4-PW	10545
5592	S4-R	9039	FCR-P	4245	S4-W	9693												
5593	S4-R	9040	FCR-P	3930	S4-W	9689							S3.5	4625			S4-W	9774
5594	S4-R	9041	FCR-P	3928	S4-W	9764												
5595	S4-R	9042	FCR-P	3922									FCR-P	3187	S4-W	9892		
5596	S4-R	9043	FCR-P	3925			S4-W	9779	FCR-R	4485			FCR-P	4248	FCR-U	4492	S4-W	10750
5597	S4-R	9044	FCR-P	3929									FCR-P	3939	S4-W	10736		
5598	S4-R	9045	FCR-P	3934	S4-W	9767			FCR-R	4495			FCR-U	4560	FCR-U	4562	S4-W	10752
5599	S4-R	9046	FCR-P	4250	S4-W	9699												
5600	S4-R	9047	FCR-P	3941	S4-W	9702			S4-R	9144			S4-R	9138				
5601	S4-R	9048	FCR-P	3906	S4-W	9701												
5602	S4-R	9049	FCR-P	4254	S4-W	9690											S3.5	4611
5603	S4-R	9050	FCR-P	4252									FCR-P	3942			S4-W	9671
5604	S4-R	9051	FCR-P	4235	S4-W	9696			S4-W	9768								
5605	S4-R	9052	FCR-P	3904											FCR-U	4494	S4-W	10381
5606	S4-R	9053	FCR-P	4241	S4-W	9698											S3.5	4618
5607	F-SS	4564	F-SS	4566	S4-W	9763												
5608	F-SS	4565	F-SS	4571	F-SS	4565	S4-W	9775										
5609	F-SS	4566	F-SS	4564	S4-W	9772			FCR-U	4494			FCR-P	4242				
5610	F-SS	4567			S4-W	9770												
5611	F-SS	4568			S4-W	9754			FCR-R	4502	S4-R	10215					S4-R	10303
5612	F-SS	4569											S4-W	10354				
5613	F-SS	4570											FCR-P	4246	S4-W	10383		
5614	F-SS	4571	F-SS	4565	F-SS	4571	S4-W	9780	S3.5	4627								
5615	F-SS	4572					S4-W	9778	S3.5	4646								
5616	F-SS	4573							FCR-U	4557			FCR-P	3943	FCR-P	3904	S4-W	10152
5617	S3.5	4600																
5618	S3.5	4601															S3.5	4621
5619	S3.5	4602																
5620	S3.5	4603																
5621	S3.5	4604																
5622	S3.5	4605																
5623	S3.5	4606															S4-W	9722
5624	S3.5	4607																
5625	S3.5	4608																
5626	S3.5	4609																
5627	S3.5	4610													S3.5	4629		
5628	S3.5	4611			S3.5	4613												
5629	S3.5	4612													S3.5	4611	S4-W	9690
5630	S3.5	4613			S3.5	4611									S3.5	4612		
5631	S3.5	4614																
5632	S3.5	4615															S4-R	9149
5633	S3.5	4616																
5634	S3.5	4617																
5635	S3.5	4618															S4-W	9763
5636	S3.5	4624																
5637	S3.5	4625											S4-W	9689				
5638	S3.5	4626																
5639	S3.5	4627							S4-W	9780								
5640	S3.5	4628											S4-R	10783	S4-W	9838		
5641	S3.5	4629													S3.5	4610		
5642	FCR-U	4559													S4-R	10232		
5643	S3.5	4620			S4-R	9032			S4-R	9362	S4-PW	10680	S4-W	9834				
5644	S3.5	4621							S4-R	9215	S4-R	9022	S4-W	9218				
5645	S3.5	4622			S4-R	9005	S4-R	9031	S4-W	9679	S4-PW	10621					S4-W	9271
5646	S3.5	4623							S4-R	9022	S4-W	9267						
5647	S3.5	4630															S3.5	4641
5648	S3.5	4631															S3.5	4602
5649	S3.5	4632																
5650	S3.5	4633																
5651	S3.5	4634																

desirable that, instead of the 3,500 gallon ones as many Jubilees as possible should get the larger Stanier tenders instead. Four old WD Stanier tenders made available after the Second World War for instance, were restored and attached to Jubilees and from 1958/59 there was a programme to get rid of the last forty-odd 3,500 gallon tenders still running with Jubilees on the London Midland Region. These came from 8F 2-8-0s and while many LMR Jubilees planned to be so fitted were eventually dealt with, exceptions remained. 45609 was withdrawn early on, in 1960, while 45704, a Crewe North engine to the end, went to its maker with its Fowler

Loco	Orig Type	Orig No	1936 Type	1936 No	1937-1939 Type	1937-1939 No	1940-1943 Type	1940-1943 No	1944-1947 Type	1944-1947 No	1948-1951 Type	1948-1951 No	1952-1955 Type	1952-1955 No	1956-1959 Type	1956-1959 No	Final Type	Final No
5652	S3.5	4635																
5653	S3.5	4636															S4-PW	10545
5654	S3.5	4637														S4-W	9692	S4-R	9366
5655	S3.5	4638																
5656	S3.5	4639																
5657	S3.5	4640															S4-W	9686
5658	S3.5	4641																
5659	S3.5	4642															S4-W	10126
5660	S3.5	4643															S4-W	10095
5661	S3.5	4644																
5662	S3.5	4645			S4-R	9139							S4-W	9161	S4-R	9130		
5663	S3.5	4646							S4-R	9778							S4-W	9838
5664	S3.5	4647											S4-W	9701	S4-W	9787		
5665	S3.5	4648																
5666	S3.5	4649															S4-W	9695
5667	S4-R	9137							S4-R	9153								
5668	S4-R	9138											S4-R	9144				
5669	S4-R	9139			S4-R	9155												
5670	S4-R	9140																
5671	S4-R	9141																
5672	S4-R	9143													S4-R	9148		
5673	S4-R	9144							S4-W	9701								
5674	S4-R	9145																
5675	S4-R	9146									S4-W	9270						
5676	S4-R	9147																
5677	S4-R	9148													S4-W	10504		
5678	S4-R	9149															S3.5	4622
5679	S4-R	9150	FCR-P	3927							FCR-U	4498						
5680	S4-R	9151																
5681	S4-R	9152																
5682	S4-W	9153							S4-R	9137								
5683	S4-R	9154																
5684	S4-R	9155			S3.5	4645												
5685	S4-R	9156																
5686	S4-R	9157																
5687	S4-R	9158											S4-PW	10586			S4-R	9084
5688	S4-R	9159																
5689	S4-R	9160																
5690	S4-W	9161											S4-R	9139				
5691	S4-R	9162											S4-W	9828				
5692	S4-R	9163							S4-W	9710	S4-W	9717					S4-R	9162
5693	S4-R	9329									S4-R	9015						
5694	S4-R	9330																
5695	FCR-P	3923													S4-R	10780	S4-W	9766
5696	FCR-P	3921											FCR-P	3944			FCR-P	3911
5697	FCR-P	4243											FCR-R	4502			S4-W	10042
5698	FCR-P	4251					S4-W	9773			FCR-U	4472			S4-W	10206		
5699	FCR-P	3917					S4-W	9776										
5700	FCR-P	3913											FCR-R	4474	S4-W	10168		
5701	FCR-P	3945									FCR-P	3898			S4-R	10248		
5702	FCR-P	3940											FCR-P	4240	S4-W	9778	S4-PW	10621
5703	FCR-P	3935			S4-R	9130							FCR-P	3940			FCR-R	4508
5704	FCR-P	4246									FCR-R	4502	FCR-R	4477	S4-R	10758	S4-W	10367
5705	FCR-P	4240											FCR-P	4252	S4-W	10747	S4-R	9128
5706	FCR-P	4226									FCR-U	4513	FCR-P	3901			FCR-P	3921
5707	FCR-P	3936									FCR-P	4240	FCR-P	3931	S4-R	10294		
5708	FCR-P	4248											FCR-P	3929	S4-W	10356		
5709	FCR-P	3931											FCR-P	3898	S4-W	10328		
5710	FCR-P	3909									FCR-P	3940	FCR-P	4244	FCR-P	3901		
5711	FCR-P	3937																
5712	FCR-P	3898											S4-R	10777				
5713	FCR-P	4244							FCR-P	4244	FCR-P	3944	FCR-P	4243				
5714	FCR-P	3911							FCR-P	4171	FCR-P	3911					FCR-P	3944
5715	FCR-P	3944									FCR-P	4244	FCR-R	4508			FCR-P	3940
5716	FCR-P	4243									FCR-P	3989					FCR-U	4513
5717	FCR-P	3933									FCR-R	4500						
5718	FCR-P	3908											FCR-P	4243				
5719	FCR-P	4238											FCR-U	4489	S4-W	10093		
5720	FCR-P	3901													FCR-P	4244		
5721	FCR-P	3902			S4-W	9755					FCR-R	4501			S4-W	10067		
5722	FCR-P	3938			S4-W	9759					FCR-R	4484	FCR-P	3909	FCR-P	3187	S4-R	10787
5723	FCR-P	3905			S4-W	9758			FCR-U	4512			FCR-P	4246	S4-W	10330		
5724	FCR-P	4247			S4-W	9771					FCR-R	4508	FCR-P	3944	S4-W	9719		
5725	FCR-P	4242									S4-R	10302			S4-W	10306		
5726	S4-R	9130			FCR-P	3935			FCR-R	4505			FCR-R	4484	FCR-P	3923	S4-W	10204
5727	S4-R	9127							S4-R	9028	S4-R	9022	S4-R	9023				
5728	S4-R	9362					S4-R	9025			S4-W	9719			FCR-P	3908		
5729	S4-R	9363					S4-R	9362	S4-W	9723	S4-W	9716	S3.5	4620				
5730	S4-R	9364					S4-W	9720	S4-W	9709	S3.5	4623						
5731	S4-R	9365									S4-W	9247	S4-R	9347			S3.5	4619
5732	S4-R	9366							S4-W	9665			S4-W	9725	S4-W	9722		
5733	S4-R	9367																
5734	S4-R	9368																
5735	S4-R	9369																
5736	S4-R	9370											S4-W	9755				
5737	S4-R	9371																
5738	S4-R	9066																
5739	S4-R	9065													S4-W	10535		
5740	FCR-P	3926			S4-W	9760					FCR-U	4497	FCR-U	4561			S4-R	9065
5741	S4-R	9125													S4-R	9128	S4-W	10747
5742	S4-R	9128													S4-R	9125	S4-W	10354

FCR-R	Fowler 3500 gallon snap-head rivets with beaded tanks
FCR-U	Fowler 3500 gallon snap-head rivets with non-beaded tanks
FCR-P	Fowler 3500 gallon flush rivets panelled
F-SS	Fowler 3500 gallon straight sided
S3.5	Stanier 3500 gallon
S4-R	Stanier 4000 gallon riveted
S4-W	Stanier 4000 gallon welded
S4-PW	Stanier 4000 gallon part riveted / part welded

Tender axlebox covers were plain on Fowler and early Stanier riveted tenders. Most of the Stanier 3,500 gallon tenders had cross-ribbed cover plates as did the welded and part-welded tenders and later repairs/replacements.

Note: The table is derived from various published material, photographs and so on. Some of these are contradictory, and wherever possible the data has been verified to eliminate the error. The date ranges for the tender pairings are based mainly on the tenders at the end of each period, except for the main swapping 'episodes' described in the text. For example, 1937-1939 uses data at 1/1/40, 1940-1943 uses data at 1/1/44 and so on. Tenders would often be swapped and the table is only a guide to the type carried by each locomotive. Once again the golden rule of 'find a photograph' applies if a particular combination needs to be pinned down to a particular time.

tender. While this was going on, however, 3,500 gallon tenders *reappeared* on some other Jubilees! Others were left still running with 3,500 gallon tenders in Scotland and on the North Eastern Region; substitution in these 'foreign parts' was regarded as pointless, though some later did indeed get 4,000 gallon tenders, presumably redundant from other Stanier locos. Despite all this, some examples retained the same tender for their entire working lives, such as 45651, and there were others.

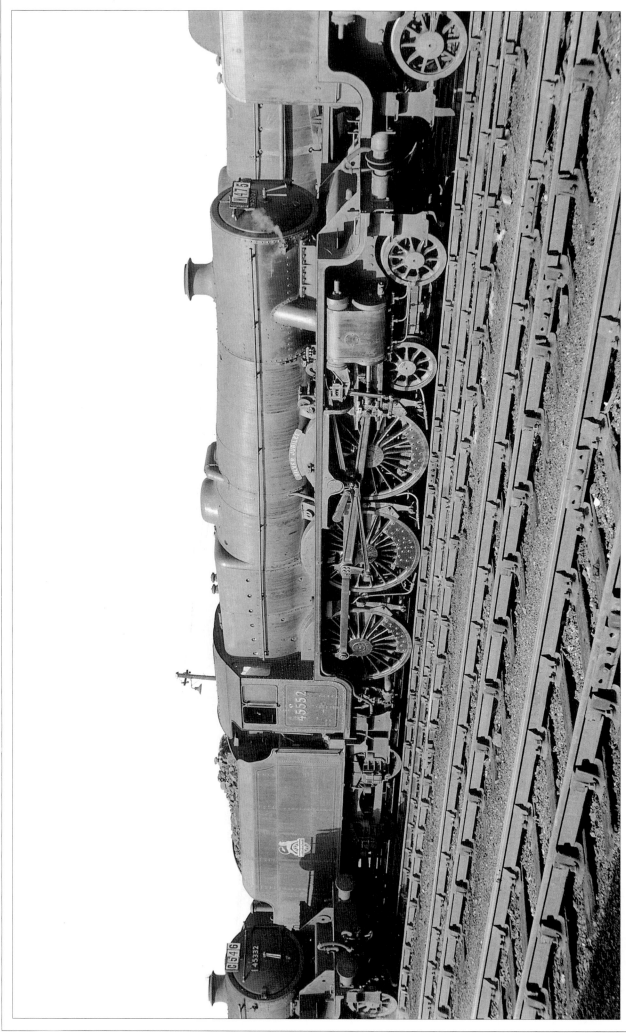

SILVER JUBILEE in BR green, Carlisle Upperby, 3 August 1953. The numbers and letters had been painted white before this and the raised '4' took a time to appear. Towards the end some numerals fell off or were pinched and wooden ones, carefully crafted by the Crewe North joiner, substituted. Photograph J. Robertson, The Transport Treasury.

4. THE RECORD

Health Warning
As pointed out in the earlier volumes of this series, *The Books of* the Coronations, Royal Scots, Princess Royals, Merchant Navys and West Countrys/Battle of Britains, railway company Engine Record Cards, while containing much useful and even fascinating information, should be regarded as a *guide* to what happened to the engines, not an unimpeachable document to be afforded the status of gospel. It seems to be stating the obvious that the Record Cards only show what was written on them at the time but the temptation to read and interpret too much should be resisted. As pointed out before in books in this series, the Cards are a marvellous, fascinating, invaluable record of what happened but they are often infuriatingly silent on events that we enthusiasts half a century or more later consider of vital interest and importance. They were filled in, by hand, by clerks and naturally enough contain errors of omission (quite a few) and commission (a few). I shudder at the thought of my own Friday afternoon standards in an office job many decades ago...

Dates of leaving and entry to works were of course to some extent nominal and a day or two either side should always be assumed. Worse, the works were not above 'fiddling' dates slightly at the beginning or the end of a month to enhance the monthly figures, either of engines 'in' or engines 'out'. It was thus not entirely unknown for a locomotive to be out on the road with the figures showing it still in works and

vice versa – for a few days at least. Breathless 'shocks' and 'revelations' in the railway press about the occasional contradictions, Record Card versus sightings are great fun, but fairly pointless, and are (given the above) easily explained.

Sheds...
As with all BR steam locomotives, the record fades from about 1959-60 as the people involved realised their charges were on the way out. No one responsible for the Cards bothered to record the last 'seeing out' mileages on the LMR or other Regions where the Jubilees ended up. The same was true of allocations and many shed moves at the end, while they were mostly recorded in the pages of contemporary magazines and journals, did not find their way onto the Record Cards. Many of these 'last gasp' allocations (sometimes meaningless paper ones) have nevertheless been added at the end of the 'Sheds' section.

Works...
It is a surprising thing but the LMS Record Cards do not specifically denote the particular works carrying out the repairs. A tiny minority of individual repairs/overhauls *do* have a particular works attached to the period of the work itself (these are duly noted) but as for the rest of the repairs – who really knows? With other classes it is simple; all the Pacifics, for instance, whether Western or Northern Division, LMR or ScR, were overhauled (apart from some exceptional repairs) at Crewe. The same was true of the Royal

Scots but larger, more widely dispersed classes, were different. The English Jubilees were certainly overhauled at Crewe, with Derby doing some of the more Casual work while Scottish ones were done at St Rollox. Horwich seems not to have played a part except maybe in exceptional circumstances. Of course, the Central Shopping Bureau would occasionally move engines around too occasionally, to even out workloads if one works was behind for whatever reason, and 'owning' Regions to an extent had responsibility for fitting AWS and speedos in the early 1960s. It is certainly strange that the works is not, generally, recorded on the cards in the form of a heading, such as 'owning' works. Locomotives were always allocated by 'painted number' to particular works for 'CME' attention whenever required, and there they would go except in special circumstances. I'd be happy to be enlightened in this matter (as others) by readers.

Works Codes
Classification of works jobs varied over the years and the best we have come up with is: HG Heavy General; NC Non-Classified; LS Light Service and HS Heavy Service. These last two evolved by BR times into LI Light Intermediate and HI Heavy Intermediate. Terms changed or were misapplied by staff coming from other traditions; LO would thus be Light Overhaul and LC Light Casual. TO (as in 45560 at Corkerhill in 1951) is probably an error, and should maybe have been EO... One extra since the

SILVER JUBILEE, as made ready by the company's PR people. It is married to a tender (odd in itself in having two painted panels) it was not paired with in 'life', actually going into service with a 3,500gallon Fowler type tender. This was the 'real' 5552 before the name was thought of and it swopped identities with 5642.

days of *The Book of the Coronation Pacifics* is the (Rect) which simply means 'rectification' and typically took place a day or two after a major repair – that is, tightening up bits that had come loose and loosening bits that were too tight. They seldom took very long – often only a day. (EO) was 'Engine Order', under which some jobs seem to have ordered out of the normal run of things.

The Record Cards represent an unmatched body of endlessly fascinating data, and if the reader (like Graham Onley below) gets half as much fun perusing the information as I have had in compiling it, I'll be content.

Reflections... By Graham Onley

I enjoy digging out pieces of new information which I may have missed at the time it mattered, and the Irwell Press *Books of* the Royal Scot, Princess, Coronation, Merchant Navy, West Country/Battle of Britains and Standard classes have allowed just that. Having had a preview of the content of *The Book of The Jubilee 4-6-0s*, I know that there is enough minutiae contained therein to keep me going on many a winter's night. It is not for me to attempt to quote it all, I am sure other readers will do that between them, but I could give a few appetisers, in no particular order, being merely led from one to another as we might all have been during the quieter moments of spotting sessions by the lineside all those long years ago. Take a deep breath, and consider the following:-

Sometimes, official records are incomplete, or even in obvious error. Where the truth is known, this has been 'worked in'. The North Eastern and Western Regions, which received a number of former LMS sheds upon regional boundary changes during 1956 to 1958, perversely ceased recording mileages and transfers of the Jubilees they inherited.

There is no sign on the record cards of the fitting of double chimneys to 5553, 5684, 45742 and 45596, although there is no doubting the facts.

Many readers will remember with distaste the yellow striped finale of many of the class. Photographs exist of many of the recipients, but there is doubt in the case of engines withdrawn from approximately late July to mid-September 1964. Withdrawals either side of those dates fall into 'not received yellow stripe: 105,' 'received stripe: 60' or 'in doubt 26'. Make your own list!

The distinction between pairings with Fowler low sided, Fowler high straight sided, or Stanier tenders will assist many of us in pinning down dates of half-forgotten sightings. In the late 1950s many Jubilees lost their Fowler tenders, acquiring Stanier types from 8F 2-8-0s, but it is possible to overlook that a good number, usually Scottish Region ones or, oddly, ex-Scottish examples such as 45704, did in fact retain their Fowlers to the end.

Similarly, works visits dates may explain unusual sightings, such as my own of Farnley Junction's 45646 storming southwards through Roade cutting on 24 March 1959. Likewise, my own often recalled 'missed by ten minutes' (if the notebooks of newly enlisted spotters were to be believed) of Bristol's 45685 at Blisworth in August 1956, now appears almost certainly to have been fact, despite my scepticism over the intervening years!

Some 'odd' transfers will be noticed during the course of many of the Jubilees' careers, depending on an individual reader's 'era'. Look at 5612 to Bath, 5648 to Stafford, 45628 to Neasden, and others to Carstairs and Aberdeen.

Many Jubilees spent periods in store during 1937 and 1938; whether they did so in other pre-war years is not known. Where later 1960s storage details are on the record cards, this information is given with the engine history. It may explain the oft-queried lack of sightings of 'common' engines over a period. Some of the class were stored on more than one occasion; some managed four such episodes, which may have lengthened survival times.

Many of the class were transferred so often that they cannot now be looked upon as having a 'regular' home. This makes the longevity of engines such as 45658 and 45659 at Leeds Holbeck particularly noteworthy. Indeed Holbeck has a whole list of long-serving engines, and not only Jubilees, the reason for which is yet to be discovered. Blackpool held onto 45571 from before the Second World War to the time when it was transferred away due to redundancy. Newton Heath was another shed to hang on to its Jubilees – see 45642, 45701, 45702 as examples. There are many more examples to be trawled. Some probable 'paper transfers' (or errors) spoil otherwise proud records; 45659 of Holbeck is one, without which it would have matched 45658. Only a handful of Jubilees managed a one shed career, though some managed to work out their lives in a single division – look at 45556 (Western Division) and 45717 (Central Division). There may be others.

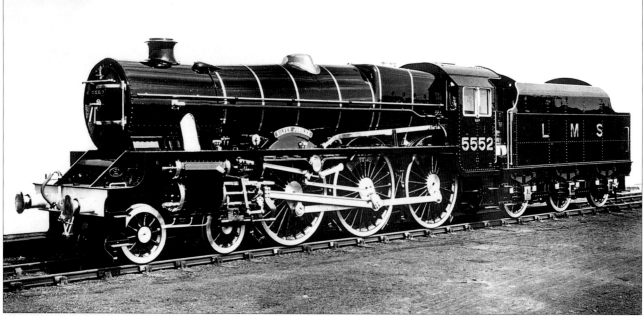

The second manifestation of 5552; this of course was actually 5642, which had ran around so numbered for a few months. The glorious livery is high-gloss varnished black with raised chrome-finish nameplates, numbers and letters. It was classy stuff; even the handrails and their knobs, boiler bands, window beading, smokebox door handles, hinges and other parts also got the chrome finish. As Rowledge and Reed point out, the tender in this second official picture is not the original of either engine, but a Stanier 4,000 gallon one taken from 5559.

45552 SILVER JUBILEE
Built Crewe 1/12/34 as 5642
Named 17/4/35
5642 acquires 5552's identity 29/4/35
Renumbered 5552 to 45552 9/51

REPAIRS
28/3/35-24/4/35**LO**
(5642 substitutes
for the original 5552)
8/8/35-4/9/35**LS**
2/10/36-5/11/36**LS**
Record Ends

SHEDS
Crewe North 1/12/34
Rugby 12/1/35
Camden 29/4/35
Preston 4/1/36
Apparently a gap
in record (though 5552 was
at Longsight 31/1/47) until
Carlisle Upperby 12/50
Bushbury 2/56
Carlisle Upperby 3/56
Edge Hill 4/56
Crewe North 6/61

TENDERS

No	Fitted
4619	1/12/34 (as first 5642)
9006	29/4/35 (as second 5552)

Record Ends

MILEAGES
1934   5,329
1935   55,007
1936   63,877
Record Ends
Withdrawn 9/64
'This amended card supplied
by Crewe A/STAT 24/3/36'
Card for post-1936 now lost

BOILERS
First boiler 8748
(as 5642 and 5552)

No	Fitted	From
8741	21/9/40	5554
8752	3/43	5581
8600	27/2/45	5633

Record Ends

5552 goes into service for Triplex safety glass – Jubilees and Black 5s were popular for this sort of works outing right through to the end of the 1950s, with the 'headboards' often made up at the local shed. Photograph E.M. Johnson Collection.

45553 CANADA

Built Crewe 29/5/34
Named 3/37
Renumbered 5553 to 45553 week ending 30/7/49

BOILERS
First boiler 8466

No	Fitted	From
8565	10/2/37	5615
8561	22/5/40	5642
8613	5/1/43	5646
8735	3/1/48	5647
8634	24/3/52	45585
8629	15/3/57	45554
8634	26/5/62	45619

REPAIRS
21/2/35-12/3/35**LS**
4/11/35-26/11/35**LS**
17/12/36-24/2/37**HG**
5/7/37-4/8/37**HO**
6/3/39-4/4/39**LS**
1/5/40-22/5/40**HG**
2/1/42-24/1/42**HS**
1/12/42-5/1/43**HG**
17/4/44-4/5/44**HS**
8/8/45-31/8/45**HS**
12/11/47-3/1/48**HG**
21/6/49-27/7/49**HI**
23/1/50-18/2/50**LC**
22/8/50-15/9/50**HL**
21/1/52-24/3/52**HG**
16/5/53-20/6/53**HI**
14/4/54-18/5/54**HI**
30/1/55-23/2/55**LC(EO)**
26/9/55-22/10/55**HI**
14/2/57-15/3/57**HG**
29/7/58-18/8/58**NC(EO)(Rugby)**
8/12/58-10/1/59**LI**
7/4/59-17/4/59**NC(EO)AWS fitted**
7/6/60-2/7/60**LI speedo fitted**
   ? -26/5/62**HG**

TENDERS

No	Fitted
4560	29/5/34*
4558	20/9/34*
4560	4/10/34*
4562	14/11/36*
4507	15/3/57*
10301	18/8/58 ex-48046

*Fowler

SHEDS
Camden 26/5/34
Preston 2/6/34
Bushbury 25/8/34
Rugby 19/1/35
Crewe North 2/3/35
Camden 8/6/35
Rugby 5/10/35
Aston 30/12/39
Leeds (loan) 27/7/40
Leeds 24/8/40
Crewe North (loan) 9/11/40
Crewe North 7/12/40
Carlisle Upperby 23/5/42
Crewe North 28/3/49
Trafford Park (loan) 24/9/49
Trafford Park 22/10/49
Longsight 2/6/51
Crewe North 9/6/56
Camden 14/7/56
Crewe North 8/9/56
Trafford Park 15/9/56
Crewe North 10/11/56
Carlisle Upperby 15/12/56
Crewe North 5/1/57
Llandudno Jct 26/11/60
Crewe South 31/12/60
Crewe North 23/6/62

MILEAGES

1934	38,509
1935	58,570
1936	53,513
1937	40,473
1938	50,278
1939	44,466
1940	40,242
1941	46,045
1942	33,337
1943	40,352
1944	37,788
1945	36,066
1946	37,767
1947	21,318
1948	49,499
1949	47,827
1950	59,781
1951	44,794
1952	56,124
1953	53,858
1954	51,896
1955	47,244
1956	58,953
1957	45,770
1958	43,561
1959	49,554
1960	47,292

Mileage at 31/12/50 735,831;
mileage at 31/12/60 1,234,877
Withdrawn week ending 7/11/64

45554 ONTARIO

Built Crewe 5/6/34
Named 11/3/36
Renumbered 5554 to 45554
week ending 6/11/48

BOILERS
First boiler 8467

No	Fitted	From
8741	3/2/38	5648
8466	21/9/40	5586
8628	7/10/44	5568
8612	3/11/48	45570
8623	16/3/51	45568
8629	29/10/53	45660
8743	23/1/57	45594

SHEDS
Preston 2/6/34
Bushbury 25/8/34
Rugby 19/1/35
Camden 1/7/39
Longsight 7/10/39
Millhouses loan 18/11/39
Millhouses 9/12/39
Nottingham 12/4/47
Edge Hill 19/10/57
Probably on loan until
Edge Hill 8/11/58
Crewe North 10/6/61

MILEAGES

1934	33,908
1935	49,096
1936	49,376
1937	48,752
1938	48,576
1939	42,867
1940	51,363
1941	47,026
1942	40,736
1943	41,420
1944	52,365
1945	40,533
1946	47,809
1947	34,411
1948	33,345
1949	47,833
1950	49,094
1951	46,487
1952	51,294
1953	59,135
1954	59,586
1955	56,759
1956	59,762
1957	62,201
1958	40,941
1959	47,489
1960	37,047

Stored 29/11/63-17/12/63, 16/1/64-15/6/64
Mileage at 31/12/50 758,510, mileage at 31/12/60
1,279,211
Withdrawn week ending 7/11/64

REPAIRS
18/6/35-28/6/35**LS**
24/2/36-11/3/36**LS**
4/5/36-17/6/36**HO**
17/3/37-7/4/37**LS**
26/1/38-17/2/38**HG**
9/9/39-26/9/39**LS**
14/8/40-21/9/40**HG**
Damaged by enemy action
at Saltley 20/4/41
24/2/42-25/3/42**LS**
3/11/42-5/12/42**HS**
26/3/43-22/4/43**LO**
10/9/43-20/10/43**HS (damage repair)**
16/9/44-7/10/44**HG**
9/10/45-14/11/45**HS**
15/1/47-21/2/47**HS**
19/1/48-16/2/48**LO Derby**
27/8/48-3/11/48**HG**
14/12/49-6/1/50**HI**
12/2/51-16/3/51**HG**
13/8/52-4/9/52**HI**
22/9/53-29/10/53**HG**
5/11/54-1/12/54**HI**
28/1/55-10/2/55**LC(EO) Trials on**
Lickey Incline 1955
15/11/55-14/12/55**LC(EO)**
18/12/56-23/1/57**HG**
14/8/58-12/9/58**LI**
13/10/59-30/10/59**NC(EO) AWS fitted**
31/12/59-3/2/60**HI**
23/11/60-6/1/61**LC(EO)**
6/62 speedo fitted

TENDERS

No	Fitted
4561	5/6/34*
10226	6/1/50

*Fowler

5553 CANADA in the 1946 black, a livery that remained fairly effective even under a considerable burden of grime. Photograph The Transport Treasury.

45555 QUEBEC
Built Crewe 18/6/34
Named 8/2/37
Renumbered 5555 to 45555 week ending 17/4/48

BOILERS
First boiler 8468

No	Fitted	From
8465	21/1/37	5642
8469	12/11/38	5628
8618	8/12/42	5573
8746	8/2/47	5618
8751	21/6/52	45562
8630	7/2/56	45583
8622	19/3/60	45606

TENDERS

No	Fitted
4562	18/6/34*
4560	14/11/36*
3913	19/3/55*
4499	13/4/57*
10365	6/10/58 ex-48648
*Fowler	

MILEAGES

1934	32,735
1935	45,240
1936	45,851
1937	50,903
1938	52,783
1939	48,876
1940	32,917
1941	44,985
1942	33,159
1943	47,813
1944	43,464
1945	47,818
1946	45,099
1947	46,447
1948	52,282
1949	53,253
1950	42,364
1951	53,659
1952	56,730
1953	54,459
1954	55,256
1955	48,480
1956	57,461
1957	40,946
1958	38,044
1959	51,300
1960	55,117

Mileage at 31/12/50 765,989, mileage at 31/12/60 1,277,441
Withdrawn week ending 17/8/63

REPAIRS
22/5/35-7/6/35**LO**
26/10/35-12/11/35**LS**
11/8/36-15/8/36**LO**
12/11/36-8/2/37**HG**
10/10/38-12/11/38**HG**
24/11/39-9/12/39**HS**
22/3/41-8/4/41**LS**
19/11/42-8/12/42**HG**
9/6/44-23/6/44**LS**
12/3/46-5/4/46**LS**
11/1/47-8/2/47**HG**
27/3/48-16/4/48**LS**
25/5/49-16/6/49**LI**
12/12/50-11/1/51**LI**
5/5/52-21/6/52**HG**
17/9/53-15/10/53**HI**
22/2/55-19/3/55**HI**
16/12/55-7/2/56**HG**
21/3/57-13/4/57**HI**
15/11/57-18/1/58**HI**
29/1/58-7/2/58**NC(EO Rect)**
25/8/58-6/10/58**LC(EO)**
30/10/58-28/11/58**LC(EO)**
2/5/59-13/6/59**LC(EO) AWS fitted**
16/2/60-19/3/60**HG**
3/5/61-15/6/61**HI speedo fitted**

SHEDS
Preston 23/6/34
Bushbury 25/8/34
Camden 7/6/35
Rugby 5/10/35
Willesden 11/6/38
Rugby 24/9/38
Aston 27/1/40
Carlisle Upperby 11/1/41
Farnley Jct (loan) 26/8/44
Farnley Jct 30/9/44
Crewe North (loan) 9/12/44
Crewe North 13/1/45
Camden 19/6/48
Edge Hill (loan) 3/9/49
Willesden 1/10/49
Crewe North 8/10/49
Carlisle Upperby 29/4/50
Longsight 7/7/51
Crewe North 12/6/54
Camden 7/8/54
Bushbury 14/8/54
Carlisle Upperby 7/11/59
Crewe South 7/1/61

45556 NOVA SCOTIA

Built Crewe 22/6/34
Named 8/3/37
Renumbered 5556 to 45556 week ending 2/4/49

BOILERS
First boiler 8469

No	Fitted	From
8616	23/2/37	5586
8587	17/10/38	5615
8574	30/9/41	5582
8751	25/1/45	5648
8611	23/8/47	5617
8469	13/6/50	45611
8587	2/5/55	45565
8609	30/9/60	45572

TENDERS

No	Fitted
4563	22/6/34*
9757	29/4/39
4503	2/7/48*
4483	2/5/55*
10216	21/11/58
*Fowler	

MILEAGES

1934	32,918
1935	64,616
1936	66,359
1937	50,229
1938	51,388*
1939	65,031
1940	45,409
1941	40,322
1942	54,668
1943	53,631
1944	45,693
1945	62,125
1946	63,969
1947	47,327
1948	49,880
1949	37,889
1950	56,535
1951	24,062
1952	57,660
1953	52,734
1954	54,940
1955	47,994
1956	49,059
1957	45,992
1958	46,059
1959	48,242
1960	40,860

stored serviceable 38 days
stored 18/9/62-16/6/63
stored 26/9/63-17/11/63
**Mileage at 31/12/50 887,989,
mileage at 31/12/60 1,355,591
Withdrawn week ending 5/9/64**

REPAIRS
13/2/35-23/2/35**HG**
10/10/35-30/10/35**LS**
12/1/37-8/3/37**HG**
19/9/38-17/10/38**HS**
26/2/40-9/3/40**LS**
16/9/41-30/9/41**HG**
10/5/43-27/5/43**LS**
22/5/44-27/6/44**HS**
18/12/44-25/1/45**HG**
6/2/46-4/3/46**LS**
21/8/46-9/9/46**LO**
26/6/47-23/8/47**HG**
21/6/48-2/7/48**NC**
8/3/49-30/3/49**LI**
18/11/49-21/12/49**LC**
8/5/50-13/6/50**HG**
5/11/51-24/11/51**LI**
25/8/52-20/9/52**HI**
22/9/53-14/10/53**HI**
16/3/55-2/5/55**HG**
23/2/57-23/3/57**HI**
27/10/58-21/11/58**HI**
29/4/59-25/5/59**LC(EO) Rugby**
4/10/59-23/10/59**NC(EO) AWS fitted**
12/8/60-30/9/60**HG speedo fitted**

SHEDS
Preston 14/7/34
Bushbury 25/8/34
Camden 20/4/35
Willesden 15/10/35
Camden 28/8/37
Willesden 1/10/38
Crewe North 29/10/38
Camden 31/12/38
Willesden 8/4/39
Camden 28/2/42
Crewe North 31/10/42
Longsight 2/6/45
Crewe North 12/6/54

45557 NEW BRUNSWICK

Built North British Loco Co Ltd 29/6/34
Named 10/36
Renumbered 5557 to 45557 week ending 15/5/48

MILEAGES

1934	31,948
1935	62,643
1936	61,395
1937	59,485
1938	83,037
1939	63,276
1940	59,844
1941	56,958
1942	49,559
1943	65,503
1944	61,753
1945	58,341
1946	53,292
1947	49,952
1948	63,940
1949	63,552
1950	53,166
1951	67,319
1952	62,417
1953	64,929
1954	59,828
1955	57,610
1956	43,529
1957	65,915
1958	67,614
1959	54,296
1960	38,692

stored 24/9/62-17/12/62
**Mileage at 31/12/50 997,644,
mileage at 31/12/60 1,579,793
Withdrawn week ending 19/9/64**

SHEDS
Camden 7/7/34
Crewe North 21/7/34
Camden 2/2/35
Willesden 5/10/35
Camden 28/8/37
Kentish Town 30/7/38
Bristol 16/9/39
Derby 15/6/46
Kentish Town 20/9/47
Derby 21/11/59
Burton 18/11/61
Derby 6/64

TENDERS

No	Fitted
9004	29/6/34
3918	31/10/36* ex-6131
9761	6/7/39
4486	15/3/47*
4648	9/5/51
4486	8/8/51*
4246	11/1/57*
4497	4/4/59*
10329	22/4/60
*Fowler	

BOILERS
First boiler 8587

No	Fitted	From
8560	25/2/37	5610
8630	20/6/38	5600
8756	24/2/40	5604
8741	4/6/43	5552
8569	21/12/45	5575
8613	14/5/48	5553
8567	6/9/50	45558
8615	27/6/53	45569
8567	11/1/57	45561
8561	2/5/62	45641

REPAIRS
16/10/35-1/11/35**L**
28/12/36-10/3/37**HG** (63)
14/6/38-28/6/38**HS** (13)
20/2/39-21/3/39**HS** (26)
21/6/39-24/7/39**LO** (29)
24/1/40-24/2/40**HG** (28)
17/2/41-14/3/41**LS** (23)
27/12/41-17/1/42**LS** (19)
19/9/42-14/10/42**LO** (22)
10/5/43-4/6/43**HG** (23)
12/2/44-2/3/44**LS** (17)
15/9/44-10/10/44**LO** (22)
1/3/45-5/4/45**LS** (31)
16/11/45-21/12/45**HG** (31)
25/2/47-15/3/47**LS** (17)
3/4/48-14/5/48**HG** (36)
1/2/49-28/2/49**HI** (24)
17/8/49-8/9/49**HC** (20)
27/11/49-6/12/49**NC Derby**
11/1/50-17/2/50**LI** (32)
10/7/50-6/9/50**HG** (50)
16/10/50-8/11/50**LC** (20)
1/9/51-4/10/51**HI** (28)
2/6/52-30/6/52**HI** (24)
19/5/53-27/6/53**HG** (34)
26/7/54-24/8/54**HI** (25)
26/8/54-2/9/54**NC(EO Rect)**
12/11/54-25/11/54**LC(EO)** (11)
15/2/55-7/3/55**LC(EO)** (17)
30/9/55-20/10/55**HI** (17)
26/11/56-11/1/57**HG** (38)
25/11/57-2/1/58**HI** (31)
26/6/58-14/8/58**LC(EO)** (42)
21/2/59-4/4/59**LI** (35)
5/3/60-22/4/60**HI** speedo fitted – AWS
probably never fitted
?-2/5/62**HG**

45558 MANITOBA
Built North British Loco Co Ltd 6/7/34
Named 27/10/36
Renumbered 5558 to 45558 week ending 4/9/48

BOILERS
First boiler 8588

No	Fitted	From
8758	12/11/37	5660
8599	16/7/40	5564
8626	26/3/42	5578
8582	8/6/44	5562
8567	19/9/46	5662
8754	22/2/50	45649
8746	10/12/54	45651
8624	25/3/59	45564

TENDERS

No	Fitted
9005	6/7/34
4622	17/5/35
9149	approx.1963
4615	19/4/64

MILEAGES

Year	Mileage
1934	35,378
1935	44,957
1936	53,922
1937	57,592
1938	54,819*
1939	60,288
1940	60,870
1941	62,266
1942	65,566
1943	61,827
1944	59,528
1945	68,706
1946	51,661
1947	41,151
1948	49,808
1949	51,961
1950	39,972
1951	38,320
1952	48,029
1953	44,799
1954	32,238
1955	56,164
1956	40,037
1957	47,648
1958	55,126
1959	45,627
1960	37,596
1961	32,091
1962	27,716**
1963	22,966

*80 days stored serviceable
** stored 1/10/62-20/10/62
Mileage at 31/12/50 920,272; mileage at 31/12/63 1,448,629
Withdrawn week ending 15/8/64

REPAIRS
12/4/35-26/4/35**LO**
31/10/35-18/11/35**LS**
8/10/36-27/10/36**LS**
9/10/37-29/11/37**HG**
2/3/39-12/4/39**HS**
24/6/40-16/7/40**HG**
29/12/41-15/1/42**HS**
24/2/42-26/3/42**HO**
24/12/42-4/2/43**HS**
18/9/43-15/10/43**HS**
23/5/44-8/6/44**HG**
21/10/44-3/11/44**LO**
4/6/45-27/6/45**LS**
24/8/46-19/9/46**HG**
14/8/47-1/10/47**LS**
3/8/48-3/9/48**HS**
5/1/50-22/2/50**HG**
13/3/50-11/4/50**HC**
6/10/51-31/10/51**LI**
28/5/53-26/6/53**HI**
12/11/54-10/12/54**HG**
23/5/56-27/6/56**LI**
27/10/57-20/11/57**HI**
16/2/59-25/3/59**HG AWS fitted**
7/11/60-8/12/60**HI speedo fitted**

SHEDS
Camden 7/7/34
Crewe North 21/7/34
Camden 2/2/35
Willesden 5/10/35
Camden 6/2/37
Crewe North 11/2/37
Preston (loan) 18/12/37
Crewe North 1/1/38
Camden (loan) 16/4/38
Crewe North 20/4/38
Camden 2/7/38
Willesden 1/10/38
Camden 2/12/39
Leeds (loan) 28/9/40
Leeds 26/10/40
Trafford Park 12/10/46
Crewe North (loan) 13/12/47
Crewe North 31/1/48
Edge Hill (loan) 16/9/50
Patricroft 2/12/50
Newton Heath immediately prior to withdrawal

Green 45559 BRITISH COLUMBIA, then a Patricroft engine, at Polmadie shed 9 May 1953. Photograph J. Robertson, The Transport Treasury.

45559 BRITISH COLUMBIA

Built North British Loco Co Ltd 9/7/34
Named 13/1/37
Renumbered 5559 to 45559 week ending 27/11/48

TENDERS

No	Fitted
9006	9/7/34
4619	10/4/35
9247	13/9/62
4644	*see 45661*

REPAIRS

3/12/35-20/12/35**LS**
3/12/36-13/1/37**HG**
30/9/37-27/10/37**HS**
18/6/38-11/7/38**LS**
18/7/39-16/8/39**HG**
11/3/40-26/3/40**LO**
19/10/40-13/11/40**LS**
25/8/41-10/9/41**LO**
30/10/41-22/11/41**HG**
10/8/42-22/8/42**LS**
19/3/43-3/4/43**LS**
13/9/43-25/9/43**LO**
11/2/44-3/3/44**LS**
1/8/44-22/8/44**HG**
25/6/45-2/8/45**HS**
10/12/45-17/1/46**LO**
31/12/46-24/1/47**HS**
5/6/47-1/7/47**LO**
14/9/48-23/11/48**HG**
26/11/48-6/12/48**TRO**
1/11/49-21/11/49**LI**
15/12/50-11/1/51**HI**
17/9/51-20/10/51**HC**
24/10/52-26/11/52**HG**
1/3/54-1/4/54**HI**
7/4/54-30/4/54**NC(EO Rect)**
12/5/54-1/6/54**LC(EO)**
14/7/55-13/8/55**HI**
22/3/56-21/4/56**HC**
12/8/57-12/9/57**HG**
14/3/58-9/4/58**HC**
14/8/59-12/9/59**LI** AWS fitted
24/10/60-1/12/60**LI** speedo fitted

MILEAGES

Year	Miles
1934	28,770
1935	58,773
1936	56,966
1937	65,121
1938	66,215
1939	55,391
1940	52,174
1941	48,024
1942	70,151
1943	61,757
1944	44,895
1945	53,128
1946	66,265
1947	42,299
1948	35,388
1949	50,001
1950	51,317
1951	48,657
1952	46,151
1953	59,018
1954	43,156
1955	44,420
1956	48,839
1957	51,731
1958	52,903
1959	44,489
1960	48,018

Mileage at 31/12/50 906,635; at 31/12/60 1,394,017
Withdrawn week ending 20/10/62

BOILERS
First boiler 8589

No	Fitted	From
8574	1/1/37	5624
8594	20/10/37	5564
8628	16/8/39	5660
8611	22/11/41	5658
8619	22/8/44	5592
8589	23/11/48	5627
8635	26/11/52	45599
8569	12/9/57	45588

SHEDS

Camden 7/7/34
Crewe North 21/7/34
Camden 2/2/35
Willesden 5/10/35
Camden 6/2/37
Willesden 1/10/38
Camden 2/12/39
Patricroft 10/5/47
Derby 11/59
Blackpool 2/7/60

45560 PRINCE EDWARD ISLAND

Built North British Loco Co Ltd 11/7/34
Named 2/9/36
Renumbered 5560 to 45560 week ending 14/8/48

BOILERS
First boiler 8590

No	Fitted	From
8620	15/6/37	5590
8746	23/10/39	5641
8557	15/1/44	5603
8590	10/8/48	5584
8614	27/1/53	45651
8557	21/12/54	45564
8736	3/8/57	45576

TENDERS

No	Fitted
9007	11/7/34
2863	16/12/35* ex-6127
3903	27/1/39*
9777	23/4/40
9062	20/6/47
9714	16/9/49
9362	31/7/51

***Fowler**

REPAIRS

25/11/35-16/12/35**LS**
18/8/36-2/9/36**LS**
17/5/37-30/6/37**HG**
13/5/38-10/6/38**LS**
3/2/39-17/3/39**LO**
23/10/39-28/11/39**HG**
29/7/40-3/9/40**LS**
7/1/41-27/1/41**LO**
10/7/41-9/8/41**LS**
30/10/41-15/11/41**LO**
20/2/42-10/4/42**LS**
5/2/43-10/3/43**HS**
3/12/43-15/1/44**HG**
13/6/45-20/7/45**LS**
29/10/46-5/12/46**HS** St Rollox
12/3/48-10/8/48**HG** St Rollox
31/5/49-17/9/49**LI** St Rollox
20/9/49-23/9/49**NC Rect** St Rollox
5/7/50-19/8/50**HI** St Rollox
9/4/51-24/4/51**LC** St Rollox
13/6/51-2/8/51**LI** St Rollox
5/12/51-19/12/51**LC (TO)** Corkerhill
22/3/52-4/4/52**LC** St Rollox
6/5/52-20/5/52**LC(EO)** St Rollox
12/12/52-27/1/53**HG**
4/1/54-3/2/54**HI**
1/12/54-21/12/54**HG**
27/4/56-23/5/56**HI**
13/6/57-3/8/57**HG**
2/9/58-17/10/58**LI**
12/3/60-27/4/60**HI** AWS and speedo fitted
16/12/60-11/1/61**LC(EO)**

MILEAGES

Year	Miles
1934	36,669
1935	64,300
1936	57,421
1937	69,074
1938	64,150
1939	50,515
1940	72,537
1941	59,487
1942	49,169
1943	45,866
1944	49,020
1945	48,829
1946	48,260
1947	50,097
1948	31,765
1949	34,496
1950	49,354
1951	36,829
1952	38,638
1953	54,783
1954	51,174
1955	63,459
1956	56,738
1957	52,475
1958	45,070
1959	45,304
1960	42,742

Mileage at 31/12/50 881,009; at 31/12/60, 1,368,221
Stored 4/10/63, withdrawn week ending 30/11/63

SHEDS

Camden 7/7/34
Crewe North 21/7/34
Preston 3/11/34
Camden 13/7/35
Willesden 5/10/35
Carnforth 8/2/36
Crewe North 9/1/37
Leeds 11/9/37
Carlisle Kingmoor (loan) 10/1/42
Carlisle Kingmoor 24/1/42
Corkerhill 21/11/42
Nottingham (loan) 30/8/52
Nottingham 13/9/52
Edge Hill 19/10/57
Possibly on loan until
Edge Hill 8/11/58
Crewe North 10/6/61

45561 SASKATCHEWAN
Built North British Loco Co Ltd 13/7/34
Named 4/6/36
Renumbered 5561 to 45561 week ending 15/5/48

SHEDS
Camden 14/7/34
Crewe North 21/7/34
Preston 6/10/34
Longsight 18/7/36
Carlisle Upperby 3/10/36
Edge Hill 2/5/42
Crewe North 30/11/46
Bristol (loan) 13/9/47
Bristol 25/10/47
Trafford Park 5/1/57
Kentish Town 6/7/58
Trafford Park 25/7/59
Kentish Town 7/11/59
Burton 20/1/62
Derby 26/1/63

REPAIRS
27/5/35-17/6/35LS
21/5/36-4/6/36LS
3/12/36-29/1/37HG
8/2/38-1/3/38HS
5/12/38-5/1/39HS
16/8/39-2/9/39LO
11/1/40-26/1/40LS
30/9/40-12/10/40LO
31/5/41-18/6/41HG
14/3/42-21/4/42LS
6/3/43-20/3/43LO
9/2/44-18/3/44LS
16/8/44-30/8/44LO
23/3/45-5/5/45HG
26/3/46-11/5/46HS
13/5/47-10/6/47LS
5/4/48-10/5/48HG
17/11/48-8/12/48LO
31/5/49-13/6/49LI
12/12/49-10/1/50HI
17/7/50-29/8/50HG
29/8/51-3/10/51LI
18/11/52-18/12/52LI(EO)
8/2/53-25/2/53LC
19/11/53-19/12/53HG
22/9/54-30/10/54HI
10/10/55-7/11/55HI
16/5/56-17/5/56NC(EO)
21/10/56-21/12/56HG
10/1/58-5/2/58LI(EO)
23/5/58-2/7/58LC(TO)
12/1/59-27/1/59LC(EO) Rugby
16/4/59-16/5/59HI
21/5/60-25/7/60HG speedo fitted; AWS
probably never fitted

MILEAGES

Year	Mileage
1934	34,137
1935	62,368
1936	64,815
1937	60,276
1938	55,002
1939	55,564
1940	35,807
1941	44,860
1942	34,472
1943	41,947
1944	37,539
1945	40,817
1946	44,105
1947	59,609
1948	60,319
1949	64,594
1950	61,044
1951	60,027
1952	64,849
1953	59,197
1954	66,760
1955	58,280
1956	54,213
1957	52,217
1958	54,252
1959	63,622
1960	47,883

Stored 15/10/62-21/1/63
**Mileage at 31/12/50 857,275; at
31/12/60 1,438,575**
Withdrawn week ending 19/9/64

TENDERS

No	Fitted
9008	13/7/34
3912	4/6/36 *ex-6149
9762	25/8/39
4492	8/12/48*
4496	18/12/52*
4557	30/10/54*
3933	17/5/56*
4554	10/12/57*
3190	5/2/58*
10387	2/7/58 ex-48613

*Fowler

BOILERS
First boiler 8591

No	Fitted	From
8589	13/1/37	5559
8624	16/2/38	5594
8566	18/6/41	5652
8739	5/5/45	5603
8759	10/5/48	5656
8736	29/8/50	45600
8567	19/12/53	45557
8628	21/12/56	45653
8740	25/7/60	45633

5562 ALBERTA at its home shed, Holbeck, late in the 1930s. Red livery, gravity sanding, 'knobs' on the sandhole filler caps. Photograph W. Hermiston, The Transport Treasury.

45562 ALBERTA

Built North British Loco Co Ltd 8/8/34
Named 21/2/36
Renumbered 5562 to 45562 week ending 30/10/48

BOILERS
First boiler 8592

No	Fitted	From
8745	17/6/37	5652
8607	18/10/39	5577
8582	22/7/41	5659
8607	7/4/44	5635
8751	9/10/47	5556
8467	7/2/52	45632
8626	1/6/56	45648
8598	2/12/58	45605

REPAIRS
4/2/36-21/2/36**LS**
25/8/36-27/8/36**LO**
1/1/37-10/2/37**LO**
? - 3/7/37**HG**
1/9/38-28/9/38**LS**
28/1/39-3/3/9**LO**
11/9/39-18/10/39**HG**
3/7/40-8/8/40**LS**
16/6/41-22/7/41**HG**
1/5/42-26/5/42**HS**
31/10/42-2/1/43**LS**
21/3/44-7/4/44**HG**
11/11/44-2/12/44**LO**
17/4/45-5/5/45**LS**
6/12/45-12/1/46**HO**
6/10/46-4/11/46**LS**
11/8/47-9/10/47**HG**
1/10/48-28/10/48**LS**
5/10/49-28/10/49**LI**
26/11/50-5/1/51**HI**
31/12/51-7/2/52**HG**
13/10/52-8/11/52**HI**
16/10/53-6/11/53**LI**
25/11/54-22/12/54**LI**
14/4/56-1/6/56**HG**
27/1/57-13/3/57**LC Derby**
8/5/57-14/6/57**HI**
29/10/58-2/12/58**HG**
? - 25/6/59**LC(EO)**
26/11/59-19/12/59**LC**
? - 6/2/60**NC(EO)**
? - 16/9/60**NC(EO)**
20/3/61-25/4/61**HI**
AWS, speedo fitted; date
not recorded

SHEDS
Preston 11/8/34
Longsight 18/7/36
Rugby 3/10/36
Patricroft 20/2/37
Blackpool 22/5/37
Patricroft (loan) 12/6/37
Patricroft 3/7/37
Leeds 11/9/37
Farnley Junction 3/64
Leeds 11/66

TENDERS

No	Fitted
9009	8/8/34
3903	21/2/36* ex-6143
2863	27/1/39*
9774	20/3/40

*Fowler

MILEAGES

1934	31,657
1935	65,104
1936	57,303
1937	49,536
1938	85,482
1939	52,337
1940	67,895
1941	53,342
1942	63,679
1943	60,817
1944	58,587
1945	52,019
1946	56,551
1947	54,841
1948	63,751
1949	68,253
1950	59,722
1951	68,234
1952	60,523
1953	70,674
1954	67,832
1955	72,087
1956	58,607
1957	53,533

Mileage at 31/12/50 1,000,876
Withdrawn approx. 9/67

45563 AUSTRALIA

Built North British Loco Co Ltd 9/8/34
Named 23/1/36
Renumbered 5563 to 45563 week ending 4/6/49

REPAIRS
8/1/36-23/1/36**LS**
7/7/36-22/7/36**LO**
23/11/36-5/2/37**HG**
18/1/38-2/2/38**LS**
4/1/39-8/2/39**HG**
8/4/40-27/4/40**LS**
16/5/40-7/6/40**LO**
12/6/40-25/6/40**LO**
25/11/40-14/12/40**LO**
28/4/41-17/5/41**LS**
3/3/42-25/3/42**LS**
5/11/42-5/12/42**HS**
23/9/43-6/11/43**HG**
8/12/45-2/1/46**LS**
8/10/47-22/11/47**HG**
2/5/49-31/5/49**LI**
22/4/50-12/5/50**LC**
15/1/51-23/2/51**HG**
23/6/52-9/8/52**HI**
4/12/52-24/12/52**LC**
18/11/53-10/12/53**HI**
7/3/55-6/4/55**HI**
23/2/56-10/4/56**HG**
16/4/56-20/4/56**NC(EO Rect)**
23/9/57-2/11/57**HG**
14/11/59-14/12/59**LC(TO)**
19/12/59-23/1/60**HI AWS**
?-10/62 **no speedo fitted**

TENDERS

No	Fitted
9010	9/8/34
3897	23/1/36* ex-6111
9756	29/4/39
4496	22/11/47*
4492	24/12/52*
4495	6/4/55*
10418	14/12/59

*Fowler

SHEDS
Preston 11/8/34
Camden 27/3/37
Preston (loan)
Holyhead 17/7/37
Crewe North 28/5/38
Longsight 2/7/38
Willesden 23/8/41
Camden 4/4/42
Crewe North 17/6/44
Longsight 29/7/44
Carlisle Upperby 19/8/44
Patricroft 28/5/49
Warrington 9/63

BOILERS
First boiler 8593

No	Fitted	From
8584	20/1/37	5634
8738	8/2/39	5630
8742	6/11/43	5598
8566	22/11/47	5578
8581	23/2/51	45614
8575	10/4/56	45602
8564	2/11/57	45584

MILEAGES

1934	23,910
1935	68,850
1936	50,194
1937	57,455
1938	61,704
1939	60,024
1940	45,375
1941	58,538
1942	38,241
1943	62,904
1944	46,437
1945	32,287
1946	32,299
1947	38,054
1948	46,256
1949	47,232
1950	42,995
1951	48,328
1952	46,880
1953	40,221
1954	47,403
1955	40,008
1956	44,366
1957	43,659
1958	51,571
1959	38,112
1960	43,559

Stored 29/10/62-8/4/63
Mileage at 31/12/50 812,755; at
31/12/60 1,256,862
Withdrawn week ending 27/11/65

45564 NEW SOUTH WALES

Built North British Loco Co Ltd 18/8/34
Named 27/1/36
Renumbered 5564 to 45564 week ending 9/4/49

BOILERS
First boiler 8594

No	Fitted	From
8599	28/7/37	5569
8467	6/6/40	5607
8581	21/8/43	5589
8586	16/3/46	5566
8591	26/8/50	45576
8557	30/7/54	45582
8618	20/9/54	45627
8624	6/7/57	45565
8617	19/9/58	45598

REPAIRS
13/1/36-27/1/36**LS**
18/5/36-23/5/36**LO**
28/9/36-15/10/36**LS**
21/6/37-16/8/37**HG**
24/5/38-8/6/38**LO**
27/1/39-28/2/39**HS**
20/5/40-6/6/40**HG**
28/5/42-13/6/42**LS**
31/7/43-21/8/43**HG**
13/9/44-28/9/44**LS**
23/2/46-16/3/46**HG**
16/8/47-7/10/47**LS St Rollox**
20/10/47-25/10/47**NCRect St Rollox**
9/3/49-9/4/49**LI St Rollox**
14/6/50-26/8/50**HG St Rollox**
14/1/52-9/2/52**LI St Rollox**
29/9/52-4/11/52**LI**
8/12/52-22/12/52**NC(EO)**
2/2/53-14/2/53**LC(EO) Derby shed**
20/5/53-23/6/53**LC(EO)**
19/6/54-30/7/54**HG**
24/8/54-20/9/54**HC(EO)**
5/11/55-15/11/55**NC(EO) Derby**
4/12/55-28/12/55**LI**
1/6/57-6/7/57**HG**
9/8/58-19/9/58**HG**
16/11/59-18/12/59**HI**
8/8/60-24/9/60**LC(EO)**
28/5/61-28/6/61**HI**
**AWS, speedo fitted after 2/60,
dates not recorded**

MILEAGES

1934	26,878
1935	74,849
1936	60,459
1937	60,454
1938	62,188
1939	62,669
1940	44,234
1941	48,641
1942	50,724
1943	57,836
1944	58,496
1945	31,358
1946	49,484
1947	43,636
1948	47,153
1949	61,201
1950	47,042
1951	58,262
1952	39,796
1953	52,918
1954	50,178
1955	53,084
1956	65,567
1957	58,715

Mileage at 31/12/50 887,302
Withdrawn week ending 18/7/64
after 'paper transfer'?
to Newton Heath 7/64

TENDERS

No	Fitted	
9011	18/8/34	
3914	27/1/36*	ex-6138
9697	16/8/37	

*Fowler

SHEDS
Preston 18/8/34
Longsight 25/7/36
Willesden 14/11/36
Camden 6/2/37
Willesden 8/5/37
Camden 28/8/37
Willesden 25/9/37
Camden 20/3/43
Crewe North 10/6/44
Carlisle Upperby 31/3/45
Carlisle Kingmoor (loan) 12/10/46
Carlisle Kingmoor 2/11/46
To Perth at some point (was still at
Kingmoor 21/12/47) before going to
Derby (loan for first fortnight) 30/8/52
Leeds 25/7/53

45564 NEW SOUTH WALES at Corkerhill on 20 June 1959. There's BR green somewhere under that grime; second BR emblem. Photograph Hamish Stevenson.

A Holbeck engine from 1953 to the end of its life, NEW SOUTH WALES was familiar the length of the Midland main line and over the old G&SW route. Here it is, pretty as a picture, with a down train at Sanquhar on 12 August 1961. Photograph J.L. Stevenson, courtesy Hamish Stevenson.

45565 VICTORIA

Built North British Loco Co Ltd 18/8/34
Named 24/2/36
Renumbered 5565 to 45565 5/48

BOILERS
First boiler 8595

No	Fitted	From
8597	4/37	5567
8617	30/6/39	5602
8468	10/4/43	5612
8576	9/46	5627
8587	9/3/51	45617
8624	9/10/54	45614
8589	23/2/57	45569
8628	5/5/61	45561

REPAIRS
8/3/35-8/4/35**LO**
6/2/36-24/2/36**LS**
1/9/36-16/9/36**LS**
some records missing

- 17/12/46**HG**
12/8/47-28/8/47**TRO**
10/1/48-16/2/48**HS**
5/5/48-21/5/48**NC Derby**
2/1/49-28/1/49**LI**
15/11/49-12/12/49**LI**
4/1/51-9/3/51**HG**
9/5/52-31/5/52**LI**
14/11/52-11/12/52**LC(EO)**
28/7/53-21/8/53**LI**
24/8/54-9/10/54**HG**
10/11/55-8/12/55**LI**
9/1/57-23/2/57**HG**
28/5/57-4/7/57**LC(EO)**
5/5/58-31/5/58**LI**
31/8/59-28/10/59**HI**
- 20/9/60**NC(EO)**
20/3/61-5/5/61**HG (probable
date of AWS/speedo fitting)**

MILEAGES

1934	25,847
1935	60,629
1936	59,443
1951	60,150
1952	64,843
1953	70,385
1954	62,818
1955	65,242
1956	74,412
1957	59,578

Mileage at 31/12/50 969,559
Withdrawn 1/67

SHEDS
Preston 18/8/34
Blackpool 22/5/37
'Carlisle' – probably
Upperby (loan) 12/6/37
'Carlisle' 3/7/37
Sheffield 11/9/37
Millhouses 25/9/37
Leeds 28/10/50
Low Moor 6/62
Wakefield 2/65
Low Moor 6/65

TENDERS

No	Fitted
9012	18/8/34
3900	24/2/36* ex-6105
9768	c.1939
9696	16/11/46
10152	20/5/61

*Fowler

45566 QUEENSLAND

Built North British Loco Co Ltd 25/8/34
Named 23/4/36
Renumbered 5566 to 45566 week ending 26/6/48

BOILERS
First boiler 8596

No	Fitted	From
8576	25/3/37	5626
8468	25/1/39	5656
8601	27/7/40	5615
8586	18/8/43	5569
8629	26/1/46	5569
8582	11/8/49	45597
8757	19/9/53	45643
8560	2/8/56	45646
8611	5/7/58	45585

REPAIRS
16/2/35-13/3/35**LO**
2/4/36-23/4/36**LS**
21/1/37-13/4/37**HG**
26/3/38-2/5/38**LS**
6/12/38-25/1/39**HG**
20/12/39-19/1/40**LS**
2/7/40-27/7/40**HO**
2/10/40-25/10/40**LS**
5/5/41-3/6/41**LO**
30/9/41-1/11/41**LS**
17/7/42-10/9/42**LS**
22/1/43-23/2/43**LO**
20/7/43-18/8/43**HG**
5/6/44-19/6/44**LS**
13/12/44-18/1/45**LO**
21/5/45-15/6/45**LS**
5/1/46-26/1/46**HG**
26/2/47-17/4/47**HS**
29/5/48-26/6/48**LS**
20/6/49-11/8/49**HG**
15/8/49-20/8/49**NCRect**
22/8/49-27/8/49**NCRect**
21/6/50-25/7/50**LI**
8/8/51-29/8/51**HI**
30/6/52-9/8/52**HI**
10/8/53-19/9/53**GEN**
30/7/54-3/9/54**LI**
29/9/55-20/10/55**LI**
13/6/56-2/8/56**HG**
17/9/57-1/11/57**HI**
31/5/58-5/7/58**HG**
4/8/59-18/9/59**HI**
26/10/60-2/12/60**LI**
(Dates not recorded – speedo fitted; AWS probably not)

SHEDS
Preston 18/8/34
Patricroft 1/2/36
Longsight 13/11/37
Camden 28/5/38
Leeds (loan) 2/7/38
Leeds 16/7/38
Derby 23/9/39
Normanton 16/3/40
Leeds 20/4/40

TENDERS

No	Fitted
9013	25/8/34
3932	23/4/36* ex-6169
3924	25/1/37*
9766	18/9/39
10780	9/10/62

*Fowler

MILEAGES

Year	Mileage
1934	17,532
1935	59,776
1936	59,989
1937	55,164
1938	63,623
1939	67,147
1940	43,850
1941	57,571
1942	58,310
1943	68,015
1944	70,502
1945	67,620
1946	50,210
1947	50,042
1948	60,905
1949	54,651
1950	66,202
1951	56,028
1952	67,972
1953	66,625
1954	67,041
1955	69,744
1956	64,391
1957	62,531

Mileage at 31/12/50 971,109
Withdrawn week ending 17/11/62

5566, as yet without a name, at Camden in 1935. Behind it of course, stands the 'Turbomotive' (see *The Book of the Princess Royal Pacifics*.) Photograph W. Hermiston, The Transport Treasury.

45567 SOUTH AUSTRALIA

Built North British Loco Co Ltd 18/8/34
Named 16/3/36
Renumbered 5567 to 45567 week ending 6/11/48

No	Fitted	From
10034	20/4/37	NEW
9789	1/3/40	5741
9221	15/2/41	5689
9336	15/2/46	5733
9213	2/11/50	45666
9213	23/4/55	45567
9256	12/4/61	45733

BOILERSREPAIRS
27/4/35-28/5/35LO
2/3/36-16/3/36LS
27/2/37-30/4/37HG
7/2/38-18/2/38LO
15/6/38-25/7/38LS
30/11/38-9/1/39LO
20/1/40-1/3/40HG
8/11/40-23/11/40LO
9/1/41-15/2/41HO
14/8/41-30/8/41HS
11/1/43-27/1/43LS
24/4/44-10/5/44LS
29/1/46-15/2/46HG
19/5/47-20/6/47LS
1/3/48-25/3/48LO
18/9/48-5/11/48HS
21/9/50-2/11/50HG
20/5/52-12/6/52LI
24/10/53-17/11/53LI
12/2/55-23/4/55HG
27/4/55-10/5/55NC(EO Rect)
26/8/56-20/9/56LI
6/2/58-1/3/58LI
4/6/59-4/7/59HI AWS fitted
2/3/61-12/4/61HG speedo fitted
First boiler 8597

MILEAGES

Year	Miles
1934	21,765
1935	63,583
1936	68,400
1937	50,247
1938	49,579
1939	44,945*
1940	39,974
1941	38,513
1942	32,229
1943	42,266
1944	41,374
1945	37,934
1946	40,058
1947	46,941
1948	45,827
1949	55,113
1950	43,248
1951	52,455
1952	45,832
1953	45,200
1954	54,662
1955	42,172
1956	52,009
1957	51,332
1958	47,529
1959	49,040
1960	49,545

*54 days stored unserviceable
Mileage at 31/12/50 761,996
Withdrawn week ending 30/1/65

TENDERS

No	Fitted
9014	18/8/34
3924	16/3/36* ex-6128
3932	25/1/37*
9688	30/4/37

*Fowler

SHEDS
Crewe North 18/8/34
Aston 8/9/34
Preston 10/11/34
Patricroft 1/2/36
Crewe North 14/1/39
Patricroft 22/7/39
Carlisle U pperby 16/9/39
Edge Hill 11/10/47
Carlisle Upperby 5/6/48*
Longsight 5/6/48*
Edge Hill 13/11/48
Crewe North 10/6/61
Aston 6/1/62
Crewe North 23/6/62
Birkenhead 22/12/62
Crewe North 19/1/63
Llandudno Jct 9/64
Crewe North 1/65
*same dates on card!

45567 SOUTH AUSTRALIA leaving Birmingham New Street with the 6.25pm to Heysham, 20 July 1961. Fitted with speedo, AWS and electrification flashes – a very good view of the AWS protection plate. Photograph Michael Mensing.

Another Holbeck Jubilee, 45568 WESTERN AUSTRALIA, at the former Caledonian shed in Edinburgh, Dalry Road, 3 February 1951. Steam sanding and 'recess' sand filler caps; vacuum pump bracket still attached to crosshead. Photograph J. Robertson, The Transport Treasury.

45568 WESTERN AUSTRALIA

Built North British Loco Co Ltd 25/8/34
Named 21/9/36
Renumbered 5568 to 45568 week ending 23/10/48

REPAIRS
2/10/35-21/10/35**LS**
- 2/10/36**TRO**
26/10/36-9/11/36**LS**
26/2/37-5/3/37**LO**
5/6/37-15/7/37**HG**
10/8/37-18/8/37**LO**
21/1/38-1/7/38**HS**
21/11/38-16/12/38**LO**
10/8/39-29/9/39**HG**
30/9/40-15/10/40**LS**
5/1/42-7/2/42**HG**
22/1/43-19/2/43**LS**
26/10/43-27/11/43**HS**
5/6/44-15/7/44**HG**
22/8/44-5/10/44**LO**
15/3/45-19/5/45**HS**
15/10/45-10/11/45**LO**
4/3/46-2/4/46**HS**
3/3/37-25/4/47**HG**
31/1/48-6/2/48**TRO**
19/2/48-22/3/48**LO**
9/9/48-20/10/48**LS**
11/3/49-7/4/49**LC**
17/8/49-15/9/49**HI**
30/1/50-2/3/50**LC**
25/9/50-15/12/50**HG**
7/9/51-9/10/51**HI**
13/11/52-12/12/52**HI**
26/11/53-28/12/53**HG**
29/12/53-5/1/54**NC(EO Rect)**
25/8/54-1/10/54**HI**
11/4/55-11/5/55**LC(EO)**
22/4/56-29/5/56**LI**
8/4/57-4/6/57**HG**
9/8/58-12/9/58**HG**
8/2/60-21/4/60**HI**
- 27/1/61**NC(EO)**
AWS fitted, speedo probably fitted, before 4/61

MILEAGES
1934	24,215
1935	58,475
1936	55,947
1937	47,340
1938	47,418
1939	55,856
1940	78,077
1941	66,693
1942	68,818
1943	45,741
1944	50,303
1945	54,061
1946	52,092
1947	48,570
1948	55,760
1949	60,280
1950	45,872
1951	71,348
1952	51,143
1953	60,232
1954	70,620
1955	58,832
1956	62,350
1957	60,012

Mileage at 31/12/50 915,515
Withdrawn week ending 25/4/64 after 'paper transfer'? to Newton Heath 4/64

TENDERS
No	Fitted
9015	25/8/34
3907	21/9/36* ex-6145
4569	4/6/57*HSS
10741	21/4/60 ex-48716

***Fowler**
HSS=high straight sided

SHEDS
Crewe North 18/8/34
Camden 8/9/34
Preston 10/11/34
Patricroft 1/2/36
Blackpool 22/5/37
Crewe North 26/6/37
Leeds 11/9/37
Damaged by enemy action
Prior to 19/12/40
Toton (loan) 27/7/46
Leeds 14/9/46
Nottingham (loan) 25/12/48
Leeds 5/2/49

BOILERS
First boiler 8598
No	Fitted	From
8602	23/6/37	5572
8594	29/9/39	5559
8628	7/2/42	5559
8604	15/7/44	5606
8623	25/4/47	5603
8570	15/12/50	45641
8632	28/12/53	45649
8578	4/6/57	45625
8613	12/9/58	45654

45569 TASMANIA

Built North British Loco Co Ltd 25/8/34
Named 10/2/36
Renumbered 5569 to 45569 week ending 4/12/48

MILEAGES

Year	Mileage
1934	26,987
1935	43,951
1936	53,695
1937	55,501
1938	73,831
1939	73,746
1940	54,986
1941	53,720
1942	34,455
1943	66,585
1944	52,349
1945	42,045
1946	49,991
1947	60,857
1948	52,714
1949	67,603
1950	71,966
1951	55,385
1952	68,442
1953	68,012
1954	72,375
1955	57,034
1956	58,918
1957	70,466

Mileage at 31/12/50 934,982
Withdrawn week ending 25/4/64
after 'paper transfer'? to Patricroft.

BOILERS

First boiler 8599

No	Fitted	From
8753	2/7/37	5655
8586	18/8/39	5595
8629	5/6/43	5662
8621	17/11/45	5602
8615	1/12/48	45613
8589	16/5/53	45559
8619	15/1/57	45614
8737	18/1/62	45656

TENDERS

No	Fitted
9016	25/8/34
3916	10/2/36* ex-6147
9694	27/7/37

*Fowler

SHEDS

Shed	Date
Crewe North	25/8/34
Camden	8/9/34
Crewe North	24/11/34
Rugby	9/3/35
Derby	11/9/37
Kentish Town	9/7/38
Saltley	6/9/41
Leeds	31/10/42

REPAIRS

25/1/36-10/2/36**LS**
13/9/36-18/9/36**LO**
26/5/37-27/7/37**HG**
25/8/38-26/9/38**HS**
8/4/39-28/4/39**TRO**
17/7/39-18/8/39**HG**
7/10/40-19/10/40**LS**
21/6/41-19/7/41**LS**
6/6/42-27/6/42**LO**
15/9/42-10/10/42**LO**
10/5/43-5/6/43**HG**
25/5/44-10/6/44**HS**
27/1/45-24/3/45**LO**
13/4/45-30/5/45**HS**
29/10/45-17/11/45**HG**
25/10/46-6/12/46**LS**
25/8/47-8/10/47**HS**
20/9/48-1/12/48**HG**
6/12/49-28/12/49**HI**
6/2/51-27/2/51**LI**
6/10/51-10/11/51**HI**
16/4/52-10/5/52**LC(EO)**
21/5/52-22/5/52**NC(Rect)**
13/4/53-16/5/53 **HG**
20/3/54-22/4/54**HI**
16/8/55-9/9/55**HI**
12/9/55-22/9/55**NC(EO Rect)**
23/11/56-15/1/57**HG**
26/6/55-7/8/58**LI**
21/11/59-29/12/59**HI**
21/4/60-31/5/60**LC(EO)**
28/9/60-19/11/60**LC**
? -18/1/62**HG**

AWS and probably speedo
fitted before 5/61. Retained
first BR emblem at 5/61.
May have received second
style at HG of 1/62

Another Holbeck Jubilee in Scotland. 45569 TASMANIA in BR green but looking decidedly unkempt, at Dalry Road shed in the 1950s. Photograph The Transport Treasury.

45570 NEW ZEALAND on a siding at Kentish Town shed, July 1953. Photograph J. Robertson, The Transport Treasury.

45570 NEW ZEALAND

Built North British Loco Co Ltd 25/8/34
Named 15/1/36
Renumbered 5570 to 45570 week ending 19/6/48

SHEDS
Crewe North 25/8/34
Camden 8/9/34
Crewe North 17/11/34
Carlisle Upperby 29/6/35
Edge Hill 18/4/36
Camden 18/7/36
Willesden 17/10/36
Edge Hill 29/5/37
Trafford Park (loan) 9/7/38
Trafford Park 6/8/38
Bristol 11/10/47
Derby 26/5/51
Millhouses 15/6/57
Canklow 1/62
Darnall 6/62

REPAIRS
2/1/36-16/1/36**LS**
2/7/36-21/7/36**LO**
18/2/37-22/3/37**HS**
23/8/37-21/9/37**HG**
22/4/38-16/5/38**LO**
28/8/38-11/10/38**LS**
21/1/39-15/2/39**LO**
7/6/39-26/6/39**LO**
6/11/39-21/12/39**HG**
7/8/40-4/9/40**LS**
22/3/41-17/4/41**LO**
24/12/41-22/1/42**HS**
14/1/43-20/2/43**HG**
7/11/43-9/11/43**LO**
14/12/43-18/1/44**LS**
27/12/44-14/2/45**HG**
29/11/45-29/12/45**LS**
5/7/46-1/8/46**LO**
5/6/47-9/8/47**HS**
21/4/48-15/6/48**HG**
16/5/49-10/6/49**LI**
19/3/50-6/4/50**LI**
8/4/51-12/5/51**HG**
12/8/52-12/9/52**HI**
2/2/54-27/2/54**LI**
16/8/54-14/9/54**LC(EO)**
4/2/55-4/3/55**LI**
8/5/56-23/6/56**HG**
8/5/58-30/5/58**HI**
9/9/59-9/10/59**HI**
   ?   -16/11/61**HG**
Dates not recorded;
speedo probably fitted,
AWS probably not

MILEAGES

Year	Mileage
1934	25,086
1935	62,709
1936	53,794
1937	56,200
1938	57,300
1939	50,267
1940	53,229
1941	44,472
1942	53,555
1943	61,028
1944	56,767
1945	47,351
1946	44,000
1947	41,060
1948	58,829
1949	64,572
1950	60,128
1951	54,077
1952	49,435
1953	46,918
1954	44,158
1955	44,003
1956	48,205
1957	47,567

Mileage at 31/12/50 890,347
Withdrawn week ending 29/12/62
(Stored prior to withdrawal)

BOILERS
First boiler 8600

No	Fitted	From
8610	27/8/37	5580
8755	21/12/39	5655
8561	20/2/43	5553
8612	14/2/45	5593
8594	15/6/48	5596
8608	12/5/51	45607
8741	23/6/56	45636
8636	16/11/61	45661

TENDERS

No	Fitted
9017	25/8/34
4249	16/1/36* ex-6164
9700	21/9/37

***Fowler**

45571 SOUTH AFRICA

Built North British Loco Co Ltd 1/9/34
Named 4/5/36
Renumbered 5571 to 45571 week ending 16/10/48

SHEDS
Camden 8/9/34
Crewe North 17/11/34
Carlisle 19/1/35
Edge Hill 18/4/36
Carlisle Upperby 9/5/36
Blackpool (loan) 12/6/37
Blackpool 3/7/37
Speke Junction 16/11/63

MILEAGES

Year	Mileage
1934	13,040
1935	63,420
1936	55,524
1937	45,691
1938	41,146
1939	46,135
1940	42,212
1941	36,810
1942	45,237
1943	47,489
1944	42,954
1945	47,058
1946	46,554
1947	31,897
1948	43,526
1949	35,833
1950	58,506
1951	45,838
1952	51,538
1953	54,740
1954	40,494
1955	48,916
1956	45,798
1957	49,377
1958	46,036
1959	43,446
1960	45,078

Mileage at 31/12/50 743,032; at
31/12/60 1,214,293
Withdrawn week ending 16/5/64

REPAIRS
30/3/36-4/5/36**LS**
12/9/36-19/9/36**LO**
27/2/37-19/3/37**HS**
5/1/38-24/1/38**LO**
30/4/38-2/6/38**HG**
5/12/39-30/12/39**LS**
7/9/40-21/9/40**HS**
3/4/41-22/4/41**LO**
4/6/42-17/7/42**HG**
14/6/43-3/7/43**LS**
2/10/44-19/10/44**HS**
26/3/46-16/4/46**HG**
28/11/47-7/1/48**HS**
10/1/48-13/1/48**NC(Rect)**
1/9/48-15/10/48**LO**
31/8/49-4/11/49**HG**
25/9/51-19/10/51**LI**
17/1/53-10/2/53**HI**
3/9/54-8/10/54**HG**
2/8/56-25/8/56**LI**
17/3/58-26/4/58**HG**
16/3/59-2/4/59**NC(EO) AWS fitted**
4/1/60-6/2/60**HI**
 ? -11/61 **speedo fitted**

BOILERS
First boiler 8601

No	Fitted	From
8579	17/5/38	5641
8762	17/7/42	5585
8585	16/4/46	5573
8622	4/11/49	45615
8585	8/10/54	45600
8612	26/4/58	45628

TENDERS

No	Fitted
9018	1/9/34
3943	4/5/36* ex-6146
4493	8/10/54*
3939	26/4/58*
10575	2/4/59
9462	5/1/60

*Fowler

45572 EIRE at Holyhead shed, 29 March 1959; 45684 JUTLAND alongside. With an 82E shedplate, the engine is a long way from its Bristol home, Barrow Road having passed to the Western Region just over a year before. It had come off Crewe Works on or about 14 March which would explain its presence here. Photograph Hamish Stevenson.

45572 EIRE

Built North British Loco Co Ltd 1/9/34
Named IRISH FREE STATE 24/3/36; renamed EIRE 19/7/38
Renumbered 5572 to 45572 week ending 14/8/48

TENDERS

No	Fitted
9019	1/9/34
4239	24/3/36* ex-6154
9691	3/6/37
*Fowler	

REPAIRS
16/2/35-7/3/35**LO**
9/3/36-24/3/36**LS**
24/3/37-3/6/37**HG**
5/6/38-19/7/38**LS**
21/11/38-9/1/39**LO**
17/10/39-7/11/39**HG**
10/6/40-20/6/40**LO**
20/11/40-7/12/40**LS**
19/3/42-18/4/42**HS**
26/12/42-8/2/43**HG**
22/7/43-20/8/43**LO**
30/6/44-28/7/44**LS**
14/5/45-12/6/45**HG**
29/5/47-5/7/47**HS**
6/1/48-11/2/48**LS**
20/2/48-6/3/48**NC**
13/7/48-14/8/48**LO**
16/12/48-7/3/49**HG**
18/10/49-8/11/49**LC**
16/5/50-9/6/50**HI**
23/4/51-11/5/51**LI**
21/4/52-20/5/52**HI**
20/6/53-17/8/53**HG**
16/9/53-8/10/53**LC(EO)**
3/5/54-2/6/54**HI**
3/6/54-21/6/54 **NC(EO Rect)**
1/4/55-30/4/55**HI**
20/4/56-18/5/56**HI**
22/5/56-13/6/56**NC(EO Rect)**
30/4/57-20/6/57**HG**
2/2/59-14/3/59**LI**
29/4/60-18/6/60**HG** speedo fitted;
AWS probably not

SHEDS
Crewe North 8/9/34
Carlisle Upperby 6/10/34
Edge Hill 18/4/36
Carlisle Upperby 9/5/36
Sheffield 11/9/37
Millhouses 25/9/37
Trafford Pk 11/2/39
Bristol 11/10/47
Leeds 1/10/55
Bristol 15/10/55
Shrewsbury 9/61
Willesden 4/1/64
('paper transfer')

BOILERS
First boiler 8602

No	Fitted	From
8596	18/5/37	5566
8602	17/10/39	5568
8591	8/2/43	5631
8609	12/6/45	5643
8621	7/3/49	45569
8561	17/8/53	45644
8609	20/6/57	45660
8631	18/6/60	not recorded

MILEAGES

1934	24,094
1935	60,120
1936	59,636
1937	57,748
1938	50,165
1939	54,631
1940	64,820
1941	57,308
1942	43,296
1943	55,678
1944	51,686
1945	48,848
1946	21,976
1947	41,078
1948	43,935
1949	55,727
1950	64,450
1951	61,812
1952	68,858
1953	53,727
1954	64,535
1955	64,609
1956	62,009
1957	62,058
1958	63,176
1959	56,642
1960	59,520
1961	47,532
1962	24,569
1963	32,188

Mileage at 31/12/50 855,196; at 31/12/60 1,472,142
Withdrawn week ending 4/1/64

45573 NEWFOUNDLAND

Built North British Loco Co Ltd 29/9/34
Named 10/2/36
Renumbered 5573 to 45573 week ending 11/9/48

MILEAGES

1934	16,088
1935	62,366
1936	57,793
1937	50,710
1938	66,482
1939	45,270
1940	53,484
1941	51,264
1942	53,777
1943	52,434
1944	49,478
1945	46,097
1946	49,087
1947	60,065
1948	58,657
1949	64,663
1950	62,175
1951	58,917
1952	70,239
1953	73,156
1954	65,426
1955	61,940
1956	61,806
1957	72,332

Mileage at 31/12/50 899,890
Withdrawn Aug/Sept 1965

BOILERS
First boiler 8703

No	Fitted	From
8740	18/3/38	5647
8618	8/5/40	5599
8585	8/8/42	5613
8741	30/3/46	5557
8588	11/9/48	45663
8739	22/12/51	45622
8761	22/10/55	45638
8571	2/11/57	45631

TENDERS

No	Fitted
9020	29/9/34
3919	10/2/36* ex-6101
9769	4/10/39
*Fowler	

SHEDS
Crewe North 29/9/34
Carlisle Upperby 6/10/34
Camden 17/7/37
Willesden 28/8/37
Trafford Park (loan) 3/9/38
Trafford Park 17/9/38
Millhouses 11/2/39
Leeds 13/4/46

REPAIRS
24/1/36-10/2/36**LS**
24/9/36-24/10/36**LO**
12/4/37-29/4/37**HS**
6/3/38-5/4/38**HG**
31/3/39-29/4/39**HS**
19/4/40-8/5/40**HG**
2/12/40-4/2/41**LO**
2/2/42-28/2/42**LS**
15/6/42-8/8/42**HG**
16/6/43-2/7/43**HS**
30/11/43-30/12/43**LO**
23/6/44-26/7/44**LS**
20/11/44-16/12/44**LO**
6/9/45-7/9/45**LO**
18/1/46-30/3/46**HG**
29/5/47-7/8/47**HS**
17/7/48-11/9/48**HG**
24/9/49-18/10/49**HI**
6/11/50-7/12/50**LI**
24/1/51-22/2/51**HC**
19/11/51-22/12/51**HG**
12/12/52-8/1/53**LI**
11/1/54-6/2/54**HI**
15/10/54-6/11/54**LC(EO)**
6/9/55-22/10/55**HI**
29/10/56-30/11/56**HI**
15/9/57-2/11/57**HG**
27/9/58-31/10/58**HI**
-/24/9/59**NC(EO)**
25/6/60-13/8/60**LI**
-/26/8/60**NC(EO)**
-/2/11/60**NC(EO)**
Dates not recorded;speedo probably fitted, AWS probably not

45573 NEWFOUNDLAND runs along tender first at Bellahouston, 16 May 1959. Photograph Hamish Stevenson.

45574 INDIA

Built North British Loco Co Ltd 29/9/34
Named 26/5/36
Renumbered 5574 to 45574 week ending 2/7/49

MILEAGES

Year	Mileage
1934	6,397
1935	62,596
1936	54,672
1937	42,296
1938	51,009
1939	40,018
1940	39,314
1941	49,300
1942	48,869
1943	49,902
1944	39,731
1945	46,695
1946	46,939
1947	33,220
1948	40,800
1949	45,304
1950	54,317
1951	38,371
1952	49,065
1953	46,224
1954	50,787
1955	44,995
1956	42,003
1957	48,842
1958	44,379
1959	50,151
1960	41,260

stored 21/11/64-15/5/65
**Mileage at 31/12/50 751,379; at
31/12/60 1,207,456**
Withdrawn March 1966

REPAIRS
8/10/34-19/10/34**LO**
2/11/34-26/11/34**LO**
4/5/36-26/5/36**LS**
5/10/36-20/10/36**LO**
22/2/37-6/4/37**HS**
17/11/37-13/12/37**HG**
12/3/38-23/3/38**LO**
1/6/39-24/7/39**LS**
15/2/41-15/3/41**HG**
5/1/42-24/1/42**LO**
17/8/42-12/9/42**LS**
11/8/43-31/8/43**LS**
11/9/44-30/9/44**HG**
11/2/46-15/3/46**HS**
13/10/47-14/11/47**LS**
17/11/47-18/11/47**NC**
19/5/49-2/7/49**HG**
6/7/50-10/8/50**LI**
10/11/51-18/12/51**LI**
10/6/53-4/7/53**LI**
3/1/55-5/2/55**HG**
14/12/55-18/1/56**HC**
11/12/56-17/1/57**HI**
21/4/58-16/5/58**LI**
5/1/59-6/2/59**LI AWS fitted**
9/11/59-26/11/59**LC(EO)**
27/6/60-20/8/60**HG speedo fitted**

TENDERS

No	Fitted
9021	29/9/34
3939	26/5/36* ex-6115
3933	18/12/51*
4242	5/2/55*
4485	18/1/56*
4496	17/1/57*
3907	6/2/59*
10367	26/11/59
10758	19/5/62

*Fowler

SHEDS
Crewe North 29/9/34
Carlisle Upperby 6/10/34
Aston 10/11/34
Shrewsbury 20/4/35
Camden 6/7/35
Willesden 5/10/35
Carlisle Upperby 9/11/35
Preston (loan) 24/4/37
Carlisle Upperby 8/5/37
Blackpool (loan) 12/6/37
Blackpool 3/7/37
Carlisle Kingmoor 9/64
Leeds 6/65

BOILERS
First boiler 8604

No	Fitted	From
8588	29/11/37	5558
8572	15/3/41	5662
8617	30/9/44	5620
8466	2/7/49	45614
8605	5/2/55	45650
8597	20/8/60	45611

45575 MADRAS
Built North British Loco Co Ltd 29/9/34
Named 13/11/37
Renumbered 5575 to 45575 week ending 21/8/48

TENDERS

No	Fitted
9022	29/9/34
4623	4/9/47
9022	17/11/47
9023	27/11/47
9366	18/8/48
4637	6/3/57

REPAIRS
24/11/34-13/12/34**LO**
1/7/36-17/7/36**LS**
18/1/37-2/2/37**LO**
10/3/37-14/4/37**LO**
5/10/37-13/11/37**HG**
19/9/38-2/11/38**LO**
21/9/39-19/10/39**LS**
28/8/40-14/9/40**HG**
25/6/41-9/8/41**LS**
25/5/42-1/7/42**HS**
19/4/43-22/5/43**LS**
30/8/43-26/11/43**LO**
18/5/44-10/6/44**LO**
22/5/45-12/7/45**HG**
30/12/46-5/2/47**HS** St Rollox
12/1/48-16/2/48**LS** St Rollox
1/3/48-4/3/48**NC(Rect)** St Rollox
24/6/48-19/8/48**LO** St Rollox
29/10/49-14/1/50**HG** St Rollox
5/5/50-17/5/50**LC** St Rollox
11/4/51-17/5/51**LI** St Rollox
3/1/52-18/1/52**LC(EO)** St Rollox
11/2/52-22/2/52**LC(EO)** St Rollox
26/2/52-5/3/52**LC(EO)** St Rollox
11/4/52-7/5/52**LC(EO)** Perth shed
25/6/52-16/8/52**HI** St Rollox
5/5/53-15/6/53**HG**
5/1/54-7/1/54**LC(TO)** Derby
7/9/54-5/10/54**HI**
15/10/55-24/11/55**HI**
24/7/56-18/9/56**HG**
28/10/57-29/11/57**LI**
14/2/59-13/3/59**HI**
9/6/59-1/8/59**LC(EO)**
20/4/60-3/6/60**HG** speedo fitted;
AWS probably never fitted

MILEAGES

1934	14,296
1935	69,201
1936	75,524
1937	45,767
1938	71,240
1939	66,987
1940	45,260
1941	42,268
1942	41,999
1943	16,616
1944	44,114
1945	42,309
1946	49,233
1947	44,628
1948	38,800
1949	37,778
1950	50,865
1951	51,495
1952	35,109
1953	57,038
1954	58,286
1955	54,408
1956	69,590
1957	57,052
1958	63,410
1959	49,459
1960	60,649

Mileage at 31/12/50 796,885; at
31/12/60 1,353,381
Withdrawn week ending 15/6/63

BOILERS
First boiler 8605

No	Fitted	From
8595	13/11/37	5565
8569	14/9/40	5636
8744	12/7/45	5604
8750	14/1/50	45644
8752	15/6/53	45636
8750	18/9/56	45601
8582	3/6/60	45658

SHEDS
Crewe North 29/9/34
Camden 13/7/35
Carlisle Upperby 5/10/35
Carlisle Kingmoor 18/1/36
Corkerhill 8/2/36
Polmadie 21/10/39
Carlisle Kingmoor 11/5/40
Corkerhill 28/9/40
Perth 1/4/50
Kentish Town 30/8/52
Loan at first then
Kentish Town 13/9/52
Nottingham 30/5/59
Kentish Town 20/6/59
Derby 16/12/61
Burton 7/4/62

45575 MADRAS at Corkerhill, its home through the 1940s, on 17 September 1949. Photograph A.G. Ellis, The Transport Treasury.

45576 BOMBAY

Built North British Loco Co Ltd 29/9/34
Named 9/12/37
Renumbered 5576 to 45576 week ending 19/6/48

BOILERS
First boiler 8606

No	Fitted	From
8751	9/12/37	5645
8595	3/5/41	5575
8591	2/2/46	5572
8744	24/6/50	45575
8736	8/5/54	45561
8760	21/5/57	45582

REPAIRS
25/2/36-1/4/36LS
7/9/36-25/9/36LO
5/4/37-7/5/37LS
19/10/37-9/12/37HG
9/9/38-14/10/38LO
21/4/39-29/5/39HS
1/7/40-26/7/40LS
11/4/41-3/5/41HG
15/8/41-20/9/41LO
2/11/42-5/12/42HS
4/1/43-22/2/43LO
20/10/43-3/12/43LS
14/1/44-25/4/44LO
4/8/44-22/8/44HO
31/12/45-2/2/46HG
19/2/47-4/4/47LS St Rollox
25/11/47-24/12/47LO St Rollox
8/5/48-17/6/48HS St Rollox
26/4/49-17/6/49HI St Rollox
1/5/50-24/6/50HG St Rollox
1/3/51-23/3/51NC St Rollox
29/10/51-24/11/51HI St Rollox
3/12/51-3/12/51NC(TO) St Rollox
29/10/52-4/12/52HI
15/12/52-23/12/52NC (EO Rect)
7/4/54-8/5/54HG
26/1/56-18/2/56HI
12/4/57-21/5/57HG
5/9/58-10/10/58HI
Dates not recorded; speedo probably fitted, AWS probably never

MILEAGES

1934	18,766
1935	69,989
1936	59,976
1937	52,204
1938	59,174
1939	60,405
1940	51,806
1941	30,559
1942	39,113
1943	37,451
1944	27,848
1945	44,174
1946	60,658
1947	43,774
1948	46,095
1949	49,187
1950	42,572
1951	45,385
1952	38,570
1953	41,226
1954	52,716
1955	44,920
1956	57,638
1957	57,737

Mileage at 31/12/50 793,751
Withdrawn week ending 29/12/62
(Stored prior to withdrawal)

TENDERS

No	Fitted
9023	29/9/34
9022	27/11/47
9215	27/4/49
9329	6/5/50
10686	18/7/51
9258	20/11/51

SHEDS
Crewe North 29/9/34
Carlisle Upperby 5/10/35
Carlisle Kingmoor 18/1/36
Corkerhill 11/4/36
Polmadie 20/8/38
Corkerhill 22/2/41
Millhouses 30/8/52
Loan at first then
Millhouses 13/9/52
Canklow 1/62
Darnall 6/62

45577 BENGAL

Built North British Loco Co Ltd 29/9/34
Named 30/3/37
Renumbered 5577 to 45577 week ending 10/4/48

BOILERS
First boiler 8607

No	Fitted	From
8743	6/6/39	5587
8616	25/9/43	5620
8564	31/5/47	5581
8749	1/12/51	45579
8565	7/8/53	45587
8577	11/9/57	45617

REPAIRS
15/3/35-9/4/35LS
15/5/36-18/6/36LS
5/5/37-25/5/37LO
1/9/37-30/9/37LS
1/8/38-6/9/38LO
30/3/39-6/6/39HG
11/6/40-29/6/40HS
26/8/41-27/9/41LS
19/6/42-1/8/42LS
12/11/42-9/12/42LO
11/8/43-25/9/43HG
11/11/43-15/12/43-LO
12/5/45-27/6/45HS
14/3/46-17/4/46LS
17/4/47-31/5/47HG St Rollox
5/8/47-22/8/47LO St Rollox
12/11/47-14/11/47LO St Rollox
19/3/48-8/4/48LO St Rollox
15/7/48-29/7/48LO Kilmarnock
4/8/48-11/8/48NC St Rollox
27/5/49-9/7/49LI St Rollox
16/6/50-12/8/50HI St Rollox
17/10/51-1/12/51HG St Rollox
12/5/52-23/5/52NC(EO) St Rollox
15/9/52-20/10/52HI
13/6/53-7/8/53HG
31/5/54-23/6/54LI
25/9/54-26/10/54HC(EO)
6/6/55-30/6/55LI
8/6/56-24/7/56LI
6/8/57-11/9/57HG
6/4/59-8/5/59LI
21/7/60-3/9/60LI speedo fitted;
AWS probably never fitted

MILEAGES

1934	21,052
1935	69,611
1936	63,928
1937	41,373
1938	55,935
1939	44,238
1940	53,324
1941	51,593
1942	45,778
1943	43,558
1944	56,635
1945	52,237
1946	48,171
1947	39,865
1948	38,699
1949	40,239
1950	45,668
1951	38,663
1952	58,235
1953	60,589
1954	60,365
1955	66,418
1956	62,685
1957	63,097

Mileage at 31/12/50 811,904
Withdrawn week ending 5/9/64

TENDERS

No	Fitted
9024	29/9/34
9719	2/5/47
9027	27/5/47
9364	7/7/49
9278	21/11/51
9696	19/5/62

SHEDS
Crewe North 6/10/34
Carlisle Upperby 5/10/35
Carlisle Kingmoor 18/1/36
Bristol 30/8/52
Loan at first then
Bristol 13/9/52
Shrewsbury 9/61

45575 MADRAS stands at Balornock (St Rollox) shed, 19 May 1951. MADRAS had been a Scottish engine most of its life, though in the celebrated 'mass exchange' (see Graham Onley's Appendix One) it was soon to move south, to Kentish Town. Throughout the 1950s the Scottish Jubilees ran rather lower annual mileages than the English ones, while returning somewhat higher availability figures. This was doubtless the result of geography and geology; the sort of distances available either side of the border and, crucially, better water. Photograph J.L. Stevenson, courtesy Hamish Stevenson.

A super show at Carlisle on 20 August 1952, as 45577 BENGAL, with domeless boiler, pilots 45568 WESTERN AUSTRALIA on an up express. Photograph J. Robertson, The Transport Treasury.

45578 UNITED PROVINCES

Built North British Loco Co Ltd 29/9/34
Named 3/3/38
Renumbered 5578 to 45578 week ending 11/12/48

SHEDS

Crewe North 6/10/34
Carlisle Upperby 2/2/35
Carlisle Kingmoor 18/1/36
Crewe North 11/4/42
Loan at first then
Crewe North 9/5/42
Carlisle Upperby 13/6/42
Longsight 5/2/44
Crewe North 5/4/47
Longsight 26/11/49
Carlisle Upperby 21/1/50
Crewe North 13/6/53
Longsight 19/9/53
Crewe North 20/6/59
Edge Hill 12/9/59
Crewe North 10/6/61
Aston 6/1/62
Newton Heath 17/3/62

REPAIRS

17/4/36-9/5/36**LS**
21/10/36-3/11/36**LO**
31/5/37-1/7/37**LS**
11/1/38-3/3/38**HG**
8/3/39-30/3/39**LS**
14/2/40-27/4/40**LS**
17/5/41-12/6/41**HS**
28/11/41-10/1/42**HG**
21/11/42-10/12/42**LS**
11/8/43-28/8/43**LO**
14/12/43-14/1/44**LO**
22/6/44-22/7/44**HS**
26/5/45-20/6/45**HG**
5/8/46-17/9/46**HS**
8/9/47-22/10/47**HG**
18/11/48-7/12/48**LS**
13/6/49-16/8/49**HG**
24/3/51-13/4/51**LI**
21/11/52-30/12/52**HG**
5/10/53-3/11/53**HI**
25/1/54-17/2/54**NC(EO)**
18/1/55-14/2/55**HI**
12/4/56-10/5/56**LI**
25/6/57-8/8/57**HG**
8/9/58-22/10/58**HG**
25/5/59-13/6/59**NC AWS fitted**
9/4/60-14/5/60**LI speedo fitted**
20/12/60-19/1/61**LC(EO)**
6/4/61-1/5/61**LC(EO)**

MILEAGES

Year	Mileage
1934	21,136
1935	62,068
1936	64,163
1937	58,945
1938	63,539
1939	58,252
1940	39,153
1941	34,272
1942	44,174
1943	37,482
1944	46,348
1945	66,219
1946	49,221
1947	44,196
1948	36,796
1949	38,771
1950	48,303
1951	38,654
1952	42,496
1953	49,561
1954	57,532
1955	47,204
1956	57,834
1957	55,874
1958	50,320
1959	55,662
1960	42,466

Mileage at 31/12/50 813,038; at 31/12/60 1,310,641
Withdrawn week ending 30/5/64

BOILERS
First boiler 8608

No	Fitted	From
8626	3/3/38	5596
8573	10/1/42	5595
8566	20/6/45	5561
8632	22/10/47	5593
8602	16/8/49	45594
8748	30/12/52	45615
8634	8/8/57	45553
8559	22/10/58	45655

TENDERS

No	Fitted
9025	29/9/34
9363	17/5/41

Polmadie's 45579 PUNJAB at Kingmoor,
21 August 1952. Photograph J. Robertson,
The Transport Treasury.

45579 PUNJAB

Built North British Loco Co Ltd 29/9/34
Named 2/10/36
Renumbered 5579 to 45579 week ending 4/9/48

SHEDS
Crewe North 6/10/34
Carlisle Upperby 2/2/35
Aberdeen 7/12/35
Carlisle Kingmoor 8/4/39
Polmadie 18/3/50
Kentish Town 30/8/52
Loan at first, then
Kentish Town 13/9/52
Derby 21/11/59
Saltley 4/3/61
Burton 18/11/61
Derby 22/6/63

REPAIRS
30/8/36-2/10/36LS
27/5/37-28/6/37LO
22/2/38-4/3/38LS
2/5/38-23/5/38HO
2/2/39-8/3/39HG
26/4/40-25/5/40LS
2/11/40-23/11/40LO
23/8/41-25/9/41HS
23/3/42-14/5/42HG
25/1/43-9/3/43LO
29/6/43-27/7/43LS
8/5/44-8/6/44LS
2/8/44-30/8/44LO
7/4/45-30/6/45LS
12/7/45-1/9/45LO
21/11/46-18/1/47HG St Rollox
21/8/47-3/10/47LO St Rollox
7/11/47-17/12/47LS St Rollox
2/8/48-4/9/48LO St Rollox
8/11/48-22/12/48LO St Rollox
8/4/49-27/5/49LI St Rollox
8/6/49-21/6/49NC(Rect) St Rollox
19/7/49-20/8/49LC St Rollox
21/10/49-12/11/49LC St Rollox
5/12/49-7/2/50HI St Rollox
7/8/50-22/8/50LC St Rollox
30/4/51-25/8/51HG St Rollox
24/3/52-14/4/52LC Polmadie shed
16/10/52-28/11/52LI
20/6/53-14/8/53LC(EO)
26/3/54-24/4/54LI
15/5/54-27/5/54NC(EO Rect)
10/6/55-5/7/55HG
7/11/55-6/12/55LC(EO)
19/11/56-22/12/56HI
5/7/57-7/8/57LC(EO)
14/8/57-31/8/57NC(EO Rect)
25/3/58-19/4/58HI
17/3/59-29/4/59HG
25/9/59-28/10/59LC(EO)
6/10/60-8/11/60HI speedo fitted; AWS
probably never fitted

MILEAGES
Year	Mileage
1934	19,883
1935	65,431
1936	67,597
1937	58,604
1938	59,438
1939	63,632
1940	49,076
1941	51,663
1942	49,993
1943	45,063
1944	41,097
1945	30,252
1946	47,558
1947	39,823
1948	29,776
1949	25,933
1950	42,934
1951	39,155
1952	39,732
1953	52,831
1954	57,754
1955	52,965
1956	61,509
1957	60,170
1958	67,046
1959	49,031
1960	48,822

**Mileage at 31/12/50 787,752; at
31/12/60 1,316,768**
Withdrawn week ending 15/8/64

TENDERS
No	Fitted
9026	29/9/34
9015	2/10/36
9032	7/11/40
9720	26/11/40
9364	26/8/41
9679	12/5/44
9270	30/8/44
9146	3/5/49
9271	9/2/50
9778	?

BOILERS
First boiler 8609
No	Fitted	From
8752	23/5/38	5646
8750	8/3/39	5644
8631	14/5/42	5647
8749	18/1/47	5607
8753	25/8/51	45580
8586	5/7/55	45645
8578	29/4/59	45568

PUNJAB in earlier guise - it's possible to 'spot the differences', beginning with the smokebox saddle... Photograph Gavin Whitelaw Collection.

45580 BURMA

Built North British Loco Co Ltd 6/10/34
Named 18/2/38
Renumbered 5580 to 45580 week ending 7/5/49

TENDERS

No	Fitted
9027	6/10/34
9190	8/2/45
10618	8/6/50
9264	12/4/51

REPAIRS
30/4/36-29/5/36LS
12/5/37-24/6/37HG
21/11/38-17/12/38LS
8/6/39-24/6/39LO
5/9/39-4/10/39LO
23/4/40-17/5/40LS
5/9/40-5/10/40LO
30/4/41-27/5/41HS
1/7/41-21/8/41HO
22/5/42-27/6/42HG
27/2/43-1/4/43LS
8/11/43-21/1/44LS
7/9/44-14/10/44LO
25/11/44-11/1/45LO
2/4/45-2/6/45LS
1/12/45-21/12/45LO
8/7/46-24/8/46HG
22/12/47-28/1/48HS St Rollox
22/3/49-5/5/49LI St Rollox
2/5/50-8/6/50HI St Rollox
25/10/50-21/4/51HG St Rollox
1/4/52-29/4/52LI St Rollox
11/9/53-10/10/53LI
19/11/54-10/12/54LI
25/11/55-2/1/56HG
24/5/56-21/6/56LC(EO)
28/8/57-21/9/57LI
8/8/58-11/9/58LI
13/9/58-8/10/58NC(EO Rect)
11/4/60-6/6/60HG AWS, speedo fitted

SHEDS
Crewe North 6/10/34
Carlisle Upperby 2/2/35
Aberdeen 7/12/35
Carlisle Kingmoor 8/4/39
St Rollox 24/6/39
Carlisle Kingmoor 7/10/39
Blackpool 30/8/52
Loan at first, then
Blackpool 13/9/52
Warrington 22/6/63
Newton Heath 9/64

BOILERS
First boiler 8610

No	Fitted	From
8757	24/6/37	5659
8751	21/8/41	5576
8465	27/6/42	5624
8753	24/8/46	5654
8571	21/4/51	45645
8604	2/1/56	45664
8593	6/6/60	45589

MILEAGES

Year	Mileage
1934	14,153
1935	72,028
1936	73,841
1937	48,656
1938	65,730
1939	53,031
1940	43,931
1941	34,385
1942	54,870
1943	41,798
1944	30,285
1945	36,188
1946	51,447
1947	57,547
1948	64,240
1949	59,535
1950	47,375
1951	46,584
1952	49,810
1953	35,089
1954	53,462
1955	44,771
1956	55,178
1957	52,721
1958	51,179
1959	52,883
1960	37,052

Mileage at 31/12/50 849,040; at 31/12/60 1,327,769
Withdrawn week ending 12/12/64

45580 BURMA at Kingmoor shed, 25 May 1952; BR lined green, St Rollox big cabside number below tablet catcher bracket and 6P below the number. Smokebox char not brushed off running plate but tender coaled 'to the gunwales'. Photograph A.G. Ellis, The Transport Treasury.

45581 BIHAR AND ORISSA

Built North British Loco Co Ltd 6/10/34
Named 30/3/38
Renumbered 5581 to 45581 week ending 17/4/48

REPAIRS
2/3/37-9/4/37**LS**
19/3/38-30/3/38**LS**
15/2/39-17/3/39**HS**
15/5/40-10/7/40**HS**
26/12/40-18/1/41**LS**
4/12/41-19/1/42**HS**
11/1/43-1/3/43**HG**
24/8/43-22/9/43**LS**
14/10/43-18/12/43**LS**
4/9/44-14/10/44**LS**
3/1/45-10/2/45**LO**
29/10/45-13/12/45**HS**
1/5/46-7/6/46**LO**
18/1/47-15/3/47**HG** St Rollox
5/3/48-15/4/48**LS** St Rollox
17/6/48-1/7/48**LO** St Rollox
20/4/49-10/6/49**LI** St Rollox
4/7/49-15/7/49**LC** St Rollox
18/8/50-30/9/50**HI** St Rollox
26/4/51-5/5/51**LC** St Rollox
15/6/51-30/6/51**LO** St Rollox
15/8/52-31/12/52**HG** St Rollox
5/1/53-10/1/53**NC(EO)** St Rollox
7/2/53-21/3/53**LC(EO)**
22/7/54-20/8/54**LI**
21/3/55-16/4/55**LC**
16/8/56-22/9/56**HI**
22/2/57-23/3/57**LC(EO)**
6/5/57-3/6/57**LC(EO)**
8/3/58-2/5/58**HG**
13/2/59-11/3/59**LC** Rugby
7/11/59-11/12/59**LI**
-/29/11/60**NC(EO)**
AWS, speedo, fitted
before 9/63

MILEAGES
1934	15,195
1935	66,406
1936	65,481
1937	62,663
1938	60,183
1939	70,040
1940	45,025
1941	44,520
1942	50,373
1943	34,903
1944	49,752
1945	37,884
1946	55,371
1947	57,742
1948	61,535
1949	51,595
1950	45,991
1951	52,658
1952	31,244
1953	40,126
1954	45,870
1955	43,147
1956	37,849
1957	37,657

Mileage at 31/12/50 874,659
Withdrawn July/August 1966

BOILERS
First boiler 8611

No	Fitted	From
8752	17/3/39	5579
8564	1/3/43	5618
8599	15/3/47	5583
8616	31/12/52	45584
8574	2/5/58	45642

SHEDS
Crewe North 6/10/34
Carlisle Upperby 2/2/35
Perth 7/12/35
Carlisle Kingmoor 5/12/36
Farnley Jcn 13/9/52
Loan at first, then
Farnley Jcn 13/9/52

TENDERS
No	Fitted
9028	6/10/34
9077	9/9/44
9261	13/2/48
9077	10/3/48
10524	30/7/51

45582 CENTRAL PROVINCES

Built North British Loco Co Ltd 24/11/34
Named 13/10/36
Renumbered 5582 to 45582 week ending 5/2/49

MILEAGES
1934	1,738
1935	69,390
1936	62,570
1937	55,613
1938	55,630
1939	55,417
1940	51,523
1941	42,703
1942	30,430
1943	54,742
1944	38,096
1945	42,650
1946	53,363
1947	40,501
1948	58,314
1949	58,050
1950	47,588
1951	53,676
1952	46,482
1953	51,689
1954	51,639
1955	50,245
1956	50,864
1957	48,386
1958	49,190
1959	48,668
1960	32,265

Mileage at 31/12/50 818,318; at
31/12/60 1,301,422
Withdrawn week ending 8/12/62

BOILERS
First boiler 8612

No	Fitted	From
8574	6/1/38	5559
8761	26/6/41	5620
8579	14/6/46	5646
8557	3/2/49	45560
8760	26/2/54	45663
8615	8/3/57	45557

SHEDS
Crewe North 24/11/34
Edge Hill 23/2/35
Crewe North 30/4/35
Shrewsbury 5/10/35
Perth 7/12/35
Carlisle Kingmoor 5/12/36
Preston 6/9/52
Loan at first, then
Preston 13/9/52
Carnforth 9/9/61

REPAIRS
5/9/36-13/10/36**LS**
19/4/37-10/5/37**LO**
25/11/37-6/1/38**HG**
6/10/38-1/11/38**LO**
19/7/39-2/9/39**LS**
29/6/40-16/7/40**LS**
21/5/41-26/6/41**HG**
18/4/42-30/7/42**LO**
11/9/42-28/10/42**HS**
12/1/44-5/2/44**LS**
9/6/44-7/7/44**LO**
17/11/44-16/12/44**LO**
26/3/45-25/4/45**LO**
13/5/46-14/6/46**HG**
8/11/47-6/12/47**HS** St Rollox
20/12/48-3/2/49**HG** St Rollox
26/1/50-4/3/50**LI** St Rollox
24/3/50-4/4/50**NC(Rect)** St Rollox
2/7/51-8/8/51**LI** St Rollox
4/9/52-18/10/52**HI**
30/1/54-26/2/54**HG**
4/8/55-20/8/55**LI**
12/1/57-8/3/57**HG**
20/10/58-15/11/58**HI**
23/9/59-6/10/59**NC(EO)** AWS fitted
29/6/60-12/8/60**LI** speedo fitted
12/12/60-20/1/61**LC(EO)**

TENDERS
No	Fitted
9029	24/11/34
9362	2/3/50
9265	8/8/51

45583 ASSAM

Built North British Loco Co Ltd 24/11/34
Named 29/1/38
Renumbered 5583 to 45583 week ending 23/10/48

BOILERS
First boiler 8613

No	Fitted	From
8633	28/1/38	5603
8599	23/5/42	5558
8757	11/1/47	5644
8579	29/4/49	5582
8630	11/3/53	45637*
8468	23/12/55	45615
8610	5/10/60	45609

*destroyed at Harrow 10/52 but boiler nevertheless 'repaired'. Presumably new one built using same number.

REPAIRS
24/10/36-4/12/36**LS**
20/5/37-8/6/37**LO**
13/12/37-28/1/38**HG**
15/5/39-14/6/39**LS**
26/3/40-19/4/40**HS**
22/2/41-22/3/41**LS**
26/9/41-15/10/41**LO**
1/4/42-23/5/42**HG**
26/11/42-26/1/43**LO**
10/4/43-19/6/43**LS**
4/10/43-19/11/43**LO**
19/1/44-25/3/44**LO**
9/10/44-11/11/44**LS**
9/8/45-28/9/45**LS**
6/2/46-16/3/46**LO**
12/10/46-11/1/47**HG** St Rollox
13/5/47-9/8/47**HO** St Rollox
14/9/48-19/10/48**LS** St Rollox
11/3/49-29/4/49**HC** St Rollox
20/8/49-25/8/49**LC** St Rollox
6/1/50-8/2/50**LC** St Rollox
15/5/50-17/6/50**LI** St Rollox
2/8/51-15/9/51**HI** St Rollox
2/2/53-12/3/53**HG**
1/5/53-15/5/53**NC(EO Rect)**
28/7/53-21/8/53**LC(EO)**
1/10/54-29/10/54**LI**
10/11/55-23/12/55**HG**
26/5/57-21/6/57**HI**
4/12/57-7/1/58**LC(EO)**
12/1/59-7/2/59**HI** AWS fitted
30/8/60-5/10/60**HG** speedo fitted

MILEAGES

Year	Mileage
1934	221
1935	70,521
1936	72,258
1937	66,392
1938	46,696
1939	52,343
1940	38,688
1941	25,473
1942	41,684
1943	27,630
1944	27,898
1945	51,806
1946	33,186
1947	31,770
1948	29,990
1949	29,430
1950	39,883
1951	38,762
1952	48,284
1953	43,049
1954	45,818
1955	46,191
1956	58,230
1957	46,132
1958	50,910
1959	50,075
1960	41,462

Mileage at 31/12/50 685,869; at 31/12/60 1,154,782
Withdrawn week ending 24/10/64

SHEDS
Crewe North 24/11/34
Shrewsbury 5/10/35
Perth 7/12/35
St Rollox 10/7/37
Polmadie 2/10/37
St Rollox 19/2/38
Loan at first, then
St Rollox 11/6/38
Polmadie 8/10/38
St Rollox 17/6/39
Carstairs 16/9/39
Polmadie 25/11/39
Carlisle Upperby 30/8/52
Loan at first, then
Carlisle Upperby 13/9/52
Crewe North 29/1/55
Carlisle Upperby 17/9/55
Edge Hill 7/4/56
Crewe North 5/9/59
Edge Hill 12/9/59
Llandudno Jct 19/11/60
Crewe North 10/6/61
Llandudno Jct 16/9/61
Aston 23/9/61
Warrington 21/10/61

TENDERS

No	Fitted
9030	24/11/34

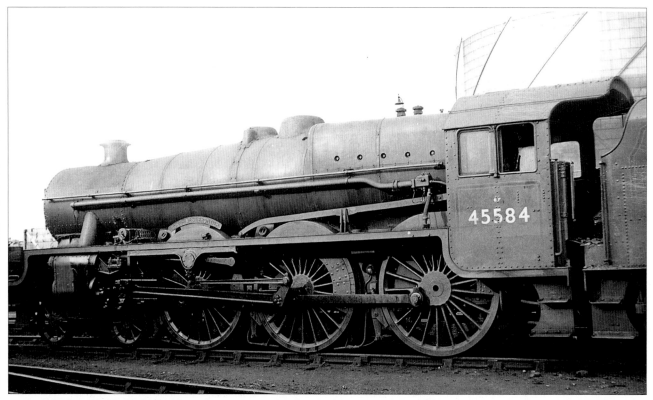

45584 NORTH WEST FRONTIER at Shrewsbury; BR lined green, small 'English' numbers, 6P above. Photograph R.K. Blencowe.

45584 NORTH WEST FRONTIER

Built North British Loco Co Ltd 1/12/34
Named 12/2/38
Renumbered 5584 to 45584 week ending 27/3/48

BOILERS
First boiler 8614

No	Fitted	From
8589	21/6/38	5610
8609	9/7/42	5644
8590	27/5/43	5645
8616	25/3/48	5577
8564	30/8/52	45577
8745	27/9/57	45604
8587	8/6/61	45556

REPAIRS
29/12/36-23/1/37**LS**
30/4/37-4/6/37**LO**
16/3/38-29/3/38**LS**
30/5/38-21/6/38**HO**
30/8/38-20/10/38**LO**
1/5/39-26/5/39**LS**
26/3/40-23/4/40**HS**
24/4/41-24/5/41**LS**
4/6/42-9/7/42**HG**
13/1/43-10/2/43**LO**
26/3/43-27/5/43**HS**
24/2/44-5/4/44**HS**
16/8/44-20/9/44**LO**
24/12/45-2/2/46**LS**
18/2/47-28/3/47**LS St Rollox**
23/4/47-26/4/47**LO St Rollox**
17/2/48-25/3/48**HG St Rollox**
8/10/48-23/10/48**LO St Rollox**
18/6/49-6/8/49**HI St Rollox**
17/11/50-30/12/50**LI St Rollox**
16/7/51-22/8/51**LC(EO) St Rollox**
7/7/52-30/8/52**HG St Rollox**
11/3/53-23/4/53**HI**
26/7/54-2/9/54**HI**
28/9/54-14/10/54**Horwich Painting Only**
14/4/55-10/5/55**LC(EO)**
5/3/56-5/4/56**LI**
23/8/57-27/9/57**HG**
4/4/59-9/5/59**LI AWS fitted**
24/4/61-8/6/61**HG speedo fitted**

MILEAGES

Year	Miles
1934	4,954
1935	76,336
1936	65,483
1937	60,262
1938	52,072
1939	60,761
1940	53,648
1941	42,044
1942	43,679
1943	40,509
1944	40,839
1945	56,336
1946	46,592
1947	35,400
1948	40,152
1949	41,569
1950	27,999
1951	44,039
1952	34,595
1953	52,556
1954	47,799
1955	51,565
1956	52,626
1957	43,988
1958	57,878
1959	50,355
1960	37,838

Mileage at 31/12/50 788,635; at 31/12/60 1,261,874
Withdrawn week ending 3/10/64

TENDERS

No	Fitted
9031	1/12/34
9005	4/12/41
4621	25/2/42
9828	18/5/63

SHEDS
Crewe North 1/12/34
Patricroft 9/3/35
Camden 20/4/35
Shrewsbury 5/10/35
Perth 7/12/35
Polmadie 13/11/37
Perth 27/11/37
Polmadie 25/6/38
Blackpool 13/9/52
Loan at first, then
Blackpool 13/9/52
Saltley 9/3/63
Willesden 30/11/63
Blackpool 4/64
Carlisle Kingmoor 9/64
'paper transfer'?

45585 HYDERABAD

Built North British Loco Co Ltd 1/12/34
Named 30/6/36
Renumbered 5585 to 45585 week ending 15/5/48

TENDERS

No	Fitted
9032	1/12/34
3915	29/1/37* ex-6104
9781	19/7/40
4498	19/10/48*
10303	8/8/50
10215	13/6/64

*Fowler

BOILERS
First boiler 8615

No	Fitted	From
8747	30/6/37	5654
8762	18/8/39	5658
8747	14/4/42	5641
8565	23/2/45	5601
8634	12/5/48	5651
8573	22/11/51	45592
8611	4/6/55	45556
8761	11/4/58	45573

REPAIRS
9/6/36-30/6/36**LS**
28/9/36-4/10/36**LO**
-1/2/37**TRO**
10/6/37-23/7/37**HG**
- 9/9/37**TRO**
25/11/38-5/1/39**LS**
28/3/39-3/4/39**LO**
5/7/39-18/8/39**HG**
5/3/40-5/4/40**LO**
20/1/41-10/2/41**LS**
25/3/42-14/4/42**HG**
7/7/43-9/7/43**LO**
11/9/43-30/9/43**LS**
6/6/44-14/7/44**LO**
29/1/45-23/2/45**HG**
17/9/45-13/10/45**LS**
15/5/46-27/6/46**HS**
13/5/47-7/6/47**LS**
13/3/48-12/5/48**HG**
12/9/48-19/10/48**LO**
15/7/49-13/8/49**HI**
9/2/50-9/3/50**LC Derby**
23/6/50-8/8/50**HI**
8/10/51-22/11/51**HG**
27/5/53-19/6/53**LO**
14/5/54-12/6/54**LI**
26/4/55-4/6/55**HG**
14/11/56-21/12/56**HI**
12/2/58-11/4/58**HG**
9/6/59-1/8/59**HI**
27/2/61-19/4/61**HI Speedo fitted**
AWS never fitted

MILEAGES

Year	Miles
1934	415
1935	55,647
1936	59,932
1937	50,052
1938	61,522
1939	60,300
1940	49,549
1941	50,721
1942	45,772
1943	50,654
1944	41,933
1945	45,804
1946	45,569
1947	53,023
1948	46,483
1949	56,055
1950	43,522
1951	45,499
1952	58,973
1953	51,239
1954	48,349
1955	43,617
1956	30,648
1957	61,418
1958	53,911
1959	61,386
1960	53,589

Mileage at 31/12/50 816,953; at 31/12/60 1,325,582
Withdrawn week ending 9/5/64

SHEDS
Crewe 1/12/34
Willesden 6/7/35
Carlisle Upperby 20/7/35
Rugby 14/11/36
Derby 11/9/37
Millhouses 6/1/40
Derby 4/11/44
Millhouses 9/12/44
Trafford Park 12/10/46
Kentish Town 16/11/46
Derby 20/9/47
Bristol (loan) 22/11/52
Returned to
Derby 24/1/53
Kentish Town 29/6/57
Neasden 3/10/59
Kentish Town 21/11/59
Leicester 16/1/60
Newton Heath 1/7/61
Leicester 23/9/61
Burton 18/11/61
Derby 26/1/63

45586 MYSORE

Built North British Loco Co Ltd 15/12/34
Named 2/4/36
Renumbered 5586 to 45586 week ending 3/7/48

SHEDS
Given simply as 'Western Division' at first
Kentish Town 10/2/35
Longsight 6/4/35
Crewe North 20/4/35
Willesden 6/7/35
Preston 2/5/36
Willesden 8/8/36
Camden 28/8/37
Willesden 25/9/37
Trafford Park (loan) 30/7/38
Trafford Park 6/8/38
Camden (loan) 20/8/38
Willesden 17/9/38
Camden 30/4/43
Edge Hill 9/10/43
Longsight (loan) 16/6/45
Edge Hill 18/8/45
Crewe North 1/10/49
Bushbury (loan) 27/9/52
Return from loan to
Crewe North 18/10/52
Bushbury 26/2/55
Crewe North 30/7/55
Edge Hill 20/9/58
Crewe North 20/6/59
Edge Hill 12/9/59
Llandudno Jnc 6/2/60
Camden 11/6/60
Aston 17/9/60
Crewe North 23/6/62
Crewe South 4/8/62

MILEAGES

Year	Mileage
1934	1,738
1935	69,708
1936	58,422
1937	44,299
1938	64,955
1939	54,594
1940	40,582
1941	45,427
1942	36,383
1943	38,286
1944	39,724
1945	43,210
1946	48,915
1947	48,357
1948	47,558
1949	50,770
1950	45,488
1951	33,764
1952	50,230
1953	50,498
1954	49,260
1955	55,449
1956	37,139
1957	43,542
1958	47,019
1959	37,774
1960	41,795

Stored 6/10/63-16/12/63, 20/10/64-withdrawal
Mileage at 31/12/50 778,416; at 31/12/60 1,224,886
Withdrawn week ending 23/1/65

REPAIRS
16/3/36-2/4/36**LS**
5/1/37-9/3/37**HG**
26/5/37-18/6/37**LO**
29/10/37-14/12/37**LO**
12/12/38-6/2/39**HS**
17/10/39-29/11/39**TRO**
10/7/40-31/7/40**HG**
6/7/42-1/8/42**LS**
7/1/43-9/3/43**HO**
24/11/43-6/1/44**LS**
26/3/45-27/4/45**HG**
1/2/46-28/2/46**LO**
13/1/47-8/2/47**HS**
16/7/47-26/8/47**LO**
14/5/48-3/7/48**HG**
17/3/50-18/4/50**HI**
23/8/51-12/10/51**HG**
23/10/51-1/11/51**NC EO**
14/3/53-13/4/53**HI**
6/10/54-27/10/54**LI**
23/5/56-17/8/56**HG**
23/9/56-15/10/56**NC(EO Rect)**
9/11/57-7/12/57**HI**
6/3/59-9/4/59**LI AWS fitted**
17/11/59-14/12/59**NC(EO)**
13/1/61-16/2/61**HG Speedo fitted**

TENDERS

No	Fitted
9033	15/12/34
3942	2/4/36* ex-6148
3899	13/4/53*
4504	27/10/54*
3929	7/12/57*
10742	14/12/59

*Fowler

BOILERS
First boiler 8616

No	Fitted	From
8466	22/2/37	5553
8635	31/7/40	5628
8758	9/3/43	5622
8747	27/4/45	5585
8569	3/7/48	5557
8636	12/10/51	45626
8756	17/8/56	45603
8752	16/2/61	45651

5586 MYSORE in the 1930s, in red with the 1936 block style – vacuum pump still in place on the left-hand crosshead. Photograph W. Hermiston, The Transport Treasury.

45587 BARODA leaving Rugby past No.4 box with a down semi-fast on 18 August 1959. Still with Fowler tender; AWS but no speedometer fitted. Photograph Peter Groom.

45587 BARODA

Built North British Loco Co Ltd 8/12/34
Named 15/5/36
Renumbered 5587 to 45587 week ending 3/7/48

REPAIRS

20/4/36-11/5/36LS
10/2/37-16/4/37HG
-21/6/37TRO
26/10/37-5/11/37LO
4/5/38-25/5/38LS
18/2/39-17/4/39HG
9/7/40-24/7/40LS
7/10/40-12/11/40LO
14/8/41-23/9/41HG
2/2/42-28/2/42LO
29/10/42-28/11/42HS
17/3/43-16/4/43LO
23/8/43-18/9/43HS
2/11/43-8/12/43LO
27/6/44-26/7/44HG
10/5/45-28/6/45HS
11/10/46-29/10/46LS
22/4/48-3/7/48HG
17/9/48-18/11/48LO
30/5/49-25/6/49LI
24/7/50-24/8/50LI
2/10/50-11/11/50HC
28/3/51-19/4/51LC
11/9/51-3/10/51HI
25/2/52-25/3/52LC
25/2/53-28/3/53HG
21/4/54-17/5/54LI
28/5/55-24/6/55LI
6/7/55-7/7/55NC(EO Rect)
30/12/56-1/2/57HG
14/12/57-11/1/58HI
9/2/59-20/3/59HG AWS fitted
29/3/60-20/4/60LC(TO)
29/7/61-31/8/61HI speedo fitted

TENDERS

No	Fitted
9034	8/12/34
4237	11/5/36* ex-6112
9765	15/9/39
4507	18/11/48*
4240	1/2/57*
4248	11/1/58*
4496	20/3/59*
9247	?
*Fowler	

BOILERS

First boiler 8617

No	Fitted	From
8743	5/4/37	5650
8584	17/4/39	5563
8596	23/9/41	5604
8626	26/7/44	5558
8565	3/7/48	5585
8595	28/3/53	45653
8594	1/2/57	45592
8590	20/3/59	45636

MILEAGES

1934	2,113
1935	69,250
1936	54,901
1937	64,655
1938	66,702
1939	70,279
1940	40,151
1941	43,011
1942	34,983
1943	53,398
1944	70,252
1945	57,633
1946	51,584
1947	46,728
1948	43,516
1949	64,030
1950	53,528
1951	42,854
1952	52,624
1953	58,802
1954	52,312
1955	53,157
1956	56,351
1957	50,979
1958	56,628
1959	48,887
1960	40,575

Mileage at 31/12/50 886,714; at
31/12/60 1,399,883
Withdrawn week ending 15/12/62

SHEDS

Crewe North 8/12/34
Edge Hill 23/2/35
Crewe North 30/4/35
Willesden 6/7/35
Carnforth 8/2/36
Crewe North 9/1/37
Kentish Town 11/9/37
Derby 23/9/39
Leeds 13/6/42
Nottingham (loan) 18/10/47
Leeds 20/12/47
Crewe North (loan) 17/2/51
Crewe North 3/3/51
Longsight 28/7/51
Preston 18/6/55
Longsight 17/9/55
Crewe North 14/6/58
Longsight 20/9/58
Bushbury 30/5/59
Longsight 1/8/59
Crewe North 10/6/61
Carnforth 5/5/62

45588 KASHMIR
Built North British Loco Co Ltd 15/12/34
Named 9/10/36
Renumbered 5588 to 45588 week ending 18/6/49

REPAIRS
8/8/35-4/9/35**LO**
23/9/36-8/10/36**LS**
17/6/37-28/7/37**HG**
21/1/39-15/2/39**LS**
22/1/40-17/2/40**HG**
4/8/41-30/8/41**HS**
18/5/42-16/6/42**LS**
4/8/42-20/8/42**LO**
8/9/42-26/9/42**LO**
8/7/43-7/8/43**HG**
5/7/44-27/7/44**LS**
15/11/45-8/12/45**LS**
26/4/47-13/6/47**HG**
23/5/49-16/6/49**LI**
18/9/50-6/10/50**HI**
9/1/52-22/2/52**HG**
6/2/53-3/3/53**HI**
25/10/54-26/11/54**HI**
3/12/54-13/12/54**NC(EO Rect)**
20/1/56-10/2/56**LI**
15/3/57-11/5/57**HG**
26/3/59-30/4/59**LI AWS fitted**
5/6/61-28/7/61**HG speedo fitted**

SHEDS
Crewe North 22/12/34
Edge Hill 23/2/35
Crewe North 20/4/35
Willesden 6/7/35
Rugby 8/2/36
Preston 13/6/36
Blackpool 22/5/37
Carlisle Upperby 19/10/57
Carlisle Kingmoor 7/7/62

TENDERS
No	Fitted
9035	15/12/34
3910	8/10/36* ex-6120
9695	4/9/37
9153	4/6/62

*Fowler

BOILERS
First boiler 8618

No	Fitted	From
8622	13/7/37	5592
8600	17/2/40	5596
8568	7/8/43	5617
8740	13/6/47	5600
8569	22/2/52	45586
8595	11/5/57	45587
8742	28/7/61	45620

MILEAGES
Year	Mileage
1934	87
1935	54,936
1936	56,267
1937	54,271
1938	50,319
1939	40,824
1940	43,707
1941	55,030
1942	43,168
1943	54,222
1944	58,253
1945	45,262
1946	46,131
1947	49,081
1948	44,498
1949	49,296
1950	42,460
1951	48,519
1952	54,955
1953	54,539
1954	43,842
1955	46,077
1956	50,935
1957	47,249
1958	47,601
1959	53,260
1960	28,448

Stored 10/9/62-19/11/62, 21/11/64-date unrecorded
Mileage at 31/12/50 787,812; at 31/12/60 1,263,237
Withdrawn week ending 1/5/65

45588 KASHMIR, beautifully lit, on a special (Lockerbie-Dumfries) at Shieldhall, 15 April 1963. Photograph Desmond Coakham, The Transport Treasury.

45589 GWALIOR

Built North British Loco Co Ltd 15/12/34
Named 21/2/36
Renumbered 5589 to 45589 week ending 5/6/48

MILEAGES

1934	1,054
1935	73,454
1936	59,045
1937	44,691*
1938	49,586*
1939	46,909
1940	44,605
1941	75,371
1942	56,977
1943	58,605
1944	50,075
1945	45,527
1946	56,052
1947	60,782
1948	60,365
1949	59,143
1950	64,793
1951	43,816
1952	64,358
1953	58,862
1954	61,306
1955	57,050
1956	54,216
1957	59,734

*1937 stored 7 days serviceable,
*1938 stored 80 days serviceable
Mileage at 31/12/50 907,034
Withdrawn March 1965

BOILERS
First boiler 8619

No	Fitted	From
8598	26/10/37	5568
8581	21/6/40	5662
8571	26/6/43	5637
8583	26/4/46	5664
8597	25/8/49	45605
8599	28/2/53	45581
8593	1/3/57	45651
8596	15/1/60	45619

TENDERS

No	Fitted
9036	15/12/34
3899	21/2/36* ex-6107
4238	28/2/53*
3899	30/5/58*
10288	15/1/60

*Fowler

SHEDS
Crewe North 22/12/34
Preston 2/5/36
Edge Hill 2/10/37
Crewe North 27/11/37
Camden (loan) 18/12/37
Crewe North 1/1/38
Camden (loan) 16/4/38
Crewe North 30/4/38
Camden 2/7/38
Willesden 1/10/38
Crewe North 10/2/40
Leeds 9/11/40
Loan at first, then
Leeds 7/12/40
Kentish Town (loan) 2/12/50
Leeds 16/12/50
Longsight 19/9/53
(This entry, though clear on
the record, was not effected)
Wakefield 6/64

REPAIRS
23/4/35-13/5/35**LO**
4/2/36-21/2/36**LS**
11/6/36-24/6/36**LO**
9/1/37-28/1/37**LO**
20/4/37-7/5/37**HS**
4/10/37-10/11/37**HG**
30/8/38-14/9/38**LO**
12/6/39-28/6/39**LS**
29/5/40-21/6/40**HG**
7/4/41-26/4/41**LO**
5/1/42-11/2/42**LS**
12/6/42-25/7/42**LO**
8/6/43-26/6/43**HG**
12/2/44-18/3/44**LO**
1/1/45-17/1/45**LS**
2/8/45-20/9/45**LO**
28/2/46-26/4/46**HG**
6/4/47-17/5/47**LS**
29/4/48-1/6/48**HS**
10/12/48-2/2/49**LC**
13/7/49-25/8/49**HG**
22/8/50-14/9/50**HI**
24/1/52-27/2/52**LI**
22/1/53-28/2/53**HG**
26/2/54-29/3/54**HI**
19/3/55-16/4/55**LI**
16/1/56-15/2/56**LI**
12/11/56-19/12/56**LC**
11/1/57-1/3/57**HG**
  ? -25/3/57**NC(EO Rect)**
5/5/58-30/5/58**LI**
  ? -10/9/58**NC(EO Rect)**
8/12/59-15/1/60**NC**
  ? -25/11/60**NC(EO)**
  ? -16/8/61**LI**
**Dates not recorded; speedo proba-
bly fitted, AWS possibly**

45590 TRAVANCORE

Built North British Loco Co Ltd 22/12/34
Named 11/6/37
Renumbered 5590 to 45590 week ending 2/10/48

REPAIRS
3/12/35-19/12/35**LS**
5/4/37-11/6/37**HG**
10/3/38-29/3/38**LS**
18/1/39-20/2/39**HS**
17/1/40-16/2/40**HG**
16/12/40-8/1/41**LO**
3/3/41-28/3/41**HS**
17/6/42-25/7/42**LS**
14/1/43-22/2/43**HG**
26/11/43-12/1/44**LS**
7/6/44-15/7/44**LS**
6/3/45-30/3/45**LS**
30/11/45-27/12/45**HG**
21/10/46-15/11/46**LS**
11/8/47-1/11/47**HS**
8/8/48-29/9/48**LS**
14/11/49-4/1/50**HG**
26/9/50-18/11/50**HI**
21/3/52-19/4/52**HI**
23/4/52-26/4/52**NC(Rect)**
23/5/53-25/6/53**HI**
12/6/54-4/8/54**HG**
15/2/56-20/3/56**LI**
16/1/57-13/2/57**LC(EO)**
13/1/58-12/2/58**HG**
23/4/59-29/5/59**LI**
26/8/60-6/10/60**LI**
**Dates not recorded – speedo
probably fitted, AWS possibly.**

MILEAGES

1934	403
1935	74,801
1936	70,239
1937	59,419
1938	85,624
1939	69,287
1940	51,979
1941	58,909
1942	66,252
1943	52,668
1944	60,169
1945	48,543
1946	64,974
1947	40,205
1948	50,469
1949	41,587
1950	49,601
1951	50,517
1952	48,127
1953	50,301
1954	54,163
1955	50,252
1956	48,343
1957	48,300

Mileage at 31/12/50 945,129
Withdrawn week ending 11/12/65

BOILERS
First boiler 8620

No	Fitted	From
10035	17/5/37	New
9785	16/2/40	5737
9215	28/3/41	5670
9335	22/2/43	5715
9201	27/12/45	5720
10036	4/1/50	45739
9196	4/8/54	45709
9340	12/2/58	45740
9328	28/4/62	45723

TENDERS

No	Fitted
9037	22/12/34
3896	31/12/35* ex-6110
9692	11/6/37

*Fowler

SHEDS
Crewe North 22/12/34
Preston 25/4/36
Derby 11/9/37
Kentish Town 9/7/38
Trafford Park 30/9/39
Bristol 28/10/39
Millhouses 12/4/47
Nottingham (loan) 17/2/51
Derby (loan) 10/3/51
Millhouses 21/4/51
Agecroft 3/3/62
Newton Heath 22/6/63
Warrington 9/63

45591 UDAIPUR

Built North British Loco Co Ltd 22/12/34
Named 21/4/36
Renumbered 5591 to 45591 week ending 25/9/48

REPAIRS
24/5/35-7/6/35**LO**
26/7/35-8/8/35**LO**
31/3/36-21/4/36**LS**
29/1/37-8/2/37**LO**
23/6/37-16/7/37**HS**
24/6/38-28/7/38**HG**
3/7/39-2/8/39**HS**
17/12/41-3/1/42**HG**
23/10/43-11/11/43**LS**
3/2/45-16/3/45**HG**
30/10/45-22/11/45**LO**
21/6/46-30/7/46**HS**
20/2/47-1/4/47**HG**
26/8/47-10/10/47**LO**
30/6/48-22/9/48**LS**
23/1/49-24/3/49**HC**
10/12/49-24/1/50**HI**
28/7/51-25/8/51**HG**
23/9/52-30/10/52**HC**
25/7/53-25/8/53**LI**
26/8/53-1/9/53**NC(EO Rect)**
20/8/54-7/9/54**LC**
3/8/55-10/9/55**HG**
5/1/57-5/2/57**LI**
30/5/58-25/6/58**LI**
10/2/60-26/3/60**HG** AWS fitted
12/8/60-13/9/60**LC(EO)**
5/5/61-7/6/61**HI** speedo fitted

BOILERS
First boiler 8621

No	Fitted	From
8603	11/7/38	5573
8584	3/1/42	5587
8574	16/3/45	5556
8743	1/4/47	5597
8559	25/8/51	45602
8753	10/9/55	45579
8749	26/3/60	45600

TENDERS

No	Fitted
9038	22/12/34
3920	21/4/36* ex-6126
9753	28/3/39
4504	22/9/48*
4470	7/9/54*
4503	10/9/55*
10545	26/3/60
*Fowler	

SHEDS
Crewe North 22/12/34
Rugby 19/1/35
Edge Hill 23/2/35
Newton Heath 30/3/35
Crewe North 7/6/35
Rugby 19/10/35
Willesden 31/1/42
Rugby 28/2/42
Longsight 9/5/42
Willesden 21/6/47
Camden 5/7/52
Willesden 20/9/52
Crewe North 12/6/54
Camden 11/7/56
Crewe North 8/9/56*
Trafford Park 8/9/56*
Crewe North 10/11/56
same dates on card!

MILEAGES

1934	932
1935	59,130*
1936	53,375
1937	43,480
1938	45,284
1939	40,554
1940	32,582
1941	34,337
1942	54,907
1943	48,974
1944	57,174
1945	54,715
1946	58,013
1947	33,915
1948	26,173
1949	36,766
1950	38,048
1951	28,064
1952	43,856
1953	41,722
1954	46,203
1955	43,078
1956	57,533
1957	44,452
1958	48,750
1959	50,284
1960	43,143

*36 days stored serviceable
Stored 15/10/62-8/4/63, 20/9/63-
withdrawal
**Mileage at 31/12/50 718,359; at
31/12/60 1,165,444**
Withdrawn week ending 26/10/63

45591 UDAIPUR coaled and ready for the next turn at Shrewsbury shed, 21 July 1954. As usual with this angle of view the difference in width between the cab and the Fowler tender is quite marked. Photograph Brian Morrison.

45592 INDORE

Built North British Loco Co Ltd 29/12/34
Named 22/1/36
Renumbered 5592 to 45592 week ending 5/6/48

BOILERS
First boiler 8622

No	Fitted	From
8632	2/6/37	5602
8619	2/2/40	5594
8748	13/6/44	5618
8573	23/3/49	45630
8594	24/8/51	45570
8558	6/10/56	45605
8595	6/4/62	45588

MILEAGES

1934	112
1935	79,955
1936	59,482
1937	47,297
1938	58,165
1939	44,443
1940	58,654
1941	57,200
1942	42,978
1943	61,039
1944	47,595
1945	26,842
1946	41,938
1947	36,347
1948	43,647
1949	47,252
1950	56,749
1951	43,646
1952	48,270
1953	50,690
1954	55,345
1955	50,824
1956	47,359
1957	52,692
1958	45,493
1959	47,845
1960	48,782

stored 26/9/63-26/10/63
**Mileage at 31/12/50 809,695; at
31/12/60 1,300,641**
Withdrawn week ending 26/9/64

REPAIRS

2/1/36-22/1/36**LS**
19/2/37-2/3/37**LO**
29/4/37-25/6/37**HG**
8/6/38-13/7/38**LS**
5/1/40-2/2/40**HG**
29/1/41-11/2/41**HS**
27/8/41-18/9/41**LO**
25/3/42-11/4/42**LS**
25/6/42-11/8/42**LO**
18/2/43-8/3/43**LO**
25/8/43-14/9/43**LS**
27/5/44-13/6/44**HG**
14/5/46-4/6/46**LS**
14/2/47-11/3/47**LO**
3/1/48-3/2/48**HS**
16/4/48-31/5/48**LO**
12/2/49-23/3/49**HG**
20/4/49-22/4/49**NC**
3/4/50-26/4/50**LI**
21/7/51-24/8/51**HG**
9/6/52-29/7/52**HI**
14/11/53-11/12/53**HI**
11/3/54-6/4/54**LC(EO)**
14/1/55-5/2/55**HI**
21/8/56-6/10/56**HG**
16/2/58-3/4/58**HI**
25/5/58-24/6/58**LC**
6/1/60-19/2/60**HI AWS fitted**
 ?   -6/60 **speedo fitted**

TENDERS

No	Fitted
9039	29/12/34
4245	22/1/36* ex-6160
9693	25/6/37

*Fowler

SHEDS
Crewe North 29/12/34
Preston 25/4/36
Aston 25/7/36
Camden 28/8/37
Crewe North 4/9/37
Holyhead 4/6/38
Camden 1/7/39
Carlisle Upperby 22/4/44
Edge Hill 11/10/47
Carlisle Upperby 5/6/48*
Longsight 5/6/48*
Camden (loan) 30/4/49
Longsight 21/5/49
Crewe North 24/6/50
Bushbury (loan) 16/2/52
Crewe North 15/3/52
Carlisle Upperby 21/2/53
Camden 13/6/53
Bushbury 30/5/59
Camden 1/8/59
Carnforth 2/1/60
Bushbury 12/3/60
Carnforth 21/5/60
Newton Heath 6/64
same dates on card!

45592 INDORE on the Camden turntable, 19 May 1958. Photograph J. Robertson, The Transport Treasury.

45593 KOLHAPUR

Built North British Loco Co Ltd 31/12/34
Named 22/5/36
Renumbered 5593 to 45593 week ending 4/12/48

TENDERS

No	Fitted
9040	31/12/34
3930	20/12/35* ex-6123
9689	14/5/37
4625	25/1/52
9774	?
*Fowler	

REPAIRS

6/5/36-22/5/36**LS**
15/10/36-1/11/36**LO**
22/2/37-14/5/37**HG**
20/4/38-23/5/38**LS**
1/5/39-9/6/39**HG**
21/2/41-13/3/41**LS**
26/2/42-14/3/42**HS**
16/1/43-25/1/43**LO**
21/8/43-9/9/43**HG**
28/11/44-9/12/44**HS**
26/3/46-29/4/46**LS**
8/7/47-28/8/47**HG**
12/11/48-3/12/48**LS**
16/1/50-25/2/50**HG**
6/3/50-14/3/50**NC(Rect)**
22/1/51-16/2/51**LI**
12/3/51-19/3/51**NC**
5/6/52-28/6/52**HI**
31/10/53-27/11/53**HI**
14/7/55-11/8/55**HG**
26/1/57-23/2/57**LI**
29/11/58-2/1/59**LI**
11/4/59-25/4/59**NC(EO) AWS fitted**
27/9/59-6/11/59**LC**
18/11/60-23/12/60**HG speedo fitted**
1/4/61-28/4/61**NC(EO Rect)**

SHEDS

Crewe North 31/12/34
Carlisle Upperby 8/2/36
Leeds 27/11/37
Carlisle Upperby 29/1/38
Longsight 20/11/43
Preston 14/7/51
Carlisle Upperby 8/9/51
Carlisle Kingmoor 17/9/60
Willesden 4/3/61
Aston 10/6/61
Burton 23/11/63
Patricroft 9/64
Newton Heath 1/65
Leeds 4/65

BOILERS

First boiler 8623

No	Fitted	From
8754	26/4/37	5656
8736	9/6/39	5635
8612	9/9/43	5615
8632	9/12/44	5616
8593	28/8/47	5620
8465	25/2/50	45618
-	11/8/55	-
-	23/12/60	-

MILEAGES

1934	-
1935	70,391
1936	63,373
1937	56,978
1938	68,303
1939	57,815
1940	46,505
1941	43,126
1942	43,629
1943	36,167
1944	57,963
1945	69,481
1946	57,637
1947	50,496
1948	58,768
1949	65,603
1950	59,527
1951	47,140
1952	48,997
1953	48,804
1954	53,768
1955	45,648
1956	53,723
1957	49,437
1958	43,566
1959	49,866
1960	40,355

stored 6/11/62-16/6/63, 9/9/63-18/11/63
Mileage at 31/12/50 905,762;
at 31/12/60 1,387,066
Withdrawn Sept/Oct 1967.
PRESERVED

45593 KOLHAPUR in the last dark days, at Willesden without nameplate on 8 July 1964, and working from Burton shed (16F). Photograph J.L. Stevenson, courtesy Hamish Stevenson.

45594 BHOPAL leaving York for the south on 10 February 1961, carrying a crude painted 41C (Millhouses) shed code. Photograph The Transport Treasury.

45594 BHOPAL

Built North British Loco Co Ltd 12/1/35
Named 20/3/36
Renumbered 5594 to 45594 week ending 12/2/49

TENDERS

No	Fitted
9041	12/1/35
3928	20/3/36* ex-6134
9764	9/9/39

*Fowler

REPAIRS

7/3/36-20/3/36**LS**
31/8/36-11/9/36**LO**
16/4/37-4/5/37**HS**
4/1/38-24/1/38**HG**
4/9/38-30/9/38**LO**
20/12/38-21/2/39**HS**
23/10/39-12/12/39**HG**
27/5/40-24/6/40**HS**
8/8/41-17/9/41**LS**
21/4/42-15/5/42**LO**
6/1/43-1/3/43**HG**
14/12/43-10/2/44**HS**
9/3/44-18/3/44**LO**
12/6/45-29/6/45**LS**
18/1/46-16/3/46**HG**
23/5/47-30/6/47**LS**
23/9/48-15/10/48**TRO 'shed'**
2/12/48-8/2/49**HG**
23/5/50-19/6/50**LI**
2/10/50-24/10/50**LC Derby**
6/12/51-21/1/52**HG**
19/5/53-9/6/53**HI**
16/8/54-15/9/54**LI**
17/8/55-24/9/55**LI**
13/8/56-25/9/56**HG**
17/4/58-10/5/58**HI**
21/10/59-11/12/59**HI**
    ?   -11/61 **speedo fitted; AWS
probably never ftted**

BOILERS
First boiler 8624

No	Fitted	From
8619	7/1/38	5589
8597	12/12/39	5565
8560	1/3/43	5663
8602	16/3/46	5642
8627	8/2/49	5631
8743	21/1/52	45591
8467	25/9/56	45562
8589	21/10/61	45565

SHEDS

Crewe North 12/1/35
Derby 10/2/35
Longsight 6/4/35
Crewe North 20/4/35
Carlisle Upperby 1/9/35
Preston 25/4/36
Aston 26/9/36
Blackpool 22/5/37
Crewe North 26/6/37
Camden 3/7/37
Willesden 28/8/37
Leeds (loan) 2/7/38
Leeds 16/7/38
Millhouses 13/4/46
Canklow 1/62
Darnall 6/62

MILEAGES

1935	74,622
1936	64,831
1937	56,947
1938	63,781
1939	55,867
1940	77,201
1941	63,441
1942	64,941
1943	53,436
1944	49,613
1945	56,279
1946	55,210
1947	42,234
1948	39,018
1949	53,378
1950	52,066
1951	41,797
1952	52,834
1953	52,187
1954	52,058
1955	52,165
1956	52,201
1957	57,032

Mileage at 31/12/50 922,865
Withdrawn week ending 29/12/62
(Stored prior to withdrawal)

45595 SOUTHERN RHODESIA

Built North British Loco Co Ltd 5/1/35
Named 25/2/36
Renumbered 5595 to 45595 week ending 24/9/49

REPAIRS
10/2/36-25/2/36**LS**
24/8/36-28/8/36**LO**
23/1/37-7/4/37**HG**
26/2/38-3/5/38**HS**
5/6/39-21/7/39**HG**
29/8/40-21/9/40**LS**
1/2/41-20/3/41**LO**
29/10/41-22/11/41**HG**
20/7/42-15/8/42**LS**
18/5/43-16/6/43**LS**
10/1/44-4/3/44**HG**
7/5/45-2/6/45**HS**
28/9/46-23/10/46**HS**
29/10/47-20/12/47**HG**
22/8/49-22/9/49**LI**
3/2/51-26/2/51**HI**
12/5/52-26/6/52**HG**
11/11/52-5/12/52**NC(EO)**
29/8/53-26/9/53**LI(EO)**
5/3/55-30/3/55**LI**
17/6/55-23/7/55**LC**
10/9/56-17/10/56**HI**
27/4/57-15/6/57**HG**
17/9/58-18/10/58**LI**
31/7/59-10/9/59**LC** AWS fitted
13/9/60-12/10/60**HI** speedo fitted

TENDERS

No	Fitted
9042	5/1/35
3922	25/2/36* ex-6137
4252	13/11/52*
3187	3/10/53*
9892	18/10/58 ex-48165

*Fowler

SHEDS
Crewe North 5/1/35
Kentish Town 10/2/35
Longsight 6/4/35
Crewe North 20/4/35
Preston 2/5/36
Carlisle Upperby 26/9/36
Crewe North 6/3/37
Aston 7/4/37
Walsall 4/9/37
Bushbury (loan) 16/10/37
Crewe North 13/11/37
Camden 20/11/37
Crewe North 11/12/37
Camden 2/7/38
Leeds (loan) 30/7/38
Crewe North (loan) 11/3/44
Camden 18/3/44
Crewe North 1/4/44
Camden 22/4/44
Crewe North 10/6/44
Carlisle Upperby 19/8/44
Longsight 7/7/51
Crewe North 20/6/59
Llandudno Jcn 9/64
Crewe North 1/65

BOILERS
First boiler 8625

Fitted		From
8586	19/3/37	5636
8573	21/7/39	5634
8753	22/11/41	5655
8634	4/3/44	5619
8614	2/6/45	5624
8605	20/12/47	5632
8588	26/6/52	45573
8623	15/6/57	45618

MILEAGES

Year	Mileage
1935	77,474
1936	67,335
1937	38,819
1938	62,416
1939	76,056
1940	62,831
1941	37,503
1942	69,079
1943	60,558
1944	50,939
1945	36,718
1946	35,864
1947	36,041
1948	43,715
1949	42,075
1950	44,981
1951	52,448
1952	55,569
1953	55,522
1954	58,732
1955	43,128
1956	61,449
1957	50,340
1958	51,456
1959	52,831
1960	45,686

stored 27/9/63-10/12/63, 10/1/64-15/6/64
Mileage at 31/12/50 842,404; at 31/12/60 1,369,565
Withdrawn week ending 30/1/65

45596 BAHAMAS with its unflattering double chimney, at Upperby on 18 May 1964. Photograph Peter Groom.

45596 BAHAMAS

Built North British Loco Co Ltd 12/1/35
Named 8/6/36
Renumbered 5596 to 45596 week ending 15/5/48

BOILERS
First boiler 8626

Fitted		From
8600	9/11/37	5570
8745	2/12/39	5562
8735	3/7/42	5636
8594	5/12/44	5632
8758	10/5/48	5602
8600	24/7/52	45605
8465	27/9/55	45618
8604	5/5/61	45580

TENDERS

No	Fitted
9043	12/1/35
3925	8/6/36* ex-6129
9779	8/5/40
4485	11/10/46*
4248	18/6/54*
3922	11/12/56*
4238	12/9/58*
4492	17/1/59*
9045	23/8/60
10750	5/10/63

*Fowler

REPAIRS
23/5/36-8/6/36**LS**
29/10/37-24/11/37**HG**
13/4/39-4/5/39**LS**
21/10/39-12/12/39**HG**
23/11/40-11/1/41**HS**
15/6/42-3/7/42**HG**
13/10/43-17/11/43**HS**
30/10/44-5/12/44**HG**
20/9/46-11/10/46**HS**
4/7/47-8/8/47**LO** Derby
6/4/48-10/5/48**HG**
1/4/49-26/4/49**LC**
22/8/49-4/10/49**HI**
6/4/50-4/5/50**LC**
28/12/50-13/2/51**HI**
22/5/52-24/7/52**HG**
2/12/52-6/1/53**LC(EO)**
8/1/53-20/1/53**NC(EO Rect)EO**
24/5/54-18/6/54**HI**
31/7/55-27/9/55**HG**
28/9/55-1/10/55**NC(EO Rect)**
15/11/56-11/12/56**HI**
6/8/58-12/9/58**HI**
1/1/59-25/2/59**HC(EO) AWS fitted**
6/8/60-23/8/60**LC(TO)**
7/3/61-5/5/61**HG speedo, double chimney fitted**
4/9/61-12/10/61**LC**

SHEDS
Crewe North 12/1/35
Preston 4/5/35
Aston 4/1/36
Camden 3/7/37
Willesden 28/8/37
Crewe North 4/12/37
Camden (loan) 18/12/37
Crewe North 1/1/38
Camden (loan) 16/4/38
Crewe North 30/4/38
Camden 2/7/38
Kentish Town (loan) 30/7/38
Kentish Town 6/8/38
Derby 23/9/39
Grimesthorpe 2/3/40
Millhouses 6/9/41
Bristol 12/4/47
Crewe North (loan) 13/9/47
Crewe North 25/10/47
Edge Hill (loan) 28/8/48
Edge Hill 4/12/48
Carlisle Upperby 24/2/56
Stockport 2/7/62

MILEAGES

1935	77,365
1936	48,229
1937	51,328*
1938	60,279*
1939	72,474
1940	44,058
1941	52,298
1942	55,831
1943	53,961
1944	50,100
1945	58,311
1946	31,361
1947	47,994
1948	44,336
1949	44,848
1950	38,657
1951	41,707
1952	37,857
1953	52,408
1954	43,652
1955	43,192
1956	48,104
1957	45,131
1958	42,702
1959	48,800
1960	38,425

*1937 23 days stored serviceable
*1938 80 days stored serviceable
Mileage at 31/12/50 831,430; at 31/12/60 1,273,408
Withdrawn week ending 23/7/66
PRESERVED

45597 BARBADOS

Built North British Loco Co Ltd 12/1/35
Named 26/3/36
Renumbered 5597 to 45597 week ending 28/8/48

TENDERS

No	Fitted
9044	12/1/35
3929	31/12/35* ex-6142
3939	22/1/52*
4246	1/2/58*
10736	18/4/59

*Fowler

MILEAGES

1935	67,184
1936	58,377
1937	51,140
1938	61,586
1939	59,583
1940	64,160
1941	58,718
1942	45,396
1943	52,949
1944	61,874
1945	54,468
1946	57,459
1947	66,569
1948	64,079
1949	61,045
1950	58,179
1951	67,050
1952	68,847
1953	54,067
1954	70,093
1955	60,681
1956	56,005
1957	60,531

Mileage at 31/12/50 942,766
Withdrawn January 1965

SHEDS
Kentish Town 2/2/35
Longsight 6/4/35
Crewe North 20/4/35
Chester 8/2/36
Holyhead 11/7/36
Carlisle Upperby 26/9/36
Crewe North 6/3/37
Camden 3/7/37
Willesden 28/8/37
Bristol (loan) 18/11/39
Bristol 9/12/39
Leeds 2/3/40

BOILERS
First boiler 8627

No	Fitted	From
8606	8/2/38	5576
8621	15/8/40	5609
8743	23/10/43	5577
8582	17/10/46	5558
8609	25/4/49	45572
8597	31/3/53	45589
8581	14/9/56	45563

REPAIRS
27/5/35-12/6/35**HO**
? -14/1/36**TRO**
4/3/36-26/3/36**LS**
5/6/37-25/6/37**LS**
31/1/38-21/2/38**HG**
18/7/38-15/8/38**LO**
23/10/39-4/11/39**HS**
3/7/40-15/8/40**HG**
9/1/41-15/2/41**LO**
1/1/42-28/1/42**LS**
9/3/42-18/4/42**LO**
28/9/42-12/11/42**LO**
26/9/43-23/10/43**HG**
25/8/44-15/9/44**HS**
10/5/45-29/5/45**LO**
29/10/45-21/11/45**LS**
10/9/46-17/10/46**HG**
23/6/47-11/8/47**LS**
27/7/48-25/8/48**LS**
14/3/49-25/4/49**HG**
1/5/50-22/5/50**HI**
16/10/50-30/11/50**HC**
21/5/51-8/6/51**LI**
22/12/51-22/1/52**HI**
24/2/53-31/3/53**HG**
18/5/53-20/6/53**LC(EO)**
20/3/54-24/4/54**HI**
9/5/55-8/6/55**HI**
17/7/56-14/9/56**HG**
24/1/57-27/2/57**LC**
4/1/58-1/2/58**HI**
23/3/59-18/4/59**HI**
22/8/60-14/10/60**HI**
speedo probably fitted, AWS probably never

45597 BARBADOS working hard (though in the hot sultry conditions this is not apparent) to recover from the 50mph slack and attack the climb towards Grimston, 18 July 1958. Melton Junction is beyond the bridge in the background – this section is now part of the 'Old Dalby' test track. Photograph Peter Groom.

45598 BASUTOLAND

Built North British Loco Co Ltd 2/2/35
Named 20/4/36
Renumbered 5598 to 45598 week ending 24/4/48

TENDERS

No	Fitted
9045	2/2/35
3934	20/4/36* ex-6141
9767	28/9/39
4495	6/6/47*
4560	6/4/55*
4562	27/4/57*
10752	24/11/60
*Fowler	

REPAIRS

30/3/36-20/4/36LS
7/9/36-14/9/36LO
10/5/37-28/6/37HG
25/5/38-16/6/38LS
2/2/39-22/3/39HG
6/1/40-2/2/40LS
27/5/40-25/6/40LO
20/1/41-8/2/41HG
11/7/41-2/8/41LO
30/5/42-19/6/42LS
31/8/42-17/10/42LO
23/12/42-30/1/43LO
17/8/43-2/10/43HG
21/10/44-17/11/44HS
8/10/45-6/11/45LS
16/4/47-6/6/47HG
13/3/48-22/4/48HS
7/1/49-11/2/49LI
8/10/49-7/11/49LC
12/12/49-5/1/50TRO
17/6/50-2/8/50HG
6/6/51-2/7/51LI
16/6/52-8/8/52HG
29/12/53-6/2/54LI
7/3/55-6/4/55HG
9/4/56-7/5/56HI
26/8/56-4/10/56LC
5/4/57-27/4/57HI
3/1/58-8/2/58HG
9/3/58-16/4/58LC(EO)
3/9/59-15/10/59HI
24/10/60-24/11/60LI speedo fitted;
AWS never fitted

MILEAGES

1935	67,737
1936	65,494
1937	71,464
1938	75,917
1939	72,598
1940	57,068
1941	45,596
1942	46,891
1943	49,958
1944	48,978
1945	56,097
1946	54,059
1947	60,922
1948	57,361
1949	50,989
1950	63,063
1951	72,144
1952	52,747
1953	64,859
1954	53,517
1955	66,344
1956	64,745
1957	63,919
1958	48,395
1959	47,622
1960	40,754

Mileage at 31/12/50 944,192; at 31/12/60 1,519,238
Withdrawn week ending 24/10/64

BOILERS
First boiler 8528

No	Fitted	From
8568	7/6/37	5618
8559	22/3/39	5625
8742	8/2/41	5618
8467	2/10/43	5564
8604	6/6/47	5568
8468	2/8/50	45638
8742	8/8/52	45661
8617	6/4/55	45609
8575	8/2/58	45563

SHEDS
'Carlisle (M)'2/2/35
(presumed to be Durran Hill, closed 1936)
Crewe North 6/4/35
Edge Hill 20/6/36
Leeds 11/9/37
Bristol 16/9/39
Leeds 2/12/39
Saltley 11/5/46
Kentish Town 12/10/46
Derby 21/11/59
Burton 11/61
Bank Hall 10/64
('paper transfer')

45599 BECHUANALAND

Built North British Loco Co Ltd 26/1/35
Named 21/7/36
Renumbered 5599 to 45599 week ending 4/9/48

TENDERS

No	Fitted
9046	26/1/35
4250	5/12/35* ex-6159
9699	8/9/37
*Fowler	

MILEAGES

Year	Mileage
1935	64,192
1936	57,329
1937	52,438
1938	56,342*
1939	52,903
1940	46,563
1941	43,841
1942	46,747
1943	45,127
1944	44,238
1945	27,162
1946	54,477
1947	46,452
1948	40,094
1949	45,510
1950	45,440
1951	50,813
1952	42,190
1953	48,078
1954	48,879
1955	39,017
1956	57,998
1957	47,114
1958	51,202
1959	46,734
1960	44,923

*58 days stored serviceable
stored 10/9/62-6/2/63, 15/9/63-
withdrawal
**Mileage at 31/12/50 768,855; at
31/12/60 1,245,803**
Withdrawn week ending 15/8/64

BOILERS
First boiler 8629

No	Fitted	From
8618	25/8/37	5588
8630	4/4/40	5557
8587	22/7/44	5660
8635	18/4/47	5628
8606	29/8/52	45603
8599	17/4/57	45589

REPAIRS
24/6/36-21/7/36LS
4/2/37-25/2/37LO
18/8/37-8/9/37HG
27/2/39-24/3/39LS
9/3/40-4/4/40HG
13/9/41-27/9/41HS
23/1/43-12/2/43HS
10/6/44-22/7/44HG
4/10/45-15/11/45LS
24/2/47-18/4/47HG
31/7/48-1/9/48HS
16/1/50-3/2/50LI
27/11/50-19/1/51HI
18/8/51-13/9/51LC(EO)
17/7/52-29/8/52HG
17/4/54-13/5/54LI
31/5/54-15/6/54NC(EO Rect)
21/6/55-5/8/55HI
15/8/55-20/8/55NC(EO Rect)
8/3/57-17/4/57HG
13/2/59-20/3/59HI AWS fitted
15/3/60-5/5/60LI speedo fitted

SHEDS
Derby 2/2/35
Crewe North 28/9/35
Chester 8/2/36
Patricroft 5/9/36
Blackpool 22/5/37
Patricroft 26/6/37
Carlisle Upperby 16/9/39
Bushbury 9/3/46
Crewe North 26/4/47
Carlisle Upperby 23/8/47
Preston 10/6/50
Carlisle Upperby 15/9/51
Camden 20/9/59
Willesden 7/11/59
Rugby 14/1/61
Nuneaton 4/11/61
Rugby (loan) 23/2/63
Nuneaton 11/5/63

45599 BECHUANALAND, powerful and elegant in BR green, at Upperby (that's the new BR concrete roundhouse at the left) in the early part of the 1950s. Photograph J. Patterson, The Transport Treasury.

45600 BERMUDA

Built North British Loco Co Ltd 2/2/35
Named 22/6/36
Renumbered 5600 to 45600 week ending 31/7/48

MILEAGES

Year	Mileage
1935	60,295
1936	57,082
1937	52,650
1938	58,060
1939	55,024
1940	40,715
1941	46,370
1942	37,878
1943	38,721
1944	34,880
1945	31,941
1946	41,775
1947	45,692
1948	41,291
1949	54,627
1950	45,640
1951	41,325
1952	38,269
1953	44,281
1954	51,538
1955	50,619
1956	50,434
1957	51,036
1958	47,308
1959	39,204
1960	53,224

stored 1/10/62-8/4/63
Mileage at 31/12/50 742,641; at 31/12/60 1,209,879
Withdrawn week ending 18/12/65

BOILERS

First boiler 8630

No	Fitted	From
8759	22/2/38	5661
8748	6/12/40	5552
8740	28/11/42	5609
8736	6/2/47	5623
8585	20/2/50	45571
8749	9/7/54	45577
8625	20/6/58	-
8746	2/1/60	45558
8567	8/62	45557

SHEDS

Leeds 2/2/35
Kentish Town 27/2/35
Crewe North 6/4/35
Carlisle Upperby 4/1/36
Bushbury 9/3/46
Crewe North 19/4/47
Longsight 29/4/50
Patricroft 10/6/50
Newton Heath 1/65

REPAIRS

9/2/35-27/2/35LO
5/6/36-22/6/36LS
  ?   -31/10/36TRO
5/11/36-17/11/36LO
26/8/37-24/9/37HS
8/2/38-10/3/38HG
13/11/39-28/11/39HS
15/11/40-6/12/40HG
19/3/42-3/4/42HS
12/11/42-28/11/42HO
15/3/44-31/3/44LS
2/11/44-25/11/44LO
19/9/45-27/10/45LS
10/5/46-30/5/46LO
5/10/46-28/10/46LO
17/12/46-6/2/47HG
16/6/48-26/7/48LO
23/8/48-14/9/48HS
17/1/50-20/2/50HG
25/6/51-1/8/51HI
13/4/53-2/5/53LI
9/6/54-9/7/54HG
10/9/54-20/9/54NC(EO) St Rollox
28/10/55-19/11/55HI
14/2/56-8/3/56HC(EO)
19/12/56-19/1/57HI
18/5/58-20/6/58HG
28/10/59-2/1/60HG AWS fitted
  ?   -8/62 speedo fitted

TENDERS

No	Fitted
9047	2/2/35
3941	29/10/36* ex-6117
9701	24/9/37
9144	17/3/43
9138	22/3/52

*Fowler

45600 BERMUDA with domeless boiler and BR Class 4 chimney, at Carlisle Upperby shed, 26 August 1954. Despite earlier travails with steaming, and though they were always more 'sensitive' to deficiencies in fuel than the Black 5s, say, the Jubilees by the end of the 1930s were doing just what Stanier intended, providing a solid and reliable 'second division'. With nearly two hundred at work, the LMS could hardly have operated effectively without them. Photograph J.L. Stevenson, courtesy Hamish Stevenson.

5601 before naming, in red, on the turntable at the north end of Camden shed; two-piece smokebox saddle, vacuum pump driven off crosshead, atomiser, but no 'lug' on smokebox door. Photograph W. Hermiston, The Transport Treasury.

45601 BRITISH GUIANA

Built North British Loco Co Ltd 13/4/35
Named 20/7/36
Renumbered 5601 to 45601 week ending 23/4/49

TENDERS

No	Fitted
9048	13/4/35
3906	3/6/37* ex-6108
9702	5/10/37

*Fowler

REPAIRS

24/6/36-20/7/36**LS**
? -18/6/37**TRO**
3/9/37-5/10/37**HG**
28/2/39-14/3/39**LS**
11/6/40-1/7/40**HG**
12/10/41-5/11/41**HS**
24/3/42-24/4/42**LO**
9/9/42-25/9/42**LS**
11/3/43-7/4/43**LO**
17/8/43-2/9/43**LS**
4/3/44-21/3/44**LO**
2/12/44-16/12/44**HG**
27/4/46-15/5/46**HS**
31/1/47-27/3/47**HS**
28/10/47-4/12/47**HG**
28/3/49-22/4/49**LI**
3/4/50-16/5/50**HG**
25/5/51-16/6/51**LI**
14/5/52-11/6/52**LI**
12/9/52-3/10/52**LC(EO)**
20/10/53-24/11/53**HG**
25/3/55-27/4/55**LI**
6/6/56-27/7/56**HG**
18/12/57-18/1/58**LI**
3/12/58-2/1/59**LI**
10/3/59-20/3/59**NC(EO) AWS fitted**
28/12/59-20/2/60**HI**
10/8/61-18/9/61**HG speedo fitted**

SHEDS

Crewe North 20/4/35
Rugby 30/11/35
Willesden 16/5/36
Camden 6/2/37
Willesden 8/5/37
Camden 28/2/42
Crewe North 10/6/44
Bushbury 9/3/46
Camden 19/4/47
Crewe North 11/10/47
Camden 18/10/47
Willesden (loan) 8/10/59
Willesden 7/11/59
Newton Heath 25/6/60
Loan at first, then
Newton Heath 23/7/60

BOILERS

First boiler 8631

No	Fitted	From
8615	13/9/37	5585
8565	1/7/40	5553
8562	16/12/44	5658
8607	4/12/47	5562
8575	16/5/50	45629
8750	25/11/53	45575
8600	27/7/56	-
8745	16/9/61	45584

MILEAGES

1935	46,565
1936	55,439
1937	52,759
1938	72,465
1939	58,444
1940	35,292
1941	38,246
1942	58,030
1943	60,324
1944	47,115
1945	60,267
1946	54,312
1947	43,212
1948	63,575
1949	58,364
1950	58,564
1951	55,174
1952	55,154
1953	57,039
1954	65,326
1955	55,346
1956	54,851
1957	60,834
1958	54,300
1959	53,241
1960	44,353

Stored 17/9/62-3/12/62
Mileage at 31/12/50 862,973; at 31/12/60 1,418,591
Withdrawn week ending 26/9/64

45602 BRITISH HONDURAS

Built North British Loco Co Ltd 6/4/35
Named 7/5/36
Renumbered 5602 to 45602 week ending 27/8/49

BOILERS
First boiler 8632

No	Fitted	From
8617	6/5/37	5587
8754	30/6/39	5593
8621	21/1/44	5597
8758	6/6/45	5586
8559	22/3/48	5661
8603	7/4/51	45664
8575	11/1/54	45601
8592	8/3/56	45631
8573	4/11/60	45664

MILEAGES

1935	50,133
1936	63,742
1937	60,137
1938	55,710
1939	58,282
1940	57,028
1941	38,074
1942	52,787
1943	48,753
1944	53,007
1945	51,720
1946	42,283
1947	41,740
1948	55,031
1949	52,640
1950	53,179
1951	54,001
1952	67,894
1953	59,732
1954	64,739
1955	68,441
1956	41,977
1957	48,413

Mileage at 31/12/50 834,246
Withdrawn March 1965

SHEDS
Crewe North 20/4/35
Edge Hill 4/1/36
Derby 11/9/37
Nottingham 12/10/46
Millhouses 12/4/47
Derby 11/10/47
Bristol (loan) 12/11/49
Derby 3/12/49
Kentish Town (loan) 7/10/50
Derby 13/1/51
Bristol 26/5/51
Derby 28/4/56
Bristol 9/6/56
Derby 22/9/56
Millhouses 21/9/57
Newton Heath 3/3/62
Wakefield 9/64
Leeds 10/64

TENDERS

No	Fitted
9049	6/4/35
4254	7/5/36* ex-6135
9690	29/5/37
4611	16/5/64

*Fowler

REPAIRS
3/4/36-7/5/36**LS**
31/3/37-29/5/37**HG**
26/9/38-3/11/38**LS**
8/6/39-30/6/39**HG**
1/8/40-21/8/40**LS**
26/6/41-29/7/41**LS**
4/11/41-20/12/41**LO**
21/3/42-25/4/42**LO**
20/2/43-15/3/43**HS**
1/1/44-21/1/44**HG**
16/5/45-6/6/45**HS**
16/12/46-9/1/47**LS**
9/2/48-22/3/48**HG**
27/7/49-26/8/49**LI**
26/5/50-29/6/50**HI**
1/2/51-7/4/51**HG**
23/1/52-20/2/52**HI**
15/1/53-14/2/53**LI**
30/11/53-11/1/54**HG**
10/11/54-4/12/54**LI**
9/12/54-16/12/54**NC(EO Rect)EO**
16/1/56-8/3/56**HG**
31/10/56-15/11/56**LC(EO) Derby**
21/3/57-24/4/57**HC**
25/6/58-7/8/58**HI**
12/8/59-2/10/59**LI**
3/10/60-4/11/60**HG**
Dates not recorded; speedo
probably fitted, AWS pro-
bably never

45603 SOLOMON ISLANDS

Built North British Loco Co Ltd 17/5/35
Named 24/2/36
Renumbered 5603 to 45603 week ending 12/3/49

REPAIRS
13/8/36-3/9/36**LS**
11/6/37-19/6/37**LO**
25/10/37-18/11/37**HG**
13/6/39-26/6/39**LS**
21/10/40-14/11/40**HG**
7/11/41-6/12/41**LO**
27/7/42-28/8/42**HS**
13/11/43-27/11/43**HG**
12/2/45-8/3/45**HS**
10/9/45-13/10/45**HO**
9/4/46-1/5/46**LS**
27/1/47-3/3/47**HG**
31/12/47-22/1/48**LO**
14/2/49-10/3/49**HI**
19/6/50-25/7/50**HI**
20/3/51-10/4/51**LC**
23/7/51-7/8/51**LC**
29/3/52-3/5/52**HG**
27/4/53-16/5/53**HI**
22/1/54-23/3/54**LC**
21/10/54-12/11/54**HI**
13/8/55-1/9/55**LC**
23/3/56-28/4/56**HG**
1/10/57-6/11/57**LI**
12/11/57-18/11/57**NC(EO Rect)**
1/9/59-1/10/59**HI AWS fitted**
26/4/60-6/5/60**LC(TO)**
30/12/60-4/2/61**LI speedo fitted**

SHEDS
Camden 18/5/35
Walsall 5/10/35
Camden 3/7/37
Bushbury 28/8/37
Edge Hill 11/9/37
Crewe North 27/11/37
Willesden 20/12/40
Camden 28/2/42
Willesden 4/4/42
Longsight 30/4/43
Crewe North 5/4/47
Longsight 29/4/50
Camden 11/7/53
Edge Hill 12/6/54
Crewe North 12/2/55
Carlisle Upperby 25/8/56
Crewe North 1/9/56
Willesden 24/11/56
Crewe North 9/7/60
Willesden 24/9/60
Rugby 10/6/61
Nuneaton 4/11/61

TENDERS

No	Fitted
9050	17/5/35
4252	24/2/36* ex-6167
3922	13/11/52*
3942	16/5/53*
9671	6/5/60

*Fowler

BOILERS
First boiler 8633

No	Fitted	From
8634	1/11/37	5604
8557	14/11/40	5664
8739	27/11/43	5623
8623	8/3/45	5655
8606	3/3/47	5605
8756	3/5/52	45637
8572	28/4/56	45450

MILEAGES

1935	46,491
1936	44,319
1937	45,869
1938	57,900*
1939	59,736
1940	46,745
1941	47,508
1942	49,316
1943	56,587
1944	50,521
1945	55,472
1946	67,361
1947	40,932
1948	45,856
1949	39,710
1950	48,581
1951	44,872
1952	58,436
1953	58,270
1954	46,225
1955	49,811
1956	48,652
1957	37,008
1958	46,684
1959	39,689
1960	45,808
1961	35,826
1962	24,330

*71 days stored serviceable
Mileage at 31/12/50 802,904; at
31/12/60 1,278,359;
at 8/12/62 1,338,515
Withdrawn week ending 8/12/62

45604 CEYLON

Built North British Loco Co Ltd 2/3/35
Named 11/5/36
Renumbered 5604 to 45604 week ending 10/4/48

BOILERS
First boiler 8634

No	Fitted	From
8756	3/8/37	5658
8596	11/1/40	5572
8624	2/8/41	5561
8744	29/1/44	5664
8755	12/5/45	5612
8601	7/4/48	5625
8607	15/9/50	45601
8745	30/11/54	45618
8632	30/7/57	45568

MILEAGES

1935	57,234
1936	43,816
1937	46,154
1938	69,442
1939	56,938
1940	78,525
1941	61,502
1942	60,730
1943	54,064
1944	60,068
1945	58,787
1946	54,894
1947	36,907
1948	56,246
1949	56,766
1950	61,056
1951	66,019
1952	52,870
1953	50,195
1954	45,721
1955	54,749
1956	53,417
1957	46,007
1958	46,402
1959	49,128
1960	37,855

Stored 5/12/64-19/4/65
Mileage at 31/12/50 913,129; at 31/12/60 1,415,492
Withdrawn week ending 17/7/65

TENDERS

No	Fitted
9051	2/3/35
4235	11/5/36* ex-6150
9696	18/8/37
9754	28/7/43
9696	5/10/43
9768	16/11/46

*Fowler

SHEDS

Crewe North 6/4/35
Walsall 5/10/35
Camden 3/7/37
Crewe North 28/8/37
Millhouses 22/10/38
Loan at first, then
Millhouses 17/12/38
Leeds 21/1/39
Crewe North (loan) 20/10/51
Crewe North 10/11/51
Trafford Park 9/5/53
Crewe North 4/7/53
Patricroft 1/5/54
Crewe North 8/5/54
Bushbury 11/1/58
Crewe North 25/1/58
Carnforth 5/5/62
Carlisle Kingmoor 22/6/63
Carnforth 9/63
Warrington 7/64
Newton Heath 4/65

REPAIRS

22/4/36-11/5/36LS
18/6/37-18/8/37HG
8/6/38-19/7/38HS
9/5/39-20/6/39LO
31/8/39-4/9/39LO
12/12/39-11/1/40HG
25/7/40-23/8/40LS
4/7/41-2/8/41HG
6/5/42-13/6/42LS
22/9/42-24/10/42HS
13/1/44-29/1/44HG
21/9/44-5/10/44HS
13/3/45-12/5/45HS
3/7/46-10/8/46LS
30/12/46-15/2/47HO St Rollox
8/3/48-7/4/48HG
13/5/48-27/5/48NC Derby
20/6/49-28/7/49LI
31/7/50-15/9/50HG
24/9/51-18/10/51LI
30/12/52-23/1/53LI
24/9/53-24/10/53LC
19/10/54-30/11/54HG
2/2/56-25/2/56HI
9/5/56-5/6/56HC(EO)
10/6/57-30/7/57HG
21/8/58-23/9/58LI
24/10/58-14/11/58NC(EO)
5/5/60-17/5/60NC(EO) AWS fitted
21/11/60-31/12/60LI speedo fitted

45605 CYPRUS

Built North British Loco Co Ltd 6/4/35
Named 28/7/36
Renumbered 5605 to 45605 week ending 10/7/48

REPAIRS

13/7/36-28/7/36LS
17/5/37-1/6/37HS
31/3/38-27/4/38HG
2/1/40-16/1/40HS
13/10/40-26/10/40LO
18/2/41-19/3/41HG
9/3/42-20/4/42LS
9/10/42-14/11/42LS
9/6/43-17/7/43HG
4/10/43-6/11/43LO
31/7/44-18/8/44LS
12/10/44-28/10/44LO
27/4/45-9/6/45HS
3/10/45-14/11/45HO
4/10/46-24/10/46HG
18/12/47-31/1/48HS
5/2/48-19/2/48TRO
18/5/48-9/7/48LO Derby
28/3/49-12/5/49HG
30/4/50-19/5/50LI
1/3/51-30/3/51LI
31/3/52-7/5/52HG
23/7/52-14/8/52LC(EO)
10/8/53-4/9/53HI
9/9/54-8/10/54HI
7/1/55-29/1/55LC(EO)
11/7/55-20/8/55LI
29/5/56-28/7/56HG
14/12/56-25/1/57HC(EO)
28/5/57-11/7/57HI
17/6/58-1/8/58HG
8/6/59-31/7/59HI
17/10/60-25/11/60LI

No dates – speedo probably fitted, AWS probably never

MILEAGES

1935	50,371
1936	58,467
1937	50,867
1938	52,863
1939	45,981
1940	55,645
1941	53,852
1942	61,243
1943	45,992
1944	48,818
1945	42,450
1946	56,297
1947	62,283
1948	52,386
1949	61,920
1950	63,860
1951	62,660
1952	58,945
1953	59,127
1954	57,757
1955	60,740
1956	57,889
1957	62,092

Mileage at 31/12/50 863,295
Withdrawn week ending 29/2/64

BOILERS
First boiler 8635

No	Fitted	From
8636	7/4/38	5606
8759	19/3/41	5600
8606	17/7/43	5606
8597	24/10/46	5614
8600	12/5/49	5552
8558	7/5/52	45655
8598	28/7/56	45632
8614	1/8/58	45624

TENDERS

No	Fitted
9052	6/4/35
3904	1/6/37* ex-6113
4494	28/7/56*
4474	1/8/58*
10381	25/11/60

*Fowler

SHEDS

Camden 11/5/35
Rugby 5/10/35
Aston 10/2/40
Leeds 15/4/40
Loan at first, then
Leeds 11/5/40
Burton 2/64
(probably 'paper' transfer)

45605 CYPRUS heading north from Leeds with a down express on 21 February 1961. Fitted with AWS (no need to hoist the screw coupling up onto the drawbar hook now that nice AWS shield is there for it to rest on!) and speedo; this view also shows well the flexible coupling added at the base of the pipe leading down from the vacuum ejector. Photograph The Transport Treasury.

45606 FALKLAND ISLANDS

Built North British Loco Co Ltd 13/4/35

Named 1/9/36

Renumbered 5606 to 45606 week ending 7/5/49

TENDERS

No	Fitted
9053	13/4/35
4241	9/9/36* ex-6156
9698	26/8/37
*Fowler	

MILEAGES

1935	34,497
1936	46,738*
1937	56,472*
1938	60,636
1939	58,864
1940	52,150
1941	52,672
1942	51,361
1943	56,998
1944	37,239
1945	51,538
1946	62,356
1947	54,645
1948	49,423
1949	38,682
1950	43,569
1951	44,670
1952	47,631
1953	51,113
1954	51,249
1955	59,563
1956	50,157
1957	55,199
1958	51,609
1959	53,136
1960	53,623

*1936 25 days stored serviceable
*1937 22 days stored serviceable
Mileage at 31/12/50 807,840; at 31/12/60 1,325,790
Withdrawn week ending 27/6/64

BOILERS

First boiler 8636

No	Fitted	From
8567	11/2/38	5617
8606	21/9/40	5597
8604	2/6/43	5628
8625	3/6/44	5630
8584	24/3/48	5635
8740	9/4/52	45588
8622	13/11/54	45571
8601	10/5/58	45615

SHEDS

Crewe North 13/5/35
Derby 4/1/36
Crewe North 25/9/36
Holyhead 29/5/37
Camden 17/7/37
Crewe North 4/9/37
Willesden 20/12/40
Camden 4/4/42
Willesden 2/10/48
Crewe North 1/10/49
Willesden 8/10/49
Camden 5/7/52
Edge Hill 20/12/52
Patricroft 1/5/54
Camden 12/6/54
Carnforth 2/1/60
Camden 23/7/60
Carnforth 13/8/60

REPAIRS

16/4/35-13/5/35**LO**
25/6/35-29/7/35**LO**
28/8/36-21/9/36**LS**
10/8/37-26/8/37**LS**
17/1/38-22/1/38**LO**
7/2/38-28/2/38**HG**
9/5/38-14/5/38**LO**
21/5/38-30/5/38**LO**
13/5/39-30/5/39**LS**
22/8/40-21/9/40**HG**
28/1/42-14/2/42**LS**
9/7/42-6/8/42**LO**
17/5/43-2/6/43**HG**
19/5/44-3/6/44**HS**
24/1/45-28/2/45**LO**
24/7/45-12/9/45**HS**
14/10/46-30/10/46**LS**
5/3/47-22/4/47**LO**
7/2/48-24/3/48**HG**
1/4/49-4/5/49**HI**
11/10/50-7/11/50**LI**
20/2/52-9/4/52**HG**
16/4/52-25/4/52**NC(Rect)**
28/4/52-30/4/52**NC(Rect)**
31/10/53-21/11/53**LI**
14/10/54-13/11/54**HG**
8/12/54-16/12/54**NC(EO Rect)**
21/5/56-13/6/56**HI**
12/3/57-18/4/57**HC(EO)**
25/3/58-10/5/58**HG**
4/12/59-14/1/60**HI AWS fitted**
? -2/62 **speedo fitted**

45606 FALKLAND ISLANDS at Crewe North, 31 July 1954, on the turntable built in the 1950s to serve a new semi-roundhouse – apart from coal and ash plants all that survived of a grandiose scheme to erect a pair of complete roundhouses. The ancient and decaying sequence of LNW straight sheds, already partly demolished, stretch away towards the main line. In the left background is 45545 PLANET and, on the right, an almost new DUKE OF GLOUCESTER. Photograph J. Robertson, The Transport Treasury.

45607 FIJI

Built Crewe 29/6/34
Named 20/7/36
Renumbered 5607 to 45607 week ending 22/5/48

MILEAGES

1934	29,456
1935	72,429
1936	75,136
1937	67,675
1938	89,224
1939	78,382
1940	49,283
1941	58,746
1942	50,954
1943	53,334
1944	44,532
1945	39,379
1946	45,600
1947	49,137
1948	43,639
1949	46,670
1950	42,648
1951	54,741
1952	51,562
1953	56,500
1954	53,834
1955	52,418
1956	48,894
1957	53,970

stored 15/10/62-withdrawal
Mileage at 31/12/50 936,224
Withdrawn week ending 1/12/62

TENDERS

No	Fitted
4564	29/6/34*HSS
4566	15/2/36*HSS
9763	9/9/39
4618	16/1/63

*Fowler
HSS=high straight sided

SHEDS

Crewe North 7/7/34
Camden 21/7/34
Kentish Town 10/2/35
Millhouses 13/2/43
Nottingham 17/10/52
Millhouses 31/10/53
Agecroft 3/3/62

BOILERS
First boiler 8557

No	Fitted	From
?	10/6/36	new
8467	6/4/38	5554
8610	24/2/40	5570
8749	16/12/42	5643
8608	12/10/46	5636
8747	31/1/51	45627
8562	19/6/53	45625
8618	12/10/57	45564

REPAIRS

7/3/35-1/4/35**LS**
27/5/36-20/7/36**HG**
9/2/37-1/3/37**LS**
9/3/38-25/4/38**HG**
10/4/39-25/4/39**HS**
29/1/40-24/2/40**HG**
31/7/40-31/8/40**TRO**
17/5/41-12/6/41**LS**
6/10/41-15/11/41**LS**
16/11/42-16/12/42**HG**
14/6/43-12/7/43**LO**
19/5/44-3/6/44**LS**
7/6/45-1/8/45**HS**
30/4/46-2/5/46**TRO**
23/9/46-12/10/46**HG**
13/4/48-19/5/48**LS**
20/8/48-1/10/48**LO**
21/9/49-11/10/49**LI**
25/11/50-31/1/51**HG**
11/3/52-3/4/52**LI**
20/5/53-19/6/53**HG**
9/9/54-15/10/54**LI**
2/4/55-6/5/55**LC(EO)**
17/9/55-15/10/55**HI**
25/10/56-20/11/56**HI**
20/8/57-18/10/57**HG**
? -20/2/59**LI**
7/12/59-21/1/60**LC(EO)**
12/8/60-23/9/60**LI**

No dates – speedo probably fitted, AWS probably never fitted

45608 GIBRALTAR

Built Crewe 13/7/34
Named 13/3/36
Renumbered 5608 to 45608 week ending 2/10/48

MILEAGES

1934	35,760
1935	49,472
1936	73,117
1937	65,719
1938	74,261
1939	65,921
1940	47,671
1941	66,779
1942	56,730
1943	44,688
1944	45,058
1945	41,759
1946	49,088
1947	57,517
1948	58,643
1949	60,480
1950	62,640
1951	65,266
1952	60,110
1953	70,171
1954	72,603
1955	69,659
1956	65,040
1957	59,353

Mileage at 31/12/50 955,303
Withdrawn Aug/Sept 1965

TENDERS

No	Fitted
4565	13/7/34*HSS
4571	23/7/36*HSS
4565	15/8/39*HSS
9775	6/4/40

*****Fowler**
HSS=high straight sided

SHEDS

Crewe North 14/7/34
Camden 21/7/34
Kentish Town 28/9/35
Millhouses 23/10/42
Leeds 3/2/45
Nottingham (loan) 6/5/50
Leeds 27/5/50

BOILERS

First boiler 8558

No	Fitted	From
10032	6/4/37	New
9323	27/2/39	5703
9255	29/11/40	5725
9786	30/7/43	5673
9330	1/8/47	5684
9323	29/9/50	45720
11160	18/11/53	45676
9259	31/5/57	45702

REPAIRS

23/7/35-23/8/35**LS**
2/3/36-13/3/36**LO**
20/7/36-17/8/36**LS**
28/1/37-16/4/37**HG**
-14/7/37**TRO**
6/11/37-18/11/37**LO**
8/2/38-16/3/38**HS**
13/8/38-9/9/38**LO**
4/1/39-27/2/39**HG**
22/12/39-10/1/40**LS**
7/2/40-24/2/40**LO**
28/10/40-29/11/40**HG**
30/7/41-4/9/41**HS**
15/8/42-8/9/42**LS**
20/6/43-30/7/43**HG**
7/2/44-26/2/44**LO**
31/5/44-14/6/44**LO**
29/6/45-11/8/45**HS**
10/1/46-16/2/46**LO**
21/11/46-24/12/46**LS**
27/5/47-1/8/47**HG**
30/8/48-2/10/48**LS**
18/7/49-19/8/49**HI**
15/8/50-29/9/50**HG**
4/10/51-29/10/51**LI**
31/10/52-29/11/52**HI**
12/10/53-18/11/53**HG**
11/10/54-10/11/54**HI**
27/1/56-5/3/56**HI**
1/4/57-31/5/57**HG**
29/4/58-30/5/58**HI**
20/9/58-22/10/58**HC(EO)**
-20/12/58**NC(EO)**
29/2/60-2/4/60**LI**
-31/1/61**NC(EO)**
No dates for AWS, speedo fitting

And another Holbeck Jubilee. With 20A plates, 45608 GIBRALTAR waits to back down from Kentish Town shed to St Pancras to return north, in July 1953. That looming edifice is the cinema, flying the Union flag. Photograph J. Robertson, The Transport Treasury.

45609 GILBERT AND ELLICE ISLANDS

Built Crewe 17/7/34
Named 22/9/36
Renumbered 5609 to 45609 week ending 14/8/48

MILEAGES

1934	27,403
1935	66,237
1936	55,800
1937	70,770
1938	86,002
1939	71,251
1940	56,317
1941	66,653
1942	47,232
1943	54,778
1944	35,265
1945	35,432
1946	53,609
1947	45,887
1948	40,381
1949	61,165
1950	60,547
1951	53,991
1952	44,508
1953	40,325
1954	48,009
1955	48,892
1956	48,369
1957	40,060

Mileage at 31/12/50 934,729
Withdrawn week ending 3/9/60 from Millhouses; first 'natural' withdrawal

SHEDS

Crewe North 14/7/34
Camden 21/7/34
Kentish Town 10/2/35
Bristol 7/3/36
Leeds 6/2/37
Bristol 29/5/37
Kentish Town 25/9/37
Toton 2/3/40
Kentish Town 18/5/40
Millhouses 23/10/42
Derby 22/1/44
Millhouses 11/5/46
Derby 26/10/46
Kentish Town 20/9/47
Nottingham loan 31/1/48
Derby loan 28/2/48
Kentish Town 10/4/48
Millhouses 30/9/50

TENDERS

No	Fitted
4566	17/7/34*
4564	15/2/36*
9772	4/11/39
4494	1/10/46
3899	6/7/56
4242	16/5/58

***Fowler**

BOILERS
First boiler 8559

No	Fitted	From
8571	8/9/36	5621
8621	28/9/38	5591
8740	10/7/40	5573
8633	22/8/42	5583
8761	1/10/46	5582
8617	20/10/49	5574
8610	22/1/55	45622

REPAIRS

16/10/34-8/11/34**LO**
16/3/35-15/5/35**LS**
21/5/36-6/6/36**LO**
7/8/36-22/9/36**HG**
25/8/37-14/9/37**LS**
21/3/38-8/4/38**LO**
10/8/38-28/9/38**HG**
7/6/39-28/6/39**HS**
20/6/40-10/7/40**HG**
14/8/41-5/9/41**LS**
9/7/42-22/8/42**HG**
19/8/43-2/10/43**HS**
17/2/44-24/3/44**LO**
28/5/45-29/6/45**LS**
3/12/45-21/12/45**LO**
7/9/46-1/10/46**HG**
17/10/47-19/11/47**HS**
19/5/48-13/8/48**LS Derby**
16/10/48-28/10/48**NC(Rect) Derby**
3/2/49-26/2/49**LC**
5/9/49-20/10/49**HG**
26/4/50-25/5/50**LC**
25/1/51-16/2/51**HI**
30/3/52-1/5/52**LI**
12/8/53-19/9/53**HI**
21/12/54-22/1/55**HG**
13/6/56-6/7/56**LI**
5/4/58-16/5/58**HI**
   ? -25/6/58**NC(EO Rect)**
AWS, speedo, never fitted

45610 GHANA

Built Crewe 19/7/34
Named GOLD COAST 24/2/36
Renamed GHANA 12/12/58
Renumbered 5610 to 45610 week ending 11/6/49

TENDERS

No	Fitted
4567	19/7/34*HSS
9770	13/10/39

***Fowler**
HSS=high straight sided

MILEAGES

1934	24,634
1935	81,064
1936	67,338
1937	71,804
1938	70,372
1939	73,318
1940	55,446
1941	65,210
1942	69,058
1943	58,016
1944	65,043
1945	55,174
1946	57,782
1947	39,708
1948	47,562
1949	49,122
1950	53,795
1951	44,685
1952	47,735
1953	43,336
1954	48,111
1955	46,706
1956	44,814
1957	53,077
1958	56,644
1959	46,012
1960	42,211

stored 15/10/62-21/1/63
Mileage at 31/12/50 1,004,446; at 31/12/60 1,477,777
Withdrawn week ending 11/1/64

BOILERS
First boiler 8560

No	Fitted	From
8591	18/2/37	5561
8616	2/12/38	5556
8563	25/2/41	5614

After this date 5610 became part of the post-5665 series with different boilers

9256	30/9/43	5683
9340	19/10/45	5707
9217	6/6/49	45709
10034	13/8/53	45678
9784	15/11/57	45738

SHEDS

Longsight 21/7/34
Camden 21/7/34
Kentish Town 10/2/35
Trafford Park loan 15/6/40
Kentish Town 29/6/40
Derby 26/10/46
Kentish Town 15/6/57
Derby 29/6/57
Burton 18/11/61
Derby 26/1/63

REPAIRS

4/12/34-28/12/34**LO**
15/5/35-31/5/35**LS**
24/1/36-24/2/36**HS**
6/1/37-11/3/37**HG**
27/10/37-15/11/37**HS**
7/3/38-28/3/38**LO**
19/4/38-17/5/38**LO**
8/9/38-16/9/38**LO**
14/10/38-2/12/38**HG**
4/3/39-30/3/39**LO**
24/8/39-23/9/39**HS**
4/2/41-25/2/41**HG**
11/3/42-18/4/42**LS**
7/10/42-7/11/42**LS**
12/8/43-30/9/43**HG**
16/10/44-4/11/44**LS**
29/9/45-19/10/45**HG**
10/8/46-5/10/46**LS**
19/2/48-25/3/48**LS**
21/4/49-6/6/49**HG**
16/3/50-19/4/50**HI**
19/6/51-25/7/51**LI**
2/4/52-9/5/52**HI**
24/6/53-13/8/53**HG**
19/1/55-19/2/55**HI**
11/4/56-17/5/56**HI**
10/10/56-10/11/56**LC(EO)**
6/10/57-15/11/57**HG**
6/9/58-9/10/58**LI**
26/3/60-12/5/60**LI speedo fitted**
29/6/61-15/8/61**LI**
AWS never fitted

45611 HONG KONG at Kentish Town on 19 May 1958; domed boiler, one-piece smokebox saddle, steam sanding, recessed sand filler caps and 4,000 gallon riveted curved sided tender. Photograph The Transport Treasury.

45611 HONG KONG

Built Crewe 27/7/34
Named 24/12/36
Renumbered 5611 to 45611 week ending 13/11/48

MILEAGES

1934	21,405
1935	72,764
1936	65,187
1937	78,934
1938	55,167
1939	62,237
1940	62,402
1941	51,955
1942	48,872
1943	50,793
1944	48,763
1945	59,170
1946	56,907
1947	59,050
1948	61,117
1949	46,146
1950	51,754
1951	45,072
1952	43,766
1953	65,077
1954	55,386
1955	61,230
1956	43,791
1957	65,313
1958	62,896
1959	57,499
1960	63,607

stored 15/10/62-21/1/63
Mileage at 31/12/50 952,623; at 31/12/60 1,516,260
Withdrawn week ending 19/9/64

SHEDS
Camden 28/7/34
Kentish Town 10/2/35
Crewe North 11/9/37
Leeds 20/4/40
Loan at first, then
Leeds 11/5/40
Bristol (loan) 31/1/48
Leeds 27/3/48
Nottingham 28/5/49
Burton 18/11/61
Derby 26/1/63

TENDERS

No	Fitted
4568	27/7/34*HSS
9754	11/4/39
9696	28/7/43
9754	5/10/43
4502	30/11/46*
10215	16/12/49
10303	13/6/64

*Fowler
HSS=high straight sided

BOILERS
First boiler 8561

No	Fitted	From
8581	8/12/36	5631
8560	23/8/38	5557
8615	30/7/40	5601
8580	12/12/42	5638
8469	2/10/45	5651
8578	16/12/49	45637
8758	18/10/52	45596
8597	27/11/56	45597
8758	16/10/59	45625

REPAIRS
5/7/35-7/8/35**LS**
16/10/35-11/11/35**LO**
9/3/36-2/4/36**LO**
15/10/36-24/12/36**HG**
20/8/37-13/9/37**LS**
25/7/38-23/8/38**HG**
17/1/40-1/2/40**LS**
8/7/40-30/7/40**HO**
11/2/41-21/3/41**LS**
1/10/41-27/10/41**LO**
20/3/42-29/4/42**LS**
9/11/42-12/12/42**HG**
12/7/43-21/8/43**LO**
10/1/44-4/3/44**HS**
30/11/44-21/12/44**HS**
3/9/45-2/10/45**HG**
1/11/46-30/11/46**LS**
24/6/47-11/7/47**LO Derby**
27/9/47-14/11/47**HS**
11/10/48-8/11/48**LS**
12/10/49-16/12/49**HG**
26/6/50-3/8/50**LC**
27/12/50-25/1/51**LI**
16/9/52-18/10/52**HG**
29/1/54-23/2/54**HI**
3/5/54-27/5/54**LC(EO)**
22/3/55-3/5/55**LI**
26/9/56-27/11/56**HG**
29/3/58-25/4/58**LI**
12/9/59-16/10/59**HG**
9/11/59-30/11/59**NC(EO Rect)**
10/6/61-8/8/61**LI** speedo fitted;
AWS probably never fitted

45612 JAMAICA

Built Crewe 31/7/34
Named 23/4/37
Renumbered 5612 to 45612 week ending 25/12/48

MILEAGES

1934	34,625
1935	52,646
1936	59,912
1937	72,174
1938	72,533
1939	76,435
1940	61,613
1941	42,507
1942	46,876
1943	54,685
1944	52,968
1945	56,532
1946	43,636
1947	33,131
1948	32,382
1949	67,838
1950	70,053
1951	63,394
1952	61,199
1953	58,182
1954	66,722
1955	57,312
1956	62,351
1957	61,828
1958	60,033
1959	44,401
1960	46,385

stored 1/10/62-21/1/63
Mileage at 31/12/50 930,546; at 31/12/60 1,512,353
Withdrawn week ending 28/3/64

TENDERS

No	Fitted
4569	31/7/34*HSS
3913	18/5/57*
4473	8/8/59*
10354	5/12/59

*Fowler
HSS=high straight sided

BOILERS

First boiler 8562

No	Fitted	From
8625	12/4/37	5595
8575	14/1/39	5614
8468	12/9/40	5566
8755	10/4/43	5570
8558	7/3/45	5647
8741	21/12/48	5573
8755	24/3/53	45662
8625	22/3/56	45616
8466	26/3/58	45662

SHEDS

Camden 4/8/34
Kentish Town 6/4/35
Bath 30/8/41
Bristol 6/9/41
Leeds 10/6/44
Bristol 7/10/44
Saltley 11/5/46
Derby 21/6/47
Millhouses loan 26/7/47
Derby loan 23/8/47
Derby 1/11/47*
Kentish Town 1/11/47*
same dates on card!
Derby 21/11/59
Burton 18/11/61
Derby 26/1/63

REPAIRS

6/8/35-4/9/35**LS**
4/6/36-10/7/36**LS**
8/2/37-23/4/37**HG**
4/10/37-13/10/37**LO**
8/2/38-3/3/38**HS**
24/5/38-16/6/38**LO**
7/12/38-14/1/39**HG**
13/11/39-5/12/39**LS**
11/8/40-12/9/40**HG**
22/7/41-13/8/41**LO**
27/3/42-8/5/42**LS**
12/8/42-4/9/42**LO**
22/3/43-10/4/43**HG**
4/11/43-4/12/43**LS**
21/9/44-16/10/44**LO**
13/2/45-7/3/45**HS**
4/5/45-9/6/45**TRO**
21/9/45-26/10/45**LO**
16/2/46-28/3/46**LS**
3/3/47-2/5/47**HS**
26/9/47-17/10/47**LO Derby**
20/9/48-21/12/48**HG**
23/6/49-5/8/49**LI**
8/12/49-13/1/50**LC**
21/5/50-20/6/50**HI**
28/3/51-25/4/51**HI**
5/5/52-6/6/52**HI**
3/2/53-24/3/53**HG**
2/1/54-26/1/54**HI**
14/1/55-19/2/55**LI**
22/1/56-22/3/56**HG**
22/4/57-18/5/57**LI**
7/2/58-26/3/58**HG**
22/6/59-8/8/59**LI**
19/10/59-5/12/59**LC(EO)**
10/5/60-22/6/60**LC(EO)**
11/2/61-30/3/61**HI Speedo fitted;**
AWS never fitted

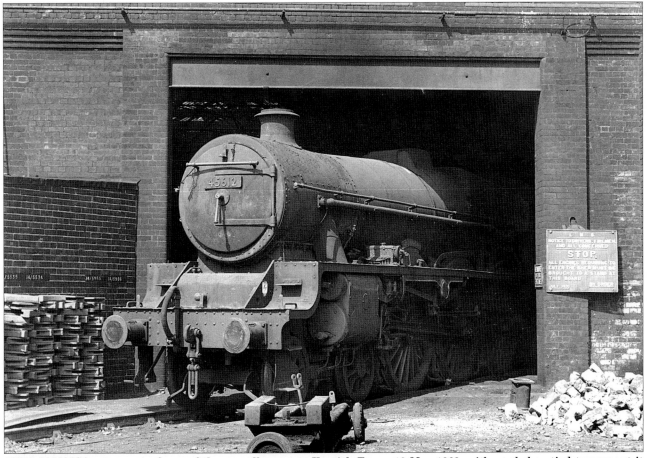

45612 JAMAICA peeps out of one of the roundhouses at Kentish Town, 19 May 1962, with smokebox tied to prevent it swinging open. 45612's disreputable condition and lack of a shedplate is a sign of the times, though the Jubilee was not withdrawn until March 1964. Photograph The Transport Treasury.

45613 KENYA

Built Crewe 6/8/34
Named 16/3/36
Renumbered 5613 to 45613 week ending 7/8/48

TENDERS

No	Fitted
4570	6/8/34*HSS
3909	17/8/57*
3904	14/9/57*
4246	28/4/59*
10383	22/4/60

*Fowler
HSS=high straight sided

SHEDS
Camden 11/8/34
Kentish Town 10/2/35
Millhouses 6/2/37
Kentish Town 27/2/37
Crewe North 11/9/37
Patricroft 18/6/38
Carlisle Upperby 16/9/39
Edge Hill 2/5/42
Carlisle Upperby 24/2/56
Longsight 3/8/57
Carlisle Upperby 17/8/57
Crewe North 14/6/58
Chester (West) 21/6/58
Crewe North 11/4/59
Edge Hill 12/9/59
Crewe South 31/12/60
Crewe North 10/6/61
Carnforth 5/5/62
Carlisle Kingmoor 22/6/63

REPAIRS
25/6/35-25/7/35LS
17/2/36-16/3/36LS
28/8/36-7/11/36HG
30/10/37-15/11/37LS
4/11/38-20/12/38HG
10/6/39-11/7/39LO
16/8/40-5/9/40LS
28/5/41-18/6/41LO
8/4/42-25/4/42HG
23/8/43-18/9/43HS
20/4/45-22/5/45LS
7/4/46-8/5/46HG
28/8/47-2/10/47LS
5/7/48-6/8/48HO
24/8/49-12/9/49LI
6/12/50-16/1/51LI
2/6/51-11/8/51HG
13/6/53-2/7/53LI
10/12/54-19/1/55HG
10/7/56-7/8/56HI
8/8/56-20/8/56NC(EO Rect)
6/8/57-14/9/57HI
12/3/59-22/4/59HI
23/4/59-28/4/59NC(EO Rect) AWS fitted
12/3/60-22/4/60LC
21/11/60-23/12/60HG speedo fitted
14/4/61-19/5/61LC(EO)

BOILERS
First boiler 8563

No	Fitted	From
8566	20/10/36	5616
8585	20/11/38	5632
8578	25/4/42	5660
8615	8/5/46	5663
8626	6/8/48	5587
8612	11/8/51	45554
8583	19/1/55	45629
8592	23/12/60	45602

MILEAGES

1934	28,574
1935	64,329
1936	55,519
1937	76,608*
1938	28,136*
1939	62,657
1940	41,978
1941	41,844
1942	40,325
1943	43,834
1944	40,344
1945	38,624
1946	46,397
1947	44,529
1948	46,402
1949	48,248
1950	47,148
1951	41,830
1952	46,320
1953	44,574
1954	46,468
1955	45,856
1956	45,773
1957	47,095
1958	38,839
1959	40,307
1960	34,526

*1937 17 days stored serviceable
*1938 71 days stored serviceable
Mileage at 31/12/50 795,496; at 31/12/60 1,227,084
Withdrawn week ending 12/9/64

45614 LEEWARD ISLANDS

Built Crewe 9/8/34
Named 11/1/37
Renumbered 5614 to 45614 week ending 1/5/48

MILEAGES

1934	30,425
1935	67,088
1936	76,702
1937	68,541
1938	79,417
1939	66,222
1940	40,446
1941	57,691
1942	61,084
1943	63,604
1944	71,118
1945	53,002
1946	56,758
1947	55,061
1948	51,219
1949	64,888
1950	50,086
1951	67,949
1952	65,879
1953	61,706
1954	62,219
1955	62,764
1956	70,223
1957	64,381
1958	52,443
1959	56,689
1960	52,542

Stored 15/10/62-21/1/63
Mileage at 31/12/50 1,013,352; at 31/12/60 1,630,147
Withdrawn week ending 11/1/64

TENDERS

No	Fitted
4571	9/8/34*HSS
4565	23/7/36*HSS
4571	15/8/39*HSS
9780	24/6/40
4627	16/1/44

*Fowler
HSS=high straight sided

BOILERS
First boiler 8564

No	Fitted	From
8575	23/12/36	5625
8563	23/11/38	5627
8575	28/11/40	5612
8597	29/7/44	5637
8466	16/9/46	5655
8581	1/3/49	5654
8624	23/12/50	45663
8619	1/1/54	45630
8620	1/11/56	45626
8625	17/12/60	45600

SHEDS
Camden 11/8/34
Kentish Town 10/2/35
Toton 2/3/40
Kentish Town 18/5/40
Newton Heath 11/7/59
Kentish Town 19/9/59
Trafford Park 27/2/60
Kentish Town 19/3/60
Derby 16/12/61
Burton 7/4/62
Derby 26/1/63

REPAIRS
24/5/35-18/6/35LS
12/5/36-27/5/36LO
16/11/36-11/1/37HG
3/6/37-7/7/37LO
15/9/37-5/10/37LS
2/3/38-1/4/38HS
11/10/38-23/11/38HG
4/5/39-21/6/39LO
31/8/39-13/10/39HS
19/10/40-28/11/40HG
23/10/41-21/11/41HS
1/12/42-31/12/42LS
13/10/43-29/10/43LS
10/7/44-29/7/44HG
1/6/45-13/7/45LS
3/1/46-6/2/46LO
16/8/46-16/9/46HG
17/10/47-22/11/47LS
31/3/48-1/5/48LO
9/11/48-1/3/49HG
29/1/50-24/2/50HI
11/3/50-18/3/50TRO
6/10/50-23/12/50HG
24/11/51-29/12/51HI
28/6/52-8/8/52HI
12/11/52-16/12/52LC(EO)
26/11/53-1/1/54HG
16/11/54-6/12/54LC(EO)
16/5/55-11/6/55LI
27/7/55-6/8/55LC(EO)
13/11/55-22/12/55LC(EO)
6/9/56-1/11/56HG
26/3/57-7/5/57LC(EO)
7/12/57-4/1/58LI
28/7/58-20/8/58LC(EO)
18/4/59-23/5/59HI
22/11/60-17/12/60HG speedo fitted;
AWS probably never fitted

45615 MALAY STATES

Built Crewe 15/8/34
Named 12/6/36
Renumbered 5615 to 45615 week ending 1/5/48

MILEAGES	
1934	19,224
1935	76,128
1936	84,753
1937	69,531
1938	73,950
1939	57,960
1940	54,817
1941	48,943
1942	61,654
1943	70,641
1944	63,160
1945	52,779
1946	56,855
1947	53,710
1948	55,695
1949	45,313
1950	68,649
1951	66,166
1952	59,412
1953	59,610
1954	65,766
1955	44,046
1956	72,942
1957	65,901
1958	59,032
1959	57,156
1960	33,881

Mileage at 31/12/50 1,013,762; at 31/12/60 1,597,674
Withdrawn week ending 8/12/62

BOILERS
First boiler 8565

No	Fitted	From
8587	15/2/37	5557
8601	14/9/38	5571
8612	27/6/40	5616
8756	27/7/43	5557
8622	19/3/46	5619
8748	11/8/49	45592
8468	29/10/52	45598
8601	26/11/55	45617
8607	21/2/58	45634

SHEDS
Camden 18/8/34
Kentish Town 10/2/35
Leicester 16/1/60
Newton Heath 8/7/61
Leicester 23/9/61
Burton 18/11/61

TENDERS

No	Fitted
4572	15/8/34*HSS
9778	23/4/40
4646	3/7/43

***Fowler**
HSS=high straight sided

REPAIRS
26/3/35-24/4/35**LO**
29/10/35-28/11/35**HS**
14/5/36-26/6/36**LS**
28/12/36-19/3/37**HG**
9/2/38-3/3/38**HS**
16/7/38-14/9/38**HG**
13/3/39-6/5/39**LO**
16/8/39-14/9/39**HS**
6/6/40-27/6/40**HG**
30/6/41-6/8/41**LS**
13/11/41-27/12/41**LO**
19/4/42-6/6/42**LS**
18/9/42-17/10/42**LO**
27/6/43-27/7/43**HG**
2/6/44-23/6/44**LS**
26/1/45-24/2/45**LS**
11/2/46-19/3/46**HG**
8/1/47-18/2/47**LS**
18/7/47-15/8/47**LO Derby**
18/3/48-26/4/48**HS**
17/8/48-22/9/48**LO**
29/4/49-11/8/49**HG**
24/10/49-19/11/49**LC**
31/8/50-3/10/50**LI**
20/8/51-15/9/51**LI**
29/9/52-29/10/52**HG**
29/10/52-7/11/52**NCRect(EO)**
31/8/53-30/9/53**LI**
1/10/53-3/10/53**NC(Rect)**
31/7/54-28/8/54**HI**
3/10/55-26/11/55**HG**
27/9/56-2/11/56**LI**
24/1/58-21/2/58**HG**
30/4/58-6/6/58**LC(EO)**
27/1/59-9/2/59**LC(EO) Rugby**
30/4/59-5/6/59**LI**
20/11/60-16/12/60**LI speedo fitted;**
AWS probably never fitted
5/6/61-1/7/61**LC(EO)**

45616 MALTA G.C.

Built Crewe 16/8/34
Named MALTA 6/8/36.
Renamed MALTA G.C. 23/10/43
Renumbered 5616 to 45616 week ending 25/9/48

MILEAGES	
1934	12,282
1935	80,121
1936	84,651
1937	70,458
1938	88,104
1939	63,720
1940	43,831
1941	60,723
1942	62,370
1943	61,623
1944	58,453
1945	58,373
1946	37,335
1947	43,491
1948	69,841
1949	57,421
1950	67,590
1951	70,579
1952	69,397
1953	56,802
1954	65,637
1955	51,006
1956	52,876
1957	53,303
1958	57,484
1959	55,921
1960	35,492

Mileage at 31/12/50 1,020,387; at 31/12/60 1,588,884
Withdrawn week ending 21/1/61

BOILERS
First boiler 8566

No	Fitted	From
9320	16/7/36	New
8612	3/3/38	5582
8632	25/4/40	5592
8596	27/10/44	5587
8760	8/11/47	5633
8574	3/4/50	45648
8625	10/5/52	45660
8568	11/2/56	-

SHEDS
Crewe North 18/8/34
Edgehill 6/10/34
Camden 27/10/34
Kentish Town 10/2/35
Bristol 11/11/39
Kentish Town 9/12/39
Nottingham 21/11/59
Leicester 23/1/60
Trafford Park 27/2/60
Leicester 19/3/60

TENDERS

No	Fitted
4573	15/8/34*HSS
4557	31/12/42*
3943	7/10/54*
3937	27/2/58*
3904	16/5/59*
10152	2/1/60

***Fowler**
HSS=high straight sided

REPAIRS
16/9/35-11/10/35**HS**
21/4/36-8/5/36**LO**
8/6/36-6/8/36**HG**
2/3/37-18/3/37**LS**
29/7/37-17/8/37**LO**
19/11/37-6/12/37**LO**
24/2/38-21/3/38**HG**
23/2/39-28/3/39**LS**
23/3/40-25/4/40**HG**
30/4/40-11/5/40**LO**
18/8/41-12/9/41**LS**
19/2/42-25/3/42**HS**
26/11/42-20/1/43**LS**
4/8/43-2/9/43**LS**
4/1/44-3/2/44**LO**
2/10/44-27/10/44**HG**
23/6/45-25/7/45**LS**
1/11/45-29/11/45**LO**
2/11/46-4/12/46**LS**
5/2/47-24/3/47**HO**
1/9/47-8/11/47**HG**
23/8/48-21/9/48**HS**
21/3/49-13/4/49**LC Derby**
24/5/49-23/6/49**LC**
17/2/50-3/4/50**HG**
10/4/50-4/5/50**NC(Rect)**
11/9/50-4/10/50**LC**
15/5/51-5/6/51**LI**
7/4/52-10/5/52**HG**
3/6/53-22/7/53**HI**
6/9/54-7/10/54**HI**
5/12/55-11/2/56**HG**
31/10/56-1/12/56**LI**
29/12/56-26/1/57**NC(EO)**
29/7/57-23/8/57**LC(EO)**
27/1/58-27/2/58**LI**
1/4/59-16/5/59**LI**
30/11/59-2/1/60**LC(EO)**
Dates not recorded – speedo probably fitted; AWS probably never

A lovely picture, capturing perfectly the balanced lines of a Jubilee. 45616 MALTA G.C. leaves Leicester with a down express 21 April 1956, passing two splendid period cars and the POTATO & FRUIT STORES. With all that steam, it looks like the fireman is 'slacking' the coal in that Fowler tender, having been in to bring coal forward during the stop. Photograph Peter Groom.

45617 MAURITIUS

Built Crewe 24/9/34

Named 7/9/37

Renumbered 5617 to 45617 week ending 5/6/48

TENDERS

No	Fitted
4600	24/9/34

REPAIRS
9/10/35-1/11/35**LS**
18/5/36-28/5/36**LO**
23/11/36-26/11/36**LO**
10/2/37-3/3/37**LS**
20/12/37-14/1/38**HG**
25/9/39-17/10/39**HS**
13/9/40-28/9/40**LO**
7/3/41-5/4/41**HG**
7/8/42-5/9/42**LS**
15/5/43-29/5/43**HS**
22/9/44-10/10/44**HG**
17/1/46-7/2/46**HS**
29/4/47-14/6/47**HG**
20/4/48-31/5/48**HS**
16/12/48-10/1/49**LC**
14/9/49-22/10/49**LI**
25/9/50-22/1/51**HG**
10/3/52-1/4/52**LI**
20/11/53-17/12/53**HI**
6/9/55-5/10/55**HG**
24/4/57-25/5/57**HG**
11/6/58-11/7/58**HI**
25/11/59-8/1/60**LI** AWS fitted
18/10/61-27/11/61**HG** speedo fitted

SHEDS
Edgehill 6/10/34
Leeds 10/2/35
Farnley Jct 22/5/37
Patricroft 26/6/37
Carlisle Upperby 6/12/41
Crewe North 5/6/43
Camden 18/10/47
Longsight 19/8/50
Crewe North 6/12/52
Trafford Park 9/5/53
Crewe North 13/6/53
Carlisle Upperby 21/9/57
Crewe North 12/10/57
Carlisle Upperby 4/10/58
Crewe South 7/1/61
Crewe North 23/6/62
Saltley 9/3/63
Willesden 30/11/63
Crewe North 8/64

BOILERS
First boiler 8567

No	Fitted	From
8592	29/12/37	5562
8568	5/4/41	5619
8620	29/5/43	5642
8611	10/10/44	5559
8587	14/6/47	5599
8601	22/1/51	45604
8577	5/10/55	45644
8606	25/5/57	45599
8602	27/11/61	45662

MILEAGES

1934	23,409
1935	71,687
1936	59,183
1937	39,767
1938	47,978*
1939	47,403
1940	41,757
1941	45,962
1942	39,812
1943	54,493
1944	50,594
1945	63,855
1946	44,682
1947	47,084
1948	53,843
1949	51,661
1950	39,514
1951	60,247
1952	56,710
1953	43,736
1954	55,319
1955	45,446
1956	58,549
1957	49,939
1958	52,058
1959	46,254
1960	49,398

*stored serviceable 58 days
stored 1/11/62-1/3/63
Mileage at 31/12/50 822,684; at 31/12/60 1,340,340
Withdrawn week ending 7/11/64

45618 NEW HEBRIDES
Built Crewe 2/10/34
Named 27/3/36
Renumbered 5618 to 45618 week ending 15/5/48

BOILERS
First boiler 8568

No	Fitted	From
8558	29/4/37	5608
8742	20/4/39	5652
8608	30/11/40	5663
8564	27/12/41	5626
8748	21/1/43	5600
8746	4/4/44	5560
8465	15/10/46	5580
8745	7/10/49	45658
8623	22/10/54	45554
8747	22/2/57	-

REPAIRS
9/1/35-26/2/35**HO**
25/2/36-27/3/36**HS**
18/8/36-22/8/36**LO**
2/3/37-8/5/37**HG**
25/11/37-24/12/37**LO**
9/5/38-24/5/38**LS**
10/11/38-10/12/38**LO**
28/1/39-20/4/39**HG**
28/11/39-13/12/39**L^S**
23/10/40-30/11/40**HG**
21/11/41-27/12/41**HS**
4/12/42-21/1/43**HS**
8/6/43-2/7/43**LO**
17/3/44-4/4/44**HG**
28/9/44-4/11/44**LS**
5/7/45-18/8/45**LS**
20/9/46-15/10/46**HG**
5/4/48-13/5/48**HS**
22/12/48-28/1/49**LC**
24/8/49-7/10/49**HG**
25/9/50-25/10/50**HI**
23/7/51-31/8/51**HI**
21/4/52-28/5/52**LI**
28/2/53-31/3/53**HI**
9/9/53-13/10/53**LC**
11/9/54-22/10/54**HG**
13/5/55-11/6/55**LC(EO)**
1/10/55-3/11/55**HI**
23/1/57-22/2/57**GEN**
11/3/57-3/4/57**NC(EO Rect)**
9/4/58-2/5/58**LI**
14/5/59-17/6/59**HI**
15/12/59-28/1/60**LC(EO)**
30/5/61-9/8/61**HI** speedo fitted;
AWS never fitted

MILEAGES

Year	Miles
1934	16,887
1935	66,707
1936	69,645
1937	56,801
1938	67,998
1939	59,484
1940	56,250
1941	46,637
1942	68,825
1943	66,364
1944	62,431
1945	73,563
1946	55,555
1947	39,906
1948	48,095
1949	55,713
1950	50,221
1951	44,484
1952	56,448
1953	52,657
1954	47,954
1955	64,851
1956	53,850
1957	49,875
1958	55,472
1959	43,589
1960	40,639

Mileage at 31/12/50 961,082; at 31/12/60 1,470,901
Withdrawn week ending 29/2/64

SHEDS
Crewe North 6/10/34
Edgehill 27/10/34
Leeds 6/4/35
Derby 25/9/37
Kentish Town 9/7/38
Bristol 16/9/39
Millhouses 11/5/46
Derby 21/6/47
Trafford Park 1/11/47
Kentish Town 5/7/58
Derby 21/11/59
Burton 18/11/61

TENDERS

No	Fitted
4601	2/10/34
4621	18/5/63

Holbeck Jubilee 5618 about 1935, 'parked up' on one of the outside turntable spurs at Sheffield Grimesthorpe shed, deep among the steel works and foundries.

45619 NIGERIA

Built Crewe 5/10/34

Named 8/4/36

Renumbered 5619 to 45619 week ending 19/6/48

MILEAGES

Year	Mileage
1934	18,441
1935	75,541
1936	66,533
1937	37,281
1938	79,541
1939	66,750
1940	59,716
1941	51,773
1942	55,668
1943	51,036
1944	55,054
1945	55,896
1946	66,710
1947	58,474
1948	55,881
1949	64,781
1950	66,682
1951	51,379
1952	62,224
1953	62,221
1954	61,840
1955	63,039
1956	79,068
1957	54,779

Mileage at 31/12/50 985,758
Withdrawn week ending 19/8/61

TENDERS

No	Fitted
4602	5/10/34

SHEDS

Crewe North 6/10/34
Longsight 27/10/34
Leeds 10/2/35

BOILERS
First boiler 8569

No	Fitted	From
8737	12/3/37	5639
8568	19/4/39	5598
8634	1/3/41	5603
8622	13/11/43	5653
8738	7/2/46	5625
8593	26/6/50	45593
8582	30/1/54	45566
8596	3/1/56	45624
8634	20/2/59	45578

REPAIRS

19/3/36-8/4/36LS
24/8/36-3/9/36LO
14/1/37-25/3/37HG
22/9/37-29/10/37LO
1/2/38-18/2/38LO
22/7/38-4/8/38HS
2/3/39-19/4/39HG
5/10/39-31/10/39LO
25/3/40-6/4/40HS
15/10/40-28/10/40LO
9/1/41-1/3/41HG
17/12/41-17/1/42LS
13/11/42-19/12/42HS
23/10/43-13/11/43HG
18/1/45-9/2/45HS
24/12/45-7/2/46HG
3/2/47-14/3/47LS
12/5/48-15/6/48HS
6/6/49-19/7/49HI
17/5/50-26/6/50HG
11/6/51-28/7/51HI
5/12/51-6/2/52HC
17/10/52-14/11/52LI
29/1/53-28/2/53LC(EO)
25/12/53-30/1/54HG
16/11/54-13/12/54HI
29/11/55-3/1/56HG
1/2/57-6/3/57LI Derby
10/12/57-18/1/58LI
-3/2/58NC(EO Rect)
-20/2/59HG
28/3/60-21/5/60LI
-24/1/61NC(EO)
Speedo, AWS fitted by 6/61

45620 NORTH BORNEO

Built Crewe 11/10/34

Named 19/3/37

Renumbered 5620 to 45620 week ending 18/9/49

MILEAGES

Year	Mileage
1934	14,023
1935	82,260
1936	72,540
1937	69,718
1938	54,426
1939	70,761
1940	46,789
1941	55,234
1942	57,039
1943	63,410
1944	56,504
1945	47,362
1946	66,734
1947	58,425
1948	55,033
1949	58,824
1950	41,175
1951	53,458
1952	55,335
1953	53,372
1954	66,008
1955	47,828
1956	57,426
1957	54,157
1958	61,222
1959	58,123
1960	56,431

Mileage at 31/12/50 970,257; at
31/12/60 1,533,617
Withdrawn week ending 12/9/64

SHEDS

Crewe North 13/10/34
Longsight 27/10/34
Leeds 10/2/35
Nottingham 17/12/49
Burton 18/11/61

TENDERS

No	Fitted
4603	11/10/34

BOILERS
First boiler 8570

No	Fitted	From
8578	8/3/37	5628
8761	4/5/39	5626
8616	9/4/41	5610
8617	31/7/43	5565
8593	17/5/44	5655
8563	21/6/47	5650
8613	12/10/50	45557
8579	5/6/53	45583
8742	9/12/55	45598
8568	17/4/61	45616

REPAIRS

12/11/35-29/11/35LS
29/4/36-2/5/36LO
21/8/36-17/9/36LS
8/1/37-19/3/37HG
20/12/37-19/1/38HS
12/7/38-22/8/38LO
16/9/38-31/10/38LO
5/4/39-4/5/39HG
15/3/40-24/4/40LS
4/7/40-26/7/40LO
3/3/41-9/4/41HG
24/10/41-9/12/41LS
6/10/42-31/10/42LS
26/6/43-31/7/43HG
20/4/44-17/5/44HS
15/1/45-21/2/45LO
19/1/46-16/2/46HS
23/9/46-8/10/46LO
21/4/47-21/6/47HG
16/8/48-14/9/48LS
13/5/49-10/6/49LI
14/11/49-3/12/49LC
10/2/50-15/2/50TRO Nottingham
19/8/50-12/10/50HG
11/1/52-9/2/52LI
18/4/53-5/6/53HG
9/6/54-1/7/54LI
8/11/55-9/12/55HG
16/2/57-14/3/57LI
19/10/57-29/11/57LC(EO)
18/6/58-16/7/58LI
6/7/59-21/8/59HI
24/2/61-17/4/61HG
18/4/61-26/4/61NC(EO Rect)
speedo fitted; AWS never fitted

The Raleigh Cycle Co. was noted for the number and variety of the excursions it chartered for its workers from the firm's home city Nottingham. On Saturday 24 May 1952 no less than eleven charters ran to Morecambe by various routes (a twelfth train had been provided for, but was not required). M964 behind gleaming green 45621 NORTHERN RHODESIA (borrowed by Nottingham from Millhouses – it was part of the mass exodus to Scotland a few weeks later) is actually on the Morecambe branch, after leaving Morecambe South Junction. Photograph E.D. Bruton.

45621 NORTHERN RHODESIA

Built Crewe 11/10/34
Named 30/7/36
Renumbered 5621 to 45621 10/48

SHEDS
Crewe North 13/10/34
Leeds 10/2/35
Bristol 2/12/39
Millhouses 2/3/40
Corkerhill 9/52
Perth 10/59
Corkerhill 4/60

REPAIRS
4/10/35-28/10/35**LS**
18/6/36-30/7/36**HG**
9/11/37-29/11/37**LS**
4/4/38-7/4/38**LO**
12/10/38-13/12/38**HG**
22/9/39-3/11/39**LS**
11/6/40-3/7/40**HG**
13/2/41-28/2/41**LO**
30/8/41-16/10/41**LS**
22/12/41-10/1/42 **Tender Only**
27/7/42-29/8/42**HS**
6/7/43-30/7/43**HS**
27/12/43-17/1/44**LO**
15/8/44-9/9/44**HS**
24/11/45-12/12/45**HG**
18/4/47-29/5/47**LS**
15/9/48-27/10/48**HG**
17/4/50-8/5/50**LI**
Record incomplete

TENDERS

No	Fitted
4604	11/10/34

Record ends

BOILERS
First boiler 8571

No	Fitted	From
9209	13/12/38	5679
9329	3/9/40	5709
11160	29/8/42	New
9214	12/12/45	5738
9777	27/10/48	45688

Record incomplete

MILEAGES

1934	19,466
1935	77,152
1936	63,562
1937	64,647
1938	70,719
1939	76,335
1940	56,267
1941	38,355
1942	45,358
1943	61,685
1944	51,428
1945	43,461
1946	46,378
1947	39,981
1948	46,710
1949	44,433
1950	49,962

Record incomplete
Mileage at 31/12/50 895,899
Withdrawn 12/62

45622 NYASALAND

Built Crewe 17/10/34
Named 10/3/36
Renumbered 5622 to 45622 week ending 19/6/48

Photograph Hamish Stevenson.

REPAIRS
17/2/36-10/3/36**HS**
16/7/36-14/8/36**HG**
22/5/37-2/6/37**LO**
19/10/37-11/11/37**LS**
24/6/38-5/8/38**HG**
12/1/39-1/2/39**LO**
16/11/39-6/12/39**HS**
23/7/40-20/8/40**HG**
8/5/42-6/6/42**LS**
18/12/42-27/1/43**HG**
27/11/43-31/12/43**HS**
29/3/44-12/4/44**LO**
6/12/44-17/1/45**HG**
13/10/45-17/11/45**LS**
27/9/46-24/10/46**LS**
29/3/47-16/5/47**LO**
5/4/48-15/6/48**HG**
14/9/48-2/10/48**TRO**
7/4/49-4/5/49**HI**
15/9/49-19/10/49**LC**
11/4/50-4/5/50**HI**
8/8/50-28/8/50**LC**
22/9/50-20/10/50**LC**
9/1/51-8/2/51**HC**
14/9/51-27/10/51**HG**
2/2/52-28/2/52**LC**
11/10/52-8/11/52**HI**
4/9/53-7/10/53**LI**
28/7/54-11/9/54**HG**
22/11/54-11/12/54**LC(EO)**
4/11/55-23/11/55**HI**
2/8/56-13/9/56**HC**
21/12/56-26/1/57**LI**
10/1/58-8/3/58**HG**
22/8/59-9/10/59**HI**
24/7/61-9/9/61**HI** speedo fitted;
AWS probably never fitted

BOILERS
First boiler 8572

No	Fitted	From
9321	29/7/36	New
8627	19/7/38	5597
8758	20/8/40	5558
8610	29/1/43	5607
8570	17/1/45	5649
8739	15/6/48	5561
8610	27/10/51	45631
8570	11/9/54	45568
8735	8/3/58	45660

SHEDS
Crewe North 20/10/34
Bushbury 5/1/35
Leeds 10/2/35
Bristol 16/9/39
Millhouses 11/5/46
Trafford Park 7/12/46
Longsight 15/9/56
Trafford Park 27/10/56
Kentish Town 5/7/58
Trafford Park 20/9/58
Kentish Town 6/12/58
Newton Heath 1/7/61
Kentish Town 15/7/61
Burton 23/3/63
Derby 6/64

TENDERS

No	Fitted
4605	17/10/34

MILEAGES

1934	10,834
1935	83,152
1936	71,103
1937	65,251
1938	67,621
1939	68,104
1940	54,761
1941	56,804
1942	59,859
1943	50,430
1944	64,613
1945	55,518
1946	63,196
1947	47,330
1948	39,963
1949	54,759
1950	46,329
1951	53,237
1952	65,782
1953	55,699
1954	50,856
1955	53,068
1956	52,346
1957	60,281
1958	46,608
1959	50,255
1960	60,726

stored 18/6/62-15/3/63
**Mileage at 31/12/50 959,627; at
31/12/60 1,508,485
Withdrawn week ending 19/9/64**

45623 PALESTINE waiting to leave Platform 7 at Birmingham New Street with the 10.35am Bournemouth West-Manchester Victoria, 3 August 1957. The view, incidentally, is from the cab of Crab 42754. Photograph Michael Mensing.

45623 PALESTINE, settled comfortably amid the ash and clinker deposits at Shrewsbury shed, 1958. Photograph The Transport Treasury.

45623 PALESTINE

Built Crewe 19/10/34
Named 23/12/36
Renumbered 5623 to 45623 week ending 19/6/48

TENDERS

No	Fitted
4606	19/10/34

REPAIRS
8/8/35-9/9/35**LS**
1/5/36-13/5/36**LO**
28/10/36-23/12/36**HG**
1/11/37-15/11/37**LS**
5/9/38-29/9/38**LS**
8/8/39-31/8/39**HG**
24/9/41-11/10/41**LS**
19/3/42-30/4/42**LO**
25/9/43-14/10/43**HG**
16/1/45-20/2/45**LS**
21/8/45-18/10/45**HO**
2/9/46-4/10/46**HG**
21/5/48-17/6/48**HS**
22/10/49-11/11/49**LI**
25/3/51-30/4/51**HG**
18/11/52-11/12/52**LI**
24/5/54-12/6/54**LC(EO)**
4/10/54-11/11/54**HG**
4/6/56-25/6/56**HI**
28/12/57-25/1/58**LI**
27/8/59-2/10/59**HG** AWS fitted; no
record of (probable) speedo fitting
14/7/61-23/8/61**LI**

SHEDS
Crewe North 20/10/34
Leeds 10/2/35
Longsight 25/7/36
Edgehill 25/9/37
Longsight 2/7/38
Rugby 19/11/38
Longsight 9/5/42
Edgehill 20/3/43
Springs Branch 12/1/57
Edge Hill 2/2/57
Crewe North 14/6/58
Longsight 30/4/60
Crewe South 31/12/60
Newton Heath 17/3/62
Loan at first, then
Newton Heath 31/3/62

BOILERS
First boiler 8573

No	Fitted	From
8583	7/12/36	5633
8739	31/8/39	5659
8736	14/10/43	5593
8592	4/10/46	5637
8633	30/4/51	45628
8738	11/11/54	45652
8469	2/10/59	45644

MILEAGES

1934	16,338
1935	60,339
1936	55,742
1937	65,733
1938	54,263
1939	39,950
1940	35,284
1941	37,036
1942	46,123
1943	50,206
1944	43,386
1945	42,572
1946	48,088
1947	56,561
1948	53,571
1949	43,555
1950	51,076
1951	42,707
1952	46,847
1953	52,180
1954	43,967
1955	50,686
1956	48,714
1957	47,855
1958	48,071
1959	45,658
1960	53,726

Mileage at 31/12/50 799,823; at 31/12/60 1,280,234
Withdrawn week ending 25/7/64

45624 ST HELENA

Built Crewe 19/10/34
Named 23/1/36
Renumbered 5624 to 45624 week ending 11/9/48

REPAIRS
1/1/36-23/1/36LS
12/5/36-17/5/36LO
10/11/36-12/12/36HG
22/11/37-9/12/37LS
12/12/38-18/1/39HG
19/4/39-12/5/39LO
10/2/40-28/2/40HS
28/3/41-18/4/41LS
16/4/42-21/5/42HG
29/6/43-24/7/43LS
11/4/45-27/4/45HG
24/10/46-11/11/46LS
3/9/47-3/10/47LO
5/8/48-9/9/48HG
26/3/50-18/4/50LI
21/5/51-22/6/51LI
23/8/52-26/9/52HG
6/10/53-30/10/53HI
14/4/54-18/5/54LC(EO)
10/6/55-6/7/55HG
31/12/56-25/1/57LI
10/3/58-19/4/58HG
9/11/59-18/12/59LI AWS fitted
14/8/61-3/10/61LI speedo fitted

SHEDS
Crewe North 20/10/34
Leeds 10/2/35
Longsight 25/7/36
Edgehill 25/9/37
Camden 1/7/39
Carlisle Upperby 10/1/42
Longsight 12/4/52
Crewe North 22/6/57
Chester (West) 20/9/58
Camden 11/4/59
Willesden 3/10/59
Loan at first, then
Willesden 7/11/59
Camden 2/7/60
Willesden 10/9/60
Camden 19/11/60
Rugby 15/4/61
Nuneaton 4/11/61

TENDERS

No	Fitted
4607	19/10/34

BOILERS
First boiler 8574

No	Fitted	From
8577	30/11/36	5627
8465	18/1/39	5555
8614	21/5/42	5632
8610	27/4/45	5622
8737	9/9/48	5660
8596	26/9/52	45635
8614	6/7/55	45560
8576	19/4/58	45652

MILEAGES

1934	15,262
1935	78,454
1936	60,268
1937	72,471
1938	59,242
1939	57,083
1940	56,457
1941	57,403
1942	38,616
1943	43,760
1944	37,414
1945	42,948
1946	43,150
1947	40,656
1948	44,455
1949	38,247
1950	42,740
1951	43,429
1952	49,082
1953	60,164
1954	56,069
1955	56,742
1956	59,315
1957	53,603
1958	42,261
1959	41,817
1960	52,220

Stored 15/9/63-withdrawal
Mileage at 31/12/50 828,626; at 31/12/60 1,343,328
Withdrawn week ending 23/11/63

45625 SARAWAK in Willesden shed yard, 14 June 1959; on the left is one of the Fowler 2-6-2T 'surface raiders' (they burned so much coal you saw them coming while still over the horizon). Photograph Peter Groom.

45625 SARAWAK

Built Crewe 24/10/34
Named 16/11/36
Renumbered 5625 to 45625 week ending 29/10/49

BOILERS
First Boiler 8575

No	Fitted	From
8559	27/10/36	5609
8625	13/2/39	5612
8623	16/6/41	5654
8738	3/1/44	5563
8601	8/9/45	5653
8562	10/3/48	5601
8578	29/11/52	45611
8758	14/12/56	45611
8585	21/11/58	45571

TENDERS

No	Fitted
4608	24/10/34

REPAIRS
25/11/35-31/12/35**LS**
13/8/36-25/8/36**LO**
6/10/36-16/11/36**HG**
8/1/38-31/1/38**LS**
8/8/38-22/8/38**LO**
2/1/39-13/2/39**HG**
22/4/40-7/5/40**LS**
31/5/41-16/6/41**HG***
28/5/42-3/7/42**HS**
16/12/43-3/1/44**HG**
6/8/45-8/9/45**HS**
2/8/46-7/9/46**HS**
24/1/48-10/3/48**HG**
6/10/49-25/10/49**LI**
12/3/51-6/4/51**HI**
24/10/52-29/11/52**HG**
24/11/53-23/12/53**LI**
28/4/55-26/5/55**HI**
10/11/56-14/12/56**HG**
4/6/57-29/6/57**LC(EO)**
13/10/58-21/11/58**HG**
10/5/60-26/5/60**NC(EO) AWS fitted**
29/11/60-7/1/61**HI speedo fitted**
23/1/61-6/2/61**NC(EO Rect)**
* *'damaged by enemy action at Nuneaton 17/5/41'*

SHEDS
Crewe North 10/11/34
Leeds 10/2/35
Longsight 25/7/36
Camden 23/8/41
Longsight 3/10/42
Camden 30/11/46
Longsight 11/1/47
Willesden 21/6/47
Camden 5/7/52
Willesden 20/9/52
Crewe North 29/1/55
Bushbury 29/10/55
Crewe North 10/12/55
Bushbury 3/8/57
Crewe North 17/8/57
Carnforth 5/5/62

MILEAGES

Year	Mileage
1934	13,701
1935	77,646
1936	62,185
1937	71,581
1938	50,901
1939	69,967
1940	57,720
1941	56,758
1942	63,134
1943	49,842
1944	66,840
1945	59,166
1946	66,393
1947	38,977
1948	42,976
1949	38,237
1950	44,130
1951	43,736
1952	30,141
1953	42,981
1954	54,253
1955	48,947
1956	42,640
1957	51,259
1958	38,142
1959	51,604
1960	37,057

Mileage at 31/12/50 930,154; at 31/12/60 1,370,914
Withdrawn week ending 7/9/63

45626 SEYCHELLES

Built Crewe 9/11/34
Named 9/4/37
Renumbered 5626 to 45626 week ending 5/3/49

REPAIRS
1/10/35-6/11/35**LS**
18/5/36-17/6/36**LO**
25/1/37-9/4/37**HG**
23/10/37-19/11/37**LO**
26/4/38-16/5/38**HS**
16/11/38-1/12/38**LO**
11/2/39-5/4/39**HG**
19/6/40-15/7/40**LS**
2/7/41-13/8/41**HS**
5/4/42-7/5/42**HS**
6/5/43-31/5/43**HS**
5/8/44-19/8/44**HG**
18/3/46-12/4/46**HS**
14/7/47-18/9/47**HG**
24/1/49-4/3/49**LI**
18/2/50-10/3/50**LI**
23/4/51-22/5/51**HG**
18/6/52-23/7/52**LI**
9/9/53-5/10/53**LI**
19/3/55-12/4/55**LI**
26/7/56-8/9/56**HG**
4/2/58-1/3/58**LI**
13/3/58-18/4/58**LC(EO)**
28/9/59-7/11/59**LI**
22/4/61-10/6/61**HG speedo fitted;**
AWS never fitted

BOILERS
First boiler 8576

No	Fitted	From
8761	22/3/37	5663
8564	5/4/39	5650
8577	13/8/41	5649
8630	19/8/44	5599
8636	18/9/47	5629
8620	22/5/51	45647
8757	8/9/56	45566
8468	10/6/61	45583

SHEDS
Longsight 17/11/34
Kentish Town 6/4/35
Millhouses 22/5/37
Derby 25/9/37
Saltley 6/9/41
Millhouses 30/6/45
Leeds 13/8/49
Derby 2/6/51
Burton 18/11/61
Annesley 17/11/62
Burton 1/63
Leeds 2/64

TENDERS

No	Fitted
4609	9/11/34

MILEAGES

Year	Mileage
1934	7,223
1935	70,506
1936	72,387
1937	40,203
1938	62,695
1939	49,519
1940	40,064
1941	39,722
1942	48,884
1943	48,523
1944	39,084
1945	39,376
1946	54,249
1947	34,908
1948	55,422
1949	48,841
1950	65,922
1951	51,925
1952	50,721
1953	47,797
1954	43,591
1955	47,967
1956	38,939
1957	51,815
1958	47,698
1959	45,944
1960	46,463
1961	33,701
1962	45,626
1963	26,680

Mileage at 31/12/50 817,528; at 31/12/60 1,290,388
Withdrawn 10/65

45626 SEYCHELLES at Crewe North, 25 July 1952; note patchwork of new painting on the tender side. Surrounding engines are Black 5s 45145 and 45099. Photograph The Transport Treasury.

This is the down 4.10pm Derby-Manchester Central corridor train (ordinary passenger train headlamp code) behind green 45626 SEYCHELLES, passing through the fine country around Darley Dale, 24 April 1953. Photograph E.D. Bruton.

45627 SIERRA LEONE

Built Crewe 13/11/34
Named 17/4/36
Renumbered 5627 to 45627 week ending 23/10/48

REPAIRS
22/11/35-12/12/35**LS**
23/3/36-17/4/36**LO**
4/6/36-8/6/36**LO**
14/10/36-1/12/36**HG**
3/1/38-17/1/38**LS**
17/8/38-5/10/38**HG**
15/4/40-29/4/40**LS**
16/9/40-30/9/40**LO**
11/4/41-7/5/41**HG**
21/8/42-10/10/42**HS**
1/9/43-9/10/43**HG**
29/3/44-18/4/44**LO**
26/6/44-5/8/44**LO**
4/8/45-25/8/45**HS**
12/1/46-11/3/46**HS**
26/8/46-12/9/46**HG**
7/10/47-15/11/47**LS**
25/8/48-19/10/48**HG**
13/11/49-22/12/49**LI**
31/10/50-8/1/51**HG**
18/2/52-27/3/52**LI**
2/1/53-24/1/53**HI**
1/3/54-30/3/54**HG**
14/4/55-12/5/55**HI**
15/9/55-22/10/55**LC(EO)**
25/7/56-30/8/56**HG**
28/5/57-29/6/57**HI**
12/8/58-17/9/58**HI**
23/5/60-30/6/60**HI speedo fitted;**
AWS never fitted

TENDERS

No	Fitted
4610	13/11/34
4629	16/6/56

SHEDS
Longsight 1/12/34
Kentish Town 6/4/35
Sheffield 29/5/37
Carlisle Upperby 11/9/37
Crewe North 12/2/38
Longsight Loan 17/12/38
Crewe North 8/2/39
Bristol 25/5/40
Loan at first then
Bristol 15/6/40
Trafford Park 29/3/47
Bristol 21/6/47
Kentish Town 1/11/47
Nottingham 19/10/57
Derby 5/7/58
Millhouses 11/9/60
Canklow 1/62
Bank Hall 3/3/62

BOILERS
First boiler 8577

No	Fitted	From
8563	13/11/36	5613
8570	5/10/38	5663
8559	7/5/41	5598
8576	9/10/43	5656
8589	12/9/46	5645
8747	19/10/48	5586
8618	8/1/51	45659
8603	30/3/54	45602
8608	30/8/56	45570
8741	31/3/62	45570

MILEAGES

1934	9,054
1935	67,079
1936	70,872
1937	88,684
1938	49,701*
1939	62,568
1940	46,440
1941	53,863
1942	48,517
1943	66,466
1944	57,882
1945	39,003
1946	55,654
1947	56,293
1948	64,799
1949	48,943
1950	58,463
1951	68,063
1952	66,672
1953	65,568
1954	68,634
1955	64,588
1956	71,998
1957	66,969
1958	57,161
1959	48,676
1960	30,736(to 11/9/60)

*stored serviceable 35 days
stored 10/9/62-18/3/63, 1/11/63-23/12/63,
3/2/64-23/3/64, 26/10/64-9/11/64,
6/9/65-9/4/66
Mileage at 31/12/50 944,281; at
11/9/60 1,553,346
Withdrawn week ending 17/9/66

45628 SOMALILAND

Built Crewe 13/11/34
Named 11/3/36
Renumbered 5628 to 45628 week ending 4/12/48

MILEAGES

1934	1,691
1935	71,937
1936	64,417
1937	67,017
1938	67,712
1939	68,529
1940	47,200
1941	49,713
1942	58,257
1943	67,980
1944	39,224
1945	55,958
1946	30,809
1947	37,894
1948	35,661
1949	51,892
1950	36,123
1951	59,453
1952	53,688
1953	67,306
1954	58,015
1955	51,458
1956	68,208
1957	42,699
1958	47,278
1959	44,359
1960	43,224

stored 9/7/62-withdrawal
Mileage at 31/12/50 852,014; at
31/12/60 1,387,702
Withdrawn week ending 8/12/62

TENDERS

No	Fitted
4611	13/11/34
4613	20/9/35

BOILERS
First boiler 8578

No	Fitted	From
8469	3/3/37	5556
8635	22/8/38	5605
8604	29/6/40	5653
8635	17/4/43	5586
8633	7/12/46	5609
8759	13/1/51	45561
8612	4/3/55	45613
8633	18/12/57	45645

SHEDS
Longsight 1/12/34
Kentish Town 6/4/35
Trafford Park 30/9/39
Longsight 15/9/56
Trafford Park 27/11/56
Kentish Town 5/7/58
Neasden 5/10/59
Kentish Town 21/11/59
Newton Heath 15/7/61
Kentish Town 23/9/61

REPAIRS
29/11/34-19/12/34**LO**
6/2/36-11/3/36**LS**
4/5/36-29/6/36**LO**
14/1/37-17/3/37**HG**
4/1/38-17/2/38**LS**
13/7/38-22/8/38**HG**
14/2/39-10/3/39 **Tender Only**
6/7/39-3/8/39**LS**
10/6/40-29/6/40**HG**
1/5/41-19/6/41**HS**
2/5/42-23/5/42**LS**
3/4/43-17/4/43**HG**
21/3/44-6/4/44**LS**
17/11/44-7/12/44**LO**
16/6/45-27/7/45**HS**
4/11/46-7/12/46**HG**
19/1/48-11/3/48**LS**
16/9/48-1/12/48**HO**
23/6/49-29/7/49**LI**
15/12/49-19/1/50**LC**
9/10/50-13/1/51**HG**
12/3/52-4/4/52**LI**
25/4/53-23/5/53**LI**
24/2/54-17/3/54**LI**
24/1/55-4/3/55**HG**
8/11/55-1/12/55**HI**
10/9/56-6/10/56**HI**
25/1/57-15/2/57**LC(EO)**
22/10/57-18/12/57**HG**
11/8/59-18/9/59**LI**
14/4/61-17/5/61**LI speedo fitted;**
AWS probably never fitted

45629 STRAITS SETTLEMENTS

Built Crewe 10/11/34

Named 2/2/37

Renumbered 5629 to 45629 week ending 6/11/48

TENDERS

No	Fitted
4612	10/11/34
4611	4/6/59
9690	16/5/64

REPAIRS
```
  ?    -24/1/36TRO
6/6/36-27/6/36LO
16/12/36-2/2/37HG
24/5/38-6/6/38LS
3/4/39-28/4/39HG
27/9/40-21/10/40LS
31/10/41-28/11/41HG
27/7/42-15/8/42LS
11/2/43-9/4/43LO
5/6/43-3/7/43LO
16/8/43-15/9/43LS
16/5/44-31/5/44LS
26/12/44-26/1/45HG
2/11/45-13/12/45HS
15/11/46-14/12/46LS
28/4/47-24/6/47HG
6/2/48-6/3/48LO
5/10/48-4/11/48LS
3/10/49-1/12/49HG
29/8/50-29/9/50LI
26/3/51-2/5/51LI
31/12/51-2/2/52LI
6/12/52-1/1/53HI
5/10/53-26/10/53HI
6/11/54-11/12/54HG
10/2/55-26/2/55LC(EO)
5/1/56-2/2/56HI
3/9/56-16/10/56LC(EO)
26/10/57-23/11/57LI
24/4/59-4/6/59HG AWS fitted
20/2/61-20/3/61LI speedo fitted
```

BOILERS
First boiler 8579

No	Fitted	From
8582	15/1/37	5632
8558	28/4/39	5618
8760	28/11/41	5630
8636	26/1/45	5652
8575	24/6/47	5638
8583	1/12/49	45589
8591	11/12/54	45564
8563	4/6/59	45632

SHEDS
```
Longsight 1/12/34
Derby 30/3/35
Rugby 11/9/37
Bristol18/11/39
Loan at first then
Bristol 9/12/39
Trafford Park 11/10/47
Longsight 10/11/56
Crewe North 14/6/58
Carnforth 5/5/62
Carlisle Kingmoor 22/6/63
```

MILEAGES

Year	Miles
1934	2,523
1935	66,575
1936	48,670
1937	56,893
1938	49,915
1939	47,140
1940	50,779
1941	41,775
1942	46,807
1943	45,192
1944	60,769
1945	58,935
1946	63,490
1947	43,440
1948	47,686
1949	49,010
1950	66,566
1951	50,525
1952	59,262
1953	57,018
1954	47,847
1955	58,657
1956	48,375
1957	49,348
1958	57,569
1959	48,033
1960	43,427

stored 21-11-64-unrecorded date
AWS fitted; speedo not fitted
Mileage at 31/12/50 846,165; at
31/12/60 1,366,226
Withdrawn week ending 1/5/65

STRAITS SETTLEMENTS at the dawn of the 1960s, carrying The Waverley headboard (i.e. St Pancras-Edinburgh Waverley) and Crewe North shedplate on 11 April 1960. AWS fitted but no speedometer; flexible hose connection visible on pipe running down from vacuum ejector. The location is not given but the best educated guess is Holbeck. A3 Pacifics took over this sort of work later in 1960. Photograph W. Hermiston, The Transport Treasury.

45630 SWAZILAND running off Dillicar troughs, south of Tebay, with an up 'special class H' freight on 26 May 1952. It was running at about 30mph, Eric Bruton recalls, at 12.18pm with the sun just breaking through the low cloud. Note longitudinal sleepers running the length of the troughs, to save ballast being washed away by the splash. A fading BRITISH RAILWAYS just visible on the tender. Photograph E.D. Bruton.

45630 SWAZILAND

Built Crewe 13/11/34
Named 1/4/36
Renumbered 5630 to 45630 week ending 3/7/48

TENDERS

No	Fitted
4613	13/11/34
4611	20/9/35
4612	11/6/59

BOILERS
First boiler 8580

No	Fitted	From
8738	22/10/36	5640
8760	6/12/38	5637
8625	25/7/41	5625
8588	20/3/44	5650
8573	15/12/45	5578
8619	18/2/49	5559
8602	12/9/53	45578
8762	7/9/57	45649

MILEAGES

1934	9,902
1935	62,399
1936	52,993
1937	61,857
1938	54,792
1939	64,808
1940	51,438
1941	40,463
1942	42,716
1943	42,592
1944	43,896
1945	34,465
1946	53,223
1947	44,739
1948	31,768
1949	47,763
1950	41,909
1951	53,996
1952	52,263
1953	45,392
1954	52,564
1955	45,108
1956	56,281
1957	46,511
1958	46,200
1959	33,417
1960	46,815
1961	19,414

**Mileage at 31/12/50 781,723;
at 31/12/60 1,260,270
Withdrawn (accident damage)
week ending 18/11/61**

REPAIRS
10/3/36-1/4/36**LS**
2/10/36-12/11/36**HG**
29/11/37-20/12/37**HS**
1/11/38-6/12/38**HG**
6/2/40-21/2/40**LS**
19/6/41-25/7/41**HG**
8/3/43-23/3/43**HS**
16/6/43-24/7/43**LO**
2/3/44-20/3/44**HG**
28/11/45-15/12/45**HS**
30/12/46-13/1/47**LS**
28/8/47-22/9/47**LO**
8/1/48-31/1/48**LS**
18/5/48-29/6/48**LO**
2/11/48-18/2/49**HG**
21/9/50-11/10/50**HI**
5/2/52-5/3/52**HI**
6/8/53-12/9/53**HG**
21/9/53-28/9/53**NC(EO)**
19/8/55-22/9/55**LI**
22/9/55-11/10/55**NC(EO Rect)**
4/8/57-7/9/57**HG**
27/8/58-3/10/58**LC(EO)**
20/12/58-11/6/59**HI AWS fitted**
4/8/60-17/9/60**LI speedo fitted**
27/6/61-22/8/61**HI**

SHEDS
Crewe North 1/12/34
Sheffield 10/2/35
Leeds 27/2/37
Sheffield 29/5/37
Carlisle Upperby 11/9/37
Edgehill 25/9/37
Longsight (loan) 21/11/42
Edge Hill 20/3/43
Crewe North 30/11/46
Carlisle Upperby 19/2/49
Preston 5/7/52
Carlisle Upperby 20/9/52
Crewe North 29/1/55
Edge Hill 19/4/58
Crewe North 26/4/58

45631 TANGANYIKA

Built Crewe 14/11/34
Named 29/1/36
Renumbered 5631 to 45631 week ending 13/11/48

REPAIRS
27/12/35-21/1/36**LS**
23/7/36-7/8/36**LO**
12/10/36-4/12/36**HG**
5/11/37-23/11/37**HG**
6/12/38-23/1/39**HG**
16/4/40-1/5/40**LS**
9/2/42-28/2/42**HS**
1/12/42-19/12/42**HG**
26/5/44-10/6/44**HS**
11/1/46-16/2/46**HS**
16/8/46-10/9/46**LO**
2/10/46-5/11/46**LO**
15/9/47-14/10/47**LS**
24/8/48-9/11/48**HG**
23/3/50-13/4/50**LI**
18/9/50-9/10/50**LC**
13/10/50-25/10/50**NC(Rect)**
16/8/51-19/9/51**HS**
7/3/53-2/4/53**LI**
23/4/54-24/5/54**HI**
6/12/55-4/2/56**HG**
17/6/57-14/8/57**HG**
26/1/59-25/2/59**LI** AWS fitted
2/3/59-14/3/59**NC(EO Rect)**
19/4/60-3/6/60**LI** speedo fitted

TENDERS
No	Fitted
4614	14/11/34

SHEDS
Crewe North 24/11/34
Llandudno Jct 2/3/35
Crewe North 1/6/35
Kentish Town 21/11/35
Crewe North 11/9/37
Patricroft 18/6/38
Carlisle Upperby 16/9/39
Farnley Jct 19/8/44
Loan at first then
Farnley Jct 30/9/44
Longsight 9/12/44
Loan at first then
Longsight 13/1/45
Carlisle Upperby 21/6/47
Longsight 28/6/47
Crewe North 10/6/61
Saltley 9/3/63

BOILERS
First boiler 8581

No	Fitted	From
8580	23/11/36	5630
8591	23/1/39	5610
8605	19/12/42	5648
8627	10/6/44	5654
8610	9/11/48	5624
8592	19/9/51	45623
8571	4/2/56	45580
8588	14/8/57	45595

MILEAGES
1934	7,786
1935	70,683
1936	65,167
1937	84,788*
1938	36,358*
1939	53,071
1940	43,424
1941	37,063
1942	33,646
1943	46,699
1944	43,143
1945	44,944
1946	51,631
1947	45,359
1948	41,482
1949	55,494
1950	51,314
1951	58,058
1952	61,866
1953	55,981
1954	51,789
1955	48,067
1956	57,206
1957	50,674
1958	57,472
1959	51,562
1960	47,653

*1937 stored serviceable 11 days
*1938 stored serviceable 80 days
stored 18/9/62-1/3/63
**Mileage at 31/12/50 812,052; at
31/12/60 1,352,380
Withdrawn week ending 22/8/64
after 'paper'
transfer to Crewe North 8/64**

45632 TONGA

Built Crewe 14/11/34
Named 17/2/36
Renumbered 5632 to 45632 week ending 7/5/49

MILEAGES
1934	6,679
1935	59,290
1936	49,557
1937	68,244
1938	52,050
1939	53,640
1940	48,145
1941	47,822
1942	55,517
1943	48,628
1944	52,916
1945	51,981
1946	63,443
1947	36,289
1948	42,274
1949	41,591
1950	54,304
1951	52,699
1952	60,827
1953	56,161
1954	53,607
1955	49,492
1956	53,435
1957	54,536
1958	48,497
1959	44,833
1960	43,260

**Mileage at 31/12/50 832,370; at
31/12/60 1,349,717
Withdrawn week ending 9/10/65**

SHEDS
Crewe North 24/11/34
Bangor 5/1/35
Crewe North 1/6/35
Kentish Town 21/11/35
Crewe North 11/9/37
Preston 1/1/38
Patricroft 11/3/39
Crewe North 16/9/39
Longsight 18/7/42
Crewe North 5/4/47
Longsight 29/4/50
Chester (West) 21/6/58
Camden 11/4/59
Carnforth 2/1/60
Carlisle Upperby 10/4/61
Stockport 21/7/62
Newton Heath 8/65

TENDERS
No	Fitted
4615	14/11/34
9149	9/4/64

BOILERS
First boiler 8582

No	Fitted	From
8585	6/1/37	5635
8614	13/9/38	5584
8594	8/4/42	5568
8605	16/9/44	5631
8467	20/8/47	5598
8598	29/10/51	45656
8563	19/4/56	45647
8560	21/2/59	45566

REPAIRS
13/1/36-17/2/36**HS**
29/8/36-21/1/37**HG**
9/9/37-28/10/37**LS**
16/8/38-13/9/38**HG**
23/2/40-9/3/40**HS**
7/3/42-8/4/42**HG**
31/3/43-16/4/43**LS**
29/5/43-10/6/43**TRO**
6/1/44-10/2/44**HS**
29/8/44-16/9/44**HG**
31/12/45-30/1/46**HS**
26/6/47-20/8/47**HG**
12/4/49-6/5/49**HI**
12/12/49-5/1/50**LC**
21/8/50-11/9/50**LI**
20/9/51-29/10/51**HG**
10/1/52-26/1/52**LC**
6/5/53-29/5/53**HI**
6/6/54-1/7/54**LI**
27/2/56-19/4/56**HG**
16/9/57-11/10/57**HI**
23/1/59-21/2/59**HG** AWS fitted
27/8/60-30/9/60**LI** speedo fitted

45633 ADEN
Built Crewe 21/11/34
Named TRANS-JORDAN 1936
Renamed ADEN 4/9/46
Renumbered 5633 to 45633 week ending 18/12/48

TENDERS

No	Fitted
4616	21/11/34

REPAIRS
27/2/36-23/3/36LS
30/3/36-4/5/36LO
22/9/36-25/11/36HG
7/9/38-30/9/38LS
21/12/38-25/1/39LO
3/10/39-18/11/39HG
24/9/41-17/10/41LS
21/8/43-14/9/43HG
3/11/43-15/12/43LO
17/1/45-27/2/45HS
14/1/46-31/1/46LS
21/7/47-2/10/47HG
29/11/48-17/12/48LS
13/2/50-8/3/50LI
27/3/50-21/4/50LC
17/5/51-16/6/51HG
11/3/52-12/3/52 **Weighing at Horwich**
3/7/52-16/8/52LI
29/10/53-1/12/53HG
24/3/55-19/5/55HG
21/5/56-12/6/56LI
27/7/57-24/8/57LI
22/11/58-15/1/59HI **AWS fitted**
19/3/60-4/5/60HG **speedo fitted**

SHEDS
Crewe North 24/11/34
Carlisle Upperby 5/1/35
Crewe North 2/3/35
Derby 21/11/35
Rugby 11/9/37
Camden 2/5/42
Longsight 3/10/42
Preston 3/11/51
Carnforth 9/9/61
Derby 9/3/63
Warrington 20/7/63

BOILERS
First boiler 8583

No	Fitted	From
8572	6/11/36	5622
8583	3/10/39	5623
8600	14/9/43	5588
8760	27/2/45	5629
8568	2/10/47	5588
8576	16/6/51	45565
8580	1/12/53	45654
8740	19/5/55	45606
8738	4/5/60	45623

MILEAGES

1934	7,523
1935	67,002*
1936	40,705
1937	61,563
1938	41,176
1939	37,840
1940	35,067
1941	36,948
1942	52,258
1943	38,893
1944	67,675
1945	56,225
1946	53,041
1947	38,349
1948	56,405
1949	60,596
1950	51,057
1951	55,208
1952	54,912
1953	53,093
1954	62,266
1955	46,884
1956	54,971
1957	47,244
1958	45,625
1959	47,853
1960	36,264

*stored serviceable 18 days
stored 5/12/64-16/10/65
Mileage at 31/12/50 802,323; at 31/12/60 1,306,643
Withdrawn week ending 16/10/65

Longsight's 45633 ADEN has just left Northchurch tunnel at about 50mph with the up 12.05pm Manchester London Road-Euston express, 2 September 1950. Tender still clearly lettered LMS – faint reminders of lining betray the livery as 1946 black. Photograph E.D. Bruton.

45634 TRINIDAD

Built Crewe 22/11/34
Named 16/5/36
Renumbered 5634 to 45634 week ending 17/12/49

TENDERS

No	Fitted
4617	22/11/34

BOILERS
First boiler 8584

No	Fitted	From
8573	24/12/36	5623
8737	8/5/39	5619
8598	25/4/44	5661
8630	20/11/47	5626
8631	29/11/51	45650
8607	3/2/55	45604
8635	14/12/57	45559

REPAIRS
5/5/36-26/5/36**LS**
14/11/36-11/1/37**HG**
23/3/38-11/4/38**LS**
14/4/39-8/5/39**HG**
14/4/41-2/5/41**LS**
9/12/42-30/12/42**LS**
26/6/43-3/7/43**LO**
29/3/44-25/4/44**HG**
27/7/45-25/8/45**LS**
23/10/46-7/11/46**LS**
30/9/47-20/11/47**HG**
24/11/49-15/12/49**LI**
10/10/51-29/11/51**HG**
1/12/51-4/12/51**NC (Rect)**
26/8/53-23/9/53**LI**
14/10/53-19/10/53**NC(EO Rect)**
1/1/55-3/2/55**HG**
11/8/56-1/9/56**LI**
31/10/57-14/12/57**HG**
27/6/58-1/8/58**LC(EO)**
25/9/59-9/11/59**HI AWS fitted**
31/8/61-12/10/61**LI speedo fitted**

SHEDS
Crewe North 24/11/34
Rugby 19/1/35
Crewe North 2/3/35
Derby 21/11/35
Rugby 11/9/37
Camden 2/5/42
Longsight 3/10/42
Edge Hill 25/1/47
Crewe North 2/10/48
Longsight 29/4/50
Crewe North 10/6/50
Camden 27/2/54
Willesden 25/9/54
Crewe North 29/1/55
Bushbury 31/12/55
Crewe North 10/3/56
Bushbury 9/3/57
Crewe North 6/4/57
Willesden 3/12/60
Crewe South 7/1/61

MILEAGES

1934	5,762
1935	66,133*
1936	41,524
1937	57,240
1938	44,756
1939	44,168
1940	31,858
1941	41,915
1942	39,123
1943	55,779
1944	57,979
1945	63,402
1946	64,581
1947	41,385
1948	57,303
1949	44,238
1950	53,205
1951	31,877
1952	56,474
1953	42,348
1954	53,883
1955	50,928
1956	52,280
1957	49,028
1958	50,186
1959	45,781
1960	54,706

*stored serviceable 36 days
**Mileage at 31/12/50 810,351; at
31/12/60 1,297,842**
Withdrawn week ending 11/5/63

45635 TOBAGO

Built Crewe 24/11/34
Named 12/6/36
Renumbered 5635 to 45635 week ending 28/5/49

TENDERS

No	Fitted
4618	24/11/34
9763	16/1/63

REPAIRS
5/3/36-16/3/36**LO**
20/3/36-31/3/36**LO**
21/5/36-19/6/36**LS**
16/10/36-29/12/36**HG**
4/1/38-25/1/38**HS**
23/2/39-11/4/39**HG**
6/9/40-19/9/40**LS**
24/7/41-16/8/41**HG**
6/12/41-27/12/41**LO**
7/7/42-26/8/42**LS**
31/1/44-8/3/44**HG**
13/3/44-28/3/44**LO**
8/5/45-31/5/45**HS**
30/11/46-27/12/46**HS**
10/12/47-17/1/48**HG**
2/5/49-28/5/49**H**
13/10/50-8/11/50**LI**
6/5/52-17/6/52**HG**
24/6/52-26/7/52**LC(EO)**
4/12/53-8/1/54**LI**
25/5/55-18/6/55**LI**
13/6/56-31/7/56**HG**
2/1/58-29/1/58**HI**
24/11/58-31/1/59**HI**
11/7/60-19/8/60**HI speedo fitted**
3/10/61-16/10/61**NC(EO) AWS fitted**

SHEDS
Crewe North 24/11/34
Rugby 19/1/35
Crewe North 2/3/35
Derby 21/11/35
Edge Hill 11/9/37
Longsight 1/7/39
Crewe North 16/9/39
Longsight 18/7/42
Newton Heath 2/1/43
Loan at first then
Newton Heath 16/1/43
Carlisle Kingmoor 8/2/64

BOILERS
First boiler 8585

No	Fitted	From
8736	14/12/36	5638
8593	11/4/39	5649
8607	16/8/41	5562
8624	8/3/44	5604
8584	31/5/45	5591
8596	17/1/48	5616
8584	17/6/52	45606
8621	31/7/56	45658

MILEAGES

1934	7,176
1935	65,245*
1936	41,538
1937	61,816
1938	62,581
1939	51,818
1940	50,743
1941	48,839
1942	49,488
1943	43,748
1944	43,027
1945	43,174
1946	37,320
1947	49,288
1948	56,342
1949	48,233
1950	46,211
1951	49,156
1952	39,713
1953	40,908
1954	50,117
1955	43,702
1956	47,501
1957	57,584
1958	42,438
1959	53,165
1960	39,417

*stored serviceable 26 days
**Mileage at 31/12/50 806,087; at
31/12/60 1,269,788**
Withdrawn week ending 12/9/64

45636 UGANDA

Built Crewe 18/12/34
Named 22/4/36
Renumbered 5636 to 45636 week ending 5/2/49

TENDERS

No	Fitted
4624	18/12/34

REPAIRS
3/4/36-22/4/36**LS**
15/12/36-28/12/36**LO**
5/2/37-5/4/37**HG**
11/6/38-29/6/38**LS**
24/8/39-6/10/39**HS**
18/1/40-16/2/40**HO**
24/2/41-3/4/41**LS**
17/1/42-28/2/42**HG**
19/6/43-14/7/43**LS**
23/10/44-11/11/44**HS**
21/5/45-21/6/45**LO**
5/5/46-22/5/46**HG**
5/7/47-11/7/47**TRO Nottingham**
13/10/47-6/12/47**LS**
22/12/48-3/2/49**HG**
7/2/49-18/2/49**NC**
10/10/49-24/10/49**TRO Nottingham**
17/4/50-22/5/50**LI**
17/5/51-8/6/51**HI**
18/8/52-17/9/52**LI**
17/3/53-24/4/53**HG**
27/1/54-23/2/54**HI**
19/1/55-15/2/55**LI**
5/9/55-10/9/55**LC(EO) Nottingham**
6/3/56-24/4/56**HG**
29/12/56-1/2/57**LC(EO)**
28/1/58-15/3/58**HG**
20/4/59-27/5/59**LI**
12/11/60-16/12/60**LI speedo fitted;**
AWS never fitted

BOILERS
First boiler 8586

No	Fitted	From
8569	16/3/37	5619
8735	16/2/40	5638
8608	28/2/42	5618
8756	22/5/46	5615
8752	3/2/49	45653
8741	24/4/53	45612
8590	24/4/56	45643
8744	15/3/58	45659

SHEDS
Crewe North 29/12/34
Carlisle Upperby 6/4/35
Carlisle Kingmoor 22/2/36
Leeds (loan) 21/5/38
Carlisle Kingmoor 11/6/38
Perth (loan) 9/7/38
Carlisle Kingmoor 29/10/38
Leeds 28/9/40
Loan at first then
Leeds 26/10/40
Derby 13/6/42
Nottingham 12/10/46
Leeds 24/9/55
Nottingham 1/10/55
Leicester 23/1/60
Newton Heath 1/7/61
Leicester 23/9/61
Burton 18/11/61

MILEAGES

1934	1,025
1935	76,392
1936	70,593
1937	67,057
1938	63,096
1939	53,802
1940	51,611
1941	65,915
1942	54,637
1943	51,969
1944	41,593
1945	45,885
1946	42,443
1947	35,105
1948	50,405
1949	42,470
1950	45,003
1951	38,994
1952	49,592
1953	59,133
1954	67,072
1955	56,127
1956	60,400
1957	65,805
1958	56,658
1959	54,420
1960	46,846
1961	41,336
1962	26,937

**Mileage at 31/12/50 859,001; at
31/12/60 1,414,048;
at 8/12/62 1,482,321
Withdrawn week ending 8/12/62**

45636 UGANDA at speed with the down Waverley, on Melton troughs 8 September 1959. The lovely Jubilee proportions are perfectly presented. Photograph Peter Groom.

45637 WINDWARD ISLANDS

Built Crewe 19/12/34
Named 27/3/36
Renumbered 5637 to 45637 week ending 4/9/48

TENDERS

No	Fitted
4625	19/12/34
9689	25/1/52

REPAIRS

2/12/35-30/12/35**LS**
3/10/36-18/11/36**HG**
31/8/37-21/9/37**LS**
11/1/38-10/2/38**LO**
27/9/38-28/10/38**HG**
5/1/40-20/1/40**HS**
22/4/41-6/5/41**LS**
15/4/42-16/5/42**LO**
14/4/43-15/5/43**HG**
31/5/43-12/6/43**LO**
2/6/44-20/6/44**HS**
23/5/45-17/7/45**LS**
18/7/46-3/9/46**HG**
13/11/47-16/12/47**HS**
27/7/48-2/9/48**LO**
1/8/49-7/9/49**HG**
24/12/49-19/1/50**LO**
9/3/51-31/3/51**LI**
16/1/52-5/3/52**HG**
6/8/52-6/9/52**LC(EO)**
AWS, speedo, never fitted

SHEDS

Crewe North 29/12/34
Rugby 19/1/35
Crewe North 30/3/35
Millhouses 21/11/35
Kentish Town 27/2/37
Preston 11/9/37
Patricroft 11/3/39
Carlisle Upperby 6/12/41
Crewe North 5/6/43
Edge Hill 19/6/48

BOILERS

First boiler 8735

No	Fitted	From
8760	2/11/36	5662
8571	28/10/38	5609
8597	15/5/43	5594
8592	20/6/44	5659
8578	3/9/46	5613
8756	7/9/49	45636
8630	5/3/52	45634

MILEAGES

1934	604
1935	57,557*
1936	48,429
1937	75,126
1938	57,966
1939	53,760
1940	56,738
1941	46,320
1942	34,047
1943	48,769
1944	51,556
1945	51,345
1946	43,259
1947	48,668
1948	44,108
1949	44,321
1950	55,096
1951	50,019
1952	30,602

*stored serviceable 36 days
Mileage at 31/12/50 817,069
Withdrawn week ending 13/12/52
(Destroyed in Harrow Accident)

The lost Jubilee. Edge Hill's 45637 WINDWARD ISLANDS (and there weren't that many 8A Jubilees) at the north end of Camden shed in 1952; vacuum bracket still on crosshead, a 'semi' cut-down smokebox Pacific stands behind. 45637, of course, was ruined in the Harrow disaster of October 1952 and partly cut up so that it could be hauled away. Photograph The Transport Treasury.

45638 ZANZIBAR

Built Crewe 19/12/34
Named 14/4/36
Renumbered 5638 to 45638 week ending 3/7/48

TENDERS

No	Fitted
4626	19/12/34

REPAIRS
28/3/36-14/4/36**LS**
22/10/36-12/12/36**HG**
12/5/38-13/6/38**LS**
29/1/39-8/3/39**HG**
3/11/39-23/11/39**HS**
16/8/41-30/8/41**LS**
22/10/41-7/11/41**LO**
19/8/42-19/9/42**HG**
8/5/43-25/5/43**HS**
22/8/44-9/9/44**HS**
15/11/45-14/12/45**LS**
3/3/47-17/4/47**HG**
3/6/48-3/7/48**HS**
19/7/48-24/7/48**NC(Rect)**
3/8/49-20/8/49**LI**
23/1/50-8/3/50**HG**
17/2/51-8/3/51**LI**
2/10/51-23/11/51**HI**
28/7/52-28/8/52**LC**
16/3/53-11/4/53**HI**
7/4/54-1/5/54**LI**
16/8/55-20/9/55**HG**
16/3/57-10/4/57**HI**
13/6/58-3/7/58**LI**
14/10/59-24/11/59**HI AWS fitted**
21/12/60-3/2/61**HG speedo fitted**

SHEDS
Crewe North 29/12/34
Derby 6/4/35
Preston 11/9/37
Crewe North 1/1/38
Carlisle Upperby 8/1/38
Crewe North 12/2/38
Longsight (loan) 5/3/38
Crewe North 2/4/38
Longsight 18/7/42
Edge Hill (loan) 21/11/42
Longsight 20/3/43
Llandudno Jct 10/9/60
Crewe North 10/6/61
Preston 16/9/61
Warrington 21/10/61

BOILERS
First boiler 8736

No	Fitted	From
8735	30/11/36	5637
8580	8/3/39	5631
8745	19/9/42	5596
8575	9/9/44	5614
8468	17/4/47	5565
8761	8/3/50	45609
8754	20/9/55	45558
8753	3/2/61	45591

MILEAGES

1934	536
1935	69,196
1936	46,682
1937	65,729
1938	67,426
1939	51,324
1940	53,887
1941	47,025
1942	52,815
1943	63,337
1944	57,186
1945	57,284
1946	68,737
1947	47,301
1948	52,315
1949	58,116
1950	56,380
1951	50,168
1952	57,818
1953	59,187
1954	58,643
1955	55,260
1956	56,737
1957	58,678
1958	50,662
1959	56,038
1960	55,509

Mileage at 31/12/50 915,276; at 31/12/60 1,473,976
Withdrawn week ending 14/3/64

45639 RALEIGH

Built Crewe 28/12/34
Named 12/6/36
Renumbered 5639 to 45639 week ending 31/7/48

TENDERS

No	Fitted
4627	28/12/34
9780	16/1/44

SHEDS
Crewe North 29/12/34
Preston 4/5/35
Millhouses 21/11/35
Kentish Town 1/10/38
Derby 20/9/47
Trafford Park (loan) 25/9/48
Derby 4/12/48
Kentish Town (loan) 17/9/49
Derby 15/10/49
Bristol (loan) 29/10/49
Derby 12/11/49
Leeds 2/6/51
Nottingham (loan) 2/6/51
Leeds 7/7/51

BOILERS
First boiler 8737

No	Fitted	From
9259	8/3/37	5699
9322	8/6/39	5702
9217	20/6/42	5697
9318	26/6/43	5691
9315	29/4/46	5727
9258	14/3/51	45706
9197	14/8/54	45740
9224	17/1/58	45686

MILEAGES

1934	40
1935	56,142
1936	52,560
1937	55,761
1938	68,127
1939	70,588
1940	55,526
1941	54,231
1942	63,708
1943	67,665
1944	66,255
1945	54,406
1946	52,356
1947	34,516
1948	47,992
1949	37,609
1950	51,030
1951	53,754
1952	56,630
1953	58,240
1954	66,371
1955	66,717
1956	60,144
1957	70,768

Mileage at 31/12/50 888,512
Withdrawn 9/63

REPAIRS
13/3/35-15/4/35**LO**
2/6/36-19/6/36**LS**
9/1/37-19/3/37**HG**
4/5/38-17/6/38**LS**
10/4/39-8/6/39**HG**
4/4/40-30/4/40**LS**
30/1/41-28/2/41**LS**
21/8/41-8/10/41**LO**
4/5/42-20/6/42**HG**
28/5/43-26/6/43**HS**
18/1/44-26/1/44**TRO**
6/5/44-25/5/44**HS**
30/3/45-28/4/45**LS**
25/3/46-29/4/46**HG**
3/6/47-6/8/47**LS**
7/6/48-29/7/48**HS**
19/11/49-28/12/49**LI**
10/5/50-13/6/50**LC**
14/6/50-23/6/50**NC(Rect)**
16/1/51-14/3/51**HG**
11/8/52-6/9/52**HI**
19/6/53-3/8/53**LI**
10/7/54-14/8/54**HG**
4/11/55-28/11/55**LI**
19/4/56-18/5/56**LC(EO)**
25/10/56-29/11/56**HI**
14/12/57-17/1/58**HG**
?   -8/2/58**NC(EO)**
22/11/58-24/12/58**HI**
8/2/60-24/3/60**LI**
21/11/60-13/1/61**LC(EO)**
No dates given; speedo probably fitted. AWS probably not

45639 RALEIGH at Kentish Town shed, beneath the familiar cathedral-like bottling stores. Photograph Peter Groom.

45640 FROBISHER

Built Crewe 31/12/34
Named 16/3/36
Renumbered 5640 to 45640 5/48

TENDERS

No	Fitted
4628	31/12/34
10783	7/1/53
9819	31/1/53
9838	19/4/58

REPAIRS

7/2/36-16/3/36**LS**
10/8/36-11/9/36**HG**
12/11/37-27/11/37**LO**
13/6/38-12/7/38**LO**
4/10/38-22/11/38**HG**
1/11/39-18/11/39**LS**
17/3/41-27/5/41**HG**
19/2/42-26/3/42**LS**
18/1/43-20/2/43**HS**
12/1/44-29/1/44**HG**
6/12/44-30/12/44**LS**
3/1/46-23/1/46**LS**
31/5/46-18/7/46**HG**
7/3/47-6/6/47**HS**
12/4/48-24/5/48**LO**
12/6/48-3/7/48**LO**
17/11/48-26/1/49**HG**
22/3/48-17/4/50**LI**
17/11/48-26/1/49**HG**
22/3/50-17/4/50**LI**
29/5/51-25/6/51**LI**
5/1/53-31/1/53**HI St Rollox**
25/6/54-14/8/54**G**
31/7/56-30/8/56**HI St Rollox**
20/3/58-19/4/58**G St Rollox**
9/5/59-29/5/59**LI St Rollox**
31/3/60-16/4/60**LC(EO) St Rollox**
9/9/60-14/10/60**HI St Rollox**
**Speedo fitted by 7/63; no
record of AWS**

SHEDS

Crewe North 29/12/34
Millhouses 21/11/35
Kentish Town 6/2/37
Derby 23/9/39
Nottingham 12/10/46
Carlisle Kingmoor 13/8/52
Loan at first then
Carlisle Kingmoor 30/8/52

BOILERS

First boiler 8738

No	Fitted	From
9327	22/11/38	5707
9338	27/5/41	5699
10038	29/1/44	5725
9326	26/1/49	5695
9343	14/8/54	45672
9322	19/4/58	-

MILEAGES

1934	-
1935	62,810
1936	57,049
1937	76,085
1938	74,112
1939	80,152
1940	52,735
1941	42,510
1942	50,375
1943	54,779
1944	42,577
1945	42,297
1946	38,367
1947	28,580
1948	25,033
1949	46,368
1950	43,812
1951	45,160
1952	38,639
1953	58,183
1954	50,928
1955	60,063
1956	59,815
1957	59,899
1958	53,960
1959	56,482
1960	43,528

Stored 19/11/62-4/3/63 (serviceable);
4/3/63-withdrawal (unserviceable)
**Mileage at 31/12/50 817,641; at 31/12/60
1,344,298**
Withdrawn week ending 7/3/64

45641 SANDWICH

Built Crewe 31/12/34

Named 5/5/36

Renumbered 5641 to 45641 week ending 18/9/48

TENDERS

No	Fitted
4629	31/12/34
4610	16/6/56

MILEAGES

Year	Mileage
1934	76
1935	72,961
1936	73,105
1937	72,213
1938	78,288
1939	56,939
1940	42,552
1941	46,906
1942	52,627
1943	62,561
1944	52,157
1945	38,554
1946	58,536
1947	54,025
1948	63,207
1949	54,552
1950	62,974
1951	68,762
1952	51,586
1953	50,919
1954	67,816
1955	60,797
1956	56,700
1957	51,089
1958	60,005
1959	60,340
1960	45,952

Mileage at 31/12/50 942,233; at 31/12/60 1,516,199

Withdrawn week ending 19/9/64

BOILERS

First boiler 8739

No	Fitted	From
8579	21/4/37	5629
8746	11/4/38	5653
8747	5/10/39	5585
8603	12/12/41	5591
8580	7/2/46	5611
8570	14/9/48	5622
8611	23/10/50	45556
8759	23/4/55	45628
8561	3/10/57	45572
8754	21/7/61	45638

SHEDS

Crewe North 29/12/34
Preston 4/5/35
Bristol 21/11/35
Kentish Town 7/3/36
Derby 28/10/39
Sheffield Grimesthorpe 2/3/40
Millhouses 6/9/41
Saltley 30/6/45
Bristol 24/11/45
Kentish Town 1/11/47
Nottingham 19/10/57
Burton 18/11/61

REPAIRS

13/4/36-5/5/36**LS**
22/2/37-6/5/37**HG**
27/12/37-28/1/38**HS**
7/3/38-20/4/38**HO**
19/9/38-14/10/38**LO**
7/2/39-4/3/39**HS**
28/8/39-5/10/39**HG**
8/11/40-22/11/40**LS**
11/12/40-6/1/41**LO**
25/4/41-5/6/41**LO**
2/1/42-12/2/42**HG**
24/11/42-26/12/42**LS**
6/4/43-1/5/43**LO**
16/3/44-5/4/44**HS**
5/5/45-29/5/45**LO**
7/12/45-7/2/46**HG**
25/1/47-4/3/47**LS**
3/11/47-12/12/47**LS**
12/8/48-14/9/48**HG**
6/9/49-30/9/49**LI**
17/10/49-14/11/49**NO(Rect)**
29/8/50-23/10/50**HG**
11/4/51-16/5/51**LC**
3/3/52-28/3/52**HI**
27/9/52-8/11/52**LI**
10/11/52-15/11/52**NC (EO Rect)**
27/11/52-2/1/53**LC(EO)**
19/11/53-18/12/53**HI**
14/3/55-23/4/55**HG**
21/4/56-30/5/56**LI**
8/8/56-20/9/56**HC(EO)**
25/8/57-3/10/57**HG**
11/10/57-14/10/57**NC (EO Rect)**
30/12/58-29/1/59**LI**
2/4/60-20/5/60**LI speedo fitted**
2/6/61-21/7/61**HG**
AWS probably never fitted

Kentish Town's 5641 SANDWICH in wholly indeterminate livery, at Dore in 1947. Photograph The Transport Treasury.

45642 BOSCAWEN

Built Crewe 10/5/34 as 5552
Named SILVER JUBILEE April 1935
Renumbered 5552 to 5642 29/4/35 without name
Named BOSCAWEN 3/4/36
Renumbered 5642 to 45642 week ending 29/5/48

TENDERS

No	Fitted
4559	10/5/34
(as 5552 and 5642)	
10232	27/1/59 ex-48506

REPAIRS
8/12/36-26/1/37HG
29/4/38-27/5/38HS
15/12/39-16/1/40HG
13/11/40-28/11/40LO
3/10/41-25/10/41LS
10/3/43-2/4/43HG
17/1/44-11/2/44HS
30/5/45-21/7/45HS
6/11/46-6/12/46LS
12/4/48-24/5/48HG
20/7/49-9/8/49HI
18/12/50-18/1/51LI
22/7/52-6/9/52HG
3/2/53-24/2/53HC
25/3/54-24/4/54HI
22/2/55-21/4/55HC
19/12/55-11/1/56LI
20/11/56-29/12/56LC(EO)
2/11/57-2/1/58HG
28/4/58-24/5/58 NC(EO)
17/6/58-1/7/58NC (EO Rect)
31/12/58-27/1/59NC(EO)
19/3/60-28/4/60HI

BOILERS
First boiler 8465

No	Fitted	From
8561	8/1/37	5611
8620	16/1/40	5560
8602	2/4/43	5572
8624	21/7/45	5635
8577	24/5/48	5649
8574	6/9/52	45616
8759	2/1/58	45641

SHEDS
As first 5552
Crewe North 1/12/34
Rugby 12/1/35
As second 5642
Camden 29/4/35
Preston 4/1/36
Farnley Jct 22/5/37
Newton Heath 4/5/40

MILEAGES
10/5/34-31/12/36
=144,629

1937	53,016
1938	43,033
1939	26,425
1940	40,629
1941	36,185
1942	39,262
1943	44,550
1944	46,660
1945	40,664
1946	35,982
1947	53,851
1948	43,240
1949	45,734
1950	42,407
1951	48,819
1952	36,700
1953	50,516
1954	45,056
1955	40,678
1956	45,050
1957	44,193
1958	43,765
1959	49,376
1960	37,549

Stored 17/9/62-3/12/62
Mileage at 31/12/50 736,267; at 31/12/60 1,177,969
Withdrawn week ending 9/1/65

Newton Heath's 45642 BOSCAWEN, the original 5552 SILVER JUBILEE, among the heathen at York shed, May 1957. Flexible hose down from vacuum ejector. Photograph A.G. Ellis, The Transport Treasury.

Beautifully lit 45643 RODNEY, a Crewe North engine off a special from the Western Division, at Dalry Road shed 6 February 1955. No flexible connection down from vacuum ejector; note also the prominent rows of rivets running laterally along smokebox. These vary from side to side, engine to engine. But that's something for the reader at home.... Photograph J. Robertson, The Transport Treasury.

45643 RODNEY

Built Crewe 4/12/34

Named 30/10/37

Renumbered 5643 to 45643 week ending 25/9/48

TENDERS

No	Fitted
4620	4/12/34
9032	24/9/37
9015	7/11/40
9176	25/5/44
9362	10/5/46
10503	21/9/48
9836	10/8/49
10680	3/11/50
9834	13/5/52

REPAIRS

3/11/36-24/11/36**LS**
12/4/37-7/5/37**LO**
6/9/37-30/10/37**LS**
4/4/38-21/4/38**LO**
6/6/38-6/7/38**HO**
28/6/39-7/7/39**LS**
7/8/40-31/8/40**LS**
16/7/41-30/8/41**HS**
6/7/42-5/9/42**HG**
22/10/43-20/11/43**LS**
5/5/44-2/6/44**LO**
5/2/45-17/3/45**HG**
26/12/45-2/2/46**HS**
13/9/47-29/10/47**LS St Rollox**
15/12/47-16/1/48**LO St Rollox**
20/8/48-22/9/48**HS St Rollox**
20/6/49-20/8/49**HG St Rollox**
25/9/50-3/11/50**LI St Rollox**
23/2/51-17/4/51**LC St Rollox**
21/5/51-16/6/51**LC St Rollox**
18/3/52-13/5/52**HI St Rollox**
7/4/53-19/5/53**HG**
15/10/54-5/11/54**LI**
26/1/56-12/3/56**HG**
10/10/57-5/11/57**LI**
16/2/59-18/3/59**LI AWS fitted**
15/6/60-26/8/60**HG speedo fitted**
7/11/60-19/11/60**NC (EO Rect)**

BOILERS

First boiler 8749

Fitted	From	
8750	5/9/42	5579
8609	2/6/44	5584
8561	17/3/45	5570
8757	20/8/49	45583
8590	19/5/53	45560
8751	12/3/56	45555
8760	26/8/60	45576

SHEDS

Crewe North 8/12/34
Rugby 19/1/35
Bushbury 23/2/35
Camden 20/4/35
Rugby 18/5/35
Aberdeen 7/12/35
Carlisle Kingmoor 8/4/39
Corkerhill 31/10/42
Carlisle Upperby 30/8/52
Loan at first then
Carlisle Upperby 13/9/52
Crewe North 29/1/55
Longsight 17/11/56
Crewe North 2/2/57
Nuneaton 15/12/62
Farnley Junction 9/11/63
Leeds 9/65

MILEAGES

1934	1,611
1935	48,640*
1936	77,381
1937	45,318
1938	58,623
1939	67,011
1940	55,471
1941	28,394
1942	48,799
1943	55,403
1944	47,823
1945	49,747
1946	42,185
1947	39,146
1948	48,080
1949	41,759
1950	49,819
1951	33,634
1952	35,131
1953	45,653
1954	46,644
1955	49,420
1956	49,289
1957	51,191
1958	52,644
1959	49,910
1960	37,722

*stored serviceable 18 days
stored 15/9/63-30/10/63
**Mileage at 31/12/50 805,210;
at 31/12/60 1,256,448
Withdrawn Jan 1966**

45644 HOWE

Built Crewe 7/12/34
Named 6/11/37
Renumbered 5644 to 45644 week ending 20/11/48

MILEAGES	
1934	3,205
1935	57,460*
1936	64,401
1937	62,548
1938	66,838
1939	60,150
1940	45,427
1941	34,497
1942	14,988
1943	51,335
1944	30,418
1945	37,790
1946	42,256
1947	44,790
1948	45,316
1949	36,134
1950	56,456
1951	40,875
1952	45,869
1953	66,043
1954	59,626
1955	52,660
1956	58,407
1957	60,349
1958	57,152
1959	54,556
1960	53,438

*stored serviceable 18 days
Stored 22/5/63-16/6/63, 18/9/63-withdrawal
Mileage at 31/12/50 754,009; at 31/12/60 1,302,984
Withdrawn week ending 23/11/63

TENDERS	
No	Fitted
4621	7/12/34
9005	25/2/42
9072	8/5/42
9215	31/8/46
9022	27/4/49
9218	20/2/52

BOILERS		
First boiler 8750		
No	Fitted	From
8609	8/10/38	5579
8757	7/5/42	5580
8750	31/8/46	5643
8561	2/11/49	45643
8577	23/10/52	45642
8469	30/6/55	45556
8594	6/6/59	45587

SHEDS
Crewe North 8/12/34
Rugby 19/1/35
Bushbury 23/2/35
Camden 20/4/35
Rugby 18/5/35
Aberdeen 7/12/35
Carlisle Kingmoor 8/4/39
Corkerhill 28/9/40
Perth 1/4/50
Longsight 30/8/52
Loan at first then
Longsight 13/9/52
Crewe South 31/12/60

REPAIRS
2/11/36-21/11/36**LS**
8/10/37-6/11/37**LS**
14/9/38-8/10/38**HS**
13/6/40-2/7/40**LS**
11/4/41-19/6/41**LS**
23/2/42-7/5/42**HG**
31/8/42-9/10/42**LO**
15/11/42-9/12/42**LO**
13/5/43-10/6/43**HS**
6/11/44-15/12/44**HS**
30/4/45-30/5/45**LO**
31/7/45-21/9/45**LO**
31/7/46-31/8/46**HG**
3/9/47-20/10/47**HS St Rollox**
10/11/47-13/11/47**NC(Rect) St Rollox**
14/10/48-20/11/48**LS St Rollox**
11/8/49-20/8/49**LC St Rollox**
10/9/49-2/11/49**HG St Rollox**
10/12/49-24/12/49**LC St Rollox**
12/7/50-13/7/50**NC St Rollox**
19/9/50-26/10/50**HI St Rollox**
3/2/51-2/3/51**NC St Rollox**
31/10/51-22/11/51**LC(TO) Perth**
24/1/52-23/2/52**LI St Rollox**
11/3/52-12/3/52**NC St Rollox**
3/9/52-23/10/52**HG**
4/1/54-22/1/54**HI**
3/2/54-8/2/54**NC(EO Rect)**
27/5/55-30/6/55**HG**
27/12/56-19/1/57**LI**
20/2/58-15/3/58**HI**
4/5/59-6/6/59**HG AWS fitted**
21/4/61-25/5/61**LI speedo fitted**

45645 COLLINGWOOD

Built Crewe 7/12/34
Named 3/9/37
Renumbered 5645 to 45645 week ending 12/6/48

REPAIRS
9/3/35-29/3/35**LO**
19/10/36-12/11/36**LS**
2/8/37-3/9/37**HG**
17/1/39-10/2/39**LS**
6/1/40-31/1/40**LS**
5/6/40-21/6/40**LO**
14/2/41-26/2/41**LO**
5/6/41-12/7/41**HS**
11/8/41-12/9/41**LO**
26/9/41-23/10/41**LO**
15/6/42-12/9/42**HG**
23/3/43-29/5/43**LO**
24/8/43-6/11/43**LS**
18/4/44-17/6/44**HO**
10/5/45-14/7/45**LS**
31/1/46-16/2/46**LO**
1/6/46-26/7/46**HG**
12/5/48-10/6/48**LS St Rollox**
12/8/49-17/9/49**LI St Rollox**
27/9/49-28/9/49**NC(Rect) St Rollox**
4/10/50-23/12/50**HG St Rollox**
7/11/51-21/11/51**LC St Rollox**
20/8/52-1/10/52**LI St Rollox**
13/11/52-17/12/52**LC(EO)**
2/9/53-6/10/53**HI**
21/4/54-15/5/54**LC**
24/12/54-28/1/55**HG**
1/3/56-27/3/56**LI**
6/9/57-10/10/57**HG**
19/6/58-8/7/58**LC(EO)**
26/1/59-28/2/59**HI AWS fitted**
13/2/61-17/3/61**HI speedo fitted**

BOILERS		
First boiler 8751		
No	Fitted	From
8590	3/9/37	5560
8589	12/9/42	5584
8571	26/7/46	5589
8586	23/12/50	45564
8633	28/1/55	45623
8748	10/10/57	45578

SHEDS
Crewe North 8/12/34
Rugby 19/1/35
Edge Hill 23/2/35
Crewe North 20/4/35
Carlisle Kingmoor 7/12/35
Corkerhill 28/9/40
Patricroft 13/9/52
Carnforth 24/8/63

TENDERS	
No	Fitted
4622	7/12/34
9005	20/5/35
9031	4/12/41
9270	17/6/44
9679	18/8/44
9818	8/6/48
10621	15/9/49
9271	2/11/63

MILEAGES	
1934	3,944
1935	47,470*
1936	65,087
1937	60,962
1938	59,151
1939	50,544
1940	41,352
1941	25,975
1942	29,071
1943	30,184
1944	38,947
1945	45,821
1946	44,211
1947	50,704
1948	49,708
1949	39,218
1950	34,005
1951	42,858
1952	27,540
1953	43,290
1954	43,140
1955	50,598
1956	46,907
1957	44,633
1958	51,200
1959	45,247
1960	23,253

*stored serviceable 36 days
stored 1/10/62-27/10/62
Mileage at 31/12/50 716,354; at 31/12/60 1,135,020
Withdrawn week ending 19/10/63

45646 NAPIER

Built Crewe 14/12/34

Named 11/9/37

Renumbered 5646 to 45646 week ending 11/12/48

TENDERS

No	Fitted
4623	14/12/34
9022	4/9/47
4623	17/11/47
9267	12/10/51

MILEAGES

1934	120
1935	66,095
1936	64,584
1937	56,354
1938	56,984
1939	59,756
1940	40,880
1941	31,394
1942	23,707
1943	41,618
1944	44,882
1945	39,025
1946	47,041
1947	44,791
1948	40,601
1949	50,736
1950	46,227
1951	20,217
1952	34,242
1953	37,941
1954	38,944
1955	42,497
1956	38,381
1957	44,691

Mileage at 31/12/50 754,795

Withdrawn week ending 28/12/63

SHEDS

Crewe North 22/12/34
Carlisle Kingmoor 7/12/35
Corkerhill 28/9/40
Farnley Jct 30/8/52
Loan at first then
Farnley Jct 13/9/52

BOILERS

First boiler 8752

No	Fitted	From
8613	11/4/38	5583
8579	13/11/42	5571
8560	9/3/46	5594
8560	27/10/51	45646*
8579	19/4/56	45620

*'Repaired on frames'.
Obviously boiler not lifted. It
is not clear if this was a rare
instance, or a rare instance
of it being recorded…

REPAIRS

22/3/35-23/3/35**LO**
14/5/36-6/6/36**LS**
16/8/37-11/9/37**LS**
22/2/38-11/4/38**HO**
17/6/39-6/7/39**LS**
12/3/40-9/4/40**LO**
26/7/40-17/8/40**LS**
11/8/41-18/9/41**HS**
6/11/41-25/2/42**LO**
8/7/42-8/8/42**HO**
2/10/42-13/11/42**HG**
23/4/43-11/6/43**LO**
21/8/43-25/9/43**LS**
23/12/43-4/2/44**LO**
30/1/45-3/3/45**HS**
11/9/45-4/10/45**LO**
11/2/46-9/3/46**HG**
18/11/46-5/2/47**HS St Rollox**
3/9/47-24/9/47**LO St Rollox**
3/11/48-11/12/48**HS St Rollox**
14/9/49-5/10/49**LC St Rollox**
1/3/50-1/4/50**LI St Rollox**
2/4/51-27/10/51**HG St Rollox**
4/3/53-10/4/53**LI**
26/10/54-19/11/54**LI**
13/2/56-19/4/56**HG**
19/8/57-7/9/57**HI**
14/2/59-18/3/59**LI**
23/3/60-14/5/60**LI**
  ? -24/1/61**NC(EO)**
**Dates not given; speedo pro-
bably fitted, AWS probably never**

Stirring scenes of smoke and steam at Polmadie on 14 April 1956 as 45645 COLLINGWOOD, a visitor from Patricroft, makes ready to leave for the south. Exquisite in lined green. Photograph J. Robertson, The Transport Treasury.

45647 STURDEE

Built Crewe 4/1/35
Named 27/4/36
Renumbered 5647 to 45647 week ending 13/8/49

TENDERS	
No	Fitted
4630	4/1/35
4641	13/6/64

BOILERS
First boiler 8740

No	Fitted	From
8631	26/1/38	5601
8558	14/3/42	5629
8735	19/1/45	5596
8620	18/10/47	5652
8563	17/2/51	45620
8566	10/1/56	45656
8583	22/4/61	45613

REPAIRS
7/4/36-27/4/36**LS**
25/2/37-9/4/37**LS**
20/1/38-14/2/38**HG**
5/10/39-31/10/39**HS**
15/2/42-14/3/42**HG**
17/4/43-1/5/43**LS**
28/1/44-19/2/44**LS**
12/12/44-19/1/45**HG**
15/4/46-6/5/46**HS**
21/8/47-18/10/47**HG**
28/10/48-3/11/48**TRO Camden**
15/7/49-9/8/49**LI**
12/1/51-17/2/51**HG**
27/9/52-18/10/52**LI**
24/9/53-21/10/53**HC**
9/8/54-25/8/54**HI**
4/12/55-10/1/56**HG**
30/1/56-24/2/56**LC(EO)**
16/2/57-21/3/57**HI**
30/5/58-20/6/58**LI**
12/9/59-23/10/59**LI AWS fitted**
8/3/61-22/4/61**HG speedo fitted**

SHEDS
Crewe North 5/1/35
Rugby 4/5/35
Longsight 9/5/42
Crewe North 5/4/47
Camden 19/6/48
Crewe North 1/10/49
Edge Hill 7/7/51
Bushbury 20/6/53
Aston 13/2/60
Saltley 9/3/63
Farnley Junction 2/64
Leeds 11/66

MILEAGES

1935	62,699
1936	60,430
1937	44,287
1938	49,468
1939	46,973
1940	33,546
1941	39,580
1942	64,264
1943	65,118
1944	47,303
1945	65,124
1946	58,759
1947	40,630
1948	52,822
1949	51,342
1950	47,450
1951	43,383
1952	47,278
1953	46,998
1954	47,228
1955	44,418
1956	56,573
1957	47,738
1958	43,634
1959	40,909
1960	45,890
1961	38,987
1962	25,666
1963	25,228

stored 13/9/62-3/3/63
Mileage at 31/12/50 829,795;
at 31/12/60 1,293,844
Withdrawn April/May 1967

45647 STURDEE, a Bushbury engine with, presumably, a Wolverhampton train, enters Euston on 29 July 1958. Just before the Second World War fourteen Jubilees had replaced Patriots at Aston and Bushbury for the Wolverhampton and Birmingham to Euston 'Two Hour' services. Photograph The Transport Treasury.

45648 WEMYSS

Built Crewe 10/1/35
Named 29/6/36
Renumbered 5648 to 45648 week ending 26/6/48

TENDERS

No	Fitted
4631	10/1/35
4602	1/3/62

MILEAGES

1935	62,841
1936	56,260
1937	47,415
1938	69,112
1939	51,972
1940	58,711
1941	55,663
1942	58,433
1943	65,534
1944	61,259
1945	59,417
1946	50,953
1947	56,475
1948	52,970
1949	60,094
1950	71,878
1951	54,136
1952	79,584
1953	64,545
1954	64,239
1955	67,410
1956	42,728
1957	53,854
1958	51,282
1959	45,246
1960	47,782

Mileage at 31/12/50 938,987; at 31/12/60 1,509,793
Withdrawn week ending 9/2/63

BOILERS
First boiler 8741

No	Fitted	From
8744	10/12/37	5651
8605	24/8/40	5661
8751	12/9/42	5580
8572	17/11/44	5574
8574	23/5/47	5591
8625	2/1/50	45660
8626	20/12/51	45613
8739	24/3/56	45573

SHEDS
Crewe North 12/1/35
Rugby 9/3/35
Crewe North 28/9/35
Stafford 1/2/36
Patricroft 20/2/37
Preston 8/5/37*
Leeds (loan) 18/11/39
Leeds 9/12/39
Longsight 26/10/46
Kentish Town 2/11/46
Derby 19/10/57
Saltley 4/3/61
Burton 18/11/61
*Record unclear – date may be 8/5/38

REPAIRS
11/6/36-29/6/36LS
8/4/37-5/5/37LS
9/11/37-28/12/37HG
?   -20/8/38TRO
14/4/39-1/5/39LS
11/6/40-24/8/40HG
12/9/41-16/10/41LS
8/12/41-3/1/42LO
22/8/42-12/9/42HG
7/10/43-3/11/43LS
1/11/44-17/11/44HG
23/11/44-6/12/44HO
6/2/46-12/3/46LS
28/3/47-23/5/47HG
22/5/48-24/6/48LS
9/2/49-10/3/49LI
9/11/49-2/1/50HG
30/12/50-23/1/51HI
25/10/51-20/12/51HG
10/3/53-10/4/53HI
15/4/53-1/5/53NC (EO Rect)
9/6/54-6/7/54HI
9/2/55-11/3/55LI
14/3/55-21/3/55NC(EO Rect)
21/1/56-24/3/56HG
28/3/56-6/4/56NC(EO Rect)
11/4/56-23/4/56NC(EO Rect)
25/7/56-24/8/56NC(EO)
26/2/57-23/3/57LI
11/5/57-28/6/57NC(EO)
4/9/57-15/10/57LC(EO)
14/7/58-22/8/58HI
19/2/59-3/4/59LC(EO)
20/8/59-25/9/59LI
14/6/60-30/7/60HI speedo fitted;
AWS probably never fitted

45649 HAWKINS

Built Crewe 10/1/35
Named 27/5/36
Renumbered 5649 to 45649 week ending 14/8/48

MILEAGES

1935	63,503
1936	61,606
1937	55,320
1938	57,920
1939	35,234
1940	50,647
1941	42,226
1942	49,386
1943	46,901
1944	39,799
1945	47,178
1946	40,694
1947	60,861
1948	37,731
1949	56,430
1950	71,823
1951	58,542
1952	70,902
1953	56,174
1954	64,439
1955	60,751
1956	56,528
1957	42,164
1958	42,018
1959	64,113
1960	49,504

Mileage at 31/12/50 817,259; at 31/12/60 1,382,394
Withdrawn week ending 5/10/63

TENDERS

No	Fitted
4632	10/1/35

BOILERS
First boiler 8742

No	Fitted	From
8593	19/4/37	5563
8577	2/3/39	5624
8570	24/6/41	5627
8577	18/11/44	5626
8754	31/7/47	5659
8632	9/11/49	5578
8762	13/11/53	45658
8584	27/4/57	45651

SHEDS
Crewe North 12/1/35
Sheffield 10/2/35
Millhouses 24/4/37
Nottingham 25/9/37
Derby 1/6/40
Kentish Town 12/10/46
Derby 21/11/59
Saltley 4/3/61
Burton 18/11/61
Derby 6/7/63

REPAIRS
16/5/36-5/6/36LS
13/2/37-22/4/37HG
28/3/38-29/4/38LS
26/7/38-12/8/38LO
27/10/38-5/11/38LO
29/12/38-2/3/39HG
7/11/39-9/12/39LO
11/7/40-31/7/40LS
7/6/41-24/6/41HG
9/3/42-11/4/42HS
19/12/42-23/1/43HS
22/9/43-30/10/43LO
30/10/44-18/11/44HG
12/11/45-5/12/45LS
17/9/46-3/10/46LO
31/5/47-31/7/47HG
12/6/48-12/8/48HS
9/9/48-9/10/48NC
20/10/48-3/11/48NC
18/11/48-10/12/48LO
11/9/49-9/11/49HG
21/11/50-21/12/50LI
31/1/51-2/3/51NC(Rect)
2/10/51-10/11/51LI EO
8/9/52-7/10/52HI
17/10/53-13/11/53HG
6/8/54-21/9/54HI
20/11/54-16/12/54LC(EO)
18/12/55-25/1/56LI
16/3/57-27/4/57HG
26/6/57-30/7/57NC(EO Rect)
15/11/58-20/12/58HI
14/5/60-18/6/60HI speedo fitted;
AWS never fitted

45650 BLAKE

Built Crewe 14/1/35
Named 18/2/37
Renumbered 5650 to 45650 week ending 19/2/49

TENDERS

No	Fitted
4633	14/1/35

MILEAGES

Year	Miles
1935	54,869
1936	61,118
1937	48,941
1938	72,817
1939	64,969
1940	66,973
1941	62,410
1942	53,647
1943	54,466
1944	63,129
1945	67,620
1946	55,372
1947	54,625
1948	57,479
1949	60,417
1950	51,975
1951	51,202
1952	66,281
1953	58,293
1954	49,851
1955	52,946
1956	70,495
1957	53,142
1958	57,963
1959	57,080
1960	35,793

Mileage at 31/12/50 950,827; at 31/12/60 1,503,873
Withdrawn week ending 19/1/63

SHEDS

Crewe North 19/1/35
Shrewsbury 20/4/35
Camden 6/7/35
Patricroft 4/1/36
Crewe North 22/5/37
Holyhead 12/6/37
Crewe North 28/5/38
Kentish Town (loan) 20/8/38
Kentish Town 17/9/38
Nottingham 19/10/57
Leicester 23/1/60
Newton Heath 1/7/61
Leicester 26/8/61
Burton 18/11/61

BOILERS

First boiler 8743

No	Fitted	From
8564	2/2/37	5614
8576	27/2/39	5566
8588	10/6/41	5574
8563	11/12/43	5610
8631	19/5/47	5579
8628	16/2/49	5554
8605	16/9/52	45595
8572	25/9/54	45659
8627	28/12/55	45655
8626	29/5/59	45562

REPAIRS

16/12/35-16/1/36**LS**
11/6/36-16/6/36**LO**
10/9/36-22/9/36**LO**
28/12/36-15/2/37**HG**
13/6/38-1/7/38**LS**
9/1/39-27/2/39**HG**
5/8/39-23/9/39**LS**
27/8/40-13/9/40**LS**
4/5/41-10/6/41**HG**
24/2/42-14/3/42**LS**
3/4/42-15/5/42**LO**
2/12/42-9/1/43**HS**
18/10/43-11/12/43**HG**
4/11/44-23/11/44**LS**
20/8/45-19/9/45**LS**
18/5/46-18/6/46**LS**
26/3/47-19/5/47**HG**
12/2/48-19/3/48**LS**
4/11/48-16/2/49**HG**
13/1/50-6/2/50**LI**
26/4/50-30/5/50**LC**
7/11/50-6/12/50**HI**
21/1/52-19/2/52**LI**
8/8/52-16/9/52**HG**
29/5/53-28/7/53**LI**
9/8/54-25/9/54**HG**
11/2/55-22/3/55**LC(EO)**
18/11/55-28/12/55**HG**
17/7/56-13/8/56**LC**
13/5/57-15/6/57**HI**
15/3/58-15/4/58**HI**
17/4/59-29/5/59**HG**
6/10/60-4/11/60**HI** speedo fitted;
AWS probably never fitted
21/8/61-18/9/61**LC(EO)**

BLAKE (with 3,500 gallon tender) at Buxworth Junction with a Manchester Central-St Pancras train, 6 July 1957. Photograph E.M. Johnson Collection.

45651 SHOVELL marvellously clean and green; a Bristol engine at York, 23 May 1955. We've seen this siding before – see 45561 in *Devil in the Detail*. Photograph The Transport Treasury.

45651 SHOVELL

Built Crewe 16/1/35
Named 29/1/36
Renumbered 5651 to 45651 week ending 25/6/49

TENDERS

No	Fitted
4634	16/1/35

MILEAGES

1935	61,407
1936	54,846
1937	47,225
1938	53,628*
1939	58,887
1940	53,578
1941	64,120
1942	68,771
1943	53,887
1944	54,222
1945	46,377
1946	49,928
1947	60,187
1948	53,767
1949	57,054
1950	58,008
1951	58,046
1952	65,113
1953	66,825
1954	65,437
1955	59,730
1956	61,805
1957	66,773

*stored serviceable 80 days
Mileage at 31/12/50 895,892
Withdrawn week ending 24/11/62

SHEDS
Crewe North 19/1/35
Camden 2/2/35
Patricroft 4/1/36
Preston 1/2/36
Patricroft 22/5/37
Carlisle 5/6/37
Camden 17/7/37
Aston 28/8/37
Walsall 25/9/37
Crewe 27/11/37
Leeds 18/11/39
Loan at first then
Leeds 9/12/39
Bristol 24/1/53
Shrewsbury 9/61

BOILERS
First boiler 8744

No	Fitted	From
8629	28/10/37	5599
8567	19/10/40	5606
8469	6/2/43	5555
8634	4/8/45	5595
8614	20/2/48	5595
8746	11/10/52	45555
8593	8/11/54	45619
8584	3/1/57	45635
8752	5/3/57	45575
8751	10/11/60	45643

REPAIRS
20/3/35-9/4/35**LO**
15/1/36-29/1/36**LS**
27/10/36-27/11/36**LS**
20/10/37-16/11/37**HG**
14/7/39-2/8/39**HS**
6/3/40-18/4/40**LO**
25/9/40-19/10/40**HG**
26/11/41-2/1/42**LS**
28/12/42-6/2/43**HG**
2/5/44-15/5/44**HS**
26/6/45-4/8/45**HG**
17/10/46-13/11/46**HS**
12/1/48-20/2/48**HG**
16/5/49-21/6/49**LI**
29/6/50-5/8/50**LI**
11/12/50-18/1/51**LC**
20/7/51-22/8/51**LI**
25/8/52-11/10/52**HG**
30/9/53-29/10/53**LI**
5/10/54-8/11/54**HG**
16/8/55-15/9/55**LI**
26/11/56-3/1/57**LI**
28/1/57-5/3/57**HC(EO)**
22/1/58-18/2/58**LI**
    ?   -27/6/59**HI**
16/9/60-10/11/60**HG**
Speedo probably fitted;
AWS probably never fitted

45652 HAWKE

Built Crewe 21/1/35

Named 3/6/37

Renumbered 5652 to 45652 week ending 16/10/48

TENDERS

No	Fitted
4635	21/1/35

MILEAGES

Year	Mileage
1935	75,988
1936	65,769
1937	60,704
1938	86,994
1939	61,050
1940	36,670
1941	41,974
1942	36,810
1943	48,812
1944	48,064
1945	48,506
1946	59,757
1947	43,033
1948	50,577
1949	40,413
1950	50,945
1951	54,399
1952	61,428
1953	67,667
1954	66,910
1955	57,160
1956	39,449
1957	47,892
1958	56,694
1959	69,433
1960	41,603

Stored 17/9/62-3/12/62, 5/12/64-unrecorded date (probably withdrawal)

Mileage at 31/12/50 856,063; at 31/12/60 1,418,698

Withdrawn week ending 16/1/65

SHEDS

Crewe North 26/1/35
Camden 2/2/35
Patricroft 4/1/36
Preston 1/2/36
Crewe North 14/11/36
Kentish Town 11/9/37
Derby 16/9/39
Sheffield 7/3/42
Bristol 13/10/45
Trafford Park (loan) 20/11/46
Bristol 22/2/47
Trafford Park 11/10/47
Longsight 27/10/56
Trafford Park 10/11/56
Kentish Town 5/7/58
Leicester 16/1/60
Kentish Town 30/4/60
Leicester 18/6/60
Newton Heath 25/6/60
Loan at first then
Newton Heath 23/7/60
Warrington 6/7/63

BOILERS

First boiler 8745

No	Fitted	From
8742	17/5/37	5649
8566	22/2/39	5613
8636	10/5/41	5605
8620	24/11/44	5617
8572	9/8/47	5648
8738	18/9/50	45619
8576	8/5/54	45633
8562	3/1/58	45607

REPAIRS

21/10/35-6/11/35**LS**
29/3/37-3/6/37**HG**
6/12/37-23/12/37**LO**
21/6/38-14/7/38**HS**
9/1/39-22/2/39**HG**
27/9/39-14/11/39**LS**
25/4/40-22/5/40**LO**
7/10/40-25/10/40**LO**
23/11/40-30/11/40**LO**
7/4/41-10/5/41**HG**
30/5/42-18/7/42**LS**
21/9/42-24/10/42**LO**
26/8/43-25/9/43**LS**
8/11/44-24/11/44**HG**
1/4/46-1/5/46**HS**
10/10/46-5/11/46**LO**
10/6/47-9/8/47**HG**
15/9/48-12/10/48**HS**
21/10/49-15/11/49**LI**
7/8/50-18/9/50**HG**
16/7/51-6/8/51**HI**
26/4/52-24/5/52**LI**
11/4/53-9/5/53**LI**
7/4/54-8/5/54**HG**
16/5/55-15/6/55**HI**
11/2/56-2/3/56**LC**
4/9/56-26/10/56**HI**
3/12/56-21/1/57**LC(EO)**
16/11/57-3/1/58**HG**
-18/6/58**LC(EO)**
5/6/59-25/7/59**HI**
22/9/60-5/11/60**LI** speedo fitted
27/3/61-26/4/61**LC(EO)**
? -2/62 **AWS fitted**

45653 BARHAM

Built Crewe 22/1/35

Named 16/4/36

Renumbered 5653 to 45653 week ending 23/10/48

TENDERS

No	Fitted
4636	22/1/35
9756	26/6/62
10545	15/11/63

MILEAGES

Year	Mileage
1935	69,398
1936	49,366
1937	50,805
1938	67,113
1939	57,170
1940	44,650
1941	49,333
1942	45,008
1943	49,225
1944	50,974
1945	26,798
1946	49,587
1947	42,455
1948	45,087
1949	56,574
1950	55,436
1951	48,396
1952	31,088
1953	57,876
1954	47,963
1955	54,676
1956	38,583
1957	58,325
1958	40,703
1959	53,729
1960	38,123

Mileage at 31/12/50 808,979; at 31/12/60 1,278,441

Withdrawn week ending 3/4/65

SHEDS

Crewe North 26/1/35
Camden 2/2/35
Patricroft 4/1/36
Preston 1/2/36
Derby 31/10/36
Preston 23/1/37
Derby 15/5/37
Preston 10/7/37
Patricroft 2/10/37
Longsight 13/4/37
Crewe North 16/9/39
Longsight 18/7/42
Newton Heath 5/12/42
Loan at first then
Newton Heath 16/1/43
Blackpool 10/4/43
Saltley 9/3/63
Blackpool 4/64
Newton Heath 6/64

BOILERS

First boiler 8746

No	Fitted	From
8604	2/2/38	5574
8622	23/5/40	5588
8601	27/9/43	5566
8752	7/6/45	5552
8595	18/10/48	5662
8628	13/12/52	45650
8603	3/11/56	45627
8558	26/6/62	45592

REPAIRS

30/3/36-16/4/36**LS**
12/4/37-7/5/37**LS**
29/5/37-1/6/37**LO**
21/10/37-28/10/37**LO**
13/1/38-16/2/38**HG**
6/6/38-30/6/38**LO**
13/5/39-29/5/39**HS**
4/5/40-23/5/40**HG**
20/11/40-19/12/40**LO**
11/2/41-26/2/41**LO**
20/8/41-4/9/41**LS**
23/10/42-14/11/42**HS**
23/8/43-27/9/43**HG**
5/2/44-17/3/44**LO**
26/2/45-14/4/45**LS**
16/5/45-7/6/45**HO**
19/10/45-29/11/45**HO**
30/12/46-23/1/47**HS**
3/6/47-23/7/47**LO**
28/1/48-17/2/48**LO**
27/8/48-18/10/48**HG**
5/12/49-29/12/49**LI**
27/3/51-14/4/51**LI**
29/10/52-13/12/52**HG**
4/10/54-28/10/54**HI**
21/8/56-3/11/56**HG**
26/8/58-25/9/58**LI**
16/5/60-24/6/60**LI** speedo, AWS, fitted

One of the Blackpool Jubilees, so highly prized for the glimpse they afforded in the south of Central Division affairs, at home at Blackpool shed, 1 June 1957. Lined green 45653 BARHAM still has the smokebox door 'lug' and seems to have its regulator blowing to judge from the jet of steam from the cylinder cocks. Regulator valves often leaked, so locos on shed and in steam were (or should have been) left with drain cocks open. Pressure therefore couldn't build up in the cylinders. Photograph The Transport Treasury.

45654 HOOD

Built Crewe 7/2/35
Named 29/5/36
Renumbered 5654 to 45654 week ending 22/1/49

MILEAGES
1935	69,974
1936	60,872
1937	52,856
1938	54,714
1939	49,880
1940	46,132
1941	43,277
1942	59,222
1943	61,618
1944	76,832
1945	46,819
1946	50,575
1947	55,528
1948	52,181
1949	58,493
1950	63,047
1951	52,923
1952	53,859
1953	46,082
1954	49,463
1955	44,258
1956	49,154
1957	52,936

Stored 15/10/62-8/4/63, 2/9/63-16/12/63,
6/1/64-9/3/64
Mileage at 31/12/50 902,020
Withdrawn week ending 25/6/66

TENDERS
No	Fitted
4637	7/2/35
9366	6/3/57

SHEDS
Camden 23/2/35
Rugby 23/11/35
Derby 11/9/37
Kentish Town 17/6/39
Derby 16/9/39
Kentish Town 14/6/41
Millhouses 30/9/50
Agecroft 3/3/62
Newton Heath 22/6/63
Stockport 3/64
Newton Heath 10/65

BOILERS
First boiler 8747
No	Fitted	From
8623	25/5/37	5593
8627	3/10/40	5622
8753	9/5/44	5595
8581	24/6/46	5564
8580	19/1/49	5641
8613	22/10/53	45620
8616	10/7/58	45581

REPAIRS
29/4/36-29/5/36**LS**
26/4/37-16/6/37**HG**
30/12/37-31/1/38**LO**
29/6/38-28/7/38**LS**
6/2/39-7/3/39**LO**
21/7/39-18/8/39**HS**
28/3/40-10/4/40**LO**
12/9/40-3/10/40**HG**
6/4/42-5/5/42**LS**
10/1/43-13/2/43**LS**
23/9/43-16/10/43**LS**
21/4/44-9/5/44**HG**
12/7/45-1/9/45**HS**
16/5/46-24/6/46**HG**
2/9/46-28/11/46**HO**
14/10/47-28/11/47**LS**
12/10/48-19/1/49**HG**
16/1/50-16/2/50**LI**
19/6/50-28/7/50**LC**
19/2/51-17/3/51**HI**
5/5/52-31/5/52**HI**
21/9/53-22/10/53**HG**
22/11/54-15/12/54**LI**
28/7/56-24/8/56**HI**
6/9/56-9/10/56**NC(EO Rect)**
8/3/57-29/3/57**LC(EO)**
18/9/57-12/10/57**LC(EO)**
10/6/58-10/7/58**HG**
23/7/59-4/9/59**HI**
20/4/60-26/5/60**HI speedo fitted;**
AWS never fitted
22/12/60-17/1/61**LC(EO)**

45655 KEITH

Built Derby 13/12/34
Named 11/6/37
Renumbered 5655 to 45655 week ending 5/2/49

TENDERS

No	Fitted
4638	13/12/34

MILEAGES

1934	119
1935	52,269
1936	56,269
1937	48,489
1938	60,344
1939	54,639
1940	60,624
1941	49,481
1942	67,336
1943	60,825
1944	62,052
1945	56,613
1946	46,024
1947	46,193
1948	38,787
1949	58,988
1950	42,577
1951	55,906
1952	49,848
1953	58,283
1954	63,084
1955	46,620
1956	60,794
1957	60,488
1958	43,914
1959	48,852
1960	45,171

stored 5/12/64-unrecorded date (probably withdrawal)
Mileage at 31/12/50 861,639; at 31/12/60 1,394,599
Withdrawn week ending 17/4/65

BOILERS
First boiler 8753

No	Fitted	From
8755	24/5/37	5657
8753	16/9/39	5569
8593	9/10/41	5635
8623	28/3/44	5625
8466	13/12/44	5554
8762	9/8/46	5571
8558	1/2/49	5612
8627	25/2/52	45594
8559	22/10/55	45591
8570	18/4/58	45622

SHEDS

Nottingham 2/2/35
Trafford Park 7/10/39
Longsight 24/6/50
Trafford Park 2/6/51
Longsight 27/10/56
Patricroft 9/3/57
Longsight 23/3/57
Crewe North 22/6/57
Llandudno Jct 26/11/60
Crewe North 10/6/61
Llandudno Jct 16/9/61
Edge Hill 23/9/61
Warrington 28/10/61

REPAIRS

23/3/36-22/4/46LS
28/9/36-2/10/36LO
22/4/37-11/6/37HG
28/6/38-3/8/38HS
3/6/39-13/6/39LO
21/8/39-28/8/39LO
16/9/39-31/10/39HG
15/10/40-8/11/40LS
8/9/41-9/10/41HG
4/6/42-21/7/42LO
8/3/43-3/4/43HS
11/3/44-28/3/44HG
16/11/44-15/12/44HS
29/8/45-15/9/45LS
19/7/46-9/8/46HG
19/11/46-6/12/46LO Derby
25/10/47-29/11/47LS
25/10/48-1/2/49HG
27/9/49-24/10/49LI
5/3/51-22/3/51HI
9/1/52-25/2/52HG
13/5/53-3/6/53HI
30/12/53-30/1/54HC
12/7/54-13/8/54HI
22/9/55-22/10/55HG
4/10/56-3/11/56HI
7/3/58-18/4/58HG
20/2/60-25/3/60LI AWS fitted
  ?   -8/62 **speedo fitted**

45656 COCHRANE

Built Derby 17/12/34
Named 4/3/36
Renumbered 5656 to 45656 week ending 1/5/48

TENDERS

No	Fitted
4639	17/12/34

MILEAGES

1934	146
1935	66,904
1936	66,640
1937	62,253
1938	58,062
1939	52,471
1940	43,218
1941	46,994
1942	56,938
1943	51,832
1944	49,955
1945	39,590
1946	52,411
1947	28,488
1948	48,807
1949	54,716
1950	53,323
1951	51,559
1952	58,805
1953	52,283
1954	51,651
1955	41,665
1956	61,782
1957	44,220

Stored prior to withdrawal
Mileage at 31/12/50 832,748
Withdrawn week ending 29/12/62

BOILERS
First boiler 8754

No	Fitted	From
8468	23/3/37	5555
8562	7/1/39	5664
8576	19/7/41	5650
8759	4/9/43	5605
8598	23/3/48	5634
8566	25/5/51	45563
8737	24/11/55	45662

SHEDS

Nottingham 2/2/35
Derby 23/9/39
Millhouses 26/10/46
Derby 13/12/47
Leeds 10/11/51
Millhouses 24/11/51
Canklow 1/62
Darnall 6/62

REPAIRS

29/1/36-4/3/36LS
23/6/36-4/7/36LO
2/10/36-9/10/36LO
17/2/37-9/4/37HG
21/2/38-22/3/38HS
20/7/38-28/7/38LO
28/11/38-7/1/39HG
21/8/39-31/8/39LO
29/1/40-17/2/40LS
3/1/41-18/1/41LO
27/6/41-19/7/41HG
9/3/42-18/4/42HS
14/8/43-4/9/43HG
30/10/44-18/11/44LS
24/2/45-2/6/45HO
17/6/46-24/7/46LS
2/2/48-23/3/48HG
12/4/48-1/5/48NC
25/5/49-24/6/49HI
5/7/50-4/8/50HI
19/2/51-21/3/51LC
14/4/51-25/5/51HC
11/1/52-9/2/52LI
27/3/53-2/5/53HI
10/5/54-2/6/54HI
11/10/55-24/11/55HG
7/1/57-8/2/57HI
28/9/57-26/10/57LC(EO)
28/8/58-25/9/58HI
4/1/60-11/2/60LI speedo fitted;
AWS probably never fitted

45657 TYRWHITT

Built Derby 17/12/34
Named 8/2/36
Renumbered 5657 to 45657 8/48

TENDERS	
No	Fitted
4640	17/12/34

MILEAGES

Year	Mileage
1934	86
1935	67,900
1936	60,090
1937	54,322
1938	67,739
1939	49,467
1940	47,748
1941	45,022
1942	56,957
1943	64,652
1944	45,763
1945	71,133
1946	47,289
1947	58,190
1948	66,350
1949	51,707
1950	68,391
1951	61,196
1952	64,829
1953	54,885
1954	56,391
1955	46,972
1956	50,159
1957	55,958
1958	52,493
1959	47,595
1960	45,661
1961	45,109
1962	20,759

Stored 10/9/62-8/4/63, 7/10/63-23/3/64
Mileage at 31/12/50 922,806; at 31/12/60 1,458,945
Withdrawn week ending 26/9/64

BOILERS

First boiler 8755

No	Fitted	From
9201	4/8/39	5685
9319	20/11/41	5666
9341	2/12/43	5674
9255	18/1/47	5676
9331	31/10/50	45710
9221	15/8/52	45733
9776	11/8/56	45715

SHEDS

Nottingham 2/2/35
Derby 23/9/39
Gloucester 14/12/40
Bristol 10/5/41
Kentish Town 1/11/47
Perth 30/8/52
Loan at first then
Perth 13/9/52
Carlisle Kingmoor 7/3/53
Bank Hall 21/7/62
Loan at first then
Bank Hall 18/8/62
Patricroft 5/64

REPAIRS

17/1/36-3/2/36**LS**
11/6/36-26/6/36**LO**
5/10/36-22/10/36**LO**
25/2/37-27/4/37**HG**
12/10/37-8/11/37**LO**
7/3/38-24/3/38**LS**
16/9/38-23/9/38**LO**
24/2/39-21/3/39**LO**
15/6/39-4/8/39**HG**
8/10/40-19/10/40**LS**
25/10/41-20/11/41**HG**
1/12/42-29/12/42**LS**
15/11/43-2/12/43**HG**
7/12/44-20/1/45**HS**
27/6/45-4/8/45**LO**
21/3/46-18/4/46**LS**
18/8/46-7/9/46**LO**
6/12/46-18/1/47**HG**
16/9/47-27/10/47**LS**
1/7/48-16/8/48**HS**
16/3/49-28/4/49**NC**
29/10/49-30/11/49**LI**
7/12/49-16/12/49**NC**
14/9/50-31/10/50**HG**
12/11/51-17/12/51**HI**
19/6/52-15/8/52**HG**
21/1/53-28/2/53**NC St Rollox**
8/1/54-30/1/54**LI St Rollox**
13/8/54-8/9/54**LC(EO) St Rollox**
2/3/55-9/4/55**HI St Rollox**
18/7/55-19/8/55**LC(EO) St Rollox**
20/6/56-11/8/56**GEN St Rollox**
24/1/57-4/2/57**NC(EO) St Rollox**
7/12/57-11/1/58**LI St Rollox**
23/3/59-11/4/59**LI St Rollox**
11/5/59-24/6/59**HC St Rollox**
17/6/60-6/8/60**HI St Rollox**
  ?   -8/62 **speedo, AWS fitted**

A Bristol Jubilee, 5657 TYRWHITT at Sheffield in the 1946 livery. Photograph The Transport Treasury.

Now a Scottish engine, 45657 TYRWHITT at Larbert, 9 May 1954; that familiar item from the 1950s and 1960s, the decaying air raid shelter, sits in the embankment. Photograph J. Robertson, The Transport Treasury.

45658 KEYES

Built Derby 18/12/34
Named 23/1/36
Renumbered 5658 to 45658 week ending 28/5/49

TENDERS

No	Fitted
4641	18/12/34
9686	13/6/64

MILEAGES

1934	153
1935	88,321
1936	70,640
1937	56,252
1938	83,696
1939	74,303
1940	58,630
1941	60,258
1942	58,412
1943	53,816
1944	58,441
1945	56,927
1946	49,540
1947	63,119
1948	61,064
1949	61,475
1950	67,151
1951	61,964
1952	57,557
1953	69,936
1954	56,633
1955	62,297
1956	65,877
1957	54,897

Mileage at 31/12/50 1,022,198
Withdrawn September 1965

BOILERS
First boiler 8756

No	Fitted	From
8762	10/6/37	5664
8611	12/7/39	5581
8562	18/10/41	5656
8745	2/11/44	5638
8762	26/5/49	5655
8621	5/9/53	45572
8582	28/3/56	45619
8586	8/1/60	45579

SHEDS
Leeds 10/2/35
This was 45658's only shed
– see also 45659 and 45701

REPAIRS
3/1/36-23/1/36LS
1/9/36-9/9/36LO
31/12/36-1/1/37LO
3/6/37-3/7/37HG
15/7/38-1/8/38HG
19/5/39-12/7/39HG
18/5/40-31/5/40LS
9/10/40-28/11/40LO
16/6/41-2/7/41LO
12/9/41-18/10/41HG
26/8/42-25/9/42LS
15/4/43-1/5/43LO
27/9/43-13/11/43HS
14/9/44-15/9/44TRO
17/10/44-2/11/44HG
12/11/45-20/12/45LS
10/5/46-24/7/46HO
18/11/46-9/12/46LO Derby
1/5/47-30/5/47LS
26/1/48-27/2/48LS
7/4/49-26/5/49HG
25/2/50-16/3/50LI
3/4/51-3/5/51LI
16/2/52-21/3/52HI
7/8/52-29/8/52LC(EO)
7/8/53-5/9/53HG
18/10/54-18/11/54HI
3/2/56-28/3/56HG
25/5/57-22/6/57LI
30/8/58-26/9/58LI
26/10/59-8/1/60HG
-9/3/61NC(EO)
12/6/61-22/7/61HI
No dates given; speedo probably fitted;
AWS probably never fitted

45659 DRAKE

Built Derby 20/12/34
Named 2/3/36
Renumbered 5659 to 45659 week ending 21/8/48

MILEAGES

Year	Mileage
1934	55
1935	77,895
1936	68,697
1937	70,689
1938	76,679
1939	70,894
1940	56,522
1941	69,433
1942	60,308
1943	57,782
1944	61,170
1945	57,921
1946	59,386
1947	53,925
1948	61,878
1949	71,332
1950	54,217
1951	66,363
1952	67,453
1953	64,494
1954	60,853
1955	60,329
1956	67,992
1957	69,581

Mileage at 31/12/50 1,028,780
Withdrawn week ending 25/5/63

SHEDS

Leeds 10/2/35
Nottingham 24/9/55
Leeds 1/10/55
Note – one week, possible 'paper'
transfer (or error?) spoiled 45659's
one-shed record

BOILERS

First boiler 8757

No	Fitted	From
8739	10/5/37	5641
8582	3/8/39	5629
8592	14/6/41	5617
8754	4/5/44	5602
8618	15/5/47	5555
8572	10/11/50	45652
8744	7/7/54	45576
8557	22/11/57	45560

TENDERS

No	Fitted
4642	20/12/34

REPAIRS

14/2/36-2/3/36**LS**
5/8/36-7/8/36**LO**
3/4/37-29/5/37**HG**
28/4/38-18/5/38**HS**
22/8/38-8/9/38**LO**
9/3/39-18/3/39**LO**
12/6/39-3/8/39**HG**
18/4/40-7/5/40**LS**
17/2/41-20/3/41**LO**
19/5/41-14/6/41**HG**
24/4/42-11/6/42**LS**
28/12/42-9/2/43**HS**
11/9/43-30/9/43**HS**
10/4/44-4/5/44**HG**
27/7/44-26/8/44**LO**
28/9/45-27/10/45**LS**
12/8/46-10/9/46**HS**
31/3/47-15/5/47**HG**
16/7/48-17/8/48**HS**
28/2/49-18/3/49**LC**
25/9/49-21/10/49**LI**
6/9/50-10/11/50**HG**
13/11/50-20/11/50**NC(Rect)**
12/12/51-17/1/52**HI**
7/7/52-19/8/52**HI**
9/5/53-20/6/53**HI**
10/6/54-7/7/54**HG**
2/6/55-5/7/55**L**
29/12/55-28/1/56**LC(EO)**
21/10/56-16/11/56**LI**
19/10/57-22/11/57**HG**
9/2/59-26/3/59**HI**
15/4/59-28/5/59**LC(EO)**
2/11/59-7/12/59**LC(EO) Derby**
? - 8/1/60**NC(Rect)**
15/3/60-14/5/60**LI**
? - 13/2/61**NC(EO)**
2/9/61-6/10/61**HI**
No dates given; speedo probably
fitted; AWS probably never fitted

45660 ROOKE

Built Derby 27/12/34
Named 1936
Renumbered 5660 to 45660 week ending 8/5/48

MILEAGES

Year	Mileage
1934	57
1935	90,269
1936	73,576
1937	64,799
1938	80,486
1939	87,034
1940	61,673
1941	63,439
1942	45,882
1943	39,885
1944	57,724
1945	43,084
1946	63,195
1947	55,702
1948	61,098
1949	54,968
1950	63,740
1951	64,075
1952	67,441
1953	66,903
1954	64,408
1955	60,547
1956	74,725
1957	51,111

Mileage at 31/12/50 1,006,611
Withdrawn June 1966

TENDERS

No	Fitted
4643	27/12/34

SHEDS

Leeds 10/2/35
Bristol 6/2/37
Leeds 27/2/37
Bristol 29/5/37
Leeds 25/9/37
Carlisle Upperby 27/11/37
Leeds 29/1/38
Derby 13/6/42
Leeds 31/10/42
Bristol (loan) 1/11/47
Leeds 27/12/47
Bristol 29/5/48
Shrewsbury 9/61
Chester 6/64
Leeds 9/64

BOILERS

First boiler 8758

No	Fitted	From
8628	22/7/37	5598
8578	10/6/39	5620
8587	28/2/42	5558
8737	26/5/44	5634
8625	5/5/48	5606
8629	18/11/49	45566
8609	14/8/53	45597
8735	16/2/57	45661
8565	30/12/57	45577

REPAIRS

17/6/36-9/7/36**LS**
22/6/37-9/8/37**HG**
28/7/38-15/8/38**HS**
18/5/39-10/6/39**HG**
26/4/40-1/6/40**LS**
14/11/40-10/12/40**LO**
28/1/42-28/2/42**HG**
30/3/42-9/5/42**LO**
18/3/43-16/4/43**HS**
21/7/43-18/9/43**LO**
25/11/43-8/1/44**HS**
12/5/44-26/5/44**HG**
13/6/44-19/7/44**LO**
30/10/45-22/11/45**HS**
30/12/46-30/1/47**LS**
24/6/47-11/7/47**LO Derby**
31/7/47-27/8/47**LO**
13/3/48-5/5/48**HG**
3/1/49-3/2/49**LI**
15/9/49-18/11/49**HG**
13/11/50-8/12/50**LI**
4/10/51-27/10/51**HI**
22/9/52-23/10/52**LI**
29/6/53-14/8/53**HG**
31/8/54-29/9/54**LI**
30/9/55-25/10/55**HI**
14/1/57-16/2/57**HG**
8/4/57-1/5/57**NC(EO Rect)**
8/11/57-30/12/57**HG**
31/12/57-1/1/58**NC(EO Rect)**
21/11/58-24/12/58**LI**
16/2/60-2/4/60**HI**
30/4/60-27/5/60**LC(EO)**
26/11/60-1/2/61**LC(EO)**
speedo fitted, date unknown
AWS never fitted

45660 ROOKE on the 9.30am St Pancras-Glasgow, entering Carlisle on 7 August 1965. Tired and yellow-striped near the end, ROOKE has the top lamp iron lowered to the right-hand side of the smokebox door, to keep the 'top' lamp in the hands of a fireman away from any overhead wires. At the same time the middle bottom iron was also moved, across to come in line with the revised upper one – as in the photograph. 'Lug' still on smokebox too; speedo but no AWS. This Jubilee caused a stir at Exeter St Davids on 15 September 1962 when it arrived on the 3.33pm Bristol to Penzance parcels. It was replaced by Hall 6988 and promptly returned light engine. Photograph J.L. Stevenson, courtesy Hamish Stevenson.

45661 VERNON

Built Derby 27/12/34
Named 4/2/36
Renumbered 5661 to 45661 week ending 13/8/49

TENDERS

No	Fitted
4644	27/12/34*
9247	10/62
10095	5/10/63

* *'to 45559 for scrapping 10/62'*

REPAIRS
13/1/36-4/2/36LS
9/9/36-25/9/36LO
15/2/37-25/3/37LS
30/6/37-17/8/37LO
6/1/38-29/1/38HG
21/7/38-2/8/38LO
2/12/38-17/12/38LO
2/5/39-20/5/39HS
27/6/40-1/8/40HG
28/3/42-23/4/42HS
9/2/44-25/2/44HG
25/7/45-8/8/45LS
27/8/46-5/10/46LS
5/1/48-10/2/48HG
25/7/49-12/8/49HI
11/3/50-31/3/50LC
17/3/51-10/4/51LI
12/11/51-19/12/51LC
1/4/52-2/7/52HG
31/8/53-5/10/53HI
10/9/54-4/10/54LC(EO)
26/4/55-20/5/55LI
25/5/56-25/5/56NC(EO) St Rollox
20/8/56-3/10/56HG
4/12/57-3/1/58LI
5/5/59-13/6/59LI
13/6/59-26/6/59NC(EO Rect)EO
15/6/61-5/8/61HG
No dates given; speedo probably fitted; AWS probably never

SHEDS
Leeds 10/2/35
Farnley Jct 22/5/37
Newton Heath 11/12/37
Farnley Jct 6/3/43
Newton Heath 1/7/44
Leeds 8/64
Wakefield 9/64
Leeds 10/64

BOILERS
First boiler 8759

No	Fitted	From
8605	13/1/38	5575
8598	1/8/40	5589
8559	25/2/44	5627
8742	10/2/48	5563
8735	2/7/52	45661
8636	3/10/56	45586
8620	5/8/61	45614

MILEAGES

1934	Nil
1935	81,240
1936	64,459
1937	38,769
1938	56,744
1939	52,149
1940	41,675
1941	45,604
1942	46,286
1943	30,362
1944	41,652
1945	43,443
1946	49,966
1947	49,917
1948	48,610
1949	41,654
1950	46,339
1951	44,868
1952	46,858
1953	56,028
1954	57,939
1955	46,416
1956	35,399
1957	51,898
1958	52,612
1959	44,020
1960	42,206

Mileage at 31/12/50 778,669; at 31/12/60 1,256,913
Withdrawn May 1965

M5661 VERNON in the curious state immediately post-Nationalisation. A Newton Heath engine, it was photographed at Polmadie; bracket on smokebox edge but no 'lug' on door. Very Black Five 5309 in background. Photograph J. Robertson, The Transport Treasury.

45661 VERNON pilots Black Five 44943 on special '2P64' past Farrington Junction south of Preston about 1961 – no doubt, given the non-corridor stock, bound for Blackpool. The picture also demonstrates the introduction of the BR train reporting number system; at one time it would have been, say, 'CXXX'. Note the lineside audience, unthinkable today, even if the vegetation had been kept down for a good enough view. The lines coming in from the right are from Lostock Hall and Southport; the train is on the West Coast main line proper. Photograph The Transport Treasury.

45662 KEMPENFELT

Built Derby 28/12/34

Named 24/9/36

Renumbered 5662 to 45662 week ending 28/8/48

REPAIRS

18/9/35-4/10/35**HS**
21/2/36-11/3/36**HO**
15/8/36-24/9/36**HG**
4/10/37-2/11/37**LS**
3/1/38-7/2/38**LO**
22/8/38-7/10/38**HG**
27/3/39-26/4/39**HS**
27/3/40-20/4/40**HG**
14/10/40-20/11/40**HO***
28/5/41-13/6/41**LS**
5/6/42-23/7/42**LS**
25/3/43-21/4/43**HG**
23/9/43-15/11/43**LO**
16/8/44-31/8/44**HS**
2/4/45-16/5/45**LS**
29/3/46-17/5/46**HG**
4/9/46-16/10/46**LO**
5/4/47-23/5/47**LO**
5/7/47-8/9/47**LS**
23/9/47-5/11/47**NC**
4/2/48-8/3/48**LO**
2/7/48-28/8/48**HG**
29/9/48-5/11/48**NC**
7/4/49-10/5/49**LC**
8/10/49-26/11/49**HI**
19/12/50-16/1/51**HI**
7/1/52-25/2/52**LI**
21/1/53-26/2/53**HG**
22/2/54-17/3/54**HI**
7/3/55-13/4/55**HG**
13/4/56-11/5/56**LI**
25/9/56-19/10/56**LC(EO)**
8/10/57-16/11/57**HG**
18/2/58-20/3/58**LC(EO)**
4/6/59-31/7/59**HI**
4/9/60-17/11/60**HG**
2/12/60-25/2/61**HC(EO)**
No dates; speedo probably
fitted; AWS never fitted
* 'damaged by enemy action
10/10/40 at Kentish Town'

MILEAGES

1934	-
1935	75,184
1936	78,586
1937	67,912
1938	76,899
1939	81,845
1940	47,103
1941	64,700
1942	64,617
1943	51,581
1944	62,015
1945	59,555
1946	52,825
1947	36,005
1948	49,577
1949	53,418
1950	68,064
1951	55,183
1952	60,331
1953	66,682
1954	71,777
1955	58,486
1956	63,180
1957	61,884

Mileage at 31/12/50 989,886
Withdrawn week ending 24/11/62

TENDERS

No	Fitted
4645	28/12/34
9139	11/3/36
9161	16/10/52

SHEDS

Bristol 10/2/35
Kentish Town 16/2/35
Derby 4/11/44
Kentish Town 2/12/44
Bristol 1/11/47
Shrewsbury 9/61

BOILERS

First boiler 8760

No	Fitted	From
8557	9/9/36	5607
8581	7/10/38	5611
8572	20/4/40	5633
8629	20/11/40	5651
8567	21/4/43	5651
8595	17/5/46	5576
8755	28/8/48	5604
8737	26/2/53	45624
8466	13/4/55	45574
8602	16/11/57	45630
8750	25/2/61	45575

45663 JERVIS

Built Derby 1/1/35

Named 5/4/37

Renumbered 5663 to 45663 week ending 7/8/48

REPAIRS

13/4/36-11/5/36**LS**
11/1/37-5/4/37**HG**
19/10/37-24/11/37**LS**
3/5/38-17/5/38**LO**
25/6/38-25/7/38**HS**
23/5/39-27/5/39**LO**
19/6/39-30/6/39**LO**
31/8/39-18/9/39**HS**
26/2/40-21/3/40**LO**
24/8/40-5/10/40**HG**
10/6/41-11/7/41**LS**
6/4/42-6/6/42**HS**
18/12/42-30/1/43**HG**
29/7/43-3/9/43**LO**
20/4/44-5/5/44**HS**
23/11/44-15/12/44**HS**
14/2/46-8/3/46**HG**
7/2/47-14/4/47**LS**
3/12/47-31/12/47**LO**
5/1/48-15/1/48**NC**
10/6/48-2/8/48**HG**
3/5/49-24/5/49**HI**
29/12/49-18/1/50**LI**
19/1/50-1/2/50**NC(Rect)**
2/6/50-3/7/50**HG**
24/7/50-5/8/50**Painting Only**
5/6/51-27/6/51**HI**
1/1/52-26/1/52**HC**
27/11/52-20/12/52**HI**
23/12/53-21/1/54**HG**
8/2/54-12/2/54**NC(Rect)**
10/2/55-11/3/55**LI**
5/5/56-7/6/56**HG**
27/6/57-10/8/57**HI**
16/2/59-21/3/59**HI**
23/2/60-11/4/60**LI**
11/4/60-20/4/60**NC(EO Rect)**
3/8/61-2/10/61**HG speedo, AWS fitted**

MILEAGES

1935	74,557
1936	67,888
1937	47,181
1938	71,229
1939	49,600
1940	46,010
1941	63,734
1942	45,150
1943	56,732
1944	60,005
1945	56,482
1946	65,526
1947	51,869
1948	63,211
1949	67,823
1950	55,742
1951	64,632
1952	60,410
1953	69,442
1954	68,023
1955	67,181
1956	71,817
1957	65,592
1958	44,948
1959	48,268
1960	38,706

Stored 1/10/62-8/4/63
Mileage at 31/12/50 942,739; at
31/12/60 1,541,758
Withdrawn week ending 24/10/64

TENDERS

No	Fitted
4646	1/1/35
9778	3/7/43
9130	10/8/57

BOILERS

First boiler 8761

No	Fitted	From
8570	16/3/37	5620
8608	18/7/38	5578
8560	5/10/40	5611
8615	30/1/43	5611
8588	8/3/46	5630
8624	2/8/48	5642
8760	3/7/50	45616
8747	21/1/54	45607
8755	7/6/56	45612
8757	2/10/61	45626

SHEDS

Derby 10/2/35
Millhouses 6/6/36
Nottingham 25/9/37
Kentish Town 1/6/40
(no entry on Card between
these two entries)
Kentish Town 1/11/47
Derby 25/1/58
Patricroft 24/10/59
Loan at first then
Patricroft 7/11/59
Warrington 14/9/63
Speke Junction 16/11/63
Warrington 7/64

45664 NELSON

Built Derby 1/1/35
Named 7/4/36
Renumbered 5664 to 45664 week ending 6/11/48

TENDERS	
No	Fitted
4647	1/1/35
9838	?

MILEAGES

Year	Mileage
1935	71,043
1936	75,088
1937	66,358
1938	78,844
1939	76,980
1940	48,523
1941	47,612
1942	41,406
1943	55,263
1944	52,818
1945	54,784
1946	51,270
1947	37,038
1948	36,834
1949	51,461
1950	29,992
1951	55,139
1952	47,157
1953	43,413
1954	49,481
1955	44,230
1956	55,603
1957	50,172

Stored 22/10/62-19/1/63, 21/1/63-8/4/63
Mileage at 31/12/50 875,316
Withdrawn May 1965

BOILERS
First boiler 8762

No	Fitted	From
8562	4/5/37	5612
8557	17/11/38	5662
8744	25/9/40	5648
8583	16/10/43	5633
8603	14/3/46	5641
8604	30/11/50	45598
8573	2/11/55	45585
8630	26/8/60	45555

SHEDS

Derby 10/2/35
Leeds 22/6/35
Kentish Town 12/10/35
Sheffield 30/9/39
Trafford Park (loan) 13/9/47
Millhouses 17/1/48
Agecroft 3/3/62
Newton Heath 22/6/63
Warrington 14/9/63
Speke Junction 16/11/63
Warrington 7/64
Leeds 4/65

REPAIRS

14/3/36-7/4/36LS
24/9/36-23/10/36LO
6/3/37-20/5/37HG
29/11/37-16/12/37LO
14/3/38-12/4/38LS
5/10/38-17/11/38HG
16/4/39-24/5/39LO
11/12/39-30/12/39LS
28/8/40-25/9/40HG
5/10/42-22/10/42LS
20/9/43-16/10/43HG
4/4/45-12/5/45LS
23/2/46-14/3/46HG
3/7/47-26/8/47LS
19/2/48-17/3/48LO
18/9/48-4/11/48LO Derby
9/4/49-11/5/49HI
13/9/50-30/11/50HG
14/5/52-14/6/52LI
9/4/54-6/5/54HI
19/9/55-2/11/55HG
16/5/57-8/6/57LI
15/9/58-17/10/58LI
4/6/59-20/8/59LC(EO)
1/7/60-26/8/60HG speedo fitted;
AWS probably never fitted
21/4/61-31/5/61LC

5664 NELSON, in red at Nottingham Midland station, about 1937. Photograph John Scott-Morgan Collection; distributed by R.S. Carpenter.

45665 LORD RUTHERFORD OF NELSON

Built Crewe 18/11/35
Named 26/11/35
Renumbered 5665 to 45665 3/49

Photograph J. Robertson, The Transport Treasury.

SHEDS
Crewe North 30/11/35
Holyhead 29/5/37
Edge Hill 25/9/37
Trafford Park 16/7/38
Leeds 13/12/41
Sheffield 14/3/42
Bristol 13/10/45
Kentish Town 1/11/47
Corkerhill 9/52
Polmadie 11/59
Corkerhill 4/60

MILEAGES
Year	Mileage
1935	5,825
1936	62,123
1937	54,172
1938	71,054
1939	50,751
1940	54,181
1941	60,188
1942	48,844
1943	59,153
1944	46,680
1945	51,612
1946	60,831
1947	53,904
1948	64,515
1949	62,702
1950	65,521

Mileage at 31/12/50 872,056
Withdrawn December 1962

TENDERS
No	Fitted
4648	18/11/35

REPAIRS
21/1/36-25/1/36**HO**
23/5/36-8/6/36**LO**
6/11/37-10/12/37**HG**
10/1/39-20/2/39**LS**
26/2/40-4/4/40**HG**
3/9/41-22/9/41**LS**
20/1/43-18/2/43**HG**
19/4/44-2/5/44**HS**
14/2/45-28/3/45**LS**
12/12/45-23/1/46**HG**
14/12/46-11/1/47**LS**
28/10/47-29/11/47**LS**
3/6/48-14/7/48**LO**
2/1/49-14/3/49**HG**
26/1/50-20/2/50**LI**
16/1/51-3/2/51**LI**
Record incomplete

BOILERS
First boiler 9256
No	Fitted	From
10037	24/11/37	New
9343	4/4/40	5723
9259	18/2/43	5671
11160	23/1/46	5621
9214	4/3/49	5621
Record incomplete		

45665 LORD RUTHERFORD OF NELSON, glistening in green, at Corkerhill shed 16 June 1957. Photograph The Transport Treasury.

45666 CORNWALLIS
Built Crewe 18/11/35
Named 1937
Renumbered 5666 to 45666 week ending 25/12/48

TENDERS

No	Fitted
4649	18/11/35

SHEDS
Crewe North 30/11/35
Longsight 28/8/37
Camden 23/8/41
Crewe North 10/6/44
Longsight 17/2/45
Crewe North 3/3/45
Bushbury 12/10/46
Edge Hill 10/5/47
Crewe North 1/10/49
Carlisle Upperby 21/2/53
Bushbury 3/8/57
Carlisle Upperby 17/8/57
Crewe North 14/6/58
Edge Hill 12/9/59
Crewe North 26/9/59
Willesden 10/12/60
Crewe South 7/1/61
Crewe North 4/8/62
Warrington 23/11/63
Loan at first then
Warrington 7/12/63

BOILERS
First boiler 9197

No	Fitted	From
9319	11/1/39	5640
9327	28/8/41	5640
9211	11/1/45	5678
9213	4/7/47	5724
9256	12/5/50	45737
9220	17/6/55	45717
9786	8/62	45674

REPAIRS
13/2/37-1/3/37**LS**
29/6/37-28/7/37**LO**
7/2/38-28/2/38**LS**
6/12/38-11/1/39**HG**
6/5/40-21/5/40**LS**
12/8/41-28/8/41**HG**
2/11/42-19/11/42**HS**
18/11/43-4/12/43**HS**
22/12/44-11/1/45**HG**
14/8/46-13/9/46**HS**
29/5/47-4/7/47**HG**
4/12/48-24/12/48**LS**
11/4/50-12/5/50**HG**
28/7/50-14/8/50**LC**
6/10/51-8/11/51**LI**
28/7/52-23/8/52**LC(EO)**
19/9/52-9/10/52**NC(EO)**
19/10/52-1/11/52**NC(EO Rect)**
3/10/53-30/10/53**HI**
14/5/55-17/6/55**HG**
7/6/57-11/7/57**LI**
25/9/58-22/10/58**LI**
13/2/60-19/3/60**HI AWS fitted**
   ?   -8/62 **speedo fitted**

MILEAGES

1935	5,869
1936	74,008
1937	66,492
1938	65,736
1939	64,349
1940	50,965
1941	67,168
1942	64,080
1943	61,085
1944	54,873
1945	55,895
1946	51,679
1947	49,176
1948	50,801
1949	56,775
1950	46,532
1951	46,475
1952	40,714
1953	39,059
1954	53,259
1955	46,129
1956	53,000
1957	44,251
1958	45,501
1959	52,132
1960	46,266

stored 29/9/63-19/11/63
Mileage at 31/12/50 885,483; at
31/12/60 1,352,269
Withdrawn week ending 17/4/65

45667 JELLICOE
Built Crewe 25/11/35
Named 25/2/37
Renumbered 5667 to 45667 week ending 23/4/49

TENDERS

No	Fitted
9137	25/11/35
9110	21/6/40
9137	15/7/40
9153	5/12/45
9695	4/6/62

MILEAGES

1935	2,542
1936	80,138
1937	72,141
1938	92,135*
1939	71,116
1940	56,423
1941	65,920
1942	69,707
1943	66,350
1944	73,539
1945	42,102
1946	54,961
1947	60,247
1948	42,577
1949	49,762
1950	50,650
1951	46,033
1952	47,656
1953	57,026
1954	57,848
1955	61,406
1956	57,859
1957	65,145
1958	45,540
1959	68,231
1960	55,243

*Second highest recorded annual
mileage; see also 45685
Stored 1/1062-18/1/63, 19/10/
64-23/1/65
Mileage at 31/12/50 950,310; at
31/12/60 1,512,297
Withdrawn week ending 23/1/65

SHEDS
Crewe North 30/11/35
Camden 3/7/37
Crewe North 4/9/37
Kentish Town 11/9/37
Derby 1/11/47
Nottingham 20/9/52
Trafford Park 30/11/57
Nottingham 29/3/58
Trafford Park 24/5/58
Nottingham 31/5/58
Burton 18/11/61
Derby 26/1/63
Bank Hall 10/64

BOILERS
First boiler 9196

No	Fitted	From
9218	8/2/38	5688
9328	3/2/40	5708
9777	2/5/42	5729
9220	21/9/44	5722
9774	2/5/47	5701
10037	12/1/52	45684
9323	18/5/54	45608
9332	31/8/56	45680
9198	21/5/60	45670

REPAIRS
6/2/37-25/2/37**LS**
12/10/37-20/10/37**LO**
1/2/38-23/2/38**HG**
3/8/38-22/8/38**LO**
7/2/39-1/3/39**LS**
1/6/39-15/6/39**LO**
26/12/39-3/2/40**HG**
2/4/41-25/4/41**HS**
3/4/42-2/5/42**HG**
13/7/43-31/7/43**LS**
23/11/43-18/12/43**LO**
5/9/44-21/9/44**HG**
30/11/45-19/1/46**HS**
25/3/47-2/5/47**HG**
22/1/48-21/2/48**LS**
29/3/49-22/4/49**HI**
12/12/49-13/1/50**HC**
7/8/50-31/8/50**HI**
28/2/51-4/4/51**LC**
28/11/51-12/1/52**HG**
30/10/52-29/11/52**LC(EO)**
11/6/53-2/7/53**LI**
28/11/53-30/12/53**LC(EO)**
14/4/54-18/5/54**HG**
16/5/55-14/6/55**HI**
14/7/56-31/8/56**HG**
30/9/57-31/10/57**HI**
25/11/58-24/12/58**LI**
20/4/60-27/5/60**HG speedo fitted;**
AWS never fitted
24/11/60-6/1/61**LC(EO)**

45668 MADDEN

Built Crewe 2/12/35
Named 4/2/37
Renumbered 5668 to 45668 week ending 30/4/49

REPAIRS
18/1/37-4/2/37LS
28/2/38-4/4/38HG
20/2/39-6/3/39HS
1/6/40-21/6/40HG
15/4/41-2/5/41LS
7/8/42-4/9/42LS
9/8/43-21/8/43HS
19/2/45-10/3/45HG
12/8/46-27/8/46LS
22/7/47-4/10/47HG
4/4/49-26/4/49LI
15/12/49-30/1/50LC
21/9/50-10/10/50HI
18/3/52-29/5/52HG
17/6/53-4/7/53LI
10/5/54-5/6/54LI
31/12/54-29/1/55LC
24/11/55-23/12/55HG
1/2/57-1/3/57LI
6/10/58-31/10/58LI
1/6/59-20/6/59NC(EO) AWS fitted
26/2/60-9/4/60HI
    ?   -6/62 **speedo fitted**

TENDERS

No	Fitted
9138	2/12/35
9144	22/3/52

SHEDS
Crewe North 7/12/35
Carnforth (loan) 20/2/37
Crewe North 20/3/37
Longsight 1/5/37
Camden 23/8/41
Crewe North 10/6/44
Bushbury 12/10/46
Patricroft 26/4/47
Derby 24/10/59
Loan at first then
Derby 7/11/59
Burton 18/11/61

BOILERS
First boiler 9198

No	Fitted	From
9196	15/3/38	5667
9788	21/6/40	5740
9327	10/3/45	5666
9333	4/10/47	5732
9777	29/5/52	45621
9774	23/12/55	45694
9344	9/6/62	-

MILEAGES

1935	5,765
1936	79,870
1937	78,482
1938	73,299
1939	59,784
1940	52,338
1941	67,853
1942	50,044
1943	60,385
1944	53,951
1945	55,785
1946	47,623
1947	39,051
1948	52,474
1949	43,948
1950	48,630
1951	53,955
1952	42,372
1953	50,013
1954	48,301
1955	43,438
1956	57,740
1957	49,919
1958	44,269
1959	49,292
1960	43,681

Stored 15/10/62-17/12/62
Mileage at 31/12/50 869,282; 31/12/60 1,352,262
Withdrawn week ending 21/12/63

5668 MADDEN in 1946 black, on the Polmadie turntable; six-hole bracket for vacuum pump still on crosshead. By the post-war period the Jubilees were less of an up-to-the-moment steam design than they had been in the 1930s, when the steaming diffculties had been put behind them. This may seem an obvious point to make, for the engines had of course grown older. But operating conditions had changed by 1945, out of all recognition from the years of the Jubilees' introduction. Coal was declining in quality, often scarce, ever more expensive and much the same could often be said of labour. New engines in this power range now had to have self emptying ashpans, rocker grates and two cylinders. Photograph J. Robertson, The Transport Treasury.

A green MADDEN at Polmadie in the usual reek, 2 October 1953. If, post-war, the Jubilees were less of a modern engine then they were, then they had been ahead of their time. They were still good, modern designs, putting in a good day's work on a tender of coal and managing eight successive days before shed examination or attention. Rowledge and Reed have pointed this out; they did 40,000 miles between piston and valve exams, 70,000 miles between wheel and axlebox attention and 150,000 miles or more before boiler repairs and general overhaul. Note different position of steam lance valve on smokebox side. Photograph J. Robertson, The Transport Treasury.

45669 FISHER

Built Crewe 4/12/35
Named 26/1/37
Renumbered 5669 to 45669 week ending 7/8/48

TENDERS

No	Fitted
9139	4/12/35
4645	5/3/36
9155	6/3/36

REPAIRS
25/8/36-28/8/36**LO**
11/1/37-26/1/37**LS**
3/10/37-6/11/37**HG**
17/7/39-2/8/39**LS**
6/8/40-29/8/40**HG**
9/7/41-21/8/41**LO**
15/12/42-2/1/43**LS**
21/3/44-5/4/44**LS**
30/8/45-22/9/45**HG**
11/9/46-26/10/46**HS**
22/10/47-3/12/47**LS**
19/6/48-7/8/48**LO**
27/5/49-25/6/49**HG**
4/9/50-21/9/50**HI**
11/2/52-7/3/52**HI**
13/4/53-13/5/53**HG**
22/4/54-25/5/54**HI**
1/9/55-28/10/55**HG**
26/6/56-11/8/56**LC(EO)**
13/8/56-21/8/56**NC(EO Rect)**
16/3/57-12/4/57**HI**
17/10/58-13/11/58**LI**
13/10/58-11/11/59**NC(EO) speedo,**
AWS, fitted
19/1/61-4/3/61**HG**

SHEDS
Crewe North 7/12/35
Carlisle Upperby 27/2/37
Crewe North 27/11/37
Carlisle Upperby (loan) 18/12/37
Crewe North 1/1/38
Camden (loan) 16/4/38
Crewe North 20/4/38
Holyhead 4/6/38
Camden 1/7/39
Willesden 4/4/42
Camden 20/3/43
Leeds (loan) 10/7/43
Camden 28/8/43
Willesden 28/4/45
Camden 4/5/46
Crewe North 10/2/51
Camden 24/3/51
Willesden 3/10/59
Rugby 10/6/61
Nuneaton 4/11/61

BOILERS
First boiler 9199

No	Fitted	From
10036	22/10/37	New
9196	29/8/40	5668
9773	22/9/45	5672
10032	25/6/49	45685
9203	13/5/53	45704
9331	28/10/55	45742
9210	4/3/61	45690

MILEAGES

Year	Miles
1935	4,186
1936	79,015
1937	54,336*
1938	50,929*
1939	57,980
1940	55,094
1941	54,669
1942	42,235
1943	61,528
1944	49,122
1945	34,092
1946	57,577
1947	59,317
1948	57,016
1949	52,364
1950	56,446
1951	53,622
1952	53,088
1953	63,442
1954	57,916
1955	45,296
1956	53,939
1957	52,644
1958	52,157
1959	45,296
1960	37,924
1961	32,896
1962	29,524
1963	8,322

*1937 Stored serviceable 31 days
*1938 Stored serviceable 80 days
Stored 29/4/63-31/5/63
Mileage at 31/12/50 825,906; at
31/12/60 1,341,230;
at 1/6/63 1,411,972
Withdrawn week ending 1/6/63

45669 FISHER at Bellahouston, running out light backwards to Corkerhill shed, 14 September 1958. The sight of this Camden engine must have stirred up the locals – it was an event comparable to Corkerhill's 45665 calling in at Camden. Photograph Hamish Stevenson.

45670 HOWARD OF EFFINGHAM

Built Crewe 17/12/35

Named 1/3/37

Renumbered 5670 to 45670 week ending 26/3/49

TENDERS

No	Fitted
9140	17/12/35

SHEDS
Crewe North 21/12/35
Carlisle Upperby 27/2/37
Patricroft 27/7/46
Edge Hill 15/10/49
Crewe North 11/6/60
Willesden 3/12/60
Rugby 14/1/61
Derby 7/12/63
Stockport 9/64

REPAIRS
15/2/37-1/3/37LS
7/5/38-9/6/38HG
1/12/39-16/12/39HS
23/12/40-22/1/41HG
15/3/43-30/3/43LS
9/10/44-21/10/44LS
25/5/46-12/6/46HG
15/12/47-27/1/48HS
7/3/49-24/3/49HI
27/1/51-31/3/51HG
22/7/52-16/8/52LI
9/9/53-13/10/53LI
27/10/54-2/12/54HG
27/9/55-20/10/55HI
15/3/57-4/4/57LI
23/4/58-23/5/58LI
15/9/59-16/10/59HG AWS fitted
    ?   -12/61 speedo fitted

BOILERS
First boiler 9200

No	Fitted	From
9215	23/5/38	5685
10036	22/1/41	5669
9222	12/6/46	5702
9206	31/3/51	45700
9198	2/12/54	45685
9330	16/10/59	45672

MILEAGES

1935	1,376
1936	83,017
1937	61,951
1938	57,407
1939	54,368
1940	47,114
1941	41,548
1942	48,099
1943	37,240
1944	37,946
1945	40,974
1946	36,875
1947	39,204
1948	51,771
1949	47,768
1950	51,176
1951	45,556
1952	51,311
1953	48,738
1954	46,820
1955	47,452
1956	54,480
1957	55,657
1958	47,932
1959	48,694
1960	54,168

Stored 14/10/62-6/2/63, 9/9/63-25/11/63
Mileage at 31/12/50 737,834; at 31/12/60 1,238,642
Withdrawn week ending 24/10/64

Ex-works and shimmering, Edge Hill's 45670 at Crewe Works. Photograph E.M. Johnson Collection.

45671 PRINCE RUPERT

Built Crewe 6/12/35
Named 22/3/37
Renumbered 5671 to 45671 week ending 30/4/49

Photograph J.L. Stevenson, courtesy Hamish Stevenson.

TENDERS

No	Fitted
9141	6/12/35

BOILERS
First boiler 9201

No	Fitted	From
9204	4/3/38	5674
9259	9/8/39	5639
9781	6/1/43	5688
9202	2/10/47	5722
9328	12/1/52	45675
10036	29/1/55	45590
9207	26/3/60	45685

REPAIRS
20/7/36-18/8/36**LO**
6/3/37-22/3/37**LS**
28/2/38-21/3/38**HG**
5/12/38-3/1/39**LS**
26/7/39-9/8/39**HO**
15/4/40-1/5/40**HS**
7/2/41-26/2/41**LS**
30/11/42-6/1/43**HG**
15/8/43-3/9/43**TRO**
19/5/44-8/6/44**L**
26/9/44-12/10/44**LO**
26/10/44-16/11/44**LO**
13/2/46-7/3/46**HS**
12/7/47-2/10/47**HG**
16/10/48-28/10/48**TRO Newton Heath**
29/3/49-29/4/49**HI**
24/6/50-28/7/50**LI**
7/12/51-12/1/52**HG**
28/1/52-9/2/52**LC**
4/6/53-20/6/53**HI**
22/12/54-29/1/55**HG**
9/1/56-21/2/56**HI**
9/5/57-5/6/57**LI**
28/7/58-25/8/58**LI**
6/12/58-20/1/59**LC(EO)**
18/3/59-3/4/59**NC(EO) AWS fitted**
3/2/60-26/3/60**HG**
　?　-5/62 **speedo fitted**

SHEDS
Crewe North 7/12/35
Carnforth 9/1/37
Crewe North 23/1/37
Edge Hill 1/5/37
Crewe North (loan) 23/1/43
Newton Heath 6/3/43
Loan at first then
Newton Heath 10/4/43
Derby 2/9/44
Loan at first then
Derby 30/9/44
Newton Heath 9/12/44
Newton Heath 13/1/45
Bank Hall 12/10/46
Farnley Jct 22/11/47
Loan at first then
Farnley Jct 3/4/48
Newton Heath 4/9/48
Longsight 19/10/57
Llandudno Jct 10/9/60
Crewe North 10/6/61
Llandudno Jct 16/9/61
Edge Hill 23/9/61
Warrington 28/10/61

MILEAGES

1935	3,303
1936	77,222
1937	63,880
1938	62,383
1939	60,328
1940	49,057
1941	39,381
1942	36,562
1943	37,739
1944	29,394
1945	46,338
1946	54,274
1947	26,879
1948	42,279
1949	47,432
1950	43,610
1951	37,774
1952	53,129
1953	56,606
1954	47,076
1955	50,472
1956	58,632
1957	53,744
1958	60,601
1959	56,463
1960	44,541

Mileage at 31/12/50 720,061; at 31/12/60 1,239,099
Withdrawn week ending 9/11/63

A Newton Heath Jubilee, 45671 PRINCE RUPERT at Beattock, 26 July 1952. Photograph J. Robertson, The Transport Treasury.

45672 ANSON

Built Crewe 10/12/35
Named 4/3/37
Renumbered 5672 to 45672 week ending 7/8/48

TENDERS

No	Fitted
9143	10/12/35

REPAIRS
15/2/37-4/3/37**LS**
24/7/37-3/9/37**LO**
1/6/38-18/7/38**HG**
8/8/38-29/8/38**LO**
2/12/39-16/12/39**LS**
11/4/41-8/5/41**HG**
6/11/42-12/12/42**LS**
23/5/44-7/6/44**HS**
7/5/45-25/5/45**HG**
26/8/46-5/10/46**LS**
4/2/47-3/3/47**LO**
12/6/48-7/8/48**HG**
17/12/48-31/1/49**LC**
9/12/49-7/1/50**LI**
20/10/50-22/11/50**HG**
20/4/52-13/5/52**LI**
27/8/52-17/9/52**LC(EO)**
15/5/53-22/5/53**LC(EO) Camden**
29/12/53-27/1/54**HG**
15/1/55-5/2/55**HI**
1/11/55-2/12/55**HC**
20/6/56-13/8/56**LI**
16/5/57-7/6/57**LC(EO)**
31/12/57-1/2/58**HG**
20/7/59-1/9/59**HI AWS fitted**
24/6/61-11/8/61**HI speedo fitted**

SHEDS
Crewe North 14/12/35
Carnforth 9/1/37
Crewe North 18/12/37
Patricroft (loan) 30/4/38
Crewe North 14/5/38
Longsight 20/3/43
Edge Hill 25/1/47
Camden 28/5/49
Bushbury 9/2/57
Camden 23/3/57
Bushbury 28/9/57
Camden 2/11/57
Carlisle Upperby 9/58
Carlisle Kingmoor 17/9/60
Willesden 4/3/61
Rugby 10/6/61
Willesden 14/12/63
Crewe North 8/64

BOILERS
First boiler 9202

No	Fitted	From
9213	22/6/38	5683
9773	8/5/41	5718
9223	25/5/44	5695
9209	7/8/48	5681
9343	22/11/50	45724
9330	27/1/54	45683
10034	1/2/58	45610

MILEAGES

Year	Mileage
1935	2,296
1936	67,546
1937	51,213
1938	57,173
1939	57,771
1940	49,197
1941	43,725
1942	53,084
1943	66,389
1944	53,546
1945	58,529
1946	52,534
1947	55,701
1948	39,211
1949	50,504
1950	55,973
1951	54,304
1952	69,724
1953	58,500
1954	55,523
1955	46,143
1956	43,065
1957	50,966
1958	51,057
1959	44,634
1960	56,974

Stored 14/10/62-6/2/63, 9/9/63-2/12/63
Mileage at 31/12/50 814,392; at 31/12/60 1,345,282
Withdrawn week ending 7/11/64

45673 KEPPEL
Built Crewe 12/12/35
Named 8/3/37
Renumbered 5673 to 45673 4/48

SHEDS
Preston 28/12/35
Carlisle Upperby 12/11/38
Longsight 12/10/46
Edge Hill 15/4/47
Preston 6/51
Carlisle Kingmoor 9/52
Perth 3/53
Corkerhill 5/60

BOILERS
First boiler 9203

No	Fitted	From
9212	8/3/38	5682
9786	22/2/41	5738
9200	17/4/43	5694
9339	18/11/44	5704
9198	17/4/48	5677
Record incomplete		

MILEAGES

1935	1,285
1936	77,927
1937	51,994
1938	62,446
1939	57,246
1940	46,875
1941	38,357
1942	35,806
1943	38,693
1944	38,961
1945	40,027
1946	45,902
1947	52,954
1948	52,698
1949	50,078
1950	68,314

Record incomplete
Mileage at 31/12/50 759,563
Withdrawn December 1962

TENDERS

No	Fitted
9144	12/12/35
9701	17/3/43
9148	approx.1956

REPAIRS
9/9/37-8/10/37**LO**
15/2/38-23/3/38**HG**
2/12/39-22/12/39**HS**
6/1/41-15/2/41**HG**
30/3/42-30/4/42**HS**
14/3/43-14/4/43**HS**
6/11/44-18/11/44**HG**
25/6/46-26/7/46**HS**
19/5/47-13/6/47**LO**
13/3/48-17/4/48**HG**
22/7/49-16/8/49**LI**
Record Ends

45673 KEPPEL, 'lug' and bracket carried on the front (45015 alongside) at St Rollox shed (the engine had newly arrived on the complement from Kingmoor) in March 1953. Photograph J. Robertson, The Transport Treasury.

45674 DUNCAN

Built Crewe 16/12/35
Named 1/4/37
Renumbered 5674 to 45674 week ending 12/6/48

TENDERS

No	Fitted
9145	16/12/35

REPAIRS
13/3/37-1/4/37**LS**
18/1/38-10/2/38**HG**
1/10/38-25/11/38**LS**
19/4/40-18/5/40**HG**
14/3/41-22/3/41**TRO**
2/3/42-26/3/42**LS**
19/8/43-9/9/43**HG**
9/11/43-10/12/43**LO**
31/8/45-27/9/45**LS**
2/12/46-21/12/46**HG**
18/5/48-9/6/48**HS**
26/1/49-18/2/49**LC**
7/7/49-26/8/49**HG**
12/1/51-31/1/51**HI**
26/3/53-23/4/53**HG**
30/12/54-19/1/55**LI**
24/1/56-7/3/56**HG**
7/9/57-2/10/57**LI**
1/12/58-2/1/59**LI**
14/4/59-30/4/59**NC(EO) AWS fitted**
4/4/60-7/5/60**HI speedo fitted**
24/10/61-30/11/61**HG**

BOILERS
First boiler 9204

No	Fitted	From
9256	24/1/38	5665
9341	18/5/40	5721
9778	9/9/43	5728
9329	21/12/46	5685
9784	26/8/49	45690
9257	23/4/53	45742
9786	7/3/56	45723
9318	30/11/61	45703

SHEDS
Crewe North 21/12/35
Preston 28/12/35
Carlisle Upperby 13/11/37
Preston 1/1/38
Patricroft 11/3/39
Crewe North 6/12/41
Saltley 9/3/63

MILEAGES

1935	1401
1936	85,514
1937	59,597
1938	50,971
1939	52,688
1940	49,933
1941	51,057
1942	60,987
1943	49,920
1944	51,987
1945	32,225
1946	50,053
1947	57,771
1948	49,351
1949	45,724
1950	53,795
1951	50,743
1952	49,097
1953	49,003
1954	51,823
1955	49,464
1956	45,674
1957	46,903
1958	50,016
1959	52,178
1960	48,258

Stored 13/9/62-1/3/63
Mileage at 31/12/50 802,974; at 31/12/60 1,296,133
Withdrawn week ending 10/10/64

45675 HARDY

Built Crewe 17/12/35
Named 18/3/37
Renumbered 5675 to 45675 week ending 4/9/48

BOILERS
First boiler 9206

No	Fitted	From
9210	3/10/38	5680
9198	29/4/41	5678
9319	9/2/44	5657
9328	20/12/46	5740
9215	20/6/51	45682
10037	26/8/54	45667
9209	10/6/58	45717

REPAIRS
3/3/37-18/3/37**LS**
29/11/37-16/12/37**LS**
1/9/38-3/10/38**HG**
12/2/40-15/3/40**HS**
29/3/41-29/4/41**HG**
13/11/42-13/12/42**LS**
13/1/44-9/2/44**HG**
3/5/45-24/5/45**HS**
27/11/45-22/12/45**LO**
1/12/46-20/12/46**HG**
18/8/48-4/9/48**LS**
13/8/49-10/9/49**HI**
19/4/50-10/5/50**HI**
24/5/51-20/6/51**HG**
30/5/52-24/6/52**HI**
3/7/53-11/8/53**LI**
15/7/54-26/8/54**HG**
19/9/55-7/10/55**LI**
17/1/57-23/2/57**HI**
12/5/58-10/6/58**HG**
13/6/58**NC(Rect)**
27/7/59-3/9/59**LI**
28/6/60-17/9/60**LI**
2/12/60-19/1/61**LC(EO)**
AWS fitted by 4/62; probably speedo at same time

SHEDS
Crewe North 21/12/35
Carlisle Upperby 11/1/36
Crewe North 8/11/41
Leeds 2/10/48
Loan at first then
Leeds 6/11/48

TENDERS

No	Fitted
9146	17/12/35
9270	3/5/49

MILEAGES

1935	469
1936	78,942
1937	58,983
1938	59,871
1939	59,143
1940	45,706
1941	42,189
1942	51,694
1943	63,658
1944	59,528
1945	53,035
1946	52,230
1947	57,208
1948	55,075
1949	64,683
1950	59,663
1951	68,077
1952	68,253
1953	66,647
1954	58,250
1955	66,893
1956	54,452
1957	59,020

Mileage at 31/12/50 862,077
Withdrawn June 1967

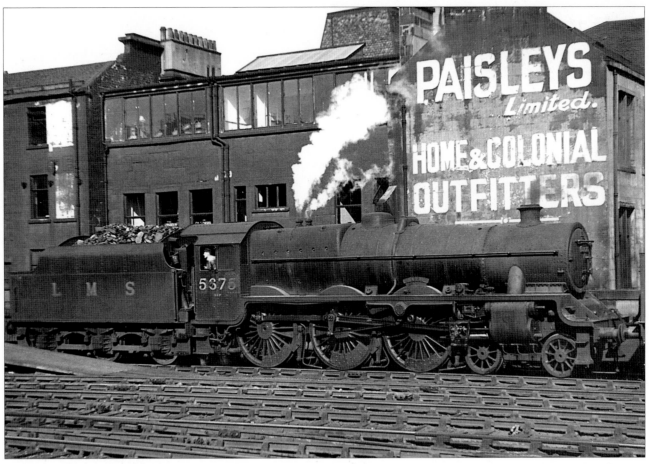

A shabby 5675 HARDY, with ancient and soot blackened backdrop, at Glasgow Central 17 May 1948. The look is anything but 'crimson lake'... Photograph J.L. Stevenson, courtesy Hamish Stevenson.

In plain black, 45675 HARDY at Kingmoor shed 24 June 1951. This was actually a very unusual livery – plain black plus BR emblem. It should, in theory, have been in Brunswick green. Photograph A. Swain, The Transport Treasury.

45676 CODRINGTON

Built Crewe 18/12/35
Named 14/5/37
Renumbered 5676 to 45676 week ending 2/10/48

TENDERS

No	Fitted
9147	18/12/35

REPAIRS
22/4/37-14/5/37**LS**
28/9/37-12/10/37**LO**
31/5/38-28/6/38**HG**
7/10/39-10/11/39**HS**
10/6/41-26/6/41**HG**
18/12/42-6/1/43**LS**
25/8/43-21/9/43**HG**
6/3/45-7/4/45**LS**
18/7/46-14/8/46**HG**
7/12/46-18/12/46**LO** St Rollox
2/1/48-14/2/48**LS**
28/8/48-28/9/48**LO**
17/3/49-14/4/9**HG**
21/4/49-22/4/49**NC(Rect)**
17/6/50-9/8/50**HI**
18/2/52-4/4/52**HI**
20/3/53-21/4/53**HG**
19/5/54-5/6/54**HI**
14/7/55-6/8/55**HI**
19/9/56-3/11/56**HG**
18/5/58-12/6/58**LI**
25/9/59-9/10/59**NC(EO) AWS fitted**
25/4/60-31/5/60**LI speedo fitted**

BOILERS
First boiler 9205

No	Fitted	From
9203	9/6/38	5673
9219	26/6/41	5679
9255	21/9/43	5608
9221	14/8/46	5567
11160	14/4/49	45665
10038	21/4/53	45719
9222	3/11/56	45726

SHEDS
Crewe North 21/12/35
Carlisle Upperby 11/1/36
Crewe North 8/11/41
Camden 5/6/48
Edge Hill 10/2/51
Camden 24/3/51
Carnforth 2/1/60
Crewe North 18/6/60
Saltley 9/3/63
Willesden 30/11/63
Crewe North 8/64

MILEAGES

Year	Mileage
1935	495
1936	75,356
1937	58,099
1938	53,262
1939	54,201
1940	51,123
1941	51,628
1942	57,537
1943	60,281
1944	61,202
1945	51,722
1946	41,682
1947	56,724
1948	49,236
1949	54,562
1950	57,225
1951	47,610
1952	49,979
1953	58,044
1954	55,543
1955	47,615
1956	48,671
1957	57,982
1958	50,154
1959	53,992
1960	44,697

Stored 16/9/62-3/3/63
Mileage at 31/12/50 834,336, at 31/12/60 1,348,623
Withdrawn week ending 26/9/64

45677 BEATTY

Built Crewe 19/12/35
Named 22/3/37
Renumbered 5677 to 45677 8/49

TENDERS

No	Fitted
9148	19/12/35

SHEDS
Crewe North 21/12/35
Carlisle Upperby 11/1/36
Crewe North 8/2/36
Carlisle Upperby 5/6/37
Camden 17/7/37
Crewe 28/8/37
Carlisle Upperby 30/11/40
Movements unknown from
30/11/40, though still at (or
back at) Upperby by 6/51
transfer
Camden 6/51
Carlisle Upperby 9/51
Polmadie 9/52
Corkerhill 8/54
Perth 9/59
Corkerhill 5/60

REPAIRS
26/8/38-10/10/38**HG**
20/4/40-4/5/40**HS**
4/1/41-25/1/41**HG**
23/12/42-28/1/43**LS**
18/5/44-2/6/44**HG**
4/2/46-1/3/46**HS**
4/11/47-19/12/47**HG**
21/7/49-12/8/49**LI**
Record Ends

BOILERS
First boiler 9207

No	Fitted	From
9211	29/10/38	5681
9344	25/1/41	5726
9198	10/6/44	5675
9216	27/12/47	5696

Record incomplete

MILEAGES

Year	Mileage
1935	56
1936	74,648
1937	60,002
1938	49,536*
1939	60,912
1940	47,454
1941	29,184
1942	42,753
1943	39,203
1944	41,347
1945	47,632
1946	38,328
1947	28,159
1948	50,864
1949	45,559
1950	47,191

*stored serviceable 38 days
Record ends
Mileage at 31/12/50 702,828
Withdrawn December 1962

45678 DE ROBECK

Built Crewe 24/12/35
Named 16/3/37
Renumbered 5678 to 45678 week ending 12/2/49

BOILERS
First boiler 9208

No	Fitted	From
9198	19/5/38	5668
9211	8/3/41	5677
9344	30/9/44	5677
10034	11/2/49	45704
9324	20/3/53	45690
9341	14/9/56	45719

MILEAGES

Year	Mileage
1935	-
1936	74,041
1937	62,052
1938	58,334
1939	60,123
1940	47,589
1941	45,013
1942	39,152
1943	42,176
1944	41,098
1945	47,273
1946	43,861
1947	30,497
1948	47,637
1949	48,267
1950	48,675
1951	37,237
1952	57,840
1953	52,562
1954	52,584
1955	42,693
1956	52,936
1957	54,021
1958	43,133
1959	49,543
1960	50,681

Mileage at 31/12/50 735,878; at 31/12/60 1,229,108
Withdrawn week ending 8/12/62

TENDERS

No	Fitted
9149	24/12/35

SHEDS
Crewe North 28/12/35
Carlisle Upperby 11/1/36
Carnforth (loan) 13/2/37
Carlisle Upperby 27/2/37
Crewe North 28/5/49
Longsight (loan; date unknown but believed to be just pre-6/52)
Crewe North 28/6/52
Bushbury 4/2/56
Crewe North 10/3/56
Edge Hill 20/9/58
Crewe North 20/6/59
Edge Hill 5/9/59
Carlisle Upperby 10/6/61
Carlisle Kingmoor 7/7/62
Stockport 8/62

REPAIRS
1/3/37-16/3/37**LS**
4/9/37-11/9/37**LO**
10/5/38-9/6/38**HG**
18/12/39-6/1/40**LS**
11/2/41-8/3/41**HG**
19/1/43-5/2/43**LS**
14/9/44-30/9/44**HG**
11/1/46-30/1/46**HS**
24/7/47-4/9/47**LS**
4/1/49-11/2/49**HG**
21/8/50-9/9/50**HI**
28/12/50-16/2/51**LC**
9/8/51-8/9/51**HI**
11/2/53-20/3/53**HG**
22/9/54-19/10/54**HI**
6/12/55-5/1/56**HI**
3/8/56-14/9/56**HG**
23/3/58-19/4/58**HI**
21/7/59-26/8/59**HI AWS fitted**
16/8/61-11/9/61**LI speedo fitted**

45678 DE ROBECK with a down train 'W225' at Crewe, still in lined black, on 25 July 1952. Obligatory 'urchins' on the famous bridge. Photograph J. Robertson, The Transport Treasury.

45679 ARMADA
Built Crewe 24/12/35
Named 29/6/37
Renumbered 5679 to 45679 8/48

BOILERS
First boiler 9209

No	Fitted	From
9219	26/11/38	5689
9785	24/5/41	5590
9224	12/5/45	5686
9788	4/5/49	5719
9339	12/5/54	45707
10035	21/11/59	45718

MILEAGES

1935	-
1936	63,943
1937	61,846
1938	52,254*
1939	50,632*
1940	43,148
1941	41,291
1942	44,788
1943	47,867
1944	37,551
1945	51,443
1946	50,417
1947	36,880
1948	40,728
1949	48,978
1950	57,362
1951	43,038
1952	53,448
1953	49,971
1954	55,099
1955	51,615
1956	53,291
1957	49,965
1958	36,668
1959	39,980
1960	39,085

*1938 stored serviceable 32 days
*1939 stored serviceable 60 days
**Mileage at 31/12/50 729,128; at
31/12/60 1,201,288**
Withdrawn week ending 29/12/62

TENDERS

No	Fitted
9150	24/12/35
3927	29/6/37* ex-6103
4498	29/8/50*
3791	14/2/53*
4498	14/3/53*

*Fowler

SHEDS

Crewe North 28/12/35
Chester 11/1/36
Preston 5/9/36
Crewe North 8/1/38
Derby 15/6/40
Bristol 21/7/45
Derby 1/9/45
Millhouses 11/5/46
Bristol 16/2/52
Carlisle Kingmoor 30/8/52
Loan at first then
Carlisle Kingmoor13/9/52
Crewe North 20/6/59
Longsight 30/4/60
Newton Heath 25/6/60

REPAIRS

13/9/38-1/11/38**HG**
20/4/40-4/5/40**LS**
30/3/41-24/5/41**HG**
27/9/42-26/10/42**LS**
1/11/43-7/12/43**LS**
26/8/44-3/10/44**LO**
24/4/45-12/5/45**HG**
2/3/46-11/4/46**HS**
13/7/46-20/8/46**HO**
13/6/47-21/8/47**HS**
10/8/48-27/8/48**LO**
21/3/49-4/5/49**HG**
31/7/50-29/8/50**HI**
5/11/51-30/11/51**H**
21/3/50-15/4/50**NC Derby**
17/6/52-5/7/52**LC**
9/1/53-14/2/53**LI St Rollox**
13/3/53-13/3/53**HC* St Rollox**
1/4/54-12/5/54**G St Rollox**
29/8/55-1/10/55**LI St Rollox**
4/4/57-2/5/57**HI St Rollox**
1/5/58-21/6/58**HI St Rollox**
28/9/59-21/11/59**GEN Cowlairs**
21/7/61-16/9/61**LI St Rollox**
*Tender only

Kingmoor's 45679 ARMADA, a further lined black example cleaned only enough to show the number, at Polmadie on 22 August 1953. In Scotland as elsewhere the Jubilees did not greatly impress at first, being regarded as hardly that much better than a Compound – a disastrous verdict. Once more superheater elements were fitted it was a different story. Photograph J. Robertson, The Transport Treasury.

45680 CAMPERDOWN

Built Crewe 31/12/35
Named 31/12/35
Renumbered 5680 to 45680 week ending 18/9/48

TENDERS	
No	Fitted
9151	31/12/35

MILEAGES	
1935	-
1936	75,940
1937	70,159
1938	62,290
1939	60,899
1940	50,722
1941	43,996
1942	44,699
1943	43,264
1944	42,223
1945	45,701
1946	40,072*
1947	38,083
1948	54,746
1949	51,882
1950	63,183
1951	56,023
1952	59,402
1953	48,421
1954	54,454
1955	56,723
1956	56,651
1957	57,802
1958	53,624
1959	57,014
1960	41,682

*'includes 2 miles running while on loan to LNER' (!)
Mileage at 31/12/50 787,859; at 31/12/60 1,329,655
Withdrawn week ending 12/1/63

BOILERS		
First boiler 9210		
No	Fitted	From
9208	25/8/38	5678
9784	22/8/41	5722
9210	29/9/45	5700
9785	5/12/49	5733
9332	23/4/52	45723
9218	11/4/56	45718
10033	2/1/62	45698

SHEDS
Crewe North 11/1/36
Stafford 18/12/36
Camden 3/7/37
Crewe North 14/8/37
Carlisle Upperby 30/11/40
Bushbury 9/3/46
Longsight 11/10/47
Edge Hill 15/10/60
Carlisle Upperby 10/6/61
Carlisle Kingmoor 7/7/62

REPAIRS
22/10/35-8/11/35**LS**
10/11/36-18/12/36**LO**
10/3/37-25/3/37**LS**
22/7/38-25/8/38**HG**
8/1/40-23/1/40**HS**
6/8/41-22/8/41**HG**
6/7/42-29/7/42**LO**
17/6/43-3/7/43**HS**
4/9/44-20/9/44**HS**
4/9/45-29/9/45**HG**
25/8/47-26/9/47**HS**
25/8/48-17/9/48**HS**
24/10/49-5/12/49**HG**
22/1/51-10/2/51**LI**
10/3/52-23/4/52**HG**
24/8/53-15/9/53**HI**
7/12/54-4/1/55**LI**
5/3/56-11/4/56**HG**
8/5/57-31/5/57**LI**
9/2/52-4/9/58**LI**
21/9/59-3/10/59**NC(EO)** AWS fitted
31/12/59-29/1/60**LI**
28/12/60-26/1/61**LC(EO)**
    ?   -1/62**HG** speedo fitted

45681 ABOUKIR

Built Crewe 31/12/35
Named 31/12/35
Renumbered 5681 to 45681 week ending 22/10/49

TENDERS	
No	Fitted
9152	31/12/35

REPAIRS
24/2/37-22/3/37**LS**
17/8/38-20/9/38**HG**
19/1/40-3/2/40**LS**
8/2/41-1/3/41**HG**
22/9/41-4/10/41**HO**
22/2/43-12/3/43**LS**
9/12/44-29/12/44**HG**
15/6/46-18/7/46**LS**
22/12/47-10/2/48**HG**
21/9/49-17/10/49**HI**
31/1/51-2/3/51**HI**
28/1/52-29/2/52**HG**
12/8/53-10/9/53**LI**
14/3/55-13/5/55**HG**
7/2/57-5/3/57**HI**
9/4/58-8/5/58**LI**
22/6/59-8/8/59**LI** AWS fitted
13/3/61-18/5/61**HG** speedo fitted

BOILERS		
First boiler 9211		
No	Fitted	From
9220	20/9/38	5690
9321	1/3/41	5687
9209	29/12/44	5724
9321	10/2/48	5687
9214	29/2/52	45665
9219	13/5/55	45689
9331	18/5/61	45669

SHEDS
Crewe North 11/1/36
Camden 3/7/37
Crewe North 28/8/37
Aston (loan) 4/5/40
Crewe North 1/6/40
Carlisle Upperby 30/11/40
Bushbury 9/3/46
Edge Hill 10/5/47
Carlisle Upperby 10/6/61
Carlisle Kingmoor 7/7/62
Blackpool 21/1/62
Loan at first then
Blackpool 18/8/62

MILEAGES	
1935	-
1936	76,918
1937	67,618
1938	60,422
1939	66,191
1940	45,315
1941	27,450
1942	43,130
1943	39,614
1944	48,903
1945	59,604
1946	43,968
1947	36,773
1948	54,036
1949	47,367
1950	43,962
1951	49,856
1952	50,713
1953	47,712
1954	50,695
1955	43,795
1956	55,163
1957	52,063
1958	46,326
1959	44,957
1960	46,310

Mileage at 31/12/50 761,311; at 31/12/60 1,248,901
Withdrawn week ending 19/9/64

45682 TRAFALGAR

Built Crewe 6/1/36
Named 6/1/36
Renumbered 5682 to 45682 week ending 19/3/49

TENDERS

No	Fitted
9153	6/1/36
9137	5/12/45

MILEAGES

1936	72,481
1937	70,297
1938	72,019
1939	69,449
1940	58,060
1941	58,595
1942	77,866
1943	72,591
1944	60,430
1945	62,222
1946	57,800
1947	62,404
1948	57,613
1949	63,670
1950	66,790
1951	58,222
1952	67,635
1953	59,968
1954	58,960
1955	62,623
1956	64,383
1957	63,614

Mileage at 31/12/50 982,487
Withdrawn June 1964

SHEDS

Crewe North 11/1/36
Kentish Town 11/9/37
Bristol 1/11/47
Trafford Park (loan) 25/9/48
Bristol 27/11/48
'Millhouses 12/10/57'
This last transfer to Millhouses shown on Record Card but not effected; 45682 stayed at Bristol until withdrawal. Someone, presumably, amended the wrong card!

BOILERS
First boiler 9212

No	Fitted	From
9199	18/1/38	5669
9315	5/4/39	5699
9195	11/4/42	5736
9206	5/1/45	5726
9215	6/3/48	5717
9209	23/4/51	45672
9326	9/10/54	45640
9787	24/11/56	45683

REPAIRS

3/4/37-3/5/37**LS**
29/12/37-2/2/38**HG**
2/3/39-5/4/39**HS**
23/2/40-7/3/40**LS**
20/12/40-6/1/41**LS**
21/3/42-11/4/42**HG**
3/3/43-27/3/43**HS**
22/1/44-15/2/44**HS**
9/12/44-5/1/45**HG**
25/7/45-7/9/45**HS**
8/4/46-3/5/46**LS**
25/11/46-2/1/47**LS**
7/1/48-6/3/48**HG**
25/2/49-18/3/49**HI**
11/2/50-3/3/50**LI**
6/3/51-23/4/51**HG**
30/4/52-29/5/52**LI**
18/4/53-16/5/53**HI**
31/8/53-1/10/53**LC**
6/9/54-9/10/54**HG**
12/11/54-24/11/54**LC(TO)**
10/10/55-2/11/55**LI**
15/10/56-24/11/56**HG**
29/12/57-28/1/58**HI**
? - 30/6/59**LI**
12/11/59-7/1/60**LC(EO)**
speedo fitted by 4/62;
AWS never fitted

45683 HOGUE

Built Crewe 16/1/36
Named 16/1/36
Renumbered 5683 to 45683 week ending 24/7/48

TENDERS

No	Fitted
9154	16/1/36

REPAIRS

15/3/37-1/4/37**LS**
4/3/38-28/4/38**HG**
19/4/39-8/5/39**LS**
21/6/40-11/7/40**HG**
29/7/41-16/8/41**HS**
11/7/42-23/7/42**TRO**
15/6/43-1/7/43**HG**
27/3/45-3/5/45**LS**
17/5/46-5/6/46**HG**
29/11/46-31/12/46**LO**
23/6/47-7/8/47**HS**
29/5/48-21/7/48**LS**
14/10/49-7/11/49**LI**
27/11/50-12/1/51**HG**
16/8/52-12/9/52**HI**
20/8/53-8/10/53**HG**
1/12/54-23/12/54**LI**
13/7/55-19/8/55**LC(EO)**
4/9/56-5/10/56**HG**
26/9/57-19/10/57**HI**
27/11/58-24/12/58**LI**
13/6/60-28/7/60**LI**

BOILERS
First boiler 9213

No	Fitted	From
9320	8/4/38	5616
9256	11/7/40	5674
10032	1/7/43	5702
9259	5/6/46	5665
9330	12/1/51	45608
9787	8/10/53	45703
9199	5/10/56	45695

SHEDS

Crewe North 18/1/36
Longsight 28/8/37
Carlisle Upperby 23/9/39
Bushbury 9/3/46
Camden 17/5/47
Crewe North 11/10/47
Millhouses 13/12/47
Loan at first then
Millhouses 31/12/47
Canklow 1/62
Darnall 6/62

MILEAGES

1936	77,810
1937	71,264
1938	65,941
1939	63,502
1940	38,080
1941	39,052
1942	41,592
1943	37,184
1944	53,142
1945	54,789
1946	52,959
1947	54,015
1948	46,627
1949	43,715
1950	46,947
1951	51,101
1952	48,057
1953	47,666
1954	47,394
1955	49,930
1956	52,403
1957	55,200

Stored prior to withdrawal
Mileage at 31/12/50 786,619
Withdrawn week ending 29/12/62

45684 JUTLAND

Built Crewe 6/2/36
Named 6/2/36
Renumbered 5684 to 45684 week ending 9/10/48

TENDERS

No	Fitted
9155	6/2/36
4645	6/3/36

SHEDS
Crewe North 8/2/36
Bushbury 10/6/39
Crewe North 16/9/39
Willesden 10/12/60
Rugby 14/1/61
Derby 7/12/63
Bank Hall 10/64

REPAIRS
14/4/37-3/5/37**LS***
14/10/37-25/10/37**LO**
28/9/38-10/11/38**HG**
29/4/40-14/5/40**HS**
6/10/41-24/10/41**HG**
10/2/43-25/2/43**LS**
27/8/43-25/9/43**HG**
1/2/45-17/2/45**LS**
10/6/46-26/6/46**HS**
4/3/47-3/4/47**HG**
21/9/48-7/10/48**LS**
8/1/49-9/2/49**LC**
5/5/50-26/5/50**HI**
12/9/51-17/10/51**HG**
12/8/53-11/9/53**LI**
10/1/55-2/4/55**HG**
16/1/57-7/2/57**HI**
14/8/58-12/9/58**LI**
13/1/60-4/3/60**HG AWS fitted**
    ? - 1/62 **speedo fitted**
*no record of double
chimney fitted 1937

BOILERS
First boiler 9214

No	Fitted	From
9206	10/11/38	5675
9207	24/10/41	5696
9330	25/9/43	5734
10037	3/4/47	5739
9315	17/10/51	45639
9781	2/4/55	45699
9196	4/3/60	45590

MILEAGES

1936	67,604
1937	56,891
1938	60,234
1939	55,489
1940	53,219
1941	54,737
1942	54,926
1943	51,484
1944	55,042
1945	58,478
1946	48,073
1947	47,580
1948	43,155
1949	42,937
1950	53,075
1951	43,138
1952	54,391
1953	50,468
1954	49,900
1955	39,741
1956	55,473
1957	49,018
1958	45,513
1959	52,113
1960	43,301

Stored 14/10/62-6/2/63, 15/9/63-
25/1/64,
12/10/64-28/6/65, 20/9/65-
unrecorded date (probably
withdrawal)
**Mileage at 31/12/50 802,924; at
31/12/60 1,285,980**
Withdrawn week ending 11/12/65

45685 BARFLEUR

Built Crewe 31/1/36
Named 31/1/36
Renumbered 5685 to 45685 5/48

MILEAGES

1936	71,807
1937	70,537
1938	93,588*
1939	71,054
1940	64,444
1941	44,660
1942	70,403
1943	66,750
1944	58,886
1945	60,601
1946	62,389
1947	50,133
1948	73,419
1951	63,598
1952	63,261
1953	69,413
1954	54,341
1955	58,460
1956	65,712
1957	62,503

*Highest recorded mileage – see
also 45667
Mileage at 31/12/50 978,354
Withdrawn March 1964

TENDERS

No	Fitted
9156	31/1/36

SHEDS
Crewe North 1/2/36
Kentish Town 11/9/37
Bristol 1/11/47

BOILERS
First boiler 9215

No	Fitted	From
9201	12/4/38	5671
9340	22/4/39	5720
9254	31/7/41	5700
9329	13/5/43	5621
10032	3/8/46	5683
9342	7/2/49	5725
9198	29/6/51	45673
9207	17/9/54	45686
9197	19/12/59	45639

REPAIRS
21/4/37-17/5/37**LS**
5/12/37-20/12/37**LO**
16/3/38-28/4/38**HG**
13/3/39-22/4/39 **HS**
22/4/40-9/5/40**HS**
30/8/41-31/7/41**HG**
25/8/41-22/9/41**LO**
11/9/42-17/10/42**HS**
17/4/43-13/5/43**HG**
8/3/44-25/3/44**HS**
10/2/45-24/2/45**LS**
20/11/45-15/12/45**HS**
1/7/46-3/8/46**HG**
14/6/47-15/8/47**LS**
29/4/48-28/5/48**HS**
31/12/48-7/2/49**HG**
10/1/50-31/1/50**LI**
28/8/50-18/9/50**LI**
28/5/51-29/6/51**HG**
11/8/52-9/9/52**HI**
10/8/53-10/9/53**HI**
27/7/54-17/9/54**HG**
23/6/55-30/7/55**LI**
16/7/56-14/8/56**HI**
21/4/57-10/6/57**HI**
9/6/58-8/8/58**LI**
4/11/59-19/12/59**HG speedo
probably fitted**
16/8/61-14/9/61**LI**
AWS never fitted

45686 ST VINCENT

Built Crewe 5/2/36
Named 5/2/36
Renumbered 5686 to 45686 week ending 3/9/49

TENDERS

No	Fitted
9157	5/2/36

MILEAGES

Year	Mileage
1936	71,159
1937	56,093
1938	56,724*
1939	55,280*
1940	53,686
1941	54,159
1942	57,984
1943	60,518
1944	58,794
1945	57,297
1946	49,674
1947	54,044
1948	48,824
1949	46,428
1950	45,306
1951	51,513
1952	45,032
1953	59,986
1954	58,556
1955	54,358
1956	34,642
1957	47,602
1958	61,014
1959	47,795
1960	42,069

*1938 stored serviceable 29 days
*1939 stored serviceable 37 days
Mileage at 31/12/50 825,970; at 31/12/60 1,328,537
Withdrawn week ending 17/11/62

BOILERS
First boiler 9216

No	Fitted	From
9205	26/9/38	5676
9224	27/11/41	5707
9200	14/3/45	5673
9779	18/3/48	5689
9207	4/10/50	45742
9224	2/2/54	45700
10032	4/12/57	-

SHEDS

Crewe North 8/2/36
Carnforth 23/1/37
Crewe North 18/12/37
Camden (loan) 10/12/38
Crewe North 8/4/39
Camden 21/2/53
Carnforth 2/1/60

REPAIRS

22/2/37-9/3/37 LS
26/8/38-26/9/38 HG
4/3/40-16/3/40 LS
8/11/41-27/11/41 HG
14/6/43-26/6/43 HS
14/6/44-1/7/44 HS
26/2/45-14/3/45 HG
5/10/46-23/10/46 LS
13/2/48-18/3/48 HG
19/7/49-31/8/49 HI
10/8/50-4/10/50 HG
29/5/52-21/6/52 HI
1/10/52-30/10/52 LC(EO)
4/1/54-2/2/54 HG
3/6/55-22/6/55 LI
9/12/56-9/1/57 LI
19/10/57-4/12/57 HG
9/12/58-22/12/58 LC(EO) Rugby
8/2/59-10/3/59 LI AWS fitted
29/4/59-20/5/59 NCRect(EO)
2/1/60-27/2/60 LC(EO)
8/5/61-9/6/61 LI speedo fitted

45686 ST VINCENT just on the Polmadie turntable, on a damp 30 July 1960. White's Chemical works, Rutherglen in the distance beyond the engine. Photograph J.L. Stevenson, courtesy Hamish Stevenson.

45687 NEPTUNE with big St Rollox numbers, at Glasgow Central on 9 June 1956. Photograph J. Robertson, The Transport Treasury.

45687 NEPTUNE

Built Crewe 10/2/36
Named 10/2/36
Renumbered 5687 to 45687 10/48

SHEDS
Crewe North 22/2/36
Carlisle Upperby 28/8/37
Crewe North 4/3/44
Carlisle Upperby 16/10/48
Corkerhill 9/52

MILEAGES

Year	Mileage
1936	66,107
1937	58,230
1938	50,254
1939	57,346
1940	43,852
1941	41,623
1942	45,827
1943	37,855
1944	45,224
1945	56,505
1946	44,694
1947	45,375
1948	49,171
1949	48,977
1950	45,765

Record ends
Mileage at 31/12/50 736,805
Withdrawn December 1962

BOILERS
First boiler 9217

No	Fitted	From
9321	1/10/38	5622
9323	25/1/41	5608
9321	8/2/45	5681
9781	27/12/47	5671
9321	29/2/52	5681

Record incomplete

TENDERS

No	Fitted
9158	10/2/36
10586	mid-1950s
9084	mid-1960s

(dates not recorded)

REPAIRS
27/1/38-10/2/38**LO**
15/8/38-27/9/38**HG**
26/2/40-16/3/40**HS**
2/1/41-24/1/41**HG**
20/3/43-3/4/43**LS**
20/1/45-8/2/45**HG**
29/8/46-28/9/46**HS**
12/11/47-24/12/47**HG**
21/9/48-9/10/48**HS**
10/2/50-2/3/50**LI**
Record incomplete

45688 POLYPHEMUS

Built Crewe 24/2/36
Named 24/2/36
Renumbered 5688 to 45688 week ending 22/5/48

TENDERS

No	Fitted
9159	24/2/36

REPAIRS
13/12/37-10/1/38**HG**
24/4/39-15/5/39**LS**
22/7/40-14/8/40**HG**
10/4/42-23/5/42**HS**
20/11/43-21/12/43**HS**
15/3/45-30/3/45**HG**
23/8/45-29/9/45**LO**
21/10/46-5/11/46**LS**
19/4/48-18/5/48**HG**
26/5/49-15/6/49**HI**
31/8/50-25/9/50**LI**
29/3/52-3/6/52**HG**
28/10/53-25/11/53**HI**
17/1/55-16/2/55**LI**
10/2/56-6/3/56**LI**
2/2/57-9/3/57**HG**
15/8/57-14/9/57**LC(EO)**
26/4/58-22/5/58**HI**
8/8/59-9/9/59**HI AWS fitted**
23/10/59-11/11/59**NCRect(EO)**
2/10/61-1/11/61**HI speedo fitted**

BOILERS
First boiler 9218

No	Fitted	From
10038	28/12/37	New
9781	4/8/40	5733
9324	23/5/42	5735
9777	30/3/45	5667
9200	18/5/48	5686
9321	3/6/52	45681
9773	9/3/57	45709

SHEDS
Crewe North 29/2/36
Carlisle Upperby 28/8/37
Longsight 1/7/39
Crewe North 16/9/39
Longsight 29/4/50
Bushbury 7/7/51
Carlisle Upperby 7/11/59
Carlisle Kingmoor 7/7/62

MILEAGES

1936	64,966
1937	65,801
1938	69,856
1939	59,133
1940	43,756
1941	58,924
1942	60,713
1943	54,879
1944	60,754
1945	54,154
1946	55,297
1947	51,750
1948	46,608
1949	48,987
1950	46,025
1951	44,397
1952	44,454
1953	52,526
1954	60,876
1955	56,359
1956	53,555
1957	50,107
1958	50,329
1959	45,888
1960	49,105

Mileage at 31/12/50 841,703; at 31/12/60 1,349,299
Withdrawn week ending 15/12/62

45689 AJAX

Built Crewe 28/2/36
Named 13/3/36
Renumbered 5689 to 45689 week ending 27/11/48

TENDERS

No	Fitted
9160	28/2/36

REPAIRS
3/4/37-19/4/37**LS**
22/8/38-23/9/38**HG**
20/1/40-9/2/40**HS**
26/12/40-18/1/41**HG**
27/6/42-25/7/42**LS**
20/12/43-5/1/44**HG**
26/3/45-25/4/45**LS**
6/12/46-28/12/46**HS**
6/9/47-16/10/47**HG**
3/11/48-25/11/48**LS**
28/4/50-19/5/50**HI**
25/5/50-26/5/50**NCRectTRO**
21/6/51-7/8/51**HG**
23/6/53-3/8/53**LI**
13/12/54-11/2/55**HG**
9/5/56-5/6/56**LI**
24/9/57-19/10/57**HI**
12/5/59-13/6/59**HG AWS fitted**
6/9/60-15/10/60**HI speedo fitted**

BOILERS
First boiler 9219

No	Fitted	From
9221	23/9/38	5691
9202	18/1/41	5694
9779	5/1/44	5731
9786	16/10/47	5608
9219	7/8/51	45708
9215	11/2/55	45675
9201	13/6/59	45734

SHEDS
Crewe North 29/2/36
Patricroft (loan) 30/4/38
Crewe North 14/5/38
Bushbury (loan) 10/3/52
Crewe North 7/6/52
Trafford Park 8/53
('Heaton Mersey 5/9/53' –
regarded as clerical error)
Longsight 9/53
Crewe North 8/3/58
Edge Hill 19/4/58
Crewe North 24/5/58
Llandudno Jct 9/64

MILEAGES

1936	65,069
1937	66,290
1938	64,817
1939	60,846
1940	50,318
1941	56,680
1942	55,053
1943	58,890
1944	62,592
1945	51,746
1946	53,176
1947	47,282
1948	50,491
1949	48,397
1950	47,801
1951	39,364
1952	52,538
1953	53,035
1954	49,696
1955	45,863
1956	56,699
1957	51,130
1958	56,182
1959	46,703
1960	44,461

Stored 23/9/63-13/12/63
Mileage at 31/12/50 839,448; at 31/12/60 1,335,119
Withdrawn week ending 12/12/64
(After 'paper' transfer to Crewe North)

Longsight's 45689 AJAX at Dalry Road shed on 2 February 1957, in another lovely low sunlit shot. Flexible hose connection on the ejector pipe, wonderful and sublime curves everywhere you look. Veteran next door is a McIntosh Caley 0-6-0. Photograph J. Robertson, The Transport Treasury.

AWS fitted 45689 AJAX (now of Crewe North) gets going at Carlisle, 20 March 1960. Photograph The Transport Treasury.

45690 LEANDER

Built Crewe 9/3/36
Named 9/3/36
Renumbered 5690 to 45690 week ending 15/5/48

TENDERS

No	Fitted
9161	9/3/36
9139	16/10/52

REPAIRS
22/2/37-8/3/37**LS**
20/6/38-3/8/38**HG**
11/1/39-30/1/39**LO**
17/4/40-7/5/40**HG**
26/12/41-14/1/42**HS**
15/7/43-7/3/43**HG**
20/11/44-6/12/44**LS**
27/10/45-27/11/45**HG**
18/3/47-24/4/47**HS**
24/3/48-11/5/48**LS**
21/2/49-12/4/49**HG**
14/1/50-4/2/50**LI**
27/9/50-20/10/50**HI**
5/7/51-3/8/51**LI**
6/2/52-1/3/52**LC**
5/5/52-23/5/52**LC**
11/10/52-15/11/52**HG**
28/1/54-26/2/54**HI**
28/7/54-8/9/54**LC(EO)**
15/8/55-14/9/55**HG**
18/11/56-12/12/56**HI**
17/10/57-15/11/57**HI**
29/11/58-3/1/59**HI**
21/3/60-6/5/60**HG** speedo probably
AWS never fitted

BOILERS
First boiler 9220

No	Fitted	From
9200	13/7/38	5670
10037	7/5/40	5665
9217	7/8/43	5639
9784	27/11/45	5680
9324	12/4/49	45694
10033	15/11/52	45705
9210	14/9/55	45710
9215	6/5/60	45689

SHEDS
Crewe North 14/3/36
Bescot (loan) 30/4/38
Crewe North 14/5/38
Bristol 13/9/47
Loan at first then
Bristol 25/10/47

MILEAGES

1936	65,500
1937	70,687
1938	59,951
1939	56,907
1940	49,688
1941	62,879
1942	57,266
1943	57,423
1944	50,505
1945	54,209
1946	63,271
1947	59,435
1948	63,445
1949	61,035
1950	57,977
1951	61,917
1952	46,962
1953	65,877
1954	56,522
1955	59,993
1956	69,340
1957	65,796

Mileage at 31/12/50 890,198
Withdrawn March 1964 PRESERVED

45691 ORION

Built Crewe 11/3/36
Named 11/3/36
Renumbered 5691 to 45691 5/49

TENDERS

No	Fitted
9162	11/3/36
9828	16/2/53

REPAIRS
13/6/38-21/7/38**HG**
2/12/39-23/12/39**LS**
14/11/41-18/12/41**HS**
13/1/43-30/1/43**HG**
13/1/44-12/2/44**LS**
7/3/45-24/3/45**LS**
25/4/45-26/5/45**LO**
23/1/46-16/2/46**LO**
27/8/46-21/9/46**HS**
21/6/47-10/10/47**HG**
28/10/47-29/11/47**LO**
15/3/49-30/4/49**LI**
28/7/50-2/9/50**LI**
18/2/52-28/6/52**G St Rollox**
15/6/53-4/7/53**LI St Rollox**
9/11/53-1/12/53**LC St Rollox**
29/7/54-25/8/54**LI St Rollox**
2/9/54-4/9/54**NC(R) St Rollox**
4/1/56-27/1/56**LI St Rollox**
1/4/57-24/5/57**G St Rollox**
22/8/58-30/9/58**HI**
22/3/60-29/4/60**LI St Rollox**
31/7/61-9/9/61**G St Rollox**
18/9/61-7/12/61**LC St Rollox**
AWS fitted by 6/62; no date for
speedo fitting

SHEDS
Crewe North 14/3/36
Polmadie 1/2/41
Carlisle Kingmoor 16/9/54
Carlisle Upperby 28/10/61
Carlisle Kingmoor 7/7/62
Blackpool 21/7/62
Loan at first then
Blackpool 18/8/62

BOILERS
First boiler 9221

No	Fitted	From
9318	27/6/38	5607
9776	30/1/43	5727
9790	10/10/47	5716
9338	28/6/52	45699
9223	24/5/57	45696
9779	9/9/61	45728

MILEAGES

1936	69,596
1937	69,249
1938	62,286
1939	58,808
1940	47,695
1941	62,955
1942	68,734
1943	59,389
1944	33,285
1945	44,030
1946	40,545
1947	26,230
1948	47,674
1949	38,503
1950	39,671
1951	44,531
1952	36,573
1953	38,222
1954	47,219
1955	49,062
1956	58,928
1957	43,068
1958	55,553
1959	57,655
1960	50,027

Mileage at 31/12/50 968,650; at
31/12/60 1,449,488
Withdrawn week ending 29/12/62

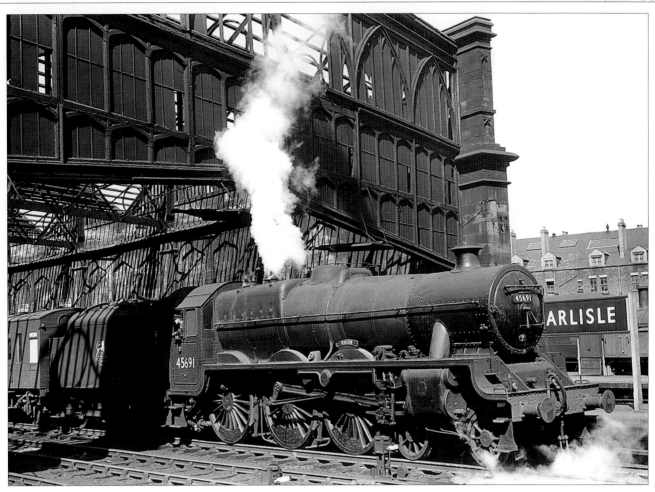

Stirring study of 45691 ORION, a Kingmoor engine with typical big St Rollox cabside numbers, on 18 April 1955. The distinctive shadow pattern of the decaying Citadel roof is wonderfully captured. Photograph J. Robertson, The Transport Treasury.

45692 CYCLOPS

Built Crewe 19/3/36
Named 19/3/36
Renumbered 5692 to 45692 6/48

TENDERS

No	Fitted
9163	19/3/36
9710	12/6/44
9596	15/7/50
9717	31/7/50

BOILERS
First boiler 9222

No	Fitted	From
9317	25/2/39	untraceable
9208	14/1/42	5680
9783	27/10/45	5730
9205	27/4/46	5729
9208	1/9/51	45680
Record incomplete		

MILEAGES

1936	55,211*
1937	54,613*
1938	55,706
1939	53,759
1940	50,747
1941	58,045
1942	53,142
1943	55,776
1944	43,648
1945	34,812
1946	36,237
1947	43,971
1948	36,865
1949	33,083
1950	34,304

*1936 stored serviceable 25 days
*1937 stored serviceable 50 days
Record ends
Mileage at 31/12/50 699,919
Withdrawn December 1962

SHEDS
Crewe North 21/3/36
Preston 26/12/37
Crewe North 25/2/39
Patricroft 22/7/39
Polmadie 1/2/41
Some missing information; believed allocated to Polmadie until transfer to Perth 8/54
Corkerhill 5/60

REPAIRS
18/8/37-13/9/37**LS**
4/1/39-8/2/39**HG**
24/5/40-6/6/40**LS**
22/12/41-14/1/42**HG**
23/1/42-18/3/42**LO**
9/6/43-17/7/43**LS**
29/5/44-14/6/44**LS**
26/9/45-27/10/45**HG**
24/12/45-1/2/46**LO**
26/2/46-27/4/46**HO**
6/10/47-13/11/47**LS**
19/6/48-30/6/48**LO**
3/7/48-24/8/48**LS**
17/12/41-3/2/50**HI**
29/5/50-14/7/50**LC**
Record incomplete

45693 AGAMEMNON

Built Crewe 19/3/36
Named 19/3/36
Renumbered 5693 to 45693 8/48

TENDERS

No	Fitted
9329	19/3/36
9215	6/5/50
9015	23/12/50

SHEDS

Crewe North 21/3/36
Longsight 29/4/39
Crewe North 22/7/39
Polmadie 1/2/41
Carlisle Kingmoor 11/4/42
Corkerhill 28/1/44

MILEAGES

1936	51,372*
1937	59,968*
1938	53,769
1939	57,841
1940	20,210
1941	46,907
1942	57,040
1943	59,533
1944	42,798
1945	52,246
1946	34,288
1947	39,697
1948	43,385
1949	42,270
1950	41,681

*1936 stored serviceable 25 days
*1937 stored serviceable 46 days
Mileage at 31/12/50 703,005
Withdrawn December 1962

BOILERS

First boiler 9223

No	Fitted	From
9258	24/12/38	5698
9322	2/1/43	5639
9254	6/3/48	5728

Record incomplete

REPAIRS

23/8/37-8/9/37**LS**
8/10/38-2/12/38**HG**
3/4/40-19/4/40**LS**
3/10/41-4/11/41**HS**
4/12/42-2/1/43**HG**
11/9/44-13/10/44**LS**
26/2/46-26/3/46**HS**
17/8/46-16/11/46**HO**
19/2/47-11/4/47**HO**
5/2/48-6/3/48**HG**
13/8/48-26/8/48**LO**
19/5/49-30/5/49**LC**
8/8/49-30/9/49**LI**
5/8/50-26/8/50**LC**
20/11/50-23/12/50**HI**

Record incomplete

45693 AGAMEMNON at Corkerhill shed, 14 November 1954; it went to the big ex-G&SW shed towards the end of the Second World War and seems to have stayed there until the end. Scottish Jubilees fared better than their English counterparts in the mid-1950s in terms of availability, probably because the better water in chalk-free Scotland meant engines could run several days more between washouts. It is difficult, however, to tease out the exact causes because, as noted earlier, distances were generally less. Water softening enacted in England from the 1930s onwards should have ironed out the differences but it was impossible to 'fix' every column at every station and every shed. Photograph J.L. Stevenson, courtesy Hamish Stevenson.

45694 BELLEROPHON

Built Crewe 25/3/36
Named 25/3/36
Renumbered 5694 to 45694 week ending 17/4/48

TENDERS

No	Fitted
9330	25/3/36

REPAIRS
15/6/37-15/7/37**LS**
3/2/38-1/3/38**LO**
19/8/38-21/9/38**HG**
6/7/39-27/7/39**LS**
1/9/39-11/10/39**LO**
24/7/40-17/8/40**HG**
28/8/40-7/9/40**LO**
19/1/42-7/2/42**LS**
6/1/43-23/2/43**HG**
3/3/44-18/3/44**LS**
17/10/44-4/11/44**LO**
20/6/45-17/7/45**HG**
29/7/46-24/8/46**HS**
24/2/47-26/4/47**HO**
6/3/48-14/4/48**LS**
19/5/48-1/6/48**NC Derby**
20/9/48-27/10/48**HG**
31/10/49-24/11/49**HI**
25/5/50-3/7/50**LC**
14/3/51-7/4/51**HI**
11/2/52-29/3/52**HG**
21/5/53-17/6/53**HI**
23/12/53-23/1/54**LC(EO)**
13/11/54-21/12/54**HG**
15/8/55-10/9/55**LC**
28/4/56-26/5/56**HI**
4/2/57-13/3/57**HI**
27/12/58-8/2/58**HG**
5/10/59-21/11/59**LI**
6/5/61-5/6/61**LI**
AWS fitted, date unknown; no record of speedo

BOILERS
First boiler 9224

No	Fitted	From
9202	21/9/38	5672
9200	17/8/40	5690
9218	23/2/43	5740
9324	17/7/45	5688
9327	27/10/48	5668
9774	29/3/52	45667
9336	21/12/54	45738
9333	8/2/58	45721

SHEDS
Crewe North 28/3/36
Preston 8/8/36
Kentish Town 11/9/37
Derby 14/6/41
Leeds 13/6/42
Bristol (loan) 3/1/48
Leeds 31/1/48
Low Moor 6/62
Wakefield 2/65

MILEAGES

1936	58,910
1937	57,584
1938	80,452
1939	62,760
1940	52,108
1941	59,069
1942	48,458
1943	56,993
1944	46,145
1945	50,446
1946	62,611
1947	56,583
1948	57,603
1949	63,712
1950	69,994
1951	64,241
1952	66,802
1953	62,783
1954	53,850
1955	66,788
1956	68,371
1957	60,254

Mileage at 31/12/50 883,428
Withdrawn January 1967

45695 MINOTAUR

Built Crewe 26/3/36
Named 26/3/36
Renumbered 5695 to 45695 week ending 16/10/48

SHEDS
Newton Heath 28/3/36
Southport 4/6/38
Newton Heath 1/10/38
Blackpool 9/12/39
Bank Hall 29/3/52
Farnley Jct 20/9/52

REPAIRS
11/8/37-6/9/37**LS**
19/12/38-2/2/39**HG**
11/7/40-7/8/40**LS**
21/11/40-24/4/41**LO**
10/10/41-8/11/41**HG**
13/11/42-12/12/42**LS**
16/8/43-11/9/43**LS**
9/11/44-24/11/44**HG**
10/8/45-28/8/45**LS**
27/4/46-1/6/46**TRO**
22/12/46-14/1/47**HS**
27/8/48-14/10/48**HG**
6/11/50-30/11/50**LI**
14/1/52-22/2/52**HG**
25/7/53-29/8/53**HI**
3/2/55-4/3/55**HI**
22/8/55-27/8/55**LC Horwich**
24/4/56-6/6/56**HG**
6/6/56-18/6/56**NC(EO Rect)**
17/6/57-6/7/57**LI**
  ? -10/57**NC(Rect)(TO)**
2/6/58-20/6/58**LC(EO)**
3/10/58-17/10/58**LC(TO)**
18/4/59-23/5/59**LI**
  ? - 23/1/61**NC(EO) probable date of AWS, speedo fitting**
25/4/61-24/5/61**HI**

TENDERS

No	Fitted
3923	26/3/36* ex-6102?
3190	6/7/57*
4484	10/10/57*
10780	17/10/58
9766	9/10/62

***Fowler**

BOILERS
First boiler 9195

No	Fitted	From
9257	2/2/39	5700
9223	8/11/41	5703
9326	24/11/44	5723
9212	14/10/48	5723
9199	22/2/52	45717
9342	6/6/56	45701

MILEAGES

1936	48,754
1937	55,638
1938	51,080
1939	45,148
1940	34,458
1941	49,088
1942	53,104
1943	56,440
1944	52,834
1945	56,738
1946	44,004
1947	45,090
1948	30,745
1949	52,065
1950	24,039
1951	53,100
1952	51,992
1953	42,770
1954	41,772
1955	39,093
1956	42,006
1957	39,337

Mileage at 31/12/50 699,225
Withdrawn week ending 29/2/64

45696 ARETHUSA
Built Crewe 2/4/36
Named 2/4/36
Renumbered 5696 to 45696 10/48

BOILERS
First boiler 9254

No	Fitted	From
9207	16/11/38	5677
9203	8/8/41	5676
9216	30/11/44	5703
9211	24/9/47	5666
9223	8/12/51	45709
9221	13/12/56	45657
9212	14/7/61	-

TENDERS

No	Fitted
3921	2/4/36* ex-6139
3791	20/1/53*
3921	3/2/53*
3944	13/12/56
*Fowler	

SHEDS
Newton Heath 4/4/36
(unrecorded transfers –
missing from sheet)
Newton Heath 30/9/44
Derby 7/1/45
Millhouses 11/5/46
Trafford Park 27/7/46
Millhouses 17/8/46
Trafford Park 30/11/46
Millhouses 21/12/46
Trafford Park 31/5/47
Millhouses 12/7/47
Trafford Park 15/11/47
Millhouses 20/12/47
Derby 29/5/48
Polmadie 30/8/52
Loan at first then
Polmadie 13/9/52
Carlisle Kingmoor 29/9/54
Crewe North 20/6/59
Aston 6/2/60
Crewe North 11/6/60
Carlisle Upperby 1/10/60
Carnforth 16/9/61
Carlisle Kingmoor 22/6/63

REPAIRS
21/9/37-11/10/37LS
17/10/38-16/11/38HG
30/11/39-14/12/39LS
5/1/40-19/1/40LO
23/7/41-8/8/41HG
13/2/43-13/3/43LS
1/2/44-26/2/44HS
15/11/44-30/11/44HG
14/8/46-5/9/46LS
2/7/47-24/9/47HG
5/10/48-25/10/48HS
8/9/49-14/10/49HI
3/6/50-26/7/50LI
1/11/51-8/12/51HG
15/11/52-13/12/52NC
25/12/52-20/1/53NC St Rollox
22/1/53-4/2/53LC St Rollox
24/6/53-10/7/53HC St Rollox
25/11/53-12/12/53HI St Rollox
10/5/55-4/6/55LI St Rollox
15/9/56-13/12/56G St Rollox
2/11/57-12/11/57NC St Rollox
- /19/9/58LI St Rollox
14/10/59-13/11/59HI St Rollox
31/5/61-14/7/61HG St Rollox; possible
date of AWS, speedo, fitting

MILEAGES

1936	50,731
1937	58,861
1938	57,177
1939	56,432
1940	44,605
1941	48,928
1942	50,145
1943	51,276
1944	47,428
1945	53,384
1946	53,348
1947	45,016
1948	52,479
1949	52,368
1950	43,789
1951	32,257
1952	46,969
1953	41,570
1954	53,807
1955	48,296
1956	38,329
1957	54,093
1958	40,767
1959	41,137
1960	44,185

stored 10/9/62-8/4/63, 24/10/63-16/3/64
Mileage at 31/12/50 765,967; at 31/12/60 1,207,377
Withdrawn week ending 18/7/64

One of Kingmoor's own, 45696 ARETHUSA in a typically crowded Kingmoor shed yard, April 1955. The Black 5 behind is 44726. Photograph W. Hermiston, The Transport Treasury.

45697 ACHILLES

Built Crewe 7/4/36
Named 7/4/36
Renumbered 5697 to 45697 5/48

BOILERS
First boiler 9255

No	Fitted	From
9217	31/10/38	5687
9257	25/2/42	5695
9316	3/10/46	5741
9329	12/1/50	45674
9254	8/7/54	45693
9195	6/2/58	45704

MILEAGES

1936	39,643
1937	54,233
1938	53,938
1939	52,984
1940	41,637
1941	34,614
1942	55,322
1943	49,708
1944	43,735
1945	36,309
1946	45,437
1947	46,499
1948	50,406
1949	39,646
1950	56,543
1951	48,370
1952	36,340
1953	51,542
1954	50,737
1955	48,863
1956	66,232
1957	54,077
1958	51,444
1959	40,929
1960	37,642
1961	45,215
1962	17,393
1963	11,058

Stored 24/9/62-8/4/63, 7/10/63-17/2/64
**Mileage at 31/12/50 700,654;
at 31/12/60 1,186,830
Withdrawn September 1967**

TENDERS

No	Fitted
4243	7/4/36* ex-6158
3940	3/4/53*
4502	6/7/54*
9694	11/7/64

45607 ended its days with a lined black tender; its attachment is not noted in the Record
***Fowler**

SHEDS
Newton Heath 18/4/36
Blackpool 2/5/36
Newton Heath 29/8/36
Blackpool 9/12/39
Carlisle Kingmoor 30/8/52
Loan at first then
Carlisle Kingmoor 13/9/52
Blackpool 18/8/62
Bank Hall 22/6/63
Farnley Junction 2/64
Leeds 3/64

REPAIRS
29/9/37-28/10/37**LS**
5/9/38-31/10/38**HG**
9/2/39-10/2/39**TO**
24/11/39-25/11/39**LO**
6/6/40-20/6/40**LS**
4/8/41-23/8/41**HS**
27/1/42-25/2/42**HG**
22/7/43-14/8/43**LS**
9/8/44-26/8/44**LS**
27/8/45-18/9/45**LS**
31/8/46-3/10/46**HG**
25/2/47-20/3/47**TO**
26/4/48-27/5/48**HS**
2/12/49-12/1/50**HG**
16/5/51-22/6/51**HI**
2/3/53-4/4/53**LI St Rollox**
31/8/53-3/10/53**LC St Rollox**
10/5/54-8/7/54**G St Rollox**
25/11/55-29/12/55**HI St Rollox**
12/3/57-3/4/57**LI St Rollox**
6/2/58-15/3/58**G St Rollox**
22/5/59-13/6/59**HI St Rollox**
1/7/59-4/7/59**NC(TO) St Rollox**
9/6/60-17/6/60**NC(EO) St Rollox**
24/10/60-26/11/60 **LI St Rollox**
29/11/60-3/12/60**NC(TO) St Rollox**
Date of AWS, speedo, unknown
Reverted to
'maintaining Works Crewe' from 6/1/64

45698 MARS

Built Crewe 8/4/36
Named 8/4/36
Renumbered 5698 to 45698 week ending 25/9/48

MILEAGES

1936	49,451
1937	61,596
1938	65,184
1939	55,625
1940	35,045
1941	43,331
1942	46,211
1943	49,366
1944	46,277
1945	51,157
1946	54,819
1947	30,685
1948	36,158
1949	51,957
1950	47,444
1951	46,975
1952	49,401
1953	55,907
1954	53,221
1955	47,703
1956	59,133
1957	53,617
1958	44,078
1959	39,690
1960	54,697

Speedo fitted
Stored 21/10/63-23/12/63, 3/2/64-23/3/64,
26/10/64-9/11/64
**Mileage at 31/12/50 724,306; at
31/12/60 1,228,728
Withdrawn week ending 23/10/65**

REPAIRS
12/8/37-7/9/37**LS**
30/8/38-22/10/38**HG**
29/6/39-14/7/39**LO**
8/1/40-3/2/40**HS**
22/11/40-7/12/40**LO**
31/5/41-25/6/41**HG**
6/8/42-1/9/42**LS**
15/1/44-5/2/44**HG**
1/3/45-31/3/45**LS**
4/6/46-20/6/46**HS**
7/8/47-11/9/47**HG**
10/9/48-24/9/48**LO**
20/6/49-25/7/49**HI**
1/4/50-20/4/50**LC**
8/12/50-5/1/51**HI**
26/2/51-30/3/51**HC**
31/3/52-15/5/52**HG**
9/6/53-29/6/53**HI**
6/8/54-28/8/54**LI**
26/9/55-5/11/55**HG**
1/1/57-30/1/57**LI**
11/4/58-10/5/58**LI**
15/4/59-29/4/59**NC(EO)**
25/9/59-13/11/59**LI**
25/11/59-11/12/59**LC(EO)**
20/2/61-25/3/61**HG speedo fitted**
2/10/61-19/10/61**NC(EO) AWS fitted**

BOILERS
First boiler 9258

No	Fitted	From
9216	22/10/38	5686
9213	25/6/41	5672
9782	5/2/44	5739
9337	11/9/47	5712
9211	15/5/52	45696
10033	5/11/55	45690
9211	25/3/61	45726

SHEDS
Newton Heath 18/4/36
Millhouses 2/10/37
Leeds 30/4/38
Derby 12/11/38
Newton Heath (loan) 10/8/40
Newton Heath 14/9/40
Bank Hall 12/10/46
Southport 8/5/48
Newton Heath 4/9/48
Bank Hall 11/9/48

TENDERS

No	Fitted
4251	8/4/36* ex-6166
9773	26/3/40
3331	24/9/48*
4470	20/4/50*
4512	28/8/54*
4470	5/11/55*
10206	29/4/59

***Fowler**

45698 MARS, dirty even for the late period – about 1964 – at an unknown location. Note speedo, AWS and welded tender. Photograph The Transport Treasury.

45699 GALATEA
Built Crewe 15/4/36
Named 15/4/36
Renumbered 5699 to 45699 week ending 22/5/48

MILEAGES

Year	Mileage
1936	47,360
1937	57,606
1938	65,702
1939	53,568
1940	58,552
1941	52,520
1942	55,136
1943	33,830
1944	44,102
1945	42,685
1946	47,145
1947	66,377
1948	69,919
1949	62,376
1950	62,991
1951	52,649
1952	63,354
1953	43,791
1954	58,069
1955	57,109
1956	58,538
1957	67,495

Mileage at 31/12/50 819,869
Withdrawn week ending 21/11/64
PRESERVED
(OR AT LEAST STILL SURVIVES)

TENDERS

No	Fitted
3917	15/4/36* ex-6118
9776	5/4/40

*Fowler

BOILERS
First boiler 9256

No	Fitted	From
9338	6/3/39	5718
9212	4/4/41	5673
9338	18/3/44	5640
9317	28/4/47	5706
9335	29/4/49	5719
9781	4/12/51	45687
9781*	11/12/53	45699
9778	3/3/55	45720
10037	13/4/60	45675

*Repaired while still in frames

SHEDS
Newton Heath 18/4/36
Millhouses 2/10/37
Derby 4/11/44
Nottingham 12/10/46
Leeds 30/11/46
Bristol 29/5/48
Shrewsbury 9/61

REPAIRS
15/6/37-17/6/37**LO**
9/8/37-27/8/37**LS**
15/11/37-8/12/37**LO**
1/2/39-6/3/39**HG**
28/3/40-16/4/40**LS**
12/3/41-4/4/41**HG**
12/1/42-31/1/42**LS**
4/2/43-11/3/43**LS**
8/4/43-13/5/43**LO**
14/2/44-18/3/44**HG**
21/3/45-26/5/45**HS**
5/9/45-10/10/45**HO**
2/7/46-6/8/46**LS**
10/3/47-28/4/47**HG**
5/4/48-19/5/48**HS**
15/3/49-29/4/49**HG**
13/3/50-4/4/50**HI**
29/12/50-18/1/51**HI**
29/10/51-4/12/51**HG**
3/3/52-3/4/52**LC Derby**
15/12/52-10/1/53**LI**
26/2/53-24/3/53**LC(EO)**
16/8/53-11/12/53**HG Derby**
22/12/54-3/3/55**HG**
27/2/56-26/3/56**HI**
29/11/56-1/1/57**LC(EO)**
12/9/57-12/10/57**HI**
2/12/58-1/1/59**LI**
16/2/60-13/4/60**HG**
speedo fitted by 9/61;
AWS never fitted

154

45699 GALATEA, the unlikely survivor of Barry, lit in a fascinating way at Willesden shed, 2 October 1963. Note the holder for the driver's nameplate below the cab window. Alec Swain did the drawings for the siting of these when he was at Euston House; it was a nice idea but proved unpopular with the majority of drivers. It was fine if the run had been a good one but if you were 45 minutes late for the third time that week there were mutterings of 'oh, driver Bloggs AGAIN – that's why we're late...' Photograph The Transport Treasury.

45700 AMETHYST

Built Crewe 20/4/36
Named BRITANNIA 20/4/36
Name removed 2/51; renamed AMETHYST 9/51
Renumbered 5700 to 45700 week ending 18/12/48

TENDERS

No	Fitted
3913	20/4/36* ex-6132
4474	11/3/55*
4510	16/7/56*
10168	13/5/59
*Fowler	

REPAIRS
19/8/37-7/9/37**LS**
24/11/38-6/1/39**HG**
6/6/40-21/6/40**LS**
22/5/41-12/6/41**HG**
4/9/42-3/10/42**LS**
3/11/43-1/12/43**LS**
23/7/45-14/8/45**HG**
21/11/46-20/12/46**LS**
11/3/47-1/5/47**LO**
21/7/48-13/12/48**HG**
14/6/49-22/7/49**LC**
1/11/49-2/12/49**HC**
18/9/50-17/10/50**HI**
19/9/51-28/9/51**NC(EO)**
1/4/52-12/6/52**HI**
25/8/53-3/10/53**HG**
15/2/55-11/3/55**HI**
18/10/56-21/11/56**HI**
16/6/58-16/7/58**HG**
23/4/59-12/5/59**LC(TO)**
3/9/59-14/10/59**HI**
3/10/60-12/11/60**LI** speedo fitted
12/9/61-27/9/61**NC(EO)** AWS fitted

BOILERS
First boiler 9257

No	Fitted	From
9254	6/1/39	5696
9210	12/6/41	5675
9197	14/8/45	5721
9206	13/12/48	5682
9224	2/12/49	45679
9344	3/10/53	45721
9336	16/7/58	45694

SHEDS
Newton Heath 25/4/36
Blackpool 7/9/57
Newton Heath 28/9/57
Derby 9/3/63
Newton Heath 6/7/63*
*believed to be in error
for Warrington

MILEAGES

1936	43,524
1937	60,760
1938	61,091
1939	48,574
1940	45,397
1941	50,187
1942	47,046
1943	45,502
1944	47,642
1945	41,893
1946	45,264
1947	40,210
1948	16,966
1949	37,163
1950	36,554
1951	45,453
1952	37,432
1953	45,266
1954	51,855
1955	51,520
1956	44,482
1957	47,828
1958	47,287
1959	44,876
1960	51,094

Stored 17/9/62-3/12/62
Mileage at 31/12/50 667,773; at 31/12/60 1,134,866
Withdrawn week ending 4/7/64

5700, our original BRITANNIA, carrying an ancient Caledonian 'semaphore' type route indicator 'somewhere in Scotland'. Smokebox lugs, vacuum pump on crosshead; steam sanding now fitted. 5700 was never a Scottish engine; in fact it was unusual in spending almost its entire career (apart from a last year or so at Derby) on the former L&Y at just two sheds, Blackpool and Newton Heath. Photograph Gavin Whitelaw Collection.

45701 CONQUEROR

Built Crewe 24/4/36

Named 24/4/36

Renumbered 5701 to 45701 week ending 22/5/48

TENDERS

No	Fitted
3945	24/4/36* ex-6109
10332	6/2/59 ex-48605

*Fowler

REPAIRS

14/9/37-7/10/37**LS**
6/2/39-7/3/39**HG**
23/4/40-9/5/40**LS**
4/11/41-26/11/41**LS**
27/10/42-17/11/42**HG**
17/3/44-1/4/44**HS**
15/11/44-28/11/44**LO**
10/7/45-25/8/45**LS**
10/1/47-14/2/47**HG**
20/4/48-21/5/48**LS**
11/7/49-30/8/49**HG**
9/6/50-1/8/50**HI**
10/7/51-17/8/51**HG**
24/1/53-24/2/53**HI**
18/6/54-28/7/54**HI**
22/9/54-13/10/54**LC(EO)**
25/1/56-12/3/56**HG**
28/9/56-24/10/56**LI**
2/4/58-1/5/58**LI**
17/1/59-6/2/59**NC(EO)**
29/9/59-6/11/59**LI**
15/4/61-8/5/61**LI** speedo
fitted
  ?   -12/61 **AWS fitted**

BOILERS

First boiler 9316

No	Fitted	From
9222	7/3/39	5692
9774	17/11/42	5720
9257	14/2/47	5697
9318	30/8/49	5740
9342	17/8/51	45685
9200	12/3/56	45703

SHEDS

Newton Heath 25/4/36
This was 45701's only shed; see also 45658 and 45659

MILEAGES

1936	46,696
1937	59,801
1938	62,359
1939	54,668
1940	47,142
1941	41,575
1942	44,860
1943	41,561
1944	50,480
1945	34,699
1946	42,615
1947	45,936
1948	44,833
1949	42,015
1950	48,386
1951	37,244
1952	48,251
1953	45,721
1954	33,716
1955	44,841
1956	46,478
1957	46,596
1958	45,252
1959	40,702
1960	46,616

Mileage at 31/12/50 707,626; at 31/12/60 1,143,043
Withdrawn week ending 23/2/63

45700 AMETHYST at Polmadie on 4 May 1957. As a Newton Heath Jubilee it could frequently be found in Glasgow; the name BRITANNIA was removed at the beginning of 1951 once 70000 was running around and the new name AMETHYST was put on in September that year. Photograph J.L. Stevenson, courtesy Hamish Stevenson.

Newton Heath's 5701 CONQUEROR in Scotland about 1936; unusually, it remained at a single shed (Newton Heath) all its working life. Photograph Gavin Whitelaw Collection.

CONQUEROR outside the Paint Shop at Crewe Works, 8 November 1959; lined green with distinct highlighted 'patches' but a plain black tender temporarily attached. This was possibly a 'works spare' for the engine to go out with during running in, while its own one was got ready. This happened at St Rollox but then the repairs to 45701 were not, presumably, that extensive (the Record gives a Light Intermediate). Perhaps its own tender was delayed... Photograph Alec Swain, The Transport Treasury.

45702 COLOSSUS

Built Crewe 5/5/36
Named 5/5/36
Renumbered 5702 to 45702 week ending 26/6/48

TENDERS

No	Fitted
3940	5/5/36* ex-6136
3898	12/11/49*
3937	20/11/53*
4240	3/3/55*
4465	24/1/57*
10248	28/2/59 ex-48521
*Fowler	

REPAIRS
5/10/37-5/11/37**LS**
22/2/39-27/3/39**HG**
28/5/40-10/6/40**LS**
1/12/41-24/12/41**HS**
26/2/43-19/3/43**HG**
22/7/44-5/8/44**LS**
20/8/45-6/9/45**LO**
9/1/46-7/2/46**HS**
27/7/47-10/9/47**LS**
15/5/48-26/6/48**LO**
12/12/49-4/1/50**LI**
16/2/51-13/4/51**HG**
24/3/52-19/4/52**HI**
2/11/53-20/11/53**HI**
4/3/54-26/3/54**LC(EO)** Horwich
29/1/55-3/3/55**HI**
21/12/55-3/2/56**LC(EO)**
12/12/56-24/1/57**HG**
9/1/58-19/2/58**HI**
10/2/59-28/2/59**NC(EO)**
22/6/59-21/8/59**LI**
8/2/61-24/3/61**LI** speedo fitted
28/4/61-11/5/61**LC(EO)**
   ?   -12/61 **AWS fitted**

BOILERS
First boiler 9322

No	Fitted	From
10032	27/3/39	5608
9222	19/3/43	5701
9196	7/2/46	5669
9259	13/4/51	45683
10038	24/1/57	45676

SHEDS
Newton Heath 9/5/36
Southport 4/6/38
Newton Heath 1/10/38
Farnley Jct 17/4/43
Crewe North (loan) 26/8/44
Bushbury 30/9/44
Willesden (loan) 7/10/44
Farnley Jct 9/12/44
Loan at first then
Farnley Jct 13/1/45
Newton Heath 9/12/50

MILEAGES

Year	Mileage
1936	40,747
1937	54,744
1938	58,821
1939	50,465
1940	50,265
1941	45,860
1942	56,058
1943	39,283
1944	39,000
1945	42,653
1946	47,931
1947	28,331
1948	36,612
1949	33,695
1950	35,391
1951	45,703
1952	50,462
1953	36,830
1954	46,833
1955	44,175
1956	41,402
1957	45,362
1958	45,622
1959	40,835
1960	45,943

Mileage at 31/12/50 659,856; at 31/12/60 1,103,023
Withdrawn week ending 27/4/63

45703 THUNDERER

Built Crewe 5/5/36
Named 5/5/36
Renumbered 5703 to 45703 week ending 9/4/49

SHEDS
Farnley Jct 9/5/36
Crewe North 6/3/43
Loan at first then
Crewe North 10/4/43
Bushbury 26/4/47
Longsight 23/8/47
Bushbury 28/5/49
Edge Hill 1/10/49
Bushbury 10/6/50
Crewe North 25/11/50
Camden 24/2/51
Bushbury 7/7/51
Camden 26/6/54
Crewe North 16/10/54
Carlisle Upperby 7/11/59
Crewe North 18/6/60
Carlisle Upperby 9/7/60
Carlisle Kingmoor 7/7/62
Blackpool 18/8/62
Carnforth 2/11/63
Warrington 7/64

REPAIRS
22/5/37-28/5/37**LO**
27/7/37-30/7/37**LO**
25/8/37-16/9/37**LS**
1/7/38-30/7/38**LO**
8/12/38-13/1/39**HG**
26/2/40-9/3/46**LS**
26/7/41-9/8/41**HS**
15/1/43-3/2/43**LS**
22/4/44-6/5/44**HG**
30/8/45-27/9/45**HS**
14/1/47-4/2/47**LS**
2/12/47-10/1/48**HG**
14/3/49-6/4/49**LI**
25/2/50-24/3/50**HI**
19/6/50-31/7/50**LC**
20/10/50-7/11/50**LC**
30/10/51-20/11/51**LI**
1/9/52-8/10/52**HG**
30/1/54-23/2/54**HI**
15/10/55-19/11/55**HG**
27/6/57-3/8/57**LI**
3/1/59-6/2/59**LI AWS fitted**
8/5/61-17/6/61**HG speedo fitted**

BOILERS
First boiler 9323

No	Fitted	From
9223	13/1/39	5693
9216	9/8/41	5698
9332	6/5/44	5737
9787	10/1/48	5711
9200	8/10/52	45688
9318	19/11/55	45734
9323	17/6/61	45737

TENDERS

No	Fitted
3935	5/5/36* ex-6139
9130	26/6/37
9778	3/8/57
10621	21/10/63
*Fowler	

MILEAGES

Year	Mileage
1936	41,300
1937	41,504
1938	36,152*
1939	49,794
1940	33,659
1941	25,800
1942	44,418
1943	55,818
1944	61,837
1945	44,075
1946	60,917
1947	41,979
1948	57,395
1949	49,840
1950	39,907
1951	49,245
1952	58,764
1953	61,729
1954	52,813
1955	48,515
1956	54,634
1957	49,429
1958	47,839
1959	50,282
1960	31,206

*1938 60 days stored serviceable
Stored 1/10/62-8/4/63
Mileage at 31/12/50 684,395; at 31/12/60 1,188,851
Withdrawn week ending 21/11/64

45704 LEVIATHAN

Built Crewe 4/5/36
Named 11/5/36
Renumbered 5704 to 45704 12/48

BOILERS
First boiler 9325

No	Fitted	From
9339	3/4/39	5719
10034	15/4/44	5709
9203	3/12/48	5738
9195	18/12/52	45725
9790	11/10/57	45713

REPAIRS
4/11/37-1/12/37**LS**
3/5/38-12/5/38**LO**
6/9/38-10/9/38**LO**
7/3/39-3/4/39**HG**
14/10/40-31/10/40**LS***
11/7/41-5/8/41**LS**
16/11/42-11/12/42**LS**
28/3/44-15/4/44**HG**
12/10/45-27/10/45**LS**
28/11/46-3/1/47**HS**
3/12/47-3/1/48**LO**
21/10/48-3/12/48**HG**
14/2/50-14/3/50**HI**
21/5/51-13/6/51**HI**
19/11/52-18/12/52**G**
29/5/54-19/6/54**HI St Rollox**
26/1/56-23/2/56**LI(EO) St Rollox**
27/2/56-3/3/56**LC St Rollox**
31/7/57-11/10/57**G St Rollox**
10/11/58-12/12/58**LI St Rollox**
22/12/59-22/1/60**LI St Rollox**
25/1/60-28/1/60**LC St Rollox**
18/2/60-18/2/60**NC St Rollox**
8/3/61-27/4/61**NC St Rollox**
* 'speed recording instruments' fitted
AWS, speedo, fitted at unknown date
Reverted to 'maintaining works Crewe'
From 6/1/64

SHEDS
Farnley Jct 16/5/36
Newton Heath 17/4/43
Farnley Jct 3/7/43
Carlisle Kingmoor 13/8/52
Loan at first then
Carlisle Kingmoor 13/9/52
Crewe North 20/6/59
Edge Hill 26/9/59
Llandudno Jct 6/2/60
Camden 11/6/60
Aston 17/9/60
Willesden 26/11/60
Rugby 14/1/61
Crewe North 22/6/63

TENDERS

No	Fitted
4246	11/5/36* ex-6161
4502	11/8/52*
3940	17/6/54*
3788	23/2/56*
3940	3/3/56*
4508	24/3/62*
*Fowler	

MILEAGES

1936	39,254
1937	37,204*
1938	42,588*
1939	42,685
1940	35,917
1941	39,995
1942	32,715
1943	46,599
1944	34,378
1945	39,956
1946	33,379
1947	33,063
1948	31,250
1949	47,317
1950	48,458
1951	35,362
1952	28,889
1953	66,865
1954	54,363
1955	54,846
1956	55,487
1957	43,524
1958	52,928
1959	50,822
1960	30,877

*1937 stored serviceable 66 days
*1937 stored serviceable 60 days
Stored 14/10/62-6/2/63, 23/9/63-
10/12/63,
23/10/64-withdrawal
**Mileage at 31/12/50 584,758; at
31/12/60 1,058,721**
Withdrawn week ending 23/1/65

45704 LEVIATHAN at Willesden shed 7 April 1964 – one of the few Jubilees to end its days with a Fowler tender. Photograph Peter Groom.

45705 SEAHORSE

Built Crewe 21/5/36
Named 21/5/36
Renumbered 5705 to 45705 week ending 15/1/49

Photograph J.L. Stevenson, courtesy Hamish Stevenson.

SHEDS
Farnley Jct 23/5/36
Blackpool 16/6/56
Newton Heath 6/64

REPAIRS
7/6/37-7/7/37**LO**
5/10/37-9/10/37**LO**
10/2/38-12/3/38**LS**
6/3/39-22/4/39**HG**
22/10/40-12/11/40**LS**
21/4/41-8/5/41**LO**
3/8/42-22/8/42**LS**
10/8/43-28/8/43**HG**
6/10/44-21/10/44**HS**
24/12/45-23/1/46**LS**
15/8/47-7/10/47**HG**
18/12/48-10/1/49**LI**
13/3/50-6/4/50**HI**
18/6/51-21/7/51**HI**
11/8/52-19/9/52**HG**
17/5/54-15/6/54**LI**
1/10/55-29/10/55**LI**
22/7/57-30/8/57**HG**
16/2/59-7/3/59**LI AWS fitted**
5/9/60-8/10/60**LI speedo fitted**

TENDERS

No	Fitted
4240	21/5/36* ex-6155
4248	6/9/49*
4502	6/4/50*
4246	11/8/52*
4477	29/10/55*
10758	7/3/59 ex-48733
10367	19/5/62
*Fowler	

BOILERS
First boiler 9324

No	Fitted	From
9316	22/4/39	5701
10035	28/8/43	5733
10033	7/10/47	5726
9337	19/9/52	45698
9255	30/8/57	45708

MILEAGES

1936	37,760
1937	36,633*
1938	50,736
1939	42,707
1940	33,825
1941	38,413
1942	36,923
1943	42,173
1944	39,646
1945	38,689
1946	43,127
1947	32,129
1948	43,761
1949	46,037
1950	44,424
1951	44,980
1952	43,645
1953	48,123
1954	39,057
1955	33,902
1956	42,712
1957	40,299
1958	47,304
1959	55,018
1960	38,758

*stored serviceable 58 days
Stored 12/11/62-8/4/63
Mileage at 31/12/50 606,983; at 1,040,781
Withdrawn week ending 6/11/65

45706 EXPRESS

Built Crewe 26/5/36
Named 26/5/36
Renumbered 5706 to 45706 week ending 14/8/48

SHEDS
Farnley Jct 6/6/36
Newton Heath 8/5/43

REPAIRS
24/1/38-26/2/38**LS**
15/12/38-24/12/38**LO**
24/6/39-29/7/39**HG**
19/11/40-5/12/40**HS**
12/1/42-23/5/42**HG**
29/11/43-3/1/44**LS**
12/1/45-8/2/45**LS**
11/6/45-13/7/45**LO**
5/11/46-29/11/46**HG**
25/10/47-29/12/47**TRO Horwich**
22/6/48-11/8/48**LS**
25/4/49-20/5/49**LC**
9/1/50-25/1/50**HI**
28/10/50-14/12/50**HG**
22/4/52-20/5/52**HI**
7/10/53-4/11/53**HI**
8/1/55-10/2/55**HI**
6/12/55-26/1/56**HI**
3/6/57-12/7/57**LI**
15/11/57-20/12/57**LC(EO)**
9/9/58-22/9/58**NC(EO)**
15/1/59-13/2/59**HI**
13/1/61-25/2/61**HG speedo fitted**
?   -12/61 **AWS fitted**

BOILERS
First boiler 9326

No	Fitted	From
9342	29/7/39	5722
9317	23/5/42	5692
9258	29/11/46	5710
9218	14/12/50	45718
9203	26/1/56	45669
9332	25/2/61	45667

TENDERS

No	Fitted
4236	26/5/36* ex-6153
4252	4/11/53*
10747	22/9/58 ex-48722
9128	5/10/63
*Fowler	

MILEAGES

1936	34,822*
1937	38,626*
1938	45,787
1939	41,573
1940	35,881
1941	42,563
1942	30,644
1943	42,876
1944	44,229
1945	31,311
1946	39,929
1947	39,951
1948	33,407
1949	42,719
1950	44,212
1951	49,521
1952	47,933
1953	42,796
1954	47,680
1955	38,391
1956	47,971
1957	40,038
1958	37,156
1959	45,829
1960	44,867

*1936 stored serviceable 18 days
*1937 stored serviceable 41 days
Mileage at 31/12/50 588,530; at 31/12/60 1,030,712
Withdrawn week ending 28/9/63

45707 VALIANT

Built Crewe 27/5/36
Named 27/5/36
Renumbered 5707 to 45707 8/48

TENDERS

No	Fitted
3936	27/5/36* ex-6140
4513	5/5/50*
3187	3/5/52*
4513	28/6/52*
3901	mid-1950s*
3921	early 1960s*
*Fowler	

BOILERS

First boiler 9327

No	Fitted	From
9224	22/10/38	5694
9340	14/10/41	5685
9195	7/8/45	5682
9339	26/8/48	5673
Record incomplete		

MILEAGES

Year	Mileage
1936	41,831
1937	49,055*
1938	49,929*
1939	45,039
1940	40,016
1941	44,515
1942	62,690
1943	51,684
1944	44,136
1945	49,419
1946	39,855
1947	50,221
1948	35,821
1949	50,816
1950	46,020

*1937 stored serviceable 11 days
*1938 stored serviceable 5 days
Record ends
Mileage at 31/12/50 701,047
Withdrawn December 1962

SHEDS

Southport 6/6/36
Crewe (loan) 13/6/36
Camden (loan) 4/7/36
Farnley Jct 10/10/36
Blackpool 19/4/41
Polmadie 9/52
Corkerhill 8/54
Polmadie 11/57
Corkerhill 4/58
Polmadie 11/59
Corkerhill 4/60

REPAIRS

27/7/37-26/8/37**LS**
19/8/38-22/10/38**HG**
19/2/40-2/3/40**LS**
15/9/41-11/10/41**HG**
13/4/43-1/5/43**LS**
14/1/44-29/1/44**LS**
9/3/44-25/3/44**HO**
23/7/45-7/8/45**HG**
29/1/47-1/3/47**LS**
19/7/48-26/8/48**HG**
28/3/50-5/5/50**LI**
Record incomplete

45708 RESOLUTION

Built Crewe 1/6/36
Named 1/6/36
Renumbered 5708 to 45708 week ending 28/8/48

TENDERS

No	Fitted
4248	1/6/36* ex-6163
4240	6/9/49*
3931	12/2/55*
4486	16/11/57*
10294	19/11/58
*Fowler	

MILEAGES

Year	Mileage
1936	26,699*
1937	48,768*
1938	42,975
1939	36,865
1940	38,403
1941	44,307
1942	50,031
1943	42,558
1944	39,932
1945	48,360
1946	43,145
1947	43,460
1948	42,842
1949	48,465
1950	42,839
1951	40,234
1952	47,197
1953	50,156
1954	43,707
1955	37,309
1956	44,178
1957	35,410

*1936 stored serviceable 65 days
*1937 stored serviceable 31 days
Mileage at 31/12/50 639,649
Withdrawn week ending 29/2/64
after 'paper transfer' to Tyseley

BOILERS

First boiler 9328

No	Fitted	From
9787	25/11/39	5739
9343	29/3/43	5665
9219	8/3/47	5742
9255	8/3/51	45657
9217	21/2/57	45737

SHEDS

Blackpool 6/6/36
Crewe (loan) 13/6/36
Camden (loan) 4/7/36
Farnley Jct 3/10/36
Blackpool 8/2/41
Newton Heath 10/4/43
Farnley Jct 8/5/43
Longsight (loan) 19/8/44
Patricroft 30/9/44
Farnley Jct 9/12/44
Loan at first then
Farnley Jct 13/1/45
Tyseley 2/64

REPAIRS

22/3/38-23/4/38**LS**
25/11/39-21/12/39**HG**
12/1/42-4/2/42**LS**
20/2/43-29/3/43**HG**
7/7/44-29/7/44**LS**
4/3/45-26/3/45**TRO**
20/11/45-7/12/45**LS**
27/12/46-8/3/47**HG**
5/8/48-26/8/48**HS**
27/9/49-14/10/49**LI**
15/1/51-8/3/51**HG**
7/4/52-14/5/52**HI**
27/7/53-31/8/53**LI**
18/1/55-12/2/55**HI**
28/11/55-23/12/55**HC**
14/1/57-21/2/57**HG**
14/10/57-16/11/57**LI**
3/11/58-19/11/58**LC(EO)**
22/6/59-5/8/59**HI**
6/2/61-14/3/61**HI**
15/3/61-22/3/61**NC(EO Rect)**
speedo probably fitted, date
unknown; AWS probably
never fitted

45709 IMPLACABLE

Built Crewe 3/6/36

Named 3/6/36

Renumbered 5709 to 45709 week ending 15/1/49

TENDERS

No	Fitted
3931	3/6/36* ex-6152
4495	15/9/45*
3931	27/5/46*
4483	10/10/53*
3929	16/1/54*
4504	30/11/57*
10366	6/11/58 ex-48649

MILEAGES

1936	24,762*
1937	50,433*
1938	73,436
1939	69,186
1940	54,347
1941	54,319
1942	35,341
1943	44,939
1944	48,627
1945	59,978
1946	50,586
1947	47,129
1948	42,596
1949	50,080
1950	48,800
1951	48,408
1952	54,975
1953	51,971
1954	62,115
1955	51,025
1956	49,327
1957	45,670
1958	47,347
1959	47,698
1960	35,678

*1936 stored serviceable 69 days
*1937 stored serviceable 32 days
Stored 27/9/62-1/3/63
Mileage at 31/12/50 754,559; at 31/12/60 1,248,773
Withdrawn week ending 23/11/63, after 'paper' transfer to Crewe North

REPAIRS

4/11/37-23/11/37**LS**
26/5/38-18/7/38**LO**
31/10/38-12/12/38**LS**
27/9/39-18/10/39**HO**
13/3/40-6/4/40**HG**
14/10/40-18/11/40**LO***
20/3/41-10/4/41**HS**
25/7/42-22/8/42**LS**
20/10/42-14/11/42**LO**
3/5/43-22/5/43**LO**
20/11/43-18/12/43**HG**
4/5/44-16/5/44**TRO**
24/11/44-23/12/44**LS**
16/6/45-12/7/45**LO**
29/4/46-27/5/46**HG**
19/9/46-8/10/46**TRO Derby**
14/4/47-15/5/47**LS**
4/12/47-2/1/48**LO**
20/11/48-11/1/49**HG**
8/4/50-2/5/50**HI**
25/9/51-22/10/51**HG**
3/10/52-8/11/52**LI**
17/12/53-16/1/54**HG**
27/5/55-24/6/55**HI**
28/1/56-25/2/56**LC(EO)**
13/10/56-13/11/56**HG**
4/11/57-30/11/57**LI**
24/1/58-29/1/58**NC(EO)**
18/10/58-6/11/58**LC**
13/6/59-31/7/59**LI AWS fitted**
14/9/60-3/11/60**LC(EO)**
    ?   -12/61 **speedo fitted**
*'**Damaged by enemy action 10/10/40**'

SHEDS

Blackpool 6/6/36
Crewe (loan) 13/6/36
Edge Hill (loan) 27/6/36
Willesden (loan) 4/7/36
Farnley Jct 10/10/36
Kentish Town 3/10/37
Saltley 6/9/41
Trafford Park (loan) 11/3/44
Saltley 22/4/44
Bristol 17/11/45
Crewe North (loan) 13/9/47
Crewe North 25/10/47
Bushbury 28/5/49
Crewe North 1/10/49
Longsight 29/4/50
Bushbury 18/6/55
Aston 13/2/60
Crewe South 31/12/60
Crewe North 23/6/62
Saltley 9/3/63
Derby 6/7/63
Saltley 14/9/63

BOILERS
First boiler 9329

No	Fitted	From
10034	6/4/40	5567
9207	18/12/43	5684
9217	27/5/46	5690
9223	11/1/49	5672
9196	22/10/51	45702
9773	16/1/54	45712
9324	13/11/56	45678

45710 IRRESISTIBLE

Built Crewe 8/6/36

Named 8/6/36

Renumbered 5710 to 45710 week ending 19/2/49

REPAIRS

27/1/38-18/2/38**LS**
15/8/38-29/8/38**LO**
5/6/39-1/7/39**HG**
29/4/41-17/5/41**LS**
15/6/42-1/8/42**HS**
14/6/43-17/7/43**HG**
7/2/45-3/3/45**LS**
14/6/46-20/7/46**HG**
23/10/47-28/11/47**LS**
31/1/49-19/2/49**HI**
26/5/50-28/6/50**HG**
1/2/52-26/2/52**LI**
24/10/52-22/11/52**LC**
1/12/53-1/1/54**HI**
13/6/55-4/8/55**HG**
24/12/56-25/1/57**LI**
24/5/57-24/5/57**LC(TO)**
2/6/58-26/6/58**LI**
3/2/59-23/2/59**NC(EO)**
10/10/59-27/11/59**HI**
21/4/61-2/6/61**HG speedo fitted**
    ?   -12/61 **AWS fitted**

TENDERS

No	Fitted
3909	8/6/36* ex-6106
3898	1/1/54*
4486	25/1/57*
4560	24/5/57*
10328	23/2/59 ex-48601

*Fowler

SHEDS

Crewe North (loan) 6/6/36
Chester 27/6/36
Farnley Jct 3/10/36
Blackpool (loan) 6/2/37
Blackpool 27/3/37
Southport 16/9/39
Newton Heath 15/6/40
Bank Hall 4/9/48
Newton Heath 11/9/48

BOILERS
First boiler 9330

No	Fitted	From
9325	1/7/39	5704
9258	17/7/43	5693
9331	20/7/46	5737
9210	28/6/50	45680
9315	4/8/55	45684
9203	2/6/61	45706

MILEAGES

1936	28,271*
1937	49,347*
1938	47,736
1939	39,327
1940	40,153
1941	54,411
1942	48,727
1943	47,090
1944	44,211
1945	45,333
1946	45,518
1947	36,990
1948	47,308
1949	48,199
1950	41,530
1951	37,932
1952	45,202
1953	43,104
1954	50,730
1955	42,975
1956	42,872
1957	41,926
1958	45,945
1959	41,306
1960	44,117

*1936 stored serviceable 41 days
*1937 stored serviceable 34 days
Mileage at 31/12/50 664,151; at 31/12/60 1,100,260
Withdrawn week ending 6/6/64

45710 IRRESISTIBLE at Polmadie, 2 August 1958; smokebox lugs, 26A shedplate. Polmadie, with no Jubilees of its own, was a distinct 'second home' for Central Division ones; well, English ones if it comes to that. Photograph Hamish Stevenson.

45711 COURAGEOUS

Built Crewe 19/6/36
Named 19/6/36
Renumbered 5711 to 45711 12/48

TENDERS

No	Fitted
3937	19/6/36* ex-6116
3940	27/7/51*
4244	mid-1950s
3901	early 1960s
*Fowler	

BOILERS

First boiler 9331

No	Fitted	From
9204	17/10/39	5671
9787	30/6/43	5708
9782	16/10/47	5698
Record incomplete		

SHEDS
Blackpool 19/6/36
Crewe North (loan) 20/6/36
Camden (loan) 4/7/36
Farnley Jct 3/10/36
Blackpool (loan) 6/2/37
Blackpool 27/3/37
Accrington 18/6/38
Blackpool 5/11/38
Southport 16/9/39
Newton Heath 15/6/40
Farnley Jct 4/9/48
Corkerhill 9/52
Polmadie 11/57
Corkerhill 4/58
Polmadie 11/59
Corkerhill 4/60

REPAIRS
10/12/37-8/1/38**HS**
13/9/39-17/10/39**HG**
31/10/40-15/11/40**LS***
25/4/42-23/5/42**LS**
8/6/43-30/6/43**HG**
2/12/44-19/12/44**LS**
18/5/46-6/6/46**LS**
28/8/47-16/10/47**HG**
9/11/48-30/11/48**LS**
7/3/50-12/4/50**HI**
*'speed recording
instruments fitted'
Record incomplete

MILEAGES

1936	30,011*
1937	45,658*
1938	50,549
1939	40,353
1940	37,662
1941	45,094
1942	46,691
1943	49,387
1944	45,036
1945	45,025
1946	54,288
1947	40,855
1948	47,724
1949	46,348
1950	40,407

*1936 stored serviceable 41 days
*1937 stored serviceable 34 days
Mileage at 31/12/50 665,088
Withdrawn December 1962

45711 COURAGEOUS in a glorious portrait at St Enoch on 18 May 1953. It has the big St Rollox numbers, though it had been in Scotland only a few months. Photograph J. Robertson, The Transport Treasury.

COURAGEOUS at Corkerhill shed on 25 October 1953, now with 4,000 gallon tender. Photograph J.L. Stevenson, courtesy Hamish Stevenson.

45712 VICTORY

Built Crewe 24/6/36
Named 24/6/36
Renumbered 5712 to 45712 week ending 23/10/48

TENDERS

No	Fitted
3898	24/6/36* ex-6144
3940	12/11/49*
4500	7/4/51*
10777	30/12/58 ex-48752

REPAIRS
3/2/38-4/3/38**LS**
1/3/39-3/3/39**LO**
11/9/39-6/10/39**HG**
21/4/41-10/5/41**HS**
22/5/41-31/5/41**TRO**
7/10/42-30/10/42**LS**
21/3/44-7/4/44**HG**
9/10/45-3/11/45**LS**
5/11/46-28/11/46**HS**
15/3/47-14/5/47**HG**
6/1/48-13/2/48**LO**
24/9/48-21/10/48**LS**
1/10/49-16/11/49**HG**
6/2/51-1/3/51**LI**
14/2/52-15/3/52**LI**
14/10/53-7/11/53**HG**
10/11/53-24/11/53**NC(Rect)**
2/3/55-29/3/55**HI**
24/11/56-29/12/56**HG**
24/1/57-31/1/57**NC(EO Rect)**
2/12/57-4/1/58**HI**
18/11/58-30/12/58**LI**
12/1/60-2/3/60**LI**
21/9/60-25/10/60**LI** speedo fitted;
AWS probably never fitted

BOILERS
First boiler 9332

No	Fitted	From
10033	11/9/39	5657
9337	7/4/44	5742
9728	14/5/47	5674
9773	16/11/49	45669
9317	7/11/53	45737
9785	29/12/56	45722

SHEDS
Crewe North (loan) 27/6/36
Camden (loan) 4/7/36
Farnley Jct 3/10/36
Blackpool (loan) 6/2/37
Blackpool 27/3/37
Newton Heath 17/10/42
Trafford Park 23/2/57
Loan at first then
Trafford Park 2/3/57
Kentish Town 5/7/58
Neasden 3/10/59
Kentish Town 21/11/59
Newton Heath 1/7/61
Kentish Town 23/9/61
Burton 20/1/62
Rowsley* 26/1/63
*almost certainly an
error for Derby*

MILEAGES

1936	29,004*
1937	44,976*
1938	47,415
1939	43,443
1940	46,839
1941	48,878
1942	45,137
1943	46,255
1944	47,416
1945	41,378
1946	47,210
1947	43,073
1948	40,604
1949	40,059
1950	49,562
1951	52,482
1952	42,561
1953	45,694
1954	55,298
1955	47,926
1956	45,544
1957	46,840
1958	49,561
1959	52,358
1960	57,062

*1936 stored serviceable 46 days
*1937 stored serviceable 34 days
Stored 1/10/62-18/1/63
Mileage at 31/12/50 661,249; at 31/12/60 1,156,575
Withdrawn week ending 30/11/63

45713 RENOWN

Built Crewe 29/6/36
Named 29/6/36
Renumbered 5713 to 45713 9/48

SHEDS
Camden (loan) 4/7/36
Farnley Jct 3/10/36
Carlisle Kingmoor 28/11/36
Bank Hall 21/7/62
Loan at first then
Bank Hall 18/8/62

REPAIRS
1/11/37-1/12/37**LS**
7/2/39-27/3/39**HS**
26/2/40-27/3/40**HG**
7/5/41-3/6/41**HS**
24/7/42-26/8/42**LS**
7/3/44-25/3/44**HG**
18/10/44-18/11/44**LO**
30/10/45-30/11/45**LS**
21/5/47-30/6/47**HG**
27/8/48-2/10/48**HS**
31/1/50-4/3/50**LI**
6/9/50-11/11/50**HC**
11/6/51-11/7/51**HI** St Rollox
30/4/52-20/9/52**G** St Rollox
30/11/53-19/12/53**HI** St Rollox
16/11/54-25/12/54**HI** St Rollox
7/10/55-5/11/55**LI** St Rollox
25/9/56-1/11/56**LC** St Rollox
17/6/57-19/9/57**G** St Rollox
29/10/57-8/11/57**NC** St Rollox
6/12/58-31/12/58**HI** St Rollox
16/1/59-20/1/59**NC(EO)** St Rollox
13/1/60-12/2/60**LI** St Rollox
20/4/61-24/4/61**LC** St Rollox
12/12/61-30/1/62**LI** St Rollox
AWS, speedo, fitted by 8/62

BOILERS
First boiler 9333

No	Fitted	From
9775	27/3/40	5727
9334	25/3/44	5714
9204	12/7/47	5731
9790	20/9/52	45691
9335	19/9/57	-

TENDERS

No	Fitted
4244	29/4/36* ex-6165
3310	9/5/45*
4244	21/9/45*
4147	14/12/46*
4345	5/4/47*
4244	28/7/47*
4171	13/2/48*
3911	31/5/48*
4014	25/11/48*
3911	5/1/49*
3944	10/7/51*
4244	17/5/52*
4243	5/11/55*

*Fowler

MILEAGES

1936	35,676*
1937	45,886
1938	70,157
1939	68,701
1940	56,931
1941	53,456
1942	56,574
1943	56,082
1944	47,962
1945	45,418
1946	54,949
1947	43,106
1948	43,842
1949	45,405
1950	40,939
1951	53,471
1952	37,355
1953	52,543
1954	54,158
1955	45,486
1956	51,715
1957	38,448
1958	52,663
1959	49,841
1960	41,793

*stored serviceable 13 days
Mileage at 31/12/50 795,084; at 31/12/60 1,272,557
Withdrawn week ending 20/10/62

45713 RENOWN taking water at St Rollox shed on 1 July 1950; Pacific 46234 DUCHESS OF ABERCORN on the right. Photograph J.L. Stevenson, courtesy Hamish Stevenson.

45714 REVENGE

Built Crewe 1/7/36
Named 1/7/36
Renumbered 5714 to 45714 4/49

SHEDS
Crewe North (loan) 4/7/36
Farnley Jct 10/10/36
Carlisle Kingmoor 28/11/36
Carnforth 16/9/61

MILEAGES
1936	32,939*
1937	48,483
1938	72,082
1939	63,520
1940	56,898
1941	64,296
1942	30,412
1943	47,696
1944	50,771
1945	40,610
1946	57,767
1947	53,929
1948	39,495
1949	42,659
1950	42,388
1951	38,166
1952	52,145
1953	57,863
1954	46,453
1955	45,289
1956	42,265
1957	47,990
1958	44,393
1959	57,882
1960	40,699

Stored 12/10/62-19/11/62
*stored serviceable 13 days
Mileage at 31/12/50 773,945; at 31/12/60 1,247,090
Withdrawn week ending 20/7/63

BOILERS
First boiler 9334
No	Fitted	From
9780	24/10/42	5732
9783	19/10/46	5692
9205	1/9/51	45692
9780	29/12/56	45732

TENDERS
No	Fitted
3911	1/7/36* ex-6124
4171	18/12/47*
4244	13/2/48*
3944	21/3/51*
3911	30/8/51*

*Fowler

REPAIRS
3/11/37-23/11/37**LS**
10/8/39-16/9/39**HG**
27/11/40-14/12/40**LS**
18/2/42-18/3/42**HS**
23/6/42-8/7/42**LO**
5/8/42-24/10/52**HO**
9/3/43-12/4/43**LS**
20/5/43-26/5/43**LS**
6/4/44-19/5/44**LS**
28/6/45-11/8/45**LS**
19/9/46-19/10/46**HG**
6/2/48-12/3/48**LS**
3/3/49-12/4/49**HI**
13/9/49-22/10/49**LC**
18/4/50-3/6/50**HI**
4/10/50-2/12/50**HI**
1/3/51-21/3/51**NC St Rollox**
16/4/51-1/9/51**G St Rollox**
18/9/52-1/11/52**LI St Rollox**
10/12/52-11/12/52**NC St Rollox**
7/4/53-25/4/53**LC(EO) St Rollox**
20/4/54-20/4/54**NC(TO)* St Rollox**
10/5/54-12/6/54**HI St Rollox**
24/8/55-17/9/55**LI St Rollox**
20/4/56-1/6/56**LC St Rollox**
16/11/56-29/12/56**G St Rollox**
24/10/57-1/11/57**LC(EO) St Rollox**
4/12/57-10/1/58**LI St Rollox**
20/3/58-25/3/58**NC(EO) St Rollox**
27/10/58-1/11/58**LC St Rollox**
30/1/59-28/2/59**HI St Rollox**
28/6/60-6/8/60**HI St Rollox**
AWS never fitted; speedo
probably fitted
*Tender only

45714 REVENGE at the north end of Citadel station, with the famous ecclesiastical end screen forming a magnificent if faded backdrop. REVENGE had been a Carlisle stalwart virtually all its life. Photograph J. Robertson, The Transport Treasury.

45715 INVINCIBLE

Built Crewe 3/7/36
Named 3/7/36
Renumbered 5715 to 45715 4/48

TENDERS

No	Fitted
3944	3/7/36* ex-6119
4244	2/4/51*
3944	17/5/52*
4508	21/9/54*
3911	19/5/56*
4508	29/5/56*
3940	3/3/62*

REPAIRS
26/1/38-12/2/38LS
15/5/39-4/7/39HG
13/3/40-13/4/40LS
23/6/41-2/8/41LS
24/6/42-20/8/42HG
10/4/43-15/5/43HS
22/9/43-25/10/43LO
9/10/44-30/11/44LS
16/10/45-10/11/45LS
3/10/46-21/12/46HG
23/3/48-29/4/48LS
28/2/49-22/4/49HI
3/9/49-17/9/49LC
8/12/49-19/1/50LI
13/2/50-4/3/50NC
1/12/50-13/1/51HI St Rollox
16/3/51-3/4/51LC St Rollox
29/10/51-9/2/52G St Rollox
28/2/52-3/3/52NC St Rollox
2/6/53-20/6/53LI St Rollox
16/9/54-28/10/54LI St Rollox
27/7/55-18/8/55LC(EO) St Rollox
25/4/56-19/5/56G(EO) St Rollox
29/5/56-29/5/56LC(TO) St Rollox
11/6/56-21/6/56LC(EO) St Rollox
29/11/57-26/12/57HI St Rollox
23/10/58HC St Rollox
17/2/59-18/3/59HI St Rollox
16/2/60-3/3/60LC(EO) St Rollox
15/4/60-28/5/60GEN St Rollox
4/1/61-6/1/61LC(EO) St Rollox
No dates given-speedo probably fitted;
AWS probably never fitted

BOILERS
First boiler 9335

No	Fitted	From
9320	28/8/42	5726
9780	21/12/46	5714
9776	9/2/52	45728
9208	19/5/56	45692
9788	28/5/60	-

SHEDS
Crewe North (loan) 4/7/36
Farnley Jct 10/10/36
Carlisle Kingmoor 28/11/36
Bank Hall 21/7/62
Loan at first then
Bank Hall 18/8/62

MILEAGES

1936	32,349*
1937	82,842
1938	70,895
1939	62,092
1940	49,744
1941	49,721
1942	49,441
1943	40,645
1944	47,441
1945	48,849
1946	39,802
1947	54,698
1948	39,330
1949	42,141
1950	41,824
1951	36,317
1952	50,364
1953	36,977
1954	43,010
1955	55,095
1956	42,265
1957	51,842
1958	47,350
1959	49,659
1960	42,706

*stored serviceable 13 days
Mileage at 31/12/50 751,814; at 31/12/60 1,207,399
Withdrawn week ending 29/12/62

45716 SWIFTSURE

Built Crewe 4/7/36

Named 4/7/36

Renumbered 5716 to 45716 2/49

SHEDS
Crewe North (loan) 4/7/36
Farnley Jct 3/10/36
Carlisle Kingmoor 28/11/36
Carlisle Upperby 28/10/61
Carlisle Kingmoor 10/3/62
Agecroft 31/7/62
Loan at first then
Agecroft 18/8/62
Newton Heath 22/6/63
Leeds 7/64

MILEAGES

1936	26,380*
1937	84,311
1938	81,587
1939	60,764
1940	52,791
1941	63,279
1942	49,946
1943	52,966
1944	50,650
1945	50,566
1946	60,631
1947	43,961
1948	32,470
1949	45,611
1950	38,020
1951	45,266
1952	22,549
1953	54,603
1954	48,122
1955	44,356
1956	51,573
1957	49,137
1958	51,777
1959	47,291
1960	44,570

*stored serviceable 35 days
Stored 22/10/62-8/4/63, 2/9/63-16/12/63,
6/1/64-23/3/64
**Mileage at 31/12/50 793,933; at 31/12/60
1,253,177**
Withdrawn week ending 12/9/64

BOILERS
First boiler 9336

No	Fitted	From
9790	8/4/43	5721
9334	28/8/47	5713
9327	10/1/53	45694
9783	7/3/57	45728

TENDERS

No	Fitted
4253	4/7/36* ex-6168
3989	7/1/50*
4513	17/12/60*

*Fowler

REPAIRS
28/2/38-7/3/38**LS**
31/5/39-18/8/39**HG**
17/10/40-30/10/40**LS**
30/1/42-5/3/42**HS**
9/3/43-8/4/43**HG**
14/9/44-13/10/44**LS**
17/1/46-20/2/46**HS**
16/6/47-28/8/47**HG**
9/9/47-10/9/47**NC(R)**
2/6/48-4/6/48**LO**
19/7/48-12/2/49**HI***
12/4/49-26/4/49**LC**
16/2/50-18/3/50**LI**
24/11/50-20/1/51**LI St Rollox**
5/2/51-12/3/51**LC St Rollox**
26/3/51-29/3/51**LC Kingmoor**
30/10/51-7/11/51**LC St Rollox**
16/6/52-10/1/53**G** St Rollox
30/1/53-31/1/53**NC St Rollox**
2/5/53-6/5/53**LC(EO) St Rollox**
9/6/54-3/7/54**LI St Rollox**
16/12/54-29/12/54**LC(EO) St Rollox**
8/2/55-23/2/55**LC(EO) St Rollox**
1/4/55-30/4/55**HI St Rollox**
4/2/57-7/3/57**G St Rollox**
17/4/58-16/5/58**HI St Rollox**
14/5/59-30/5/59**HI St Rollox**
22/3/60-1/4/60**LC(EO) St Rollox**
11/11/60-17/12/60**LI St Rollox**
24/7/61-16/8/61**LC(EO) St Rollox**
AWS never fitted
**Reverted to 'maintaining works
Crewe' from 6/1/64**
*179 days out of traffic!
** this was a mere 177 days out of
traffic, which included 106
days 'awaiting works'!

45717 DAUNTLESS

Built Crewe 21/7/36

Named 21/7/36

Renumbered 5717 to 45717 week ending 2/7/49

SHEDS
Blackpool 25/7/36
Southport 16/9/39
Newton Heath 15/6/40
Southport 3/4/48
Bank Hall 30/10/48

REPAIRS
21/12/37-19/1/38**HS**
25/2/38-5/3/38**LO**
28/6/39-7/8/39**HG**
16/9/40-5/10/40**LS**
12/3/42-4/4/42**LS**
6/7/42-7/7/42**TRO**
10/3/43-8/4/43**HG**
9/2/44-1/3/44**HS**
20/12/44-20/1/45**LS**
18/5/46-11/6/46**HS**
6/10/47-13/11/47**HG**
21/11/47-19/12/47**LO**
10/6/49-2/7/49**LI**
1/8/49-6/8/49**TRO**
26/9/50-17/10/50**HI**
27/10/51-7/12/51**HG**
23/6/52-2/8/52**LC Horwich**
25/2/53-9/4/53**LI**
14/4/53-25/4/53**NC(EO Rect)**
9/11/53-5/12/53**LC(EO)**
27/11/54-29/12/54**HG**
12/3/56-7/4/56**HI**
10/12/56-5/1/57**LC**
28/11/57-8/1/58**HG**
10/1/58-31/1/58**LC(EO)**
4/4/59-29/4/59**HI**
8/5/61-14/6/61**HI speedo fitted**
23/10/61-2/11/61**NC(EO) AWS fitted**

TENDERS

No	Fitted
3933	21/7/36* ex-6121
4242	29/12/51*
4496	29/12/54*
4248	5/1/57*
3898	8/1/58*
10750	29/4/59
9845	5/10/63

*Fowler

BOILERS
First boiler 9337

No	Fitted	From
9199	7/8/39	5682
9215	8/4/43	5590
9199	13/11/47	5734
9220	7/12/51	45726
9209	29/12/54	45682
9319	8/1/58	45725

MILEAGES

1936	19,987
1937	51,825
1938	47,927
1939	37,120
1940	43,219
1941	49,298
1942	49,655
1943	48,709
1944	52,166
1945	49,745
1946	52,802
1947	26,696
1948	41,909
1949	46,205
1950	49,867
1951	46,662
1952	58,717
1953	45,279
1954	55,087
1955	50,915
1956	49,161
1957	45,173
1958	58,168
1959	48,109
1960	49,332

Stored 7/10/63-21/10/63
**Mileage at 31/12/50 667,130; at 31/12/60
1,173,733**
Withdrawn week ending 26/10/63

45717 DAUNTLESS heads straight into the sun over Hest Bank troughs on 24 May 1952, with the up 10.50am Glasgow-Liverpool express. Its speed running past the audience on Hest Bank station was about 50mph, and Eric Bruton also noted that its green livery was grubby – 'definitely not a credit to its home shed Bank Hall'. Photograph E.D. Bruton.

AWS fitted 45717 DAUNTLESS about 1963 with almost inevitable tender change (see above) and wearing a weary and resigned air, at its home shed Bank Hall – it had been there since 1948. Photograph The Transport Treasury.

45718 DREADNOUGHT

Built Crewe 30/7/36

Named 30/7/36

Renumbered 5718 to 45718 2/49

TENDERS

No	Fitted
3908	30/7/36* ex-6125
4513	15/8/53*
3989	24/12/60*

REPAIRS
26/11/37-13/12/37**LS**
22/12/38-19/1/39**HG**
23/5/40-6/6/40**HS**
1/3/41-28/3/41**HG***
22/9/42-27/10/42**HS**
24/7/43-10/8/43**LO**
15/2/44-26/2/44**LS**
21/8/45-8/9/45**HG**
10/7/46-10/8/46**LO**
22/12/47-29/1/48**LS**
19/1/49-19/2/49**LC**
13/4/49-2/5/49**HI**
31/5/50-3/7/50**HG**
29/12/51-26/1/52**LI**
29/4/52-6/5/52**NC**
7/10/52-19/11/52**LC St Rollox**
11/7/53-15/8/53**HI St Rollox**
19/8/53-22/8/53**NC(R) St Rollox**
7/10/54-22/10/54**NC(TO) St Rollox**
17/12/54-4/2/55**G St Rollox**
19/7/56-18/8/56**LI St Rollox**
2/1/58-24/1/58**HI St Rollox**
16/6/58-2/7/58**NC(EO) St Rollox**
19/8/59-10/10/59**GEN St Rollox**
26/11/59-30/12/59**NC(EO) St Rollox**
10/11/60-23/12/60**HI St Rollox**
17/11/61-6/12/61**LC St Rollox**
**Dates not given- speedo probably
fitted, AWS probably never fitted
*'speed recording
instruments fitted'**

BOILERS

First boiler 9338

No	Fitted	From
9773	28/1/39	5725
9789	19/4/41	5567
9218	8/9/45	5694
9316	3/7/50	45697
10035	4/2/55	-
9316	10/10/59	45724

SHEDS
Blackpool 1/8/36
Preston 22/5/37
Crewe North 25/2/39
Longsight 29/4/39
Carlisle Upperby 23/9/39
Bushbury 28/5/49
Crewe North 1/10/49
Longsight 29/4/50
Bushbury 10/6/50
Carlisle Upperby 30/9/50
Longsight 7/7/51
Perth 13/9/52
Carlisle Kingmoor 14/2/53
Agecroft 21/7/62
Loan at first then
Agecroft 18/8/62

MILEAGES

1936	21,896
1937	55,508*
1938	72,902
1939	61,230
1940	45,517
1941	46,064
1942	32,010
1943	42,207
1944	45,117
1945	40,837
1946	40,389
1947	37,312
1948	40,553
1949	42,780
1950	40,506
1951	52,870
1952	50,764
1953	55,421
1954	52,033
1955	55,218
1956	54,575
1957	53,235
1958	47,459
1959	39,926
1960	55,391

*stored serviceable 18 days
**Mileage at 31/12/50 667,828; at 31/12/60
1,184,720**
Withdrawn week ending 20/10/62

Kingmoor's 45718 DREADNOUGHT puts on a super show over Beattock on 16 August 1955 with LONDON-PERTH express boards on the coaches. Just a trace of green livery lining on the cab, signs of burning on the smokebox door; driver leaning out of cab quite happily. Photograph J. Robertson, The Transport Treasury.

45719 GLORIOUS

Built Crewe 3/8/36

Named 3/8/36

Renumbered 5719 to 45719 week ending 26/2/49

BOILERS
First boiler 9339

No	Fitted	From
9197	27/2/39	5666
9342	30/4/42	5706
9335	31/5/46	5590
10038	25/2/49	5640
9341	7/3/53	45722
9202	15/3/56	45733

MILEAGES

1936	23,859
1937	63,982*
1938	65,941
1939	56,513
1940	47,798
1941	46,113
1942	53,477
1943	55,246
1944	40,952
1945	44,509
1946	52,912
1947	30,039
1948	47,751
1949	41,581
1950	46,816
1951	46,140
1952	37,555
1953	49,594
1954	51,539
1955	49,331
1956	52,766
1957	52,325
1958	43,535
1959	56,188
1960	44,863

Stored serviceable 18 days
Mileage at 31/12/50 717,489; at 31/12/60 1,201,325
Withdrawn week ending 23/3/63

SHEDS
Blackpool 22/8/36
Preston 22/5/37
Bushbury 11/3/39
Crewe North 10/6/39
Newton Heath (loan) 23/10/42
Newton Heath 16/1/43
Bank Hall 28/3/53
Blackpool 25/9/54
Bank Hall 25/6/55

TENDERS

No	Fitted
4238	3/8/36* ex-6151
4248	7/3/53*
4499	12/5/54*
4573	13/4/57*HSS
(to 48600 11/58)	
10093	28/11/58 ex-48600

*Fowler
HSS=High Straight Sided

REPAIRS
5/10/37-19/10/37**LS**
18/1/39-27/2/39**HG**
25/5/40-7/6/40**LS**
5/5/41-22/5/41**LO**
14/4/52-30/4/42**HG**
30/6/43-23/7/43**LS**
12/10/44-26/10/44**LS**
30/5/45-26/5/45**LS**
13/7/45-27/7/45**LO**
14/5/46-31/5/46**HG**
23/10/47-4/12/47**HS**
18/1/49-25/2/49**HG**
9/4/49-20/4/49**TRO**
3/8/50-29/8/50**HI**
10/9/51-5/10/51**HI**
23/1/53-7/3/53**HG**
10/4/54-12/5/54**LI**
30/1/56-15/3/56**HG**
15/3/57-13/4/57**LI**
3/11/58-28/11/58**HI**
4/4/60-31/5/60**LI**
 ?   -12/61 **AWS, speedo fitted**

45720 INDOMITABLE

Built Crewe 17/8/36

Named 17/8/36

Renumbered 5720 to 45720 9/48

BOILERS
First boiler 9340

No	Fitted	From
9774	22/4/39	5726
9201	16/5/42	5657
9323	23/8/45	5687
9778	20/5/50	45712

Record incomplete

TENDERS

No	Fitted
3901	17/8/36* ex-6122
4244	mid-1950s

*Fowler

MILEAGES

1936	17,197
1937	61,424
1938	68,547
1939	48,230
1940	43,789
1941	52,249
1942	57,507
1943	55,682
1944	48,458
1945	52,050
1946	39,563
1947	37,803
1948	43,461
1949	43,112
1950	42,427

Record ends
Mileage at 31/12/50 711,499
Withdrawn December 1962

SHEDS
Blackpool 22/8/36
Preston 22/5/37
Crewe North 26/12/37
Bescot 11/3/39
Crewe North 16/9/39
Longsight 3/10/42
Crewe North 27/3/43
Patricroft 27/7/46
Corkerhill 9/52
Perth 10/59
Polmadie 12/59
Corkerhill 4/60

REPAIRS
19/11/37-20/12/37**LS**
25/2/39-28/3/39**HG**
27/7/40-15/8/40**LS**
6/4/42-23/4/42**HG**
30/4/43-28/5/43**HS**
15/9/44-30/9/44**LS**
27/7/45-23/8/45**HG**
23/4/47-2/6/47**HS**
24/8/48-18/9/48**LS**
6/3/50-24/4/50**HS**
Record incomplete

45721 IMPREGNABLE

Built Crewe 26/8/36
Named 26/8/36
Renumbered 5721 to 45721 week ending 28/8/48

TENDERS

No	Fitted
3902	26/8/36* ex-6100
9755	11/4/39
4501	28/8/48*
10067	9/7/59

BOILERS
First boiler 9341

No	Fitted	From
9790	7/3/40	5742
9197	21/11/42	5719
9788	21/4/45	5668
9344	22/3/49	5678
9333	17/10/52	45668
9777	28/6/57	45668
9340	8/9/62	45590

REPAIRS
26/8/36**TRO**
24/1/38-4/2/38**LS**
29/8/39-14/9/39**LO**
17/2/40-7/3/40**HG**
15/12/41-3/1/42**LS**
22/10/42-21/11/42**HG**
13/3/44-27/3/44**HS**
4/4/45-21/4/45**HG**
13/1/47-1/2/47**LS**
8/9/47-8/10/47**LO**
4/8/48-28/8/48**LO**
17/12/48-22/3/49**HG**
22/7/50-15/8/50**LI**
16/4/51-14/5/51**HI**
4/9/52-17/10/52**HG**
22/10/52-3/11/52**NC(EO Rect)**
3/4/54-27/4/54**LI**
27/12/55-2/2/56**HI**
28/5/57-28/6/57**HG**
29/8/58-3/10/58**LI**
9/10/58-21/10/58**NC(EO Rect)**
26/3/59-12/5/59**NC(EO Rect)**
22/6/59-9/7/59**NC(EO)**
28/5/60-28/6/60**NC(EO) AWS fitted**
16/1/61-10/2/61**HI speedo fitted**

SHEDS
Blackpool 29/8/36
Patricroft 22/5/37
Aston 11/3/39
Bushbury 8/7/39
Crewe North 16/9/39
Bushbury 19/4/47
Willesden 21/6/47
Bushbury 28/5/49
Crewe North 1/10/49
Edge Hill 25/2/50
Crewe North 29/1/55
Carlisle Upperby 7/11/59
Crewe North 1/7/61
Burton 4/64
Bank Hall 10/64

MILEAGES

1936	19,367
1937	59,537
1938	61,543
1939	43,562
1940	45,695
1941	55,348
1942	53,389
1943	59,587
1944	60,691
1945	56,280
1946	47,154
1947	38,504
1948	27,926
1949	37,667
1950	41,714
1951	48,926
1952	37,933
1953	51,030
1954	47,905
1955	40,741
1956	46,743
1957	43,938
1958	39,140
1959	39,250
1960	44,404

Stored 25/9/63-13/12/63, 11/1/64-29/3/64, 6/1064-21/6/65, 20/9/65-withdrawal
Mileage at 31/12/50 707,964; at 31/12/60 1,147,971
Withdrawn week ending 9/10/65

45722 DEFENCE

Built Crewe 24/8/36
Named 24/8/36
Renumbered 5722 to 45722 week ending 31/7/48

BOILERS
First boiler 9342

No	Fitted	From
9784	24/4/39	5736
9220	26/4/41	5681
9202	21/4/44	5689
9341	22/5/47	5657
9785	5/9/52	45680
9257	8/9/56	45674

TENDERS

No	Fitted
3938	24/8/36* ex-6133
9759	24/6/39
4484	28/7/48*
3909	13/1/54*
4497	2/7/56*
3187	21/3/59*
10787	6/2/60
*Fowler	

REPAIRS
9/2/38-7/3/38**LS**
18/3/39-24/4/39**HG**
27/2/40-21/3/40**LO**
15/10/40-30/10/40**LS**
24/3/41-26/4/41**HO**
2/7/42-25/7/42**LS**
16/12/42-21/1/43**LO**
5/4/44-21/4/44**HG**
18/2/46-5/3/46**HS**
30/6/46-15/8/46**HO**
8/4/47-22/5/47**HG**
9/6/48-28/7/48**LS**
11/7/48-25/9/48**LO**
4/8/49-23/8/49**LI**
27/8/49-16/9/49**TRO**
9/12/50-6/1/51**LI**
21/4/51-18/5/51**LC(TO)**
26/7/52-5/9/52**HG**
9/12/53-13/1/54**HI**
14/4/55-25/5/55**LI**
6/8/56-8/9/56**HG**
5/12/57-10/1/58**HI**
20/2/59-21/3/59**LI AWS fitted**
21/12/59-6/2/60**LC(TO)**
23/2/61-19/4/61**LI speedo fitted**

SHEDS
Blackpool 29/8/36
Patricroft 22/5/37
Aston 11/3/39
Crewe North 26/10/40
Bushbury 10/6/50
Carlisle Upperby 30/9/50
Crewe North 29/1/55
Carlisle Upperby 22/10/55
Rugby Testing Station 22/9/56
Carlisle Upperby 23/3/57
Camden 22/6/57
Willesden 3/10/59
Camden 19/11/60
Willesden 3/12/60
Rugby 14/1/61

MILEAGES

1936	15,976
1937	62,008
1938	61,872
1939	45,949
1940	38,875
1941	54,842
1942	59,635
1943	52,726
1944	55,582
1945	51,937
1946	49,394
1947	49,569
1948	36,691
1949	42,679
1950	47,593
1951	43,551
1952	42,868
1953	44,481
1954	50,877
1955	44,267
1956	37,682*
1957	43,619
1958	51,154
1959	50,733
1960	40,842

*Rugby Test Station from 22/9/56
Stored 9/9/62-withdrawal
Mileage at 31/12/50 725,328; at 31/12/60 1,175,402
Withdrawn week ending 1/12/62

45722 DEFENCE fully rigged up for testing at the Rugby research plant in 1956. The plant had been open getting on for ten years before a Jubilee was tried out (they were 'second division' after all...) with a view to improving its steam/power output. Alterations were made to the draughting; chimney, taper, diameter, as well as a double blastpipe arrangement. Despite an impressive improvement 45722 did not get the double blastpipe though 45596 *was* subsequently equipped with twin exhaust – five years later! Something of the different single blastpipe dimensions tested on 45722 were applied to other engines, 45601, 45610, 45622, 45628, 45672, 45688, 45733 and 45738. No general round of alterations was embarked upon and though this may have been because the end of steam was in sight it seems strange – after all, other engines, Castles, A3s and so on got double chimneys long after the tests with DEFENCE.

45722 in more normal guise on Camden turntable, May 1958. One of the test points on the smokebox (now blanked off) is still visible to the rear of the outside steam pipe. That '22' on the fireman's side window is difficult to explain – is it a replacement window with DEFENCE's number on it or is it a 'specials' board stowed on the tender back? Photograph J. Robertson, The Transport Treasury.

45723 FEARLESS

Built Crewe 26/8/36
Named 26/8/36
Renumbered 5723 to 45723 week ending 29/5/48

BOILERS
First boiler 9343

No	Fitted	From
9326	17/2/40	5706
9212	12/4/44	5699
9332	24/5/48	5703
9786	16/1/52	45688
9328	17/11/55	45671

SHEDS
Blackpool 29/8/36
Patricroft 22/5/37
Aston 11/3/39
Longsight 21/3/42
Crewe North 7/9/57
Carlisle Upperby 12/10/57
Crewe North 1/7/61
Nuneaton 10/11/62
Rugby 23/2/63
Nuneaton 8/64

REPAIRS
26/2/38-16/3/38LS
9/8/39-12/8/39LO
12/1/40-17/2/40HG
20/2/42-13/3/42HS
2/3/43-17/3/43LS
27/3/44-12/4/44HG
28/8/45-18/9/45LS
14/7/47-23/8/47LS
26/4/48-24/5/48HG
18/6/49-21/7/49HI
6/9/49-3/10/49HC
17/4/50-9/5/50LC
31/10/50-27/11/50LI
1/12/51-16/1/52HG
23/5/53-13/6/53HI
28/6/54-4/8/54HI
3/10/55-17/11/55HG
25/4/57-18/5/57LI
21/5/58-28/6/58HI
20/12/58-13/1/59LC
11/4/59-9/5/59NC(EO) AWS fitted
20/5/59-17/6/59NC(EO)
18/7/60-27/8/60LI speedo fitted

TENDERS

No	Fitted
3905	26/8/36* ex-6114
9758	10/5/39
4512	23/8/47*
4485	4/8/54*
4246	17/11/55*
4471	15/7/56*
10330	13/1/59

MILEAGES

1936	17,106
1937	62,894
1938	60,121
1939	39,020
1940	31,121
1941	32,429
1942	57,085
1943	56,420
1944	62,651
1945	51,861
1946	54,618
1947	41,252
1948	51,644
1949	49,989
1950	48,021
1951	56,276
1952	61,929
1953	56,864
1954	49,958
1955	44,486
1956	61,499
1957	48,674
1958	42,581
1959	47,073
1960	42,541

Stored 16/1/63-6/2/63, 15/9/63-15/12/63
Mileage at 31/12/50 716,232; at 31/12/60 1,228,113
Withdrawn week ending 22/8/64

45724 WARSPITE

Built Crewe 2/9/36
Named 2/9/36
Renumbered 5724 to 45724 8/48

TENDERS

No	Fitted
4247	2/9/36* ex-6162
9771	16/10/39
4508	7/8/48*
3944	21/9/54*
3908	30/11/56*
9719	27/1/59

*Fowler

BOILERS
First boiler 9344

No	Fitted	From
9214	16/12/38	5684
9209	27/11/40	5621
9213	13/5/44	5698
9343	17/5/47	5708
9325	4/11/50	45741
9316	14/5/55	45718

REPAIRS
16/6/37-22/6/37LO
9/12/37-31/12/37LS
25/10/38-16/12/38HG
11/12/39-30/12/39LS
22/10/40-27/11/40HG
3/1/42-20/1/42LS
7/11/42-16/12/42LS
27/3/44-27/4/44HG
22/10/45-17/11/45LS
21/2/46-12/3/46LO
6/3/47-24/4/47HG
26/7/48-7/8/48NC
6/2/49-4/3/49HI
1/11/49-19/11/49LC
15/9/50-23/10/50HG
5/3/51-16/3/51LC
8/2/52-17/3/52LI
6/7/53-22/8/53HI St Rollox
16/3/55-14/5/55G St Rollox
16/6/55-21/6/55NC(EO) St Rollox
27/6/55-9/7/55LC(EO) St Rollox
6/11/56-30/11/56HI St Rollox
27/1/58-21/2/58HI St Rollox
13/6/59-11/7/59HG St Rollox
5/8/59-13/8/59NC(EO) St Rollox
20/8/59-21/8/59NC(EO) St Rollox
28/9/60-28/10/60LI St Rollox
17/4/61-17/4/61LC(EO) St Rollox
No dates; speedo probably fitted,
AWS probably never fitted

SHEDS
Low Moor 5/9/36
Farnley Jct 24/4/37
Leeds 22/5/37
Edge Hill 15/5/42
Loan at first, then
Edge Hill 27/6/42
Patricroft 27/7/46
Bushbury 3/5/47
Edge Hill 26/7/47
Crewe North 2/10/48
Bushbury 28/5/49
Edge Hill 1/10/49
Patricroft 15/10/49
Bushbury 10/6/50
Crewe North 30/9/50
Carlisle Kingmoor 9/8/52
Carlisle Kingmoor 16/8/52
Carlisle Upperby 26/7/58
Carlisle Kingmoor 13/9/58
Nuneaton 7/7/62

MILEAGES

1936	16,760
1937	71,494
1938	79,471
1939	87,634
1940	69,331
1941	71,459
1942	52,989
1943	44,483
1944	42,610
1945	35,102
1946	47,944
1947	49,317
1948	52,549
1949	42,176
1950	40,329
1951	46,939
1952	49,567
1953	53,831
1954	57,207
1955	34,386
1956	51,677
1957	57,965
1958	53,766
1959	43,113
1960	55,220

Mileage at 31/12/50 803,648; at 31/12/60 1,307,319
Withdrawn week ending 3/11/62

5724 WARSPITE in red with the block lettering, at Nottingham Midland station, 20 July 1937. Photograph J.A. Whaley, The Transport Treasury.

45724, by now in BR green of course, at Kingmoor 22 August 1952. Photograph J. Robertson, The Transport Treasury.

45725 REPULSE

Built Crewe 25/9/36
Named 26/9/36
Renumbered 5725 to 45725 week ending 4/12/48

TENDERS

No	Fitted
4242	25/9/36* ex-6157
10302	31/1/50

*Fowler

REPAIRS
23/11/37-14/12/37**LS**
11/11/38-12/12/38**HG**
6/9/39-30/9/39**HS**
22/8/40-4/10/40**HG**
19/5/41-19/6/41**LS**
6/7/42-30/7/42**LS**
11/11/42-21/11/42**LO**
19/8/43-3/9/43**HG**
12/3/45-28/3/45**HS**
25/6/46-26/7/46**HG**
9/10/47-10/11/47**LS**
19/10/48-3/12/48**HG**
1/7/49-29/7/49**TRO Millhouses**
9/1/50-31/1/50**LI**
12/2/51-10/3/51**HI**
19/5/52-28/6/52**HG**
8/12/52-9/1/53**LC(EO)**
17/8/53-18/9/53**LI**
23/8/54-24/9/54**HI**
29/1/55-17/2/55**LC(EO)**
6/3/56-29/3/56**HI**
30/7/56-14/9/56**LC**
20/9/57-23/10/57**HG**
24/11/58-24/12/58**HI**
21/10/60-26/11/60**HI**
No dates; speedo probably fitted,
AWS probably never fitted

BOILERS
First boiler 9773

No	Fitted	From
9255	12/12/38	5697
10038	4/10/40	5688
9325	3/9/43	5710
9342	26/7/46	5719
9195	3/12/48	5707
9319	28/6/52	45734
11160	23/10/57	45608

SHEDS
Low Moor 26/9/36
Farnley Jct 24/4/37
Leeds 22/5/37
Crewe North (loan) 4/9/43
Leeds 2/10/43
Bushbury 24/5/47
Loan at first then
Bushbury 21/6/47
Edge Hill 8/11/47
Kentish Town 21/8/48
Loan at first then
Kentish Town 11/9/48
Millhouses 2/10/48
Canklow 1/62
Darnall 6/62

MILEAGES

Year	Miles
1936	11,738
1937	68,685
1938	83,438
1939	82,935
1940	70,531
1941	65,059
1942	50,683
1943	54,566
1944	52,072
1945	52,930
1946	56,676
1947	39,071
1948	49,729
1949	56,467
1950	54,352
1951	51,845
1952	42,311
1953	56,593
1954	52,221
1955	50,596
1956	52,297
1957	53,036

Stored prior to withdrawal
Mileage at 31/12/50 848,932
Withdrawn week ending 29/12/62

45726 VINDICTIVE

Built Crewe 9/10/36
Named 9/10/36
Renumbered 5726 to 45726 week ending 11/12/48

TENDERS

No	Fitted
9130	9/10/36
3935	26/6/37* ex-5703
9782	21/9/40
4505	2/7/47*
4487	29/7/53*
4484	12/2/54*
3923	28/9/57*
10204	22/10/58 ex-48045

*Fowler

MILEAGES

Year	Miles
1936	8,144
1937	73,646
1938	87,314
1939	77,772
1940	65,335
1941	70,933
1942	46,965
1943	50,066
1944	41,543
1945	42,273
1946	49,214
1947	47,515
1948	47,157
1949	52,481
1950	50,634
1951	37,499
1952	46,366
1953	53,562
1954	45,886
1955	29,316
1956	50,482
1957	48,311
1958	45,422
1959	47,222
1960	47,284

Stored 26/9/63-19/11/63
Mileage at 31/12/50 810,992; at
31/12/60 1,262,342
Withdrawn week ending 20/3/65

BOILERS
First boiler 9774

No	Fitted	From
9344	16/2/39	5724
9320	21/12/40	5683
9206	3/2/42	5684
10033	8/9/44	5712
9220	2/7/47	5667
9222	1/8/51	45670
9211	4/1/56	45698
9778	4/11/60	-

SHEDS
Low Moor 10/10/36
Farnley Jct 12/12/36
Leeds 22/5/37
Edge Hill 6/6/42
Loan at first then
Edge Hill 27/6/42
Patricroft 27/7/46
Bushbury 28/5/49
Crewe North 1/10/49
Bushbury 10/6/50
Edge Hill 30/9/50
Crewe North 20/6/53
Patricroft 15/5/54
Crewe North 19/6/54
Bushbury 26/6/54
Crewe North 28/8/54
Warrington 23/11/63
Loan at first then
Warrington 7/12/63

REPAIRS
23/7/37-3/8/37**LO**
5/1/38-20/1/38**LS**
13/1/39-16/2/39**HG**
19/1/40-10/2/40**HS**
22/11/40-21/12/40**HG**
28/12/41-3/2/42**HS**
20/7/43-4/8/43**LS**
19/8/44-8/9/44**HG**
23/4/46-17/5/46**HS**
8/5/47-2/7/47**HG**
28/10/48-7/12/48**LS**
14/4/50-4/5/50**LI**
11/6/51-1/8/51**HG**
16/9/52-11/10/52**HI**
13/12/52-3/1/53**LC(EO)**
15/1/54-12/2/54**HI**
23/11/55-4/1/56**HG**
24/10/56-29/11/56**LC(EO)**
4/9/57-28/9/57**LI**
1/10/57-4/10/57**NC(EO Rect)**
10/10/58-22/10/58**NC(EO)**
31/3/59-24/4/59**HI AWS fitted**
10/10/60-4/11/60**HG speedo fitted**

45727 INFLEXIBLE

Built Crewe 12/10/36
Named 12/10/36
Renumbered 5727 to 45727 6/48

TENDERS

No	Fitted
9127	12/10/36
9028	13/7/45
9022	-
9023	-

BOILERS

First boiler 9775

No	Fitted	From
9776	27/2/40	5728
9315	17/10/42	5682
9789	2/11/45	5718
9775	3/6/50	5730

Record incomplete

MILEAGES

1936	7,629*
1937	65,249*
1938	84,935
1939	76,126
1940	56,801
1941	46,974
1942	54,762
1943	57,761
1944	51,225
1945	49,702
1946	64,865
1947	59,249
1948	51,506
1949	50,637
1950	42,880

*1936 stored serviceable 25 days
*1937 stored serviceable 46 days
Record Ends
Mileage at 31/12/50 820,301
Withdrawn December 1962

SHEDS

Willesden 17/10/36
Crewe North 2/1/37
Carlisle Kingmoor 18/4/37
St Rollox 26/4/37
Corkerhill 2/10/37
Polmadie 22/1/38
St Rollox 4/6/38
Polmadie 1/10/38
St Rollox 1/7/39
Carlisle Kingmoor 2/12/39
Record incomplete but
believed to have remained
at Kingmoor until
Perth 3/53
Corkerhill 5/60

REPAIRS

4/5/38-13/5/38**LS**
27/1/40-27/2/40**HG**
9/9/41-9/10/41**HS**
18/9/42-17/10/42**HG**
13/5/44-6/6/44**LS**
1/10/45-2/11/45**HG**
3/2/47-1/3/47**HS**
5/2/48-4/3/48**LS**
4/6/48-25/6/48**LO**
16/3/49-9/5/49**LI**
13/4/50-3/6/50**G**
Record incomplete
AWS fitted by 4/62;
Probably fitted with
Speedo

45728 DEFIANCE

Built Crewe 7/10/36
Named 7/10/36
Renumbered 5728 to 45728 10/48

TENDERS

No	Fitted
9362	7/10/36
9363	1/4/41
9025	17/5/41
9597	1/12/49
9719	12/10/56
3908	27/1/59*

*Fowler

REPAIRS

26/4/38-4/5/38**LS**
6/12/39-20/1/40**HG**
24/3/41-19/4/41**LS**
22/5/42-24/6/42**HS**
22/5/43-26/6/43**HG**
3/1/44-10/2/44**LS**
18/6/45-26/7/45**LS**
7/6/46-29/7/46**LS**
12/9/47-13/11/47**HG**
18/9/48-26/10/48**LS**
1/11/49-3/12/49**LI**
6/2/51-13/3/51**HI** St Rollox
22/9/51-15/11/51**G** St Rollox
23/2/53-21/3/53**HI** St Rollox
11/12/53-9/1/54**HI** St Rollox
18/6/55-13/8/55**LI** St Rollox
6/9/56-12/10/56**G** St Rollox
23/7/57-1/8/57**LC(EO)** St Rollox
29/10/57-7/11/57**NC** St Rollox
20/5/58-12/7/58**HI** St Rollox
1/1/59-17/1/59**LC** St Rollox
29/5/59-4/7/59**HI** St Rollox
23/8/59-3/10/59**LC** St Rollox
6/3/61-8/4/61**G** St Rollox
11/5/61-27/5/61**NC** St Rollox
No dates – speedo probably
fitted, AWS probably never
fitted

BOILERS

First boiler 9776

No	Fitted	From
9778	20/1/40	5730
9254	26/6/43	5685
9776	13/11/47	5691
9783	15/11/51	45714
9779	12/10/56	-
9775	8/4/61	-

SHEDS

Willesden 17/10/36
Crewe North 2/1/37
Carlisle Kingmoor 18/4/37
St Rollox 3/4/34
Perth 10/4/34
Carlisle Kingmoor 30/3/40
Carlisle Upperby 26/8/61
Carlisle Kingmoor 10/3/62
Agecroft 21/7/62
Loan at first then
Agecroft 18/8/62

MILEAGES

1936	6,104*
1937	66,934*
1938	72,050
1939	73,485
1940	57,387
1941	53,452
1942	54,948
1943	53,737
1944	46,092
1945	51,692
1946	51,370
1947	51,999
1948	61,348
1949	54,503
1950	57,738
1951	45,217
1952	54,918
1953	52,686
1954	60,628
1955	44,516
1956	50,366
1957	58,946
1958	49,007
1959	32,836
1960	44,393

*1936 stored serviceable 25 days
*1937 stored serviceable 46 days
Mileage at 31/12/50 812,839; at 31/12/60
1,306,352
Withdrawn week ending 20/10/62

45729 FURIOUS

Built Crewe 13/10/36
Named 13/10/36
Renumbered 5729 to 45729 6/48

BOILERS
First boiler 9777

No	Fitted	From
9205	17/1/42	5686
9208	24/1/46	5692
9789	14/10/50	45727
9325	22/10/55	45724
9789	22/10/60	-

REPAIRS
16/2/38-25/2/38**LS**
15/5/39-2/8/39**HG**
16/9/40-6/10/40**LS**
10/6/41-1/7/41**LO**
8/12/41-17/1/42**HG**
7/12/43-8/1/44**HS**
4/12/44-6/1/45**LS**
14/12/45-24/1/46**HG**
14/2/47-21/3/47**LS**
8/5/48-5/6/48**LS**
13/7/48-13/7/48**NC**
3/2/49-10/3/49**LC**
5/4/49-6/5/49**LC**
26/7/49-3/9/49**HI**
14/9/49-14/9/49**Tender repair only**
19/6/50-14/10/50**G**
28/8/51-27/9/51**HI St Rollox**
12/4/52-17/5/52**LI St Rollox**
17/12/53-16/1/54**HI St Rollox**
28/1/54-6/2/54**LC(EO) St Rollox**
24/11/54-4/12/54**LC(EO) St Rollox**
25/6/55-22/10/55**G* St Rollox**
3/9/56-13/9/56**LC(EO) St Rollox**
9/5/57-1/6/57**HI St Rollox**
4/11/58-21/11/58**HI St Rollox**
-18/12/58**NC(EO) St Rollox**
31/12/58-31/12/58**NC(EO) St Rollox**
17/9/60-22/10/60**HG St Rollox**
13/2/61-1/3/60**LC(EO) St Roll⸱** .
Speedo probably fitted; AWS never
*102 days; includes 53 days
'awaiting works'

SHEDS
Crewe North 17/10/36
Carlisle Kingmoor 18/4/37
Aberdeen 5/6/37
Carlisle Kingmoor 27/11/37
Agecroft 21/7/62
Loan at first then
Agecroft 18/8/62

TENDERS

No	Fitted
9363	13/10/36
9362	1/4/41
9176	10/5/46
9723	3/6/48
9843	3/9/49
9069	14/9/49
9716	14/10/50
9329	29/9/51
4620	22/10/55

MILEAGES

1936	8,337*
1937	40,368*
1938	69,347
1939	61,622
1940	59,740
1941	50,972
1942	55,949
1943	51,508
1944	49,609
1945	49,822
1946	54,283
1947	61,594
1948	44,461
1949	43,814
1950	46,286
1951	58,817
1952	46,358
1953	55,704
1954	52,332
1955	32,835
1956	67,688
1957	56,447
1958	48,099
1959	49,431
1960	42,196

*1936 stored serviceable 25 days
*1937 stored serviceable 46 days
Mileage at 31/12/50 777,712; at 31/12/60 1,287,619
Withdrawn week ending 20/10/62

45730 OCEAN

Built Crewe 16/10/36
Named 16/10/36
Renumbered 5730 to 45730 4/48

MILEAGES

1936	3,974*
1937	68,132*
1938	75,827
1939	70,389
1940	63,265
1941	53,220
1942	65,786
1943	54,164
1944	45,264
1945	48,485
1946	48,468
1947	56,131
1948	44,646
1949	58,988
1950	54,586
1951	48,322
1952	50,773
1953	52,750
1954	55,918
1955	56,614
1956	46,135
1957	51,244
1958	50,183
1959	43,099
1960	38,479

*1936 stored serviceable 18 days
*1937 stored serviceable 46 days
Stored 15/9/62-8/4/63
Mileage at 31/12/50 811,328; at 31/12/60 1,304,845
Withdrawn week ending 5/10/63

SHEDS
Rugby 17/10/36
Crewe North 12/12/36
Carlisle Kingmoor 18/4/37
Carnforth 16/9/61
Warrington 22/6/63

BOILERS
First boiler 9778

No	Fitted	From
9783	23/12/39	5735
9775	20/5/44	5713
9322	24/4/48	5693
9320	21/2/53	45731
9334	8/8/57	-

TENDERS

No	Fitted
9364	16/10/36
9720	26/8/41
9194	27/4/44
9709	15/5/44
4623	24/8/51

REPAIRS
7/8/37-25/8/37**LO**
12/4/38-26/4/38**LS**
3/11/39-23/12/39**HG**
28/1/41-10/2/41**LS**
21/11/41-23/12/41**LS**
31/12/42-30/1/43**HS**
13/3/44-20/5/44**HG**
8/3/45-20/3/45**LO**
26/1/46-26/2/46**LS**
1/2/47-1/4/47**HS**
10/2/48-24/4/48**HG**
29/10/48-18/11/48**LO**
9/5/49-29/6/49**LI**
23/6/50-17/8/50**LI**
1/2/51-10/2/51**LC St Rollox**
27/7/51-25/8/51**HI St Rollox**
6/11/51-16/11/51**LC St Rollox**
14/5/52-24/5/52**LC St Rollox**
30/12/52-21/2/53**G St Rollox**
5/3/54-3/4/54**HI St Rollox**
9/4/54-9/4/54**NC(EO)R St Rollox**
20/4/54-24/4/54**NC(EO) St Rollox**
23/11/54-2/12/54**LC(EO) St Rollox**
3/2/55-5/3/55**LI St Rollox**
3/3/56-6/4/56**HI St Rollox**
20/6/56-30/6/56**LC(EO) St Rollox**
18/9/56-28/9/56**LC(EO) St Rollox**
26/10/56-15/11/56**LC(EO) St Rollox**
1/7/57-8/8/57**G St Rollox**
3/2/58-20/2/58**LC(EO) St Rollox**
14/11/58-10/1/59**LI St Rollox**
30/1/59-31/1/59**NC(EO) St Rollox**
23/7/59-14/8/59**LC(TO) St Rollox**
2/7/60-20/8/60**LI St Rollox**
24/8/60-2/9/60**HC(EO) St Rollox**
6/10/60-6/10/60**NC(EO) St Rollox**
2/11/61-9/12/61**HI St Rollox**
No dates; speedo probably fitted,
AWS probably never

45731 PERSEVERANCE

Built Crewe 21/10/36

Named 21/10/36

Renumbered 5731 to 45731 12/48

BOILERS
First boiler 9779

No	Fitted	From
9204	20/11/43	5711
9320	19/4/47	5715
9204	18/12/52	45713
9782	4/7/58	-

MILEAGES

1936	6,493*
1937	42,900*
1938	74,143
1939	62,213
1940	57,703
1941	57,797
1942	50,861
1943	56,555
1944	60,347
1945	52,796
1946	57,683
1947	47,344
1948	46,343
1949	54,158
1950	55,519
1951	58,533
1952	21,314
1953	64,055
1954	60,142
1955	46,000
1956	49,448
1957	54,682
1958	47,686
1959	48,852
1960	41,016

*1936 stored serviceable 25 days
*1937 stored serviceable 46 days
**Mileage at 31/12/50 812,855; at 31/12/60
1,304,583**
Withdrawn week ending 20/10/62

SHEDS
Crewe North 24/10/36
Carlisle Kingmoor 18/4/37
Carlisle Upperby 2/9/61
Carlisle Kingmoor 7/7/62
Blackpool 21/7/62
Loan at first then
Blackpool 18/8/62

TENDERS

No	Fitted
9365	21/10/36
9213	29/11/46
9273	31/7/47
9277	18/11/48
9247	13/12/48
9701	20/8/55
9247	2/9/55
4619	13/9/61

REPAIRS
30/3/38-8/4/38**LS**
20/7/39-30/8/39**HG**
16/12/40-9/1/41**LS**
23/3/42-5/5/42**HS**
3/9/42-29/9/42**LS**
25/10/43-20/11/43**HG**
25/7/45-25/8/45**LS**
25/2/47-19/4/47**HG**
8/11/48-17/12/48**HS**
19/7/49-25/8/49**LI**
9/11/50-8/12/50**HI**
8/6/51-29/6/51**HC St Rollox**
17/5/52-18/12/52**G St Rollox**
15/1/54-12/2/54**HI St Rollox**
15/7/55-20/8/55**HI(EO) St Rollox**
31/8/55-2/9/55**LC St Rollox**
20/10/56-23/11/56**LI St Rollox**
9/8/57-24/8/57**LC(EO) St Rollox**
6/5/58-4/7/58**G St Rollox**
19/6/59-10/7/59**LI St Rollox**
16/10/59-13/11/59**LC St Rollox**
26/12/59-9/1/60**LC St Rollox**
5/9/60-17/9/60**LC(EO) St Rollox**
14/2/61-11/3/61**HI St Rollox**
No dates; speedo probably fitted,
AWS probably never

45731 PERSEVERANCE just north of Motherwell station with a down express 'W211' on 6 June 1953. Enjoy the signalling variety – that fine gantry as well as the directional arrows on those ground signals, pointing to which line they applied. Photograph J. Robertson, The Transport Treasury.

45732 SANSPAREIL

Built Crewe 29/10/36
Named 19/10/36
Renumbered 5732 to 45732 3/49

TENDERS

No	Fitted
9366	29/10/36
9665	2/4/47
9725	30/4/52
10505	12/1/56
9722	24/1/57

REPAIRS
4/3/38-21/3/38**LS**
31/5/39-7/7/39**LS**
15/7/40-3/8/40**LS**
7/12/40-27/12/40**LO**
13/6/41-10/7/41**HS**
22/12/41-4/2/42**HG**
22/9/42-21/10/42**LS**
2/12/42-12/1/43**LO**
12/2/44-4/3/44**LS**
27/4/45-5/6/45**HS**
6/3/47-6/6/47**HG**
18/1/49-12/3/49**LI**
3/9/49-30/9/49**LC**
7/7/50-26/8/50**HI**
14/9/50-19/9/50**NC**
28/11/50-21/12/50**LC***
4/2/52-10/5/52**G St Rollox**
2/5/53-23/5/53**HI St Rollox**
24/6/54-13/8/54**LI St Rollox**
30/11/55-12/1/56**HI St Rollox**
1/11/56-24/1/57**G St Rollox**
13/6/57-22/6/57**LC(EO) St Rollox**
14/11/57-19/11/57**NC St Rollox**
3/2/58-1/3/58**LI St Rollox**
6/3/58-20/3/58**HC St Rollox**
26/2/59-26/3/59**HI St Rollox**
6/11/59-25/11/59**NC St Rollox**
15/6/60-14/7/60**LI St Rollox**
*Tender only
No dates; speedo probably fitted,
AWS probably never

BOILERS
First boiler 9780

No	Fitted	From
9333	4/2/42	5713
9338	14/6/47	5699
9780	10/5/52	45715
9205	24/1/57	45714
9205	3/2/58	45732
9221	16/12/61	45696

SHEDS
Crewe North 31/10/36
Carlisle Kingmoor 18/4/37
Carlisle Upperby 10/3/62
Carlisle Kingmoor 7/7/62
Blackpool 21/7/62
Loan at first then
Blackpool 18/8/62
Stockport 12/1/63

MILEAGES

1936	5,890*
1937	40,636*
1938	80,521
1939	70,674
1940	48,278
1941	54,642
1942	41,429
1943	48,076
1944	48,737
1945	50,115
1946	56,978
1947	52,060
1948	73,411
1949	48,303
1950	38,660
1951	59,977
1952	45,233
1953	49,409
1954	49,293
1955	43,721
1956	49,979
1957	57,564
1958	54,563
1959	47,675
1960	42,120

*1936 stored serviceable 25 days
*1937 stored serviceable 46 days
**Mileage at 31/12/50 788,410; at
31/12/60 1,287,944**
Withdrawn week ending 29/2/64

45733 NOVELTY

Built Crewe 2/11/36
Named 2/11/36
Renumbered 5733 to 45733 week ending 1/10/49

TENDERS

No	Fitted
9367	2/11/36

REPAIRS
2/5/38-20/5/38**LS**
31/10/39-29/11/39**LO**
24/2/40-20/3/40**HG**
19/9/41-11/10/41**LS**
26/4/43-12/5/43**HG**
24/12/43-15/1/44**LO**
23/11/44-9/12/44**LS**
10/8/45-13/9/45**HG**
8/9/47-8/10/47**LS**
16/8/49-26/9/49**HG**
6/9/50-3/10/50**LI**
6/2/52-4/4/52**HG**
13/4/53-9/5/53**LI**
12/7/54-16/8/54**HI**
7/7/55-12/8/55**HG**
5/3/56-26/3/56**LC(EO)**
22/10/56-30/11/56**HI**
11/1/58-1/2/58**LI**
11/3/59-17/4/59**LI AWS fitted**
20/11/60-7/1/61**HG speedo fitted**

BOILERS
First boiler 9781

No	Fitted	From
10035	20/3/40	5590
9336	12/5/43	5716
9785	13/9/45	5679
9221	26/9/49	45676
9202	4/4/52	45671
9256	12/8/55	45666
9781	7/1/61	45684

SHEDS
Crewe North 7/11/36
Llandudno Jct (loan) 27/2/37
Crewe North 6/3/37
Bushbury 11/3/39
Crewe North 16/12/39
Bushbury 11/10/47
Crewe North 2/10/48
Bushbury 10/6/50
Crewe North 14/10/50
Bushbury 7/7/51
Crewe North 14/6/58
Edgehill 20/9/58
Llandudno Jct 6/2/60
Camden 11/6/60
Willesden 10/9/60
Rugby 10/6/61
Crewe North 22/6/63
Willesden 14/12/63
Crewe North 8/64

MILEAGES

1936	4,179*
1937	62,407*
1938	70,007
1939	49,050
1940	48,031
1941	47,860
1942	57,207
1943	57,015
1944	47,108
1945	67,021
1946	58,674
1947	40,281
1948	43,521
1949	29,139
1950	49,718
1951	54,723
1952	46,738
1953	42,121
1954	45,427
1955	51,892
1956	43,451
1957	62,319
1958	52,684
1959	47,564
1960	38,094

*1936 stored serviceable 25 days
*1937 stored serviceable 46 days
Stored 9/9/62-16/6/63, 26/9/63-6/12/63
**Mileage at 31/12/50 731,218; at 31/12/60
1,216,231**
Withdrawn week ending 19/9/64

45734 METEOR

Built Crewe 11/11/36
Named 11/11/36
Renumbered 5734 to 45734 week ending 18/9/48

TENDERS

No	Fitted
9368	11/11/36

REPAIRS
27/4/38-25/5/38LS
4/7/39-8/7/39LO
24/8/39-18/9/39HG
1/5/42-23/5/42LS
28/6/43-22/7/43HG
18/6/45-21/7/45LS
25/2/46-9/4/46LO
22/5/47-27/6/47HG
20/7/48-14/9/48HS
11/10/49-28/10/49HI
28/7/50-8/9/50HI
3/1/52-16/2/52HG
20/5/52-2/6/52NC
11/7/53-18/8/53LI
18/6/54-24/7/54LI
4/6/55-2/7/55HG
7/7/56-4/8/56HI
3/1/57-6/2/57LC(EO)
22/5/57-22/6/57LC(EO)
26/2/58-29/3/58HG
28/4/58-14/5/58NC(EO Rect)
6/6/59-26/6/59HI
1/7/59-6/7/59NC(EO Rect) AWS fitted
10/5/61-9/6/61LI speedo fitted

BOILERS
First boiler 9782

No	Fitted	From
9330	18/9/39	5710
9199	22/7/43	5717
9319	27/6/47	5675
9318	16/2/52	45701
9201	2/7/55	45741
9214	29/3/58	45741

SHEDS
Crewe North 21/11/36
Llandudno Jct (loan) 27/2/37
Crewe North 13/3/37
Bushbury 11/3/39
Aston 3/1/42
Bushbury 11/10/47
Crewe North 2/10/48
Longsight 29/4/50
Bushbury 7/7/51
Carlisle Upperby 7/11/59
Crewe North 9/7/60
Carlisle Upperby 1/10/60
Carlisle Kingmoor 7/7/62

MILEAGES

1936	6,214*
1937	62,268*
1938	70,908
1939	47,594
1940	33,847
1941	39,174
1942	58,786
1943	55,846
1944	44,569
1945	48,992
1946	56,601
1947	46,361
1948	39,003
1949	43,079
1950	49,959
1951	48,317
1952	48,922
1953	43,518
1954	49,041
1955	52,870
1956	54,618
1957	51,471
1958	49,835
1959	55,499
1960	49,698

*1936 stored serviceable 18 days
*1937 stored serviceable 46 days
Stored 10/9/62-9/10/62
Mileage at 31/12/50 703,201; at 31/12/60 1,206,990
Withdrawn week ending 28/12/63

45734 METEOR, a Bushbury engine, passing Harrow & Wealdstone with 'The Midlander' from Wolverhampton, 10 March 1952. London Transport Bakerloo train in reversing sidings to the left. It must have been just about here that 46242 hit the rear of that up local on 8 October and 45637/46202 met their ends. Photograph C.R.L. Coles.

45735 COMET

Built Crewe 16/11/36
Named 16/11/36
Renumbered 5735 to 45735 week ending 19/6/48
(underlines separate 'original' from 'rebuilt' information)

BOILERS
First boiler 9783

No	Fitted	From
9324	17/7/39	5705
10753	14/5/42	New
12031	31/5/44	New
10752	26/11/46	5736
12525	4/4/49	6128
10753	19/1/52	46112
12667	30/10/53	46154
12532	11/2/56	-
11726	25/5/59	45532

REPAIRS
1/6/38-17/6/38LS
14/6/39-17/7/39HG
19/10/40-2/11/40LS
3/3/41-21/3/41LO
23/3/42-14/5/42 **HG-REBUILT**

21/9/42-9/10/42LO
18/3/43-9/4/43LS
17/7/43-31/7/43LO
17/5/44-31/5/44HG
2/12/44-16/12/44LO
21/8/45-20/9/45HS
30/10/46-26/11/46HG
9/7/47-25/8/47LO
11/12/47-23/1/48LS
12/3/45-12/4/48NC
6/5/48-14/5/48NC
2/6/48-19/6/48NC
18/2/49-4/4/49HG
1/4/50-21/4/50HI
2/4/51-20/4/51LI
1/11/51-19/1/52HG **Smoke deflectors fitted**
20/12/52-28/1/53HI
1/10/53-30/10/53HG
8/9/54-28/9/54LC(EO) **Camden**
4/2/55-4/3/55LI
2/1/56-11/2/56HG
19/3/57-18/4/57HI
22/1/58-5/3/58HI
23/8/58-18/9/58LC(EO)
3/4/59-25/5/59HG **AWS fitted**
18/11/60-19/12/60LI **speedo**

TENDERS

No	Fitted
9369	16/11/36

SHEDS
Crewe North 21/11/36
Carlisle Upperby (loan) 27/2/37
Crewe North 3/4/37
Bushbury loan 4/3/39
Bushbury 11/3/39
Edge Hill 21/10/39

Leeds 6/6/42
Loan at first then
Leeds 27/6/42
Camden 10/7/43
Loan at first then
Camden 31/7/43
Crewe North (loan) 10/3/45
Camden 31/3/45
Bushbury 2/10/48
Camden 27/11/48
Preston 12/9/59
Edge Hill 17/9/60
Willesden 14/1/61
Annesley 12/10/63

MILEAGES

1936	6,057*
1937	63,196*
1938	72,532
1939	56,254
1940	46,601
1941	45,123
1942	61,044
1943	65,180
1944	65,433
1945	73,332
1946	64,209
1947	59,795
1948	47,869
1949	68,498
1950	67,455
1951	60,650
1952	70,244
1953	73,549
1954	66,605
1955	60,136
1956	55,552
1957	56,619
1958	50,398
1959	44,230
1960	42,509

*1936 stored serviceable 7 days
*1937 stored serviceable 37 days
Stored 14/10/62-10/12/62
Mileage at 31/12/50 862,578; at 31/12/60 1,443,070
Withdrawn week ending 3/10/64

The Way Ahead. The rebuilt 45735 COMET is how all the Jubilees might have looked had ideas to vastly extend the '6P' (later 7P) fleet had come to full fruit. At Camden from 1943 on top flight West Coast work (along with PHOENIX) the engine is approaching Northchurch tunnel with the up Saturday 'Lakes Express' on 2 September 1950. It has the usual two-coach strengthening set added to the four-coach through portion from Keswick via Penrith at the rear – this ran as a train in its own right through to Oxenholme, usually behind a 2-6-4T. COMET has the combined train (reporting number 'W86') and is in faded BR lined black with an equally faded BRITISH RAILWAYS on the tender. And, Eric Bruton recalls, it was doing about 60mph. Photograph E.D. Bruton.

45736 PHOENIX with the Royal Scot type smoke deflectors fitted to both of the rebuilt engines in 1950-51, at Chester on 6 September 1955. If the whole of the Jubilees as well as the Patriots and Royal Scots had indeed been so dealt with, a mighty fleet would truly have been created. The programme was abandoned with the BR Standards in prospect; in an alternative world where steam reigned on, the successors to the Jubilees would presumably have been a fleet of Britannias... Photograph J. Robertson, The Transport Treasury.

45736 PHOENIX

Built Crewe 25/11/36
Named 25/11/36
Renumbered 5736 to 45736 week ending 2/10/48

BOILERS
First boiler 9784

No	Fitted	From
9195	20/3/39	5695
10752	11/4/42	New
10753	22/2/46	5735
12036	2/10/48	6129
12205	21/12/50	46114
12656	11/4/53	45525
13891	8/6/55	45529
12206	24/5/57	46159
12540	26/5/61	46144

TENDERS

No	Fitted
9370	25/11/36
9755	4/8/52

MILEAGES

1936	4,879
1937	59,884*
1938	70,537
1939	44,389
1940	45,193
1941	47,210
1942	42,204
1943	57,260
1944	71,162
1945	64,709
1946	74,479
1947	61,067
1948	58,573
1949	66,159
1950	73,638
1951	65,407
1952	56,842
1953	56,872
1954	67,277
1955	57,054
1956	54,608
1957	56,084
1958	58,840
1959	57,526
1960	52,585

* stored serviceable 37 days
Mileage at 31/12/50 841,343; at 31/12/60 1,424,438
Withdrawn week ending 26/9/64

SHEDS

Crewe North 28/11/36
Carlisle Upperby (loan) 27/2/37
Crewe North 3/4/37
Camden 28/5/38
Willesden 1/10/38
Aston 11/3/39
Bushbury 8/7/39
Edge Hill 21/10/39

Leeds (loan) 16/5/42
Leeds (loan) 27/6/42
Camden (loan) 10/7/43
Camden 31/7/43
Crewe North 18/9/54
Holyhead 10/9/55
Longsight 7/1/56
Crewe North 25/2/56
Longsight 11/6/60
Crewe North 10/9/60
Holyhead 15/9/62
Camden 9/3/63
Holyhead 20/4/63
Willesden 22/6/63
Carlisle Kingmoor 9/63
Carlisle Upperby 7/64
Carlisle Kingmoor 9/64

REPAIRS

6/12/37-20/12/37**LS**
13/2/39-20/3/39**HG**
29/7/40-17/8/40**LS**
17/2/42-11/4/42**HG-REBUILT**

21/7/42-22/8/42**LO**
18/12/42-12/1/43**HS**
31/4/43-5/5/43**LO**
21/7/43-7/8/43**LO**
29/11/43-4/1/44**LS**
14/6/44-1/7/44**LO**
7/3/45-23/3/45**LS**
9/1/46-22/2/46**HG**
9/9/46-17/10/46**LS**
22/5/47-28/6/47**HS**
15/8/47-9/9/47**LO**
1/3/48-31/3/48**LO**
21/8/48-2/10/48**HG**
24/10/49-18/11/49**HI**
18/11/50-21/12/50**HG Smoke deflectors fitted**
21/7/51-14/9/51**LC**
9/4/52-15/5/52**LI**
1/8/52-26/8/52**LC(EO)**
13/2/53-11/4/53**HG**
2/11/53-25/11/53**LC(EO)**
23/4/54-21/5/54**HI**
15/4/55-8/6/55**HG**
21/2/56-17/3/56**HI**
10/4/57-24/5/57**HG**
29/5/57-5/6/57**NC(EO Rect)**
13/5/58-6/6/58**HI**
12/8/59-11/9/59**HI AWS fitted**
19/4/61-26/5/61**HG speedo fitted**

PHOENIX with smokebox door ajar at Willesden shed 12 October 1963; AWS and speedo fitted. 5735 and 5736 were chosen for rebuilding because they happened to be two of the 'newer' Jubilees due for heavy repair at the time, that is, when all the material was ready and the work came to start. 5735 had 130,655 miles since the last heavy repair when taken out of traffic on 23 March 1942 and 5736 had run 139,158 miles on 17 February 1942. 5735 was out of traffic for 46 weekdays returning on 14 May 1942; 5736 took one day more, and after 47 days had returned to work on 11 April. Photograph The Transport Treasury.

45737 ATLAS

Built Crewe 23/11/36
Named 23/11/36
Renumbered 5737 to 45737 week ending 13/11/48

BOILERS
First boiler 9785

No	Fitted	From
9332	6/1/40	5712
9331	5/2/44	5741
9256	27/2/46	5610
9317	24/10/49	5699
9217	26/9/53	45610
9323	18/10/56	45667
9206	2/3/61	45742

TENDERS

No	Fitted
9371	23/11/36

SHEDS
Crewe North 28/11/36
Carnforth (loan) 27/2/37
Crewe North 20/3/37
Bushbury 11/3/39
Edge Hill 21/10/39
Bushbury 9/3/46
Crewe North (loan) 24/5/47
Crewe North 21/6/47
Bushbury 5/6/48
Crewe North 2/10/48
Longsight (loan) 9/4/49
Bushbury 28/5/49
Crewe North 1/10/49
Edge Hill 25/2/50
Bushbury 7/7/51
Aston 13/2/60
Crewe North 11/6/60
Newton Heath 31/3/62

REPAIRS
3/3/38-21/3/38**LS**
5/12/39-6/1/40**HG**
12/11/41-2/12/41**HS**
8/1/44-5/2/44**HG**
7/2/46-27/2/46**HS**
24/2/48-1/4/48**HS**
18/10/48-11/11/48**LO**
10/9/49-24/10/49**HG**
6/4/51-23/4/51**HI**
18/6/52-25/7/52**LI**
1/9/53-26/9/53**HG**
6/4/54-8/5/54**LC(EO)**
12/4/55-11/5/55**LI**
30/1/56-24/2/56**LC(EO)**
12/9/56-18/10/56**HG**
30/12/57-25/1/58**LI**
28/6/58-9/8/58**LC(EO)**
10/10/59-20/11/59**HI AWS fitted**
12/12/60-2/3/61**HG speedo fitted**

MILEAGES

1936	4,857
1937	63,507*
1938	68,685
1939	51,898
1940	45,849
1941	25,991
1942	42,921
1943	37,028
1944	44,642
1945	32,413
1946	45,753
1947	35,965
1948	42,705
1949	42,720
1950	56,888
1951	55,012
1952	51,277
1953	49,013
1954	45,591
1955	52,355
1956	53,499
1957	53,166
1958	43,300
1959	45,157
1960	47,460

*stored serviceable 37 days
Mileage at 31/12/50 651,822; at 31/12/60 1,147,652
Withdrawn week ending 30/5/64

45738 SAMSON

Built Crewe 30/11/36

Named 30/11/36

Renumbered 5738 to 45738 week ending 2/7/49

BOILERS
First boiler 9786

No	Fitted	From
9214	20/1/41	5724
9203	20/8/45	5696
10035	14/2/48	5705
9336	30/12/50	45567
9784	26/8/53	45674
9317	21/3/57	45712

TENDERS

No	Fitted
9066	30/11/36

MILEAGES

1936	5,267
1937	61,345*
1938	69,835
1939	57,687
1940	53,842
1941	61,829
1942	57,995
1943	59,063
1944	53,974
1945	52,080
1946	61,448
1947	60,054
1948	52,477
1949	43,210
1950	43,774
1951	52,217
1952	49,662
1953	50,139
1954	58,415
1955	53,396
1956	51,847
1957	47,677
1958	49,196
1959	47,716
1960	49,060

*stored serviceable 43days
Mileage at 31/12/50 793,880
Withdrawn week ending 28/12/63;
at 31/12/60 1,303,205

REPAIRS
24/5/37-4/6/37**LO**
29/4/38-23/5/38**LS**
4/12/39-30/12/39**LS**
27/12/40-20/1/41**HG**
3/3/42-26/3/42**LS**
11/12/42-2/1/43**HS**
27/12/43-22/1/44**LS**
4/8/45-20/8/45**HG**
13/12/46-4/1/47**HS**
20/12/47-14/2/48**HG**
8/6/49-27/6/49**LI**
20/9/49-11/10/49**HC**
6/11/50-30/12/50**HG**
3/4/52-9/5/52**LI**
18/7/53-26/8/53**HG**
25/1/55-1/3/55**LI**
13/3/56-20/4/56**LI**
24/4/56-25/4/56**NC(EO Rect)**
24/1/57-21/3/57**HG**
19/4/58-22/5/58**HI**
8/4/60-19/5/60**HI AWS, speedo fitted**

SHEDS
Crewe North 5/12/36
Longsight (loan) 5/2/38
Crewe North 19/2/38
Bushbury 11/3/39
Camden 1/7/39
Bushbury 19/4/47
Crewe North 2/8/47
Bushbury 23/8/47
Loan at first then
Bushbury 11/10/47
Crewe North 2/10/48
Edge Hill (loan) 3/9/49
Crewe North 8/10/49
Edge Hill 25/2/50
Crewe North 10/6/50
Bushbury 7/7/51
Camden 17/11/51
Bushbury 10/5/52
Carlisle Upperby 7/11/59
Carlisle Kingmoor 7/7/62

45739 ULSTER

Built Crewe 12/36

Named 9/12/36

Renumbered 5739 to 45739 6/48

TENDERS

No	Fitted
9065	9/12/36
10535	19/12/59

MILEAGES

1936	2,946
1937	69,584*
1938	70,201
1939	56,606
1940	59,793
1941	58,803
1942	61,640
1943	65,664
1944	61,587
1945	46,150
1946	61,236
1947	53,387
1948	48,750
1949	51,538
1950	56,220
1951	66,779
1952	68,424
1953	67,247
1954	64,312
1955	63,681
1956	74,369
1957	45,966

*1937 stored serviceable 53 days
Mileage at 31/12/50 767,885
Withdrawn 1/67

BOILERS
First boiler 9787

No	Fitted	From
9782	20/9/39	5735
10037	24/9/43	5690
10036	21/10/46	5670
9340	10/11/49	5610
10032	3/11/53	-
9326	6/6/57	-

SHEDS
Crewe North 12/12/36
Bushbury 11/3/39
Camden 1/7/39
Bushbury 17/5/47
Willesden 21/6/47
Kentish Town 21/8/48
Loan at first then
Kentish Town 13/9/48
Leeds 18/9/48
Wakefield 6/64

REPAIRS
6/4/38-5/5/38**LS**
28/8/39-20/9/39**HG**
30/8/40-14/9/40**LS**
27/8/41-12/9/41**HS**
12/1/42-23/1/42**LO**
8/12/42-30/12/42**LS**
11/9/43-24/9/43**HG**
10/8/44-26/8/44**LS**
14/11/45-18/12/45**HS**
13/9/46-21/10/46**HG**
16/5/47-9/6/47**LO**
14/6/48-29/7/48**LS**
1/10/49-10/1149**HG**
16/10/50-20/11/50**LI**
4/12/50-22/12/50**LC(TO)***
7/4/51-12/4/51**LC***
26/11/51-21/12/51**HI**
6/11/52-5/12/52**LI**
21/9/53-3/11/53**HG**
6/11/53-13/11/53**2NC(Rect)EO**
29/6/54-7/8/54**LC(EO)**
25/11/54-18/12/54**HI**
24/11/55-2/1/56**HI**
27/4/57-6/6/57**HG**
18/7/58-26/8/58**LI**
16/11/59-19/12/59**HI**
?   -18/9/56**NC(EO)**
Record confused; AWS and speedo
probably fitted 1961-62
***Leeds Holbeck**

5739 ULSTER, in the block style and yet to gain its 'red hand' Ulster crest, at Crewe South 24 April 1937. The crest had apparently appeared but briefly at first and was finally refitted in January 1947. Riveted, 4,000 gallon tender. Photograph J.A. Whaley, The Transport Treasury.

45740 MUNSTER

Built Crewe 19/12/36
Named 19/12/36
Renumbered 5740 to 45740 week ending 12/6/48

TENDERS

No	Fitted
3926	19/12/36* ex-6130
9760	6/7/39
4497	10/6/48*
4561	2/4/54*
9065	6/2/60
*Fowler	

REPAIRS
23/5/38-14/6/38LS
11/10/39-17/10/39LO
21/2/40-16/3/40HG
7/4/41-22/4/41LS
10/11/41-22/11/41LS
7/12/42-29/12/42HG
5/5/44-19/5/44LS
15/5/45-20/6/45LS
18/7/46-14/8/46HG
20/3/47-19/6/47HG
8/5/48-10/6/48HS
21/5/49-24/6/49HG
6/1/50-20/1/50LC
10/7/50-7/8/50HI
18/10/51-8/11/51HI
15/3/52-1/4/52LC
28/1/53-26/2/53HI
2/3/54-2/4/54HG
11/5/55-4/6/55HI
21/4/56-16/5/56HI
30/10/57-5/12/57HG
27/8/58-23/9/58LC(EO)
26/12/59-6/2/60HI AWS fitted
14/11/60-22/12/60HI speedo fitted

BOILERS
First boiler 9788

No	Fitted	From
9218	16/3/40	5667
9328	29/12/42	5667
9318	14/8/46	5639
9197	24/6/49	45700
9340	2/4/54	-
9337	5/12/57	45705

SHEDS
Crewe North 19/12/36
Aston 11/3/39
Crewe North 26/10/40
Longsight 3/4/43
Camden 13/6/53
Bushbury 26/6/54
Willesden 24/11/56
Crewe North 9/7/60
Llandudno Jct 1/10/60
Crewe North 10/6/61
Llandudno Jct 16/9/61
Aston 23/9/61

MILEAGES

1936	132
1937	60,512*
1938	71,764
1939	43,628
1940	32,127
1941	50,087
1942	61,287
1943	62,240
1944	64,084
1945	58,130
1946	62,600
1947	47,184
1948	56,818
1949	58,283
1950	53,226
1951	52,054
1952	50,795
1953	49,728
1954	55,677
1955	54,691
1956	52,409
1957	40,407
1958	47,289
1959	45,811
1960	36,324

*stored serviceable 25 days
Stored 7/11/62-16/6/63, 9/9/63-withdrawal
Mileage at 31/12/50 782,102; at 31/12/60 1,267,287
Withdrawn week ending 26/10/63

45741 LEINSTER

Built Crewe 29/12/36
Named 29/12/36
Renumbered 5741 to 45741 week ending 29/5/48

TENDERS	
No	Fitted
9125	29/12/36
9128	5/1/56
10747	7/9/63

BOILERS
First boiler 9789

No	Fitted	From
9331	25/1/40	5711
9316	6/10/43	5705
9325	27/8/46	5725
9201	10/8/50	45590
9214	4/6/55	45681
9321	19/10/57	45688

MILEAGES

1936	-
1937	65,081*
1938	67,394
1939	46,809
1940	34,810
1941	38,459
1942	64,872
1943	56,056
1944	59,491
1945	60,894
1946	54,689
1947	44,163
1948	46,448
1949	51,685
1950	49,993
1951	38,880
1952	55,859
1953	46,009
1954	49,282
1955	55,187
1956	52,631
1957	50,651
1958	49,071
1959	54,125
1960	41,902

*stored serviceable 33 days
Mileage at 31/12/50 740,844; at 31/12/60 1,234,441
Withdrawn week ending 1/2/64

REPAIRS
2/5/38-19/5/38**LS**
1/1/40-25/1/40**HG**
4/3/42-25/3/42**LS**
22/9/43-6/10/43**HG**
20/3/45-5/4/45**LS**
30/7/46-27/8/46**HG**
4/12/47-8/1/48**LS**
30/4/48-25/5/48**LO**
6/4/49-28/4/49**HI**
16/6/50-10/8/50**HG**
17/11/51-19/12/51**HI**
1/5/53-22/5/53**HI**
31/3/54-30/4/54**LC**
25/4/55-4/6/55**HG**
2/8/56-22/8/56**HI**
21/9/57-19/10/57**HG**
10/11/58-5/12/58**HI**
26/5/59-13/6/59**NC(EO) AWS fitted**
8/9/60-5/10/60**LI speedo fitted**

SHEDS
Crewe North 2/1/37
Edge Hill (loan) 27/2/37
Crewe North 3/4/37
Aston 11/3/39
Longsight 21/3/42
Edge Hill 25/1/47
Bushbury 10/5/47
Crewe North 20/12/47
Camden 26/6/48
Bushbury 28/5/49
Crewe North 1/10/49
Bushbury 10/6/50
Edge Hill 27/1/51
Bushbury 7/7/51
Carlisle Upperby 7/11/59
Carlisle Kingmoor 7/7/62

The double chimney Jubilee and the last of the class, 45742 CONNAUGHT, running under the bridge near Northchurch with the down 2.15pm Euston-Birmingham and Wolverhampton express on Saturday 8 March 1952. The stock is that of the weekday 'Midlander'. Photograph E.D. Bruton.

45742 CONNAUGHT

Built Crewe 31/12/36

Named 31/12/36

Renumbered 5742 to 45742 week ending 13/11/48

TENDERS

No	Fitted
9128	31/12/36
9125	5/1/56
10354	18/4/64

BOILERS

First boiler 9790

No	Fitted	From
9337	8/2/40	5717
9219	11/12/43	5676
9207	12/10/46	5709
9257	21/11/49	45701
9331	22/1/53	-
9206	7/4/55	45670
10036	14/12/60	45671

REPAIRS

25/4/38-10/5/38**LS**
15/1/40-8/2/40**HG** Double chimney fitted?
25/4/42-16/5/42**HS**
23/11/43-11/12/43**HG**
18/4/45-5/5/45**LS**
18/9/46-12/10/46**HG**
10/12/47-20/1/48**HS**
4/10/48-9/11/48**LS**
18/10/49-21/11/49**HG**
6/11/50-25/11/50**LI**
21/1/52-19/2/52**HI**
18/12/52-22/1/53**HG**
29/4/53-23/5/53**LC(EO)**
5/1/54-17/2/54**HI**
9/3/55-7/4/55**HG** Double chimney removed
20/10/55-18/11/55**LC(EO)**
21/12/55-28/1/56**LC(EO)**
1/5/56-6/6/56**LI**
12/8/57-31/8/57**LI**
22/8/58-18/9/58**LI**
22/6/59-8/8/59**LC** AWS fitted
23/10/60-14/12/60**HG** speedo fitted

SHEDS

Crewe 2/1/37
Edge Hill (loan) 17/2/39
Crewe 3/4/37
Aston 11/3/39
Crewe loan 4/5/40
Aston 1/5/40
Crewe loan 14/9/40
Longsight 4/4/42
Edge Hill 25/1/47
Bushbury 10/5/47
Willesden 21/6/47
Bushbury 11/10/47
Crewe North 2/10/48
Preston 21/1/50
Bushbury 10/6/50
Longsight 28/10/50
Bushbury 7/7/51
Carlisle Upperby 7/11/59
Carlisle Kingmoor 7/7/62

MILEAGES

1937	67,508*
1938	64,058
1939	44,484
1940	29,820
1941	33,162
1942	55,016
1943	56,775
1944	62,632
1945	61,261
1946	54,836
1947	40,928
1948	49,285
1949	45,592
1950	56,275
1951	54,307
1952	45,662
1953	52,251
1954	50,026
1955	47,034
1956	46,567
1957	45,473
1958	47,758
1959	48,465
1960	41,043

*stored serviceable 33 days
Stored 21/11/64-unrecorded date
Mileage at 31/12/50 721,632; at 1,200,218
Withdrawn week ending 1/5/65

It's always nice to leave on a high note and railway photography doesn't come on a much higher note than this. CONNAUGHT with its double chimney was a Bushbury favourite until the mid-1950s especially, it is said, on the London 'two hour trains'. This exquisite portrait shows it at New Street on Sunday 13 September 1953, easing away with the 10.30 from Wolverhampton to Euston. A perfect picture! Photograph E.D. Bruton.

5. APPENDICES

APPENDIX ONE
A Fascinating Group of Transfers
(or: *vive la différence!*)
By Graham Onley

Over many years, both as spotter and as a more mature(?) enthusiast, one particular characteristic of the LMS and its successor the London Midland Region, has never ceased to amaze me. I refer to the ability to transfer all sorts of locomotives between all sorts of sheds almost without drawing breath. Even allowing for the far higher totals of locomotives compared with the other four Regions this practice was clearly most prevalent on the LMS/LMR. Anyone doubting this need only compare each Region's column inches each month in *Trains Illustrated* or any of the other contemporary journals, such as *The Railway Observer*. This state of affairs continued right up to the end of steam in 1968.

By common consent, although the old order had effectively broken down by the end of 1963, there is no doubt that the LM was still in the forefront of transfer volumes. Quite frankly, the

discovery that a Stanier 2-8-0 had moved from say, Toton to Wellingborough, or a Fowler 4F had departed Alsager for Uttoxeter, was of minimal interest to other than local watchers and most likely passed unnoticed. Strangely enough, even when the old railway boundaries began to undergo the process of change, traditional type transfers between sheds now on different Regions continued unabated. I acknowledge that eventually, hitherto impossible transfers such as Western Region pannier tanks to Scotland and the Southern Region raised a few eyebrows. In the main though, the twain rarely met!

None of this had occurred to me as a youngster on the fringes of the Northampton Duston West 'squad' in the early 1950s, and much of it was in the seemingly endless future. We tended to think of the future in terms of a full scale realisation of the results of the 1948 Exchanges, with A4s and Bullied Pacifics charging along the LMR Western Division, all with no

diminution in sightings of our domestic classes of course. Hardly surprisingly, this failed to materialise, and we were beginning to think that whatever exotic transfers had gone before, as told round the camp fires, they were a thing of the past. Then, without warning, in the summer of 1952, IT happened, and while IT had much logic, much of the vastness of the remainder of the continuing transfer to-ings and fro-ings of the ensuing 10 or 12 years still escapes me in terms of logic. Perhaps someone out there with first-hand knowledge could inform us. Imagine my quiet, unseen chuckle when recently instructed by Head Office to transfer two Scania 114 three axle tractor units from my employer's Wellingborough depot to Newton Heath depot! When I receive letters regarding commercial vehicle fleet lists, believe me, it makes me feel almost normal.

Back to IT. By the summer of 1952, the process of change from the old big four into the fashionably much-maligned British Railways that most

45581 BIHAR AND ORISSA roars away through Edge Hill, 22 August 1955. Photograph Brian Morrison.

45724 (one of the unbalanced moves) at Kingmoor 28 June 1957. 45697 ACHILLES behind. Photograph Brian Morrison.

of my generation actually came to love and accept as the norm, was well under way. The old pre-nationalisation liveries and numbering schemes that I had missed, seeing them only in magazines such as *Trains Illustrated* or *The Railway Magazine* and hearing of only through older gang members massed in our local spotting fields, had by and large, gone. If I saw the LMS initials, or BRITISH RAILWAYS in full on tenders or tank sides, I cannot honestly recollect them, oddly enough. I clearly remember seeing black-liveried Jubilees; 45574 INDIA and its Blackpool shedmate 45695 MINATOUR being the most clear in my mind. This clearly indicates that I *did* see BRITISH RAILWAYS on tenders, but I must have been too entranced by the red backed nameplates and the exquisite Fowler straight sided tenders to notice! The same LNWR style lined black on the Royal Scots is also clear in my mind. Blue Princess Royals and Coronations were no strangers to my rapt attention, yet the prolonged process of fitting smoke deflectors to the Class 7P rebuilds was an 'event' which somehow managed to bypass me. I took the advent of 'the Standards' which we saw as attempted usurpers of our indigenous classes, in my unimpressed young stride, even if a Britannia racing

through Blisworth did eventually come to excite me. But one event I have never failed to marvel at, even in later years when I came to appreciate the reasons behind it, was the exchange of Jubilees between the London Midland and the Scottish Regions in that summer of 1952 – IT.

Needless to say, the first intimation that there had been transfers of a sensational, if not exactly undreamed of nature, came through local spottings. Even then, the astonishing passage of what we took to be a 'Scottish Jubilee' on our 'half past one' would have been taken as just that – jaw-droppingly astonishing! The power was invariably, and I mean invariably, a Blackpool Jubilee – little would we have realised, probably for the first couple of occasions, that something was afoot. Then we would have wondered that the coincidence was too great, and paid greater attention to the shedplates. Once we had realised, the older gang members had probably acquired the particular 'TI' or *Railway Observer* containing the full list of transfers, which I can remember scanning disbelievingly.

Oddly enough, although thirty Jubilees were concerned in this exchange, only twelve involved me directly on a day to day basis. The other eighteen were either out of range before

the great day (although I doubt that it all occurred on one day) or despite, or possibly because of their transfer, came to be just as effectively out of range as they so infuriatingly were prior to the move. Statistically, twenty-six Jubilees were exchanged on a one for one basis, and the remaining four moved sheds. Seventeen sheds were involved as follows, with the codes of the day:

3B Bushbury
5A Crewe North
9A Longsight
10B Preston
10C Patricroft
12A Carlisle Upperby
14B Kentish Town
16A Nottingham
17A Derby
19B Millhouses
22A Bristol
24E Blackpool
25G Farnley Junction
63A Perth
66A Polmadie
67A Corkerhill
68A Carlisle Kingmoor

The straight swops were:

45560 from 67A to 16A for 45640
45575 from 63A to 14B for 45657
45576 from 67A to 19B for 45621

The scenes we could only dream of. The new engines line up; the LMS red, especially en masse like this (it was a pity it weathered poorly) must have been impressive indeed. 5606 heads 5601 (with a 'superheated converted Claughton' behind) at Crewe North shed in April 1935. The Jubilees respectively became FALKLAND ISLANDS and BRITISH GUIANA, both in September 1936.

45579 PUNJAB (see table below) arriving at platform 8 Birmingham New Street, 1 July 1961. Photograph Michael Mensing.

45577 from 68A to 22A for 45679
45579 from 66A to 14B for 45696
45580 from 68A to 24E for 45697
45581 from 68A to 25G for 45704
45582 from 68A to 10B for 45673
45583 from 66A to 12A for 45677
45584 from 66A to 24E for 45707
45643 from 67A to 12A for 45687
45645 from 67A to 10C for 45720
45646 from 67A to 25G for 45711

The unbalanced moves were:

45564 from 63A to 17A
45644 from 63A to 9A
45718 from 3B to 63A
45724 from 5A to 68A

The results were fifteen Jubilees from the LMR to the ScR and fifteen from Scotland to the LM and much ecstasy across parts of the land. On a personal note, the moves brought into my orbit 45580, 45582, 45583, 45584, 45643 and 45644; the moves took away 45697, 45707, 45718 and 45724 but these were already locked into my ABC. Taken away and escaping view were 45673 and 45687. The other eighteen might as well have been transferred from Brisbane to Sydney insofar as there was any hope of easy sightings! Needless to say, most of them did fall to my ABC over the next ten years or so.

This little exercise does raise some points worthy of consideration... Note that Leeds Holbeck (20A) was not involved in any way. This is doubtless due to the fact that, despite running probably the largest fleet of Jubilees at any shed, by the summer of 1952 none, with the sole exception of 45739, was numbered higher that the 45664 'cut off point' where non-interchangeable boilers rendered it necessary for the main works involved (Crewe and St Rollox) to keep stocks of both types. This convenience of interchangeability, it turned out, was the reason for the momentous transfers. Non-involvement also meant that 20A's long standing ownership of many of its Jubilees could continue. How was it that Holbeck clung to such as 45562, 45565, 45566, 45568, 45569, 45573, 45589, 45597, 45605, 45608, 45619, 45658, 45659 and 45739 and, once acquired during 1953, 45564, with a minimum of 'floaters'. Compare this with the records of Western Division sheds such as Camden, Crewe North, Edge Hill and Longsight.

Newton Heath (26A) was also among the leaders in fleet size, and although it ran Jubilees of both boiler types it was not involved. Newton Heath also retained a hard-core of its allocation over many years and it is interesting that 26A clung to 45635, 45642 and 45661 of the earlier variety, while doing likewise with later examples such as 45700, 45701, 45702, 45706 and 45710.

What argument, if any, did the management at Newton Heath put forward in order to ensure that the inevitable aggravation factor passed them by? Was the fact that the Western Division was a net loser of one engine, while the Midland Division managed a net gain of one an administrative error, or part of some great design we have yet to unearth? (Look at the four unbalanced moves detailed earlier.)

Why was it that the engines sent to Scotland in 1952 eventually began to look the part (that is, they gained the larger Scottish Region cab-side numerals) whereas those involved in a later, opposite direction and smaller scale exile to England in June 1959, retained their 'Scottish' appearance until withdrawal? These were 45679, 45696 and 45704 which moved from Carlisle Kingmoor to Crewe North. I acknowledge that by then Kingmoor was in fact a London Midland Region shed but in reality it was as 'Scottish' as it ever was as far as the nation's youth were concerned. All these three engines had been part of the 1952 episode and went for scrap with small Fowler tenders and large cabside numerals. Why did they miss acquiring the larger Stanier tenders like most of their fellows? Additionally, why did they never receive the standard size

cab side numerals – surely there was enough time between their 1959 transfers and withdrawal to have undergone a repaint, or did they for some mysterious reason continue to be 'shopped' at St Rollox despite their move south? This begs another question, as to why a number of other exiles from Scotland in the later, darker days of 1961-62 ultimately found themselves stored at their pre-exile sheds or works?

All the answers to the foregoing questions and no doubt many new ones (some with answers, some perhaps not) can be ferreted from within these pages

A delve into *The Railway Observer* (what pleasure those old volumes still give today) for the later months of 1952 demonstrate in cold print the events which so stirred the nation's youth at the time. The September 1952 edition shows 45724 moving to the Scottish Region at 68A during the period ended 9 August, a sort of lull before the storm. Significantly, the same notes refer to the unusual presence of 45560 and 45646, both of 67A (Corkerhill) on Crewe North shed on 10 August These were no doubt en route to their new shed, though it may not have been appreciated at the time by the writer of the notes.

In the October 1952 'RO' things really moved on apace. The period ended 6 September shows the inwards transfers to the LM of 45560, 45564,

45575, 45576, 45577, 45579, 45580, 45582, 45583, 45643, 45644, 45645 and 45646, as well as the outgoing ScR bound 45621, 45640 and 45657, hopefully all modified to the post 45664 version, along with 45665, 45673, 45677, 45679, 45687, 45696, 45697, 45711 and 45718. The same notes refer at some length to the fact that, following the transfers, all Scottish Region Jubilees then had those boilers with the larger firebox and sloping throatplates. (The post-45664 batch, which by then included the modified 45621 and 45640 and presumably, the unmentioned 45657.)

The November 'RO' records that 45581, 45584 and 45645 had arrived in England, in exchange for 45704, 45707 and 45720. The same mass of transfers only appeared in the Scottish Region notes in that same November edition, by which time much of the information was probably 'old hat' to our northern friends. Interestingly, a correspondent had gleaned the information that, as the ex-Scottish engines were invariably in poor condition, the LM had probably had a poorer deal than had the Scottish Region.

Did such niceties mightily concern us and countless grateful recipients of undreamed of 'catches'? I think you can guess the answer to *that*.

45643 RODNEY, by now relegated to the outer reaches of Nuneaton, at Rugby shed 9 October 1963. Photograph Jack Hodgkinson.

16F, as Burton became, penultimate home for 45622. Photograph R K Blencoe.

APPENDIX TWO
The Burton Jubilee Episode
By Graham Onley

Many readers will vaguely recollect the mass influx of Jubilees to Burton shed (17B) during the early 1960s. The 'paper' reality was that, although it is unimaginable that all arrived at the shed entrance on the same day, eighteen examples are nevertheless recorded on their individual record cards as transferred to Burton on Saturday 18 November 1961. This event, seismic in its proportions, nevertheless went unnoticed by the spotting 'squad' at Duston Junction West, Northampton. At that very time, we were basking in the almost daily sightings of yet more refugees from Cardiff Canton. These were the Britannia Pacifics 70024 to 70029, evacuated to Aston shed and therefore regular visitors to our patch.

I imagine that once the excitement of hosting eighteen 'new' Jubilees had sunk in with the Burton fraternity, they might possibly have been more than a little disappointed. Not one of influx had travelled from further afield than local sheds such as Saltley, Leicester, Derby and Nottingham. Once the

initial arrivals had been digested, and no doubt graded by the shed staff as good, bad or indifferent, there was a further trickle; two on Saturday 20 January 1962, and two more on Saturday 7 April 1962.

When traditional forms of shed allocations had broken down even further, another Jubilee arrived at the door on Saturday 23 March 1963, this time from the further afield, but hardly pulse-quickening Kentish Town. This was 45622 NYASALAND, which had been in store at the London end of the Midland line from Monday 18 June 1962 until it was resurrected with effect from 15 March, probably to make it ready for its move to the Midlands. 45622 was almost undoubtedly the end of Kentish Town's long association with 'the 5XPs', going back to the first days of the class, and it is extremely unlikely that the week of 15-23 March 1963 saw it storming up and down the line from St Pancras as it had since arrival on the Midland Division early in 1935.

On Saturday 23 November 1963, something slightly more attractive joined the Burton club. This was the first arrival from a non-Midland

Division shed, Aston's 45593 KOLHAPUR which had been in store since 6 November 1962 until its resurrection, though it had also worked in the summer period of 1963 from 17 June to 18 September. One of British Railways' noted 'paper transfers' then allegedly brought 45605 CYPRUS to Burton from Leeds which was not by then, of course, a Midland Division shed either. This move date was no more precise than February 1964 and withdrawal came within days, at week ending Saturday 29 February of that Leap Year.

Burton's final Jubilee incomer proved to be Crewe North's 45721, which made the short journey from headquarters during the imprecise period of April 1964. IMPREGNABLE led something of a charmed life in that it had been in store from 25 September 1963, except for what was in effect Christmas 1963 traffic purposes, until being stirred back into life for its spell at Burton, which had been recoded to an improbable 16F in September 1963. Even after leaving Burton for Bank Hall, it seems to have gone straight into store, awaiting the time from 21 June until 19 September 1965, when it would have seen service on expresses again. It is possible that IMPREGNABLE's four spells of storage was the record for the class during those ever darkening days.

In total twenty-six Jubilees found themselves officially on the Burton allocation. This includes 45605 which probably never arrived, and it should also be noted that 45626 moved to Annesley in November 1962, returning to Burton during January 1963. There may possibly be someone on the spot at that time who may question this officially recorded loan transfer!

Not all the incoming engines were withdrawn from service while based at Burton. Eight of the original influx of 18 November 1961 found themselves pressed into service from Derby from 26 January 1963. These moves were almost without doubt due to problems encountered with the new BR/Sulzer Type 4 diesels (later Class 45) during the Arctic weather conditions we endured that winter of fond memory. None of them returned to Burton.

Moves away from Burton after that time are best described as piecemeal. There were six transfers for further service, one to Derby during July 1963, one to Leeds in February 1964 (this would have been in exchange for the probably non-arriving and fit only for scrap 45605) followed by two more to Derby in June 1964. When two were transferred, one each to Bank Hall and Patricroft in October 1964, the Burton Jubilee story was over.

Lest it should be thought that the 'Burton Collection' was the only such episode there were others, it turns out, which probably made just as little

sense! When Millhouses (19B) was ejected from the London Midland Region to the Eastern Region, its small detachment of Jubilees nevertheless continued to be seen in St Pancras. Having survived the invasion of a small number of rebuilt Royal Scots onto the Midland Division, however, they could not see off the BR Sulzer Type 4s, the Peaks. With their home shed by then coded 41C, the Millhouses Jubilees would have become surplus at the same time as those which found their way to Burton. Regional thinking dictated otherwise and they went to Canklow, no less, where they may have done a little work and then on to Darnall, where it is a fair bet they did next to nothing until withdrawal. Note that Kentish Town, home for countless Jubilees over the years, provided only three of Burton's allocation, and then really only as afterthoughts, which is a little surprising.

The only other erstwhile Midland Division shed with a Jubilee allocation was the mighty Leeds Holbeck, which seemed unwilling to part with its usually long-serving engines, despite taking on a sizeable allocation of the new diesels, as befitted a shed of such rank. I reckon that the manner in which Holbeck became a sort of 'care home' for some of the class, such as STURDEE, INDIA, ROOKE and KOLHAPUR, as well as still providing a home for its own ALBERTA well into 1966 and 1967 was, bearing in mind that the shed had been part of the North Eastern Region since 1957, little short of miraculous. It probably also explains why none of Holbeck's army of Jubilees actually made it to Burton.

Unlike the 1952 exchange between England and Scotland, which, as can be read elsewhere in this book, had a firm operational basis, the ousting of Jubilees from the Midland Division sheds was a direct result of dieselisation. It might be said that this was also the reason for the 26 January 1963 exodus to Derby.

Local Burton enthusiasts must have been quite sad that none of their new arrivals was from exotic locations, but even so, they must have enoyed the three years until the last departure. What the squad at Northampton's Duston West would have given to have had 'ownership' of our own batch of Jubilees. We had long lived in hope that 'cascading' would do the trick for us, but it never happened and we had to be grateful for the many visits we had from top link engines from a host of other sheds, including, it should be noted, the 1962 visits of Burton's very own 45620 on a 7 July express, again on shed on 16 December; 45626 on a 12 March oil train, again on shed on 24 July and the famous 45649 on a fitted freight at Roade on 29 August. There were no doubt other occasions, but it has to be said that the feeling of exhilaration we would have enjoyed had these visits been in the 1950s from 'real' Midland Division sheds, was tempered to no more than a slightly raised eyebrow come 1962. The attached table attempts to put the preceding into simple form.

ENGINE	ARRIVED	FROM	DEPARTED	TO	OTHER
45557	18/11/61	Derby	6/64	Derby	
45579	18/11/61	Saltley	22/6/63	Derby	
45585	18/11/61	Leicester	26/1/63	Derby	
45598	18/11/61	Derby	10/64	Bank Hall	
45610	18/11/61	Derby	26/1/63	Derby	
45611	18/11/61	Nott'ham	26/1/63	Derby	
45612	18/11/61	Derby	26/1/63	Derby	
45615	18/11/61	Leicester			W'dn 8/12/62
45618	18/11/61	Derby			W'dn 29/2/64
45620	18/11/61	Nott'ham			W'dn 29/2/64
45626	18/11/61	Derby	2/64	Leeds	*
45636	18/11/61	Leicester			W'dn 8/12/62
45641	18/11/61	Nott'ham			W'dn 19/9/64
45648	18/11/61	Saltley			W'dn 9/2/63
45649	18/11/61	Saltley	6/7/63	Derby	
45650	18/11/61	Leicester			W'dn 19/1/63
45667	18/11/61	Nott'ham	26/1/63	Derby	
45668	18/11/61	Derby			W'dn 21/12/63
45712	20/1/62	K. Town	26/1/63	Derby	
45561	20/1/62	K. Town	26/1/63	Derby	
45575	7/4/62	Derby			W'dn 15/6/63
45614	7/4/62	Derby	26/1/63	Derby	
45622	23/3/63	K. Town	6/64	Derby	
45593	23/11/63	Aston	10/64	Patricroft	
45605	2/64	Leeds			W'dn 29/2/64
45721	4/64	Crewe North	10/64	Bank Hall	

(*possible 1/63 loan Annesley)
Some received attention at works while at Burton.